CW01023469

Cutting Edge

Art-Horror
and the
Horrific
Avant-garde

Cutting Edge

Joan Hawkins

University of Minnesota Press
Minneapolis — London

The University of Minnesota Press gratefully acknowledges permission to reprint the following. Parts of chapter 1 appeared as "Sleaze Mania" in *Film Quarterly* 53, no. 2 (2000); copyright 2000 by the Regents of the University of California, reprinted by permission. An earlier version of chapter 7 appeared as "'One of Us': Tod Browning's *Freaks*," in *Freakery: Cultural Spectacles of the Extraordinary Body*, edited by Rosemarie Garland Thomson (New York: New York University Press, 1996); copyright 1996 by New York University Press.

Published by the University of Minnesota Press
111 Third Avenue South, Suite 290
Minneapolis, MN 55401-2520
http://www.upress.umn.edu

Library of Congress Cataloging-in-Publication Data

Hawkins, Joan, 1953–
    Cutting edge : art-horror and the horrific avant-garde / Joan Hawkins
        p. cm.
"Select Filmography and Videography" : p.
Includes bibliographical references (p.) and index.
    ISBN 0-8166-3413-0 (alk. paper)
    — ISBN 0-8166-3414-9 (pbk. : alk. paper)
    1. Experimental films—Europe—History and criticism. 2. Horror films—
History and criticism. I. Title.
    PN1995.9.E96 H38 2000
    791.43'6164—dc21
99-051008

Printed in the United States of America on acid-free paper

The University of Minnesota is an equal-opportunity educator and employer.

11 10 09 08 07 06 05 04 03 02 01 00   10 9 8 7 6 5 4 3 2 1

For Skip

Contents

Acknowledgments

Like so many authors of "first books," I owe a tremendous debt of gratitude to many people and institutions.

Carol J. Clover directed the doctoral dissertation out of which this project grew. She has been an invaluable resource, a smart and savvy reader, a good adviser, and a good friend throughout the many manifestations of *Cutting Edge*. In addition, her own work on slasher films in many ways made this book possible.

Chris Anderson patiently listened to me talk my way through the beginning stages of what has become this book. He read substantial parts of the manuscript and made detailed suggestions on both argument and style. He was generous with his advice, his library, and his time; and his comments and suggestions for revision have been invaluable.

Jim Naremore, too, has been unstinting with his generosity. He always found time in his busy schedule to answer questions and to read my frequently lengthy e-mails. He read parts of the manuscript, and the chapters about *Les yeux sans visage* and Paul Morrissey owe a lot to him. As my official department "mentor," he has helped my career in more ways than I can possibly name.

Eric Schaefer and Jeffrey Sconce read substantial portions of the manuscript and made detailed suggestions for revision. Eric provided articles and information that helped me formulate my ideas for chapter 1 and provided valuable resource materials for both chapter 4 and chapter 6. Jeffrey Sconce suggested ways I could reorganize and improve the manuscript, and his own work on taste and "low" culture has been a tremendous influence on my own.

Jennifer Moore, my editor at the University of Minnesota Press, has done a lot for me, and the book owes a great deal to her. An enthusiastic supporter of the project from the beginning, she has been a sympathetic reader and a careful editor. Her tact and patience, as well as her editorial skill, are greatly appreciated. Ann Martin and the editorial boards of *Film Quarterly* and *Representations* also deserve a mention; their suggestions, questions, and critiques have been helpful. Thanks, too, to Mark Jancovich for his supportive and enthusiastic reader's report.

In addition to the people already mentioned, many colleagues and friends deserve thanks. Michael Curtin and Barbara Klinger both read parts of the manuscript and made suggestions. And both of them gave me good advice. Many of my ideas about technology were informed by conversations with Barb, who has been working on her own project in a related area; I hope she recognizes some of her influence here. Michael's suggestions for the Yoko Ono chapter were insightful, and the conversations we had about documentary cinema, politics, and ethics were instrumental to the development of my arguments. Bob Ivie has been a helpful and supportive department chair. I owe my computer, my office, and a research grant largely to his energies on my behalf. More important, perhaps, I owe the time I've spent finishing this book to him, since he has gone out of his way to keep my committee work and service obligations light during this crucial period of my career. Oscar Kenshur told me wonderful stories about art house theaters in Chicago. Nicky Evans took time away from her own research in London to track down references for me, and Rhona Berenstein similarly took time out from her own work to send me articles from the clippings files at UCLA, and the Academy of Motion Picture Arts and Sciences. In addition, Rhona's e-mail messages and the exchanges we've had over the years have provided the sense of "community" that I frequently needed.

Michael Lucey read an early version of the manuscript and made suggestions. Bill Nestrick made it possible for me to see *Sang des bêtes* and *Les yeux sans visage* on the big screen; it was Bill who first suggested that I write about *Freaks*. He passed away before the manuscript was completed, and one of my regrets is that he never had a chance to see the finished book. Rosemarie Garland Thomson published an early version of the *Freaks* chapter in her wonderful anthology *Freakery: Cul-*

tural Spectacles of the Extraordinary Body. That book and Ms. Thomson's other work in the field of disability studies has had a tremendous impact on the way I think about and through the issues of monstrosity and enfreakment, central concerns for horror. Sharon Kinoshita read theory with me—intelligently, critically, and well—and she understood that you can never approach a theoretical discussion without a good strong cup of Peet's coffee. The members of the Film History (H-Film), Film Theory, and Frameworks listservs have helped with factual information, addresses, and advice. Members of the horror and vampire listservs have similarly provided addresses, dates, and a needed nonacademic "fan" perspective.

I could never have written this book without resources and references. To begin with, I am grateful for the financial support I received from Indiana University. A paid semester's pretenure leave and two grants from Indiana University's Research and the University Graduate School (RUGS), a Summer Research Grant and a Research Grant-in-Aid award, permitted me to finish this book.

I am tremendously grateful to the staff at the Pacific Film Archive (PFA) in Berkeley, the British Film Institute in London, the University of Southern California Film Library, and the Andy Warhol Museum in Pittsburgh for their help in finding primary resources. Colleen Talty and Kris Brancolini at the Indiana University Library made it possible for me to see films I wouldn't have had the chance to see otherwise. And their impressive research skills have come in handy more times than I can remember. The Kinsey Institute made it possible for me to see adult magazines and erotica of the 1960s and 1970s. Al Zaretskie at the Museum of Modern Art Library in New York has been an invaluable resource and a good friend.

A special thanks to Shelly Diekman at the PFA, who made it possible for me to see *Rape,* Patrick Friel at Chicago Filmmakers, Dominic Angerame at Canyon Cinema, and Milos Stehlik and the staff at Facets Multimedia. Without them, this book could never have been written. Special thanks, too, to Fred Frey, Craig Ledbetter, and all the people at Sinister Cinema, European Trash Cinema, Luminous Film and Video Wurks, Video Search of Miami, and the other catalog companies mentioned in this book. There would never have been a chapter about Jess Franco without their help. And there would never have been a book at all if their catalogs hadn't shown me a side of film history I knew nothing about. To Jeff Dean and the staff at Classical Film and Music, a big thank you for all the times you found the tapes I needed, and for all your kind help and courtesy over the years. And to the staff at Plan 9, thanks for keeping your collection current and for providing a space where those of us with "special tastes" could rub elbows.

My students have made a real impact on the way I think about and watch horror films. Special thanks to Eric Beckstrom, Margaret Ervin, Aimee Hall, Cim Kearns, Darcy McKinnon, Mary O'Shea, Al Zaretskie, and all the grad students who talked horror and avant-garde with me from the start. Thanks also to the students of C 390 (Nightmare Movies), C 392 (Horror Genre), C 397 (Horror Genre), and C 792 (Theory for Troubled Times). Your journals, papers, and questions have helped keep this an interesting and exciting topic for me. Amanda, Brian, Cija, Cristina, Joe, Kyle, and Michael G.—a big thanks to you for taking so many courses and for making class both interesting and fun. Thanks to Cija Johnson also for making it possible for me to see so many movies. Thanks to Darcy McKinnon for her technical expertise and her enthusiastic participation in class, and to Christy Cousineau for her computer help. Thanks to Mary Balle-Gifford for introducing me to the work of Michael Ninn, and for telling me about her own work on pornography.

To my own teachers I owe a tremendous debt of gratitude. Ulysse Dutoit's mania for making his students appropriately identify shots (in French, no less!) taught me to really *see* a film. His class on Alain Resnais changed my life and certainly helped determine the direction my future career would take. Gary Kellard introduced me to the serious study of film and has remained a good friend and a valuable resource. Bertrand Augst taught me to appreciate both surrealism and classical Hollywood style. Donald Lowe's required historiography class at San Francisco State taught me to think critically and introduced me to the work of Michel Foucault. To this day, whenever I pick up *Discipline and Punish,* I hear his voice. Joseph Axelrod, Thanasis Maskaleris, and Manfred Wolf made the M.A. program I followed at San Francisco State a valuable learning experience. Manfred Wolf became a good friend and remains the final arbiter on all things Dutch. Paul Zimmerman taught me the importance of primary sources. Abe Evenich and Susan Zimmerman taught me the importance of probing deeper and asking harder questions. Sharon Kruzic sparked my love of French language and culture.

To my friends and family, I owe a special debt of thanks. To Julie and Chris Hawkins—for all the joy you've given me. To Ellie, my oldest and dearest friend, Carolyn, Jenny, Katharine B., Katharine S.,

Nancy C., and Nancy L., a hug of gratitude. To Suzanne and Elizabeth, thanks for providing a place for me to work when construction tore up the street in front of my house; and thanks to Jane for keeping me sane. Thanks also to my parents (who always let me watch pretty much what I wanted), to my brother (who went to Europe first), and to all my dinner and movie buddies throughout the years. Special thanks to Marianne, Mary Gordon, Vicky, and Christina, who started out as "academic support staff" and ended up as friends. On a more solemn note, my good friend Betty Vance passed away before this book was completed, and I'm sorry we never had a chance to crack that bottle of champagne we said we'd drink when this was all over.

Finally, all the love and gratitude in the world to my husband, Skip Hawkins. It's never easy to live with someone who's writing a book, and it's particularly trying to live with someone so resolutely determined to explore the dark side. Skip read every single version of this manuscript, made suggestions, asked questions, proofread, and photocopied. He watched movies that he had no desire to see and learned to see a weird kind of beauty in horror, for my sake. He kept the espresso machine turned up high and his own schedule flexible, and he helped me keep my personal monsters at bay. He was always ready to go for a walk in the park, and he always knew when it was time for spicy Thai food or a little Miles Davis. This book is dedicated to him, the one who was willing to go with me *jusqu'au bout*—all the way to the end.

Paracinema Culture and Psychotronic Style

Sleaze-Mania, Euro-trash, and High Art: The Place of European Art Films in American Low Culture

> They can keep their Bressons and their Cocteaus. The cinematic, modern marvellous is popular, and the best and most exciting films are, beginning with Méliès and Fantômas, the films shown in local fleapits, films which seem to have no place in the history of cinema.
>
> **—Ado Kyrou, *Le surréalisme au cinéma*, 1963**

O pen the pages of any horror fanzine—*Outré, Fangoria, Cinefantastique*—and you will find listings for mail-order video companies that cater to afficionados of what Jeffrey Sconce has called "paracinema" and trash aesthetics.[1] Not only do these mail-order companies represent one of the fastest-growing segments of the video market,[2] but their catalogs challenge many of our continuing assumptions about the binary opposition of prestige cinema (European art and avant-garde/experimental films) and popular culture.[3] Certainly, they highlight an aspect of art cinema generally overlooked or repressed in cultural analysis; namely, the degree to which high culture trades on the same images, tropes, and themes that characterize low culture.

In the world of horror and cult film fanzines and mail-order catalogs, what Carol J. Clover calls "the high-end" of the horror genre mingles indiscriminately with the "low-end."[4] Here, Murnau's *Nosferatu* (1921) and Dreyer's *Vampyr* (1931) appear alongside such drive-in favorites as *Tower of Screaming Virgins* (1971) and *Jail Bait* (1955). Even more interesting, European art films that have little to do with horror—Antonioni's *L'avventura* (1960), for example—are listed alongside movies that Video Vamp labels "Eurociné-trash." European art films are not easily located under separate catalog subheadings or listings. Many catalogs simply list film titles alphabetically, making no attempt to differentiate among genres or subgenres, high or low art. In *Luminous Film and Video Wurks Catalog 2.0,* for example, Jean-Luc Godard's edgy *Weekend* (1968) is sandwiched between *The Washing Machine* (1993) and *The Werewolf and the Yeti* (1975). Sinister Cinema's 1996–1997 catalog, which organizes titles chronologically, lists Godard's *Alphaville* (1965) between *Lightning Bolt* (1965) and *Zontar, the Thing from Venus* (1966).[5]

Where separate genre and subgenre headings are given, the only labels that apply are the labels important to the fans who purchase tapes. European art and experimental film titles are woven throughout catalog listings and may be found under the headings "Science Fiction," "Horror," "Barbara Steele," "Christopher Lee," "Exploitation," "Weird Westerns," and "Juvenile Schlock."[6] Where art films are bracketed off, they are often described in terms that most film historians would take pains to avoid. Instead of presenting Pier Paolo Pasolini's *Salò* (1975) as a work that explicitly links "fascism and sadism, sexual licence *[sic]* and oppression,"[7] as the *Encyclopedia of European Cinema* does, Mondo simply notes that the film "left audiences gagging."[8]

The operative criterion here is *affect:* the ability of a film to thrill, frighten, gross out, arouse, or otherwise directly engage the spectator's body. And it is this emphasis on affect that characterizes paracinema as a low cinematic culture. Paracinema catalogs are dominated by what Clover terms "body genre" films, films that, Linda Williams notes, "privilege the sensational."[9] Most of the titles are horror, porn, exploitation, horrific sci-fi, or thrillers; other non–body genre films—art films, Nixon's infamous Checkers speech, sword-and-sandal epics, and so forth—tend to be collapsed into categories dictated by the body genres that are the main focus. Part of this strategy is economic. Consumers in search of a particular title or type of film have to literally read most of a catalog to find everything that might be of interest. But the design of the catalogs also enforces a valorization of low genres and low generic categories.

Williams identifies three pertinent features shared by body genres (which she defines as porn, horror, and melodrama). "First there is the spectacle of a body caught in the grips of intense sensation or emotion" (142); the spectacle of orgasm in porn, of terror and violence in horror, of weeping in melodrama. Second, there is the related focus on ecstasy, "a direct or indirect sexual excitement and rapture," which borders on what the Greeks termed insanity or bewilderment (142–43). Visually this is signaled in films through what Williams calls the "involuntary convulsion or spasm—of the body 'beside itself' in the grips of sexual pleasure, fear and terror, and overpowering sadness" (143). Aurally, ecstasy is marked by the inarticulate cry—of pleasure in porn, of terror in horror, and of grief or anguish in melodrama (143).

Finally, body genres directly address the spectator's body. This last feature, Williams argues, most noticeably characterizes body genres as degraded cultural forms: "What seems to bracket these particular genres from others is an apparent lack of proper aesthetic distance, a sense of overinvolvement in sensation and emotion. . . . viewers feel too directly, too viscerally, manipulated by the text" (144). The body of the spectator involuntarily mimics "the emotion or sensation of the body onscreen" (143). The spectator cringes, becomes tense, screams, weeps, becomes aroused. This is such a pointed and calculated feature of body films that Mary Ann Doane, as Williams points out, "equates the violence of this emotion to a kind of 'textual rape' of the targeted . . . viewer" (144).[10]

Although Williams's assessment of the way body genres work— particularly the way they work in "specifically gendered ways" (144)—is excellent, the distinction between high and low, properly distanced and improperly involved, audience response is not as neat as Williams suggests. Consider, for example, Amos Vogel's description of *The War Games* (Peter Watkins, 1965), a British art film that is frequently listed in paracinema catalogs. "A terrifying, fabricated documentary records the horrors of a future atomic war in the most painstaking, sickening detail. Photographed in London, it shows the flash burns and firestorms, the impossibility of defence, the destruction of all life. Produced by the BBC, the film was promptly banned and became world-famous and rarely seen."[11] Similarly, Stan Brakhage's *The Act of Seeing with One's Own Eyes* (1972), which is hard to find outside experimental and avant-garde film venues, encourages an uncomfortably visceral reaction in the spectator. The chronicle of a real autopsy, the film is, Vogel writes, "an appalling, haunting work of great purity and truth. It dispassionately records whatever transpires in front of the lens: bodies sliced lengthwise, organs removed, skulls and scalp cut open with electric tools" (267). Whereas such descriptive terms as "haunting work of great purity and truth" are seldom found in paracinema catalogs, *The War Games* and *The Act of Seeing with One's Own Eyes* do address the spectator in ways that paracinema fans would appreciate. Clearly designed to break the audience's aesthetic distance, the films encourage the kind of excessive physical response that we would generally attribute to horror. Furthermore, their excessive visual force and what paracinema catalogs like to term "powerful subject matter" mark them as subversive. Banned, marginalized through being screened exclusively in museums and classrooms, these are films that most mainstream film patrons never see.

Of course, *The War Games* and *The Act of Seeing with One's Own Eyes* use sensational material differently than many body genre movies do. Seeking to instruct or challenge the spectator, not simply titillate her, films like Watkins's and Brakhage's are deemed to have a higher cultural purpose, and certainly a different artistic intent from low-genre blood-and-gore fests. That is, high culture—even when it engages the body in the same way that low genres do—supposedly evokes a different kind of spectatorial pleasure and response than the one evoked by low genres.

Supposedly. But that doesn't mean that it always does. Consider the works of the Marquis de Sade, whose books are sold in mainstream bookstores and adult bookstores and housed in university libraries. Sade's works, which the intellectual elite view as masterful analyses of the mechanisms of power and economics,[12] are also—at least if we are to take their presence in adult bookstores and magazines seriously—still regarded as sexually arousing, as masturbatory aids. Furthermore, as Jane Gallop's powerful admission that she masturbated while reading Sade demonstrates, one set of cultural uses—one kind of audience pleasure—does not necessarily preclude the other.[13]

Finally, it is not so clear that low genres seek *only* to titillate. As Laura Kipnis remarks in her famous article about *Hustler* magazine, low genres, too, can be analyzed for serious content and purpose. Using a vocabulary similar to the one generally used to analyze the powerful cultural critique mounted by the high pornography of prerevolutionary France, Kipnis writes that "*Hustler* also offers a theory of sexuality—a 'low theory.' Like [Robin] Morgan's radical feminism, it too offers an explicitly political and counterhegemonic analysis of power and the body." That it does so in a way that middle-class readers—Kipnis included—find disgusting is evidence that "it is explicit about its own class location."[14]

In a similar fashion, low cinematic genres—as Clover, Williams, Robin Wood, and others have pointed out—often handle explosive social material that mainstream cinema is reluctant to touch.[15] Carlos Clarens notes in *An Illustrated History of the Horror Film* that— for all their fabulous premises—the B thrillers that Roger Corman's studios quickly cranked out depicted a resolutely contemporary world, a world "usually ignored by Hollywood or blown up beyond recognition."[16] And Eric Schaefer has demonstrated that historically, art films that failed to get the Hays Office's coveted seal of approval were screened in bump-and-grind houses, marketed to patrons of body genre pictures as well as to European art film connoisseurs.[17]

As these examples show, the categorical difference between low and high genres, body genres and elite art—both inside and outside the cinematic beltway—is difficult to define. Even critics who make it their business to evaluate films on the basis of their artistic worth, intent, and merit sometimes find it hard to distinguish between low and high cinematic elements. Stephen Garrett's annotated article about the Production Code in *Hollywood Handbook,* for example, calls foreign films of the 1960s "erudite skin flicks,"[18] and Amos Vogel links horror, porn, avant-garde, and European art films under one heading, "subversive" cinema.[19]

If the operative criterion in paracinema culture is affect, the most frequently expressed patron desire is to see something "different," something unlike contemporary Hollywood cinema. As A. S. Hamrah and Joshua Glenn put it, "Let's face it: Hollywood films are cautious, uninventive, and bland, and young filmgoers are increasingly uninterested."[20] Paracinema fans, like the cineast elite, "explicitly situate themselves in opposition to Hollywood cinema" (Sconce, 381), and they do so in a way that academics would recognize as highly sophisticated. As Sconce notes, "the paracinematic audience recognizes Hollywood as an economic and artistic institution that represents not just a body of films, but a particular mode of film production and its accompanying signifying practices. Furthermore, the narrative form produced by this institution is seen as somehow 'manipulative' and 'repressive,' and linked to dominant interests as a form of cultural coercion" (381). Paracinema consumption can be understood, then, as American art cinema consumption has often been understood, as a reaction against the hegemonic and normatizing practices of mainstream, dominant Hollywood production.

Providing for the demand for affect-ive products and the demand for "something different"—something unlike contemporary Hollywood movies—often takes a company's list in what appears to be wildly different directions. Paracinema catalogs not only list classic films by Godard, Antonioni, and Bergman but are often the only places where European cinema fans can find video titles otherwise not available for sale in the United States. These include everything from the uncut horror films of Jess Franco to Peter Greenaway's *The Baby of Macon* (1993) to Jean-Luc Godard's historically important *Tout va bien* (1972). If "entertainment is one of the purest marketplaces in the world," as Robert Shayé, director of New Line Cinema, maintained during the 1993 GATT controversy,[21] then the alternative mail-order video industry is one of the purest (i.e., uncontaminated by any prejudice) entertainment marketplaces around. Certainly, its mail-order catalogs encourage a reading strategy much like the one that Fredric Jameson proposes in *Signatures of the Visible*. That is, they invite us to "read high and mass culture as objectively related and dialectically interdependent phenomena, as twin and inseparable forms of the fission of aesthetic production under capitalism."[22]

The Sacralization of Culture

Historically speaking, paracinema catalogs, with their leveling of cultural hierarchies and abolition of binary categories, are reminiscent of an earlier age—an age preceding what Lawrence W. Levine has called the "sacralization" of high art, when the mingling of high and low culture was commonplace.[23] In his book *Highbrow Lowbrow*, Levine describes the historical emergence of a cultural hierarchy in the United States during the late nineteenth century. Before that time there was little cultural stratification—be it of cultural products or of audiences. This was a time when opera could exist *simultaneously* as a popular and an elite art form, a time when American audiences might hear a soliloquy from *Hamlet* and a popular song in the course of an evening's entertainment at a local venue.[24] In the early nineteenth century, Levine tells us, no art form— opera, painting, theater—was "elevated above other forms of expressive culture . . . they were part of the general culture and were experienced in the midst of a broad range of other cultural genres by a catholic audience that cut through class and social lines. This situation began to change after mid-century" (149).

The change, which Levine calls "the sacralization of culture," involved the establishment of a hierarchy of cultural products and spaces. Shakespeare's works were increasingly played "straight," without the accompaniment of farce (a form of entertainment usually scheduled between acts) or popular music, and gradually acquired the patina of high art. They were seen as more culturally valuable or sophisticated than the traveling road shows that catered to "popular taste." The emergence of a growing differentiation of cultural products brought with it a nearly simultaneous differentiation of performance space and audience. Because tickets to the opera house, an edifice of high culture, commanded a much higher price than tickets to the music hall, audiences who attended performances at the opera house tended to be a much tonier crew than audiences who attended the newly devalued variety shows. More important, however, as certain cultural products picked up elite status, they also acquired a certain restrictive class inflection. Shakespeare not only moved into theaters but moved off the boards. He was transformed, as Levine tells us, "from a playwright for the general public into one for a specific audience" (56). Shakespeare became high-class and highbrow.

The reasons for the sacralization of high culture in the nineteenth century are, as Levine argues, complicated. Then as now, "culture"—as a concept—had politico-economic as well as aesthetic and social resonance, and "aesthetics by themselves cannot account for the nature of the mores and the institutions" that accompanied the historical development of high culture (228). As Levine observes, "these were shaped by the entire [historic] context—social, cultural, and economic—in which that development took place" (228). Certainly, the categorization and stratification of cultural products seems, at this remove at least, to be the logical aesthetic extension of the stratification, compartmentalization, and commodification that accompanied most cultural production during industrialization and the rise of capitalism. And as leisure activity— the freedom to not work or at least to have a wife who did not work for a salary—increasingly became both a signifier of social status and a reason for cultural consumption, it was only natural that the cultural products consumed during leisure time would themselves emerge as important signifiers of social prestige and class standing.

But while Levine stresses the need for a holistic paradigm to explain the cultural shift that occurred in the United States during industrialization, he also emphasizes the degree to which the sacralization of culture served particular partisan political goals. For Levine, cultural stratification was one logical outcome of a conservative political reformation:

> It should not really surprise us that the thrust of the Mugwumps—those independent Republicans whose devotion to the cause of orderly and

efficient civil service reform led them to desert their own party in the election of 1884—was not confined to the political sphere. Once we understand that the drive for political order was paralleled by a drive for cultural order, that the push to organize the economic sphere was paralleled by a push to organize the cultural sphere, that the quest for social authority ("the control of action through the giving of commands") was paralleled by a quest for cultural authority ("the construction of reality through definitions of fact and value"), we can begin to place the cultural dynamics of the turn of the century in clearer perspective. (228)

Certainly, we can see the way that the impetus to sacralize specific cultural products, spaces, and historic artifacts as "culture" had the same sociopolitical and economic implications in the nineteenth century that it still has today. The recent debates surrounding educational curriculum (particularly regarding the canon and which books may or may not be considered "literature" by the public schools), the concern about the free circulation of both information and images on the Internet, the disputes about continued funding for the National Endowment for the Arts and the Public Broadcasting Service, and the public lambasting of violent and sexual content in rap music, popular Hollywood cinema, and commercial television by both politicians and intellectuals demonstrate the degree to which culture, economics, and politics continue to be interrelated terms in a society very much concerned with issues of social control. Now, as in the late nineteenth century, "there is . . . the same sense that culture [in the sacralized sense of the word] is something created by the few for the few, threatened by the many, and imperiled by democracy; the conviction that culture cannot come from the young, the inexperienced, the untutored, the marginal" (252). And it is largely in opposition to this sense that "culture" is exclusionary and elitist that paracinema consumption must be understood. As Michael Weldon notes in the foreword to the *Psychotronic Video Guide*, "unlike other movie guides, nothing is omitted [here] because it's in bad taste. All of this stuff is out there. You should know about it."[25]

Paracinema and Specialty Mail-Order Houses

Specialized mail-order houses exist for a variety of reasons. Americans, Elliot Forbes notes, "have a mania for collecting; the current video-by-mail houses are the technologically inevitable descendants of the mail-order film outlets that have for years collected and traded 16 mm prints—prints junked by film companies, prints no longer needed by television stations, and sometimes pilfered prints. Obviously, the advent of the VCR has expanded film collecting exponentially. More copies can be made more easily, and more people have the equipment to view them."[26] In addition, the routine cutting of European and Asian horror films to meet U.S. standards,[27] the difficulty over copyright, and the decision not to make certain films available to a mass-market audience all have contributed to creating a consuming public whose tastes are not served by the "pure" marketplace of mainstream video and film distribution companies. Video chain stores such as Blockbuster, which limit themselves to serving a mainstream audience, have necessitated the creation of what Levine would call an unsacralized cultural space, a space where high art and low/fringe cultural products are grouped together.[28]

Paracinema catalogs provide one such space. The catalogs themselves are often cheaply made. Ranging in size from 5 by 7 to 8½ by 11, the catalogs are usually printed on newsprint or standard-grade printer paper. Most of them are thirty-five to fifty pages long, although some are longer and some—like Video Vamp's—are very short (Video Vamp usually sends out eight to ten pages). Almost all companies stress that they have more titles than the ones actually listed, and that customers who don't see what they're looking for should either visit the Web site or write (e-mail) the owner.

Companies that pay special attention to layout and graphic design (Luminous, Sinister Cinema, and Something Weird Video, for example) leave some space between the movie descriptions and break up catalog pages with black-and-white computer-scanned or photocopied images. Some companies—European Trash Cinema and Celebrity Vamp Video, for example—put out a denser product. In these catalogs, descriptions are not separated, so that the pages are filled with text. Celebrity Vamp uses a particularly tiny font, so the sheer amount of print (usually three columns of single-spaced descriptions to an 8½ by 11 page) is impressive. Occasionally a single black-and-white image will occupy the center of the page. Although European Trash Cinema's and Celebrity Vamp's catalogs are exceptionally demanding, they demonstrate the kind of committed fan "reading" that most paracinema catalogs frankly solicit. These aren't publications that the reader can simply dip into. Whereas it's not necessarily desirable (or even possible) to read an entire catalog in one sitting, the tendency is to read entries in the order in which they're given (so that you don't miss something) and mark your place as you go.

Few of the catalogs are bound. Video Search of Miami does bind its catalog, which sports a full-color cover. But most of the other companies either fold pages over to create a "booklet" effect (fastening the pages with two single staples in the center of the catalog) or—as in the case of Video Vamp—simply staple the pages in the upper-left-hand corner, like a term paper. Many of the catalogs do have covers, but these are printed on the same grade paper (newsprint or standard printer grade) as the rest of the catalog, and they seldom have color images or printing. In short, the catalogs look like something that anyone with access to a computer and a photocopier could produce. They certainly don't look like the publications of companies that—to a certain extent—depend on sales to the upscale end of the video market and cater to European art house fans.

Of course, exploitation companies are not the only places that cater to European art film fans. Other—more upscale—video companies pick up most of the art film business, and although they don't carry some of the truly obscure titles that characterize Mondo's or Cinemacabre's lists, they have a broader range of European art selections than the paracinema companies do (and their tapes are usually much better quality). Interestingly, like Mondo, they do attempt to cater to the horror tastes, as well as the art tastes, of their clients. Facets Multimedia, one of the most complete mail-order video services in the country, has listings for cult and horror films, as well as for hard-to-find avant-garde and European art titles. Even Home Film Festival, whose slogan "the best films you never saw" specifically targets a middle-class art and independent film audience, has begun carrying some horror titles—*Night of the Living Dead* (1968), *Spanish Dracula* (1931),[29] *Eyes without a Face* (1959), *Nadja* (1995), and *Mute Witness* (1995), to name just a few. That "art" companies as well as "sleaze" companies market both high-art and low-culture titles[30] suggests that the sacralization of performance culture (its division into high and low art) never completely took root among art and horror/sleaze/exploitation film fans.[31]

Of course, upscale mail-order video companies rely on a very different kind of product for the majority of their sales than do companies such as Mondo or Video Vamp. In June 1996, for example, the best-selling foreign title at Facets was Marker's *La jetée* (1964), a title that was popular at the time with film buffs because, as Facet's manager Milos Stehlik claimed, "it was adapted by Terry Gilliam for his 1995 hit *Twelve Monkeys*."[32] Ranked number two was *Bread and Chocolate* (1974), an Italian comedy that had previously been unavailable on video. Jean-Luc

Figure 1. Dracula (Carlos Villarias) waits outside Lucy's window. *Spanish Dracula.*

Godard's *Numéro Deux* (1975), Luis Puenzo's *The Official Story* (1985), and Jean-Jacques Beineix's *Diva* (1981) followed as third, fourth, and fifth in popularity, respectively.[33] The tendency here is for patrons to buy more contemporary titles or historical titles of current interest (Fox Lorber's video release of Jacques Démy's *The Umbrellas of Cherbourg* [1964], for example, which followed the film's rerelease in theaters; or the foregoing example of *La jetée*).[34]

These are titles that the horror and exploitation catalogs, for the most part, do not even bother to carry. Whereas the European *horror* film listings in exploitation publications include recent films as well as films of historical interest,[35] the European *art* films that show up in these catalogs tend to date from the height of the art cinema movement, the period that Susan Sontag elegized in her *New York Times* article "The Decay of Cinema."[36] The post-1970 auteurs mentioned by Timothy Corrigan, Thomas Elsaesser, and Jill Forbes in their studies of postwar European and postmodern cinema[37] are largely passed over in favor of the "classic" auteurs—Godard, Fellini, Antonioni, Buñuel.[38] The most frequently represented American auteur is Orson Welles. Exploitation catalogs feature, then, art film titles that don't sell well in other

venues: films of historical interest or titles that haven't been officially released. In that sense, it's not clear to what degree they actually compete
with more upscale specialty video companies. What is clear is that the
catalog companies themselves comprise and address what Dick Hebdige
might recognize as a true video subculture,[39] a subculture identified less
by a specific style than by a certain strategy of reading.[40]

In addition to art, horror, and science fiction films, paracinema
catalogs "include entries from such seemingly disparate genres" as "bad-
film," splatterpunk, "mondo" films, sword-and-sandal epics, Elvis flicks,
government hygiene films, Japanese monster movies, beach party musicals, and "just about every other historical manifestation of exploitation
cinema from juvenile delinquency documentaries to . . . pornography"
(Sconce, 372).[41] As Sconce explains, this is an "extremely elastic textual
category" and comprises "less a distinct group of films than a particular
reading protocol, a counter-aesthetic turned subcultural sensibility devoted to all manner of cultural detritus. In short, the explicit manifesto
of paracinematic culture is to valorize all forms of cinematic 'trash'
whether such films have been either explicitly rejected or simply ignored
by legitimate film culture" (Sconce, 372).

This valorization is achieved, he argues, largely through heavily
ironized strategies of cinematic reading. Connoisseurs of trash cinema
are always on the lookout for movies that are so awful they're good. But
they also consume films that are recognized by "legitimate" film culture
as masterpieces. And catalog descriptions do attempt to alert the consumer that such films might require a different reading strategy—less
heavily ironized—than other films listed in the catalog.[42] *Sinister
Cinema*'s description of *Vampyr* is a good example: "If you're looking for
a fast paced horror film with lots of action go to another movie in our
listings. If you like mood and atmosphere this is probably the greatest
horror movie ever made. The use of light, shadow, and camera angles
is translated into a pureness of horror seldom equaled, in this chilling
vampire-in-a-castle tale. One of the best."[43]

Clearly, the description serves an important economic purpose.
Customers are less likely to be disappointed, to return tapes, if they understand clearly what they're getting. But the delineation of important
stylistic elements is instructional as well as cautionary. It tells the collector what to look for, how to read a film that might seem lugubrious or
boring. That the catalog lists two versions of the film—a longer foreign-
language version and a shorter version with English subtitles—marks
the company's economic stake in serious collectors and completionists

(people who collect many versions of the same title, such as the U.S. theatrical release, the director's cut or uncut European version, the rough cut, etc.). But it also gives the catalog a curiously academic or scholarly air, which links Sinister Cinema to more upscale "serious" video companies such as Facets.

Although paracinema catalogs often tag art films as films that require a different reading strategy than *Reefer Madness* (1939) or *Glen and Glenda* (1953), they also tag certain B movies as films that can be openly appreciated on pure aesthetic grounds. In the same catalog that characterizes *Vampyr* as "one of the best," for example, the reader can also find a listing for *Carnival of Souls* (1962), a B-grade American horror film that *The Encyclopedia of Horror Movies* calls "insufferably portentous." The script, the encyclopedia tells us, "harks back to those expressionistic dramas which solemnly debated this life and the next with heavy-breathing dialogue."[44] For Sinister Cinema catalog patrons, however, the film is described in terms not unlike the ones used to describe *Vampyr*. *Carnival of Souls,* the catalog tells us, has "a riveting pipe organ music score. Seldom have the elements of sight and sound come together in such a horrifying way. A haunting film that you'll never forget. Original uncut 80 minute version."[45] Although this description does not praise *Carnival of Souls'* use of "light, shadow, and camera angles," its observation that "sight and sound come together in a . . . horrifying way" is a tribute to the film's formal style. And the use of the word "haunting" in the next-to-last line reminds the reader that schlock, too, can be beautiful. Like the surrealist film critic Ado Kyrou, the writers for paracinema publications continually remind readers that low-budget horror can sometimes be "sublime."[46]

Negotiating paracinema catalogs often calls, then, for a more complicated set of textual reading strategies than is commonly assumed. Viewing/reading the films themselves—even the trashiest films—demands a set of sophisticated strategies that, Sconce argues, are remarkably similar to the strategies employed by the cultural elite.

> Paracinematic taste involves a reading strategy that renders the bad into the sublime, the deviant into the defamiliarized and in so doing, calls attention to the aesthetic aberrance and stylistic variety evident but routinely dismissed in the many subgenres of trash cinema. By concentrating on a film's formal bizarreness and stylish eccentricity, the paracinematic audience, *much like the viewer attuned to the innovations of Godard . . .* foregrounds structures of cinematic discourse and artifice so that the

> material identity of the film ceases to be a structure made invisible in serv-
> ice of the diegesis, but becomes instead the primary focus of textual at-
> tention. (Sconce, 388; italics mine)

"Diegesis" refers to the world of the story in a film. "Diegetic" is the ad-
jective that derives from it. "Diegetic" sound, for example, refers to
sound that has a source in the film, such as a character turning on a
radio; nondiegetic sound refers to mood music on the sound track—the
music that the audience hears, but the characters in the story don't.
Sconce is using "diegesis" here to refer to all formal elements that advance the plot or are crucial to the story's meaning in some way.

Because Sconce is mainly interested in theorizing trash aesthetics, he doesn't take the "high" art aspects of the catalogs' video lists into
account. So he does not thoroughly discuss the way in which the companies' listing practices erase the difference between what is considered
"trash" and what is considered "art," through a deliberate leveling of hierarchies and recasting of categories. But his comments about "the viewer
attuned to the innovations of Godard" help to explain the heavy representation of Godard's films in these catalogs. As Godard himself repeatedly demonstrated, there is a fine line between the reading strategies demanded by trash and the reading strategies demanded by high culture.

In fact, Godard's early films are compendiums of different modes
of cultural discourse and are often preoccupied with questions of reading—both written texts and films—and of analyzing cultural and rep-
resentational codes.[47] In a scene in *My Life to Live* (Vivre sa vie, 1962),
for example, the action completely stops while a character reads a long
passage from a story by Edgar Allan Poe aloud to his lover. *Breathless*
(A bout de souffle, 1959), *A Woman Is a Woman* (Une femme est une
femme, 1961), *A Married Woman* (Une femme mariée, 1964), *Pierrot le
fou* (1965), and *Masculine/Feminine* (Masculin/féminin, 1966) all feature
characters who literally must be instructed (or who must instruct others) how to watch and project a film, how to analyze an ad, how to use
birth control, how to listen to Mozart, how to read and understand a
popular opinion poll.

Godard's films demand a reading strategy, then, much like the
one demanded by paracinema catalogs. Featuring scenes from art film
masterpieces such as Dreyer's *Passion of Joan of Arc* (Passion de Jeanne
d'Arc, 1928), prints of impressionist paintings, Mozart concertos, excerpts
from stories by Poe, magazine advertisements, billboards, nude shots
from erotica magazines, excerpts from pornographic writing (also read

Figure 2. Michel (Jean-Paul Belmondo) steals money from an unnamed woman. *Breathless,* by Jean-Luc Godard.

aloud), and pop songs, Godard's films—like paracinema catalogs—can be said to incorporate "all manner of cultural detritus" (Sconce, 372).

Although Godard's use of pop culture, advertising, and pornography has a political purpose that goes beyond the subversive aims of paracinema culture,[48] Godard has consistently acknowledged his debt to the B movies loved by paracinephiles. *Breathless* is dedicated to Monogram Pictures, a studio that occupies second place in Michael Weldon's list of production houses important to fans of what he calls psycho-tronic (paracinema) cinema.[49] *Made in USA* (1966) is dedicated to American B-movie director Sam Fuller (who also has a cameo role in *Pierrot le fou*) and to Nicholas Ray.

MacMahonism

Godard was not the only French filmmaker in 1950s and 1960s Paris who was interested in American "B" and "poverty row" film culture. As James Naremore has pointed out, many of the auteurist critics at *Cahiers du cinéma* were "mounting an attack not only on the bourgeois 'tradition of quality,' but also on certain features of both modernism and the avant-garde. . . . Despite their male bias and despite their roots in a specific fraction of postwar French society, they were opening the possibility for a new kind of intellectual activity in which many people could engage—what [Andreas] Huyssen calls 'an experimental mixing and meshing' of the old cultural domains."[50] In part, this mixing and meshing took place between the covers of *Cahiers* itself as articles lauding Douglas Sirk and Sam Fuller appeared beside articles extolling the most recent work of Jacques Rivette or Vittorio De Sica. In part, it took place within New Wave cinema production, where films such as *Breathless* and *Shoot the Piano Player* paid explicit homage to Hollywood "B" culture. Finally, it took place within the Cinéma MacMahon, one of the first theaters that—J. Hoberman and Jonathan Rosenbaum tell us—showed movies "for movies' sake."[51]

Founded by Pierre Rissient, the Cinéma MacMahon became the headquarters of what some have called a "critical sect" (25). Through the theater, Rissient fostered a macho, heroic film aesthetic that drew equally from high and low culture. Large posters of Fritz Lang, Joseph Losey, Otto Preminger, and Raoul Walsh hung in the theater lobby. And the MacMahonist journal, *Présence du cinéma,* devoted entire issues to Cecil B. DeMille, Jacques Tourneur, juvenile delinquents, and "sadisme et libertinage" [sadism and licentiousness]. Michel Mourlet, the journal's coeditor, argued that *Samson and Delilah* (Cecil B. DeMille, 1949), starring Victor Mature, was aesthetically superior to Eisenstein's *Ivan the Terrible* (1942) and launched what may well be one of the strangest cults in cinema history—the Charlton Heston cult—when he wrote a deliriously starstruck piece about the American actor. "His presence in any film—no matter what it is—suffices to incite beauty. The contained violence expressed by the somber phosphorescence of his eyes, his eagle's

Figure 3. Charlton Heston as Moses. *The Ten Commandments.*

profile, the proud arch of his eyebrows, his prominent cheekbones, the bitter and hard curve of his mouth, the fabulous power of his torso; this is what he has been given and what not even the worst director can degrade."[52]

There is more than just a little homoeroticism at work here, as Heston is extolled for the hauteur and hardness of his masculine beauty, a beauty that seems to escape the degrading controls of bad directors and on some level to exceed the bounds of the individual film itself. Heston, Mourlet argues, embodies cinema, since "by his existence alone, *outside of all film*, [he] brings a more accurate definition to cinema than films like *Hiroshima Mon Amour* or *Citizen Kane*, whose aesthetic either ignores or impugns Charlton Heston."[53] He becomes the living icon of a peculiarly masculinist aesthetic, the symbol of the machismo that MacMahonism celebrated.[54]

As Hoberman and Rosenbaum point out, the MacMahonist aesthetic was characterized by "an unabashed streak of misogyny and a taste for male bonding that celebrated acerbic macho figures such as Humphrey Bogart, Samuel Fuller, Howard Hawks, John Huston, Nicholas Ray, and John Wayne" (26). What is particularly interesting for our purposes, though, is that MacMahonism appealed to the same directors who were celebrated in the United States for providing an alternative to Hollywood and to commercialized American culture. Claude Chabrol, Jean-Luc Godard, Jean-Pierre Melville, Luc Moullet, and François Truffaut were all, Hoberman and Rosenbaum point out, "early apostles of the MacMahonist faith" (26). Two defining works of the French New Wave, *Breathless* and *Shoot the Piano Player,* fragment themselves "into a shrine of MacMahonist fetishes": the celebration of petty gangsters' ethical codes, the iconization of macho figures such as Bogart, the appearance of important figures such as Jean-Pierre Melville and important cultural signifiers such as *Cahiers du cinéma* within the works, the homage to the "style of a cheap 1950s Columbia Pictures Melodrama," and the crossing of "metaphysical absolutes with locker-room sexual humor" (28). Given the enthusiasm of French New Wave directors for the MacMahonist aesthetic sensibility, it is perhaps no surprise that Mourlet's panegyric to Charlton Heston appeared not in *Présence du cinéma* (the MacMahonist publication) but in *Cahiers du cinéma,* the publication historically noted for elevating auteurist criticism and for giving a voice to the French New Wave.[55] In this sense, *Cahiers* itself can be seen as something of a paracinematic or psychotronic publication, as it mixes paeans to what has come to be regarded as high cinematic "art" with equally enthusiastic celebrations of low culture and either ignores or reverses established cultural hierarchies in the process.

Genres and Generic Confusion

I mentioned earlier that the design of paracinema mail-order catalogs—which list titles alphabetically or chronologically and make no attempt to differentiate between high and low genres—encourages a kind of dialectical cultural reading. Certainly, it highlights an aspect of art cinema that is generally overlooked or repressed in cultural analysis; namely, the degree to which high culture trades on the same images, tropes, and themes that characterize low culture. "Film is a vivid medium," as Steven Shaviro notes.[56] And there is something vividly scandalous and transgressive about the films of Peter Greenaway, Derek Jarman, Luis Buñuel, Jean-Luc Godard, and the other European filmmakers I have mentioned.[57] In fact, European art cinema has followed a trajectory in the United States not unlike that of pure exploitation cinema, in that historically it has been seen as delving "unashamedly into often disreputable content," often "promoting it in . . . [a] disreputable manner."[58]

As Peter Lev notes, *Open City* (1945), "the first foreign-language film to earn more than a million dollars in the United States, is certainly not sexually explicit by contemporary standards. But some observers felt that *Open City's* success in the United States was based on a salacious advertising campaign."[59] Similarly, throughout the 1960s, the advertisements for Jean-Luc Godard's films tended to feature scantily clad women, images that were—American distributors felt—in keeping with the impression most Americans had of French cinema, as something sexy.[60] And as late as 1972, Pauline Kael felt it necessary to distinguish the eroticism of *Last Tango in Paris* from that of exploitation films and to stress the movie's links to the world of high culture.[61]

Michael Mayer gives a long list of reasons for the rise in popularity of foreign films in the United States after the war—the Paramount decision, which decreased the number of films produced in the United States; the increased American interest in all things foreign; the end of political isolationism; increased travel opportunities; the increased sophistication of the viewing public ("the public no longer requires complete clarity on film")—but most interesting for our purposes is the importance he places on the "violent" change in Americans' sexual mores.[62] Certainly, this is the "lesson" that Hollywood learned from the rise of art cinema. As Kristin Thompson and David Bordwell note in *Film History,* "one way of competing with television, which had extremely strict censorship," as well as with European art films, "was to make films with more daring subject matter. As a result, producers and distributors pushed the code further and further."[63]

For many Americans, however, throughout the late 1950s and early 1960s, European art cinema retained a scandalous reputation that marked its difference from Hollywood cinema (even a Hollywood cinema dedicated to "push[ing] the code further and further").[64] In 1960 the residents of Fort Lee, New Jersey, protested the opening of a "film art house" in their community. "It is a known fact that many of the foreign films are without doubt detrimental to the morals of the young and old," one pastor maintained. Apparently, the president of the borough council agreed. "I would not hesitate to pass an ordinance barring all future theatres from Fort Lee," he claimed, "if that's the only way to keep this one out."[65] And both Janet Staiger and Douglas Gomery stress the degree to which the audience for art films in the United States has always been a "special interest group."[66]

Hollywood's need to compete for art film audiences, then, should be seen more as an indication of changing audience demographics (mainstream audiences were going less and less frequently to the movies; special interest groups were going more and more) than as an index of changing mainstream tastes. The moviegoing audience was not only becoming segmented, as Janet Staiger claims,[67] but was becoming polarized (into mainstream and "alternative" or "fringe" audiences). Interestingly, the majority of historical titles on horror and exploitation video mail-order lists are drawn from films made during the era when this polarization became pronounced. Agreeing with Richard Kadrey that "everything interesting is out at the edges,"[68] the catalogs celebrate the two extreme tastes of the postwar youthful filmgoing public: low-budget horror, sci-fi, and exploitation films on the one hand, art film "classics" on the other.

In addition to these, there is an interesting array of films that, put quite simply, are difficult to categorize. There are films with high production values, European art film cachet, and enough sex and violence to thrill all but the most jaded horror fan: Roger Vadim's *Blood and Roses* (1960), Stanley Kubrick's *Clockwork Orange* (1971) Harry Kuemel's *Daughters of Darkness* (1971), Georges Franju's *Eyes without a Face* (1959), and Roman Polanski's *Repulsion* (1965) and *The Tenant* (1976), to name just a few. There are films, like Tod Browning's *Freaks* (1932), that began their career as horror or exploitation films and were later revived as art films; films, like Paul Morrissey's *Andy Warhol's*

Figure 4. The crab monster attacks in Roger Corman's *Attack of the Crab Monsters*.

Frankenstein (1973) and *Andy Warhol's Dracula* (1974), that belong to New York avant-garde culture as well as to horror; and experimental films, like the surrealist classic *Un chien andalou* (1929), that contain sequences as shocking as those in any contemporary splatter film.[69] These films promise *both* affect and "something different"; they are films that defy the traditional genre labels by which we try to make sense of cinematic history and cultures, films that seem to have a stake in both high and low art.[70]

Unlike *Nosferatu* or *Vampyr*—films that I earlier designated the "high end of horror"—these films still directly engage the viewer's body. Like the slasher films that Clover analyzes, many of them are "drenched in taboo" and encroach "vigorously on the pornographic."[71] All of them meet both Linda Williams's and William Paul's criteria for lower cinematic forms. In *Laughing Screaming,* Paul writes:

> From the high perch of an elitist view, the negative definition of the lower works would have it that they are less subtle than higher genres. More positively, it could be said they are more direct. Where lower forms are explicit, higher forms tend to operate more by indirection. Because of this

indirection the higher forms are often regarded as being more metaphorical and consequently, more resonant, more open to the exegetical analyses of the academic industry.[72]

This concurs with Williams's characterization of body genres as physically excessive, viscerally manipulative genres. For both Williams and Paul, so-called "low" genres lack "proper aesthetic distance" (Williams, 144). In fact, the title of Paul's book, *Laughing Screaming,* specifically foregrounds the kind of undistanced involuntary response—what Williams might call the ecstatic response—that direct, body genre films evoke from the audience. As Williams notes, "aurally, excess is marked by recourse not to the coded articulations of language but to inarticulate cries"—laughing, screaming—both on-screen and in the audience (143).

The films listed are nothing if not direct. There may be a "metaphorical" significance to the slashing of a woman's eye in *Un chien andalou*—in fact, feminist film theory would argue that there's a profound metaphorical significance to such an act—but that significance is very much bound up with the immediate physical jolt experienced by the spectator. Similarly, when Dracula vomits blood in *Andy Warhol's Dracula,* when Dr. Génessier peels the skin from a woman's face in *Eyes without a Face,* and when Stephan whips his wife in an excess of sadis-

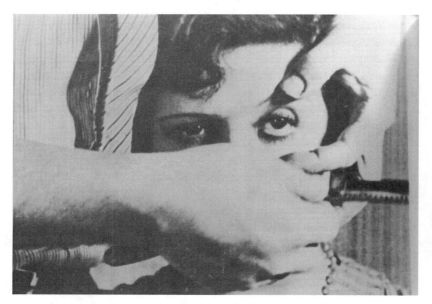

Figure 5. Prelude to the famous eye-slitting scene. Luis Buñuel wields the razor. Luis Buñuel and Salvador Dali's *Un chien andalou.*

tic sexual frenzy in *Daughters of Darkness,* the directness of the image "makes metaphoric significance seem secondary to the primary power" of the image itself (Paul, 32).

Which is not to say these films don't simultaneously operate at the high end of the horror spectrum. They do. The pacing, the blatant disregard for the cause-effect logic of classical Hollywood cinema, the strategic use of discontinuous editing, the painterly composition of certain scenes—all serve to mark these films as art cinema.[73] That the films seem to operate at both ends of the horror spectrum is at least partly responsible for the fact that the best of them were so poorly received at the time of their release. *Daughters of Darkness* was so unsuccessful in finding a generic niche, *The Encylopedia of Horror Movies* notes, that the film never received the attention it deserved. This "unsettlingly intelligent" and uncommonly beautiful film was not well received "by any of the established audiences for art cinema, horror or camp movies" (242).

A film that had an even more difficult time staking out its generic territory is Tod Browning's *Freaks* (1932). Initially made as a mainstream horror film at MGM, the film caused a scandal. Described in reviews as "loathsome" and "unwholesome," the film was pulled from mainstream distribution shortly after its initial release and leased to Dwain Esper (the prolific exploitation filmmaker), who showed it— under a variety of titles—on the exploitation circuit. Like *Daughters of Darkness,* however, the film had trouble finding an appropriate audience. Too sensational for mainstream filmgoers, the film simply wasn't sensational enough for many exploitation fans. As David Friedman notes, *Freaks* nearly caused a riot when Dwain Esper showed it to a North Carolina drive-in audience, under the sensational title *Forbidden Love.* Led by the title and advertising to expect a softcore treatment of "love" between "a beautiful woman and a midget," the crowd had no patience with a movie that Raymond Durgnat later compared to the European art films of Buñuel.[74] Esper managed to pacify the drive-in patrons by showing them a black-and-white nudist colony one-reeler that he had tucked in the trunk of his car, a film that apparently came much closer to satisfying their expectations than did Browning's creepy classic.[75] The same film—*Freaks*—was revived thirty years later as an "art film" and did very well, attracting favorable reviews by Raymond Durgnat and John Thomas and captivating such notable patrons as Emile de Antonio and Diane Arbus.[76] By 1967, David J. Skal notes, the film "had made it to the Museum of Modern Art" (21).

Finally, Michael Powell's art-horror masterpiece *Peeping Tom*

Figure 6. Director Tod Browning with his cast. Publicity still for *Freaks*.

(1960), which the *Encylopedia of Horror Movies* calls "one of the best and most disturbing films to be made in Britain," not only shocked audiences but almost ruined the director's career (135). Known for making films such as *The Life and Death of Colonel Blimp* (1943), *Black Narcissus* (1947), and *The Red Shoes* (1948), Powell had previously flirted with the sensational in his work, but never so graphically and disturbingly as he did in *Peeping Tom*. The film disgusted reviewers. Derek Hill's now infamous review for the *Tribune* perhaps best sums up the critical response. "The only really satisfactory way to dispose of *Peeping Tom* would be to shovel it up and flush it swiftly down the nearest sewer. Even then the stench would remain."[77] Interestingly, the film is now shown in art houses as well as in horror venues, and it is frequently taught—as an example of some of the best of British filmmaking—in university courses treating the history of British cinema.

In a way, hybrid genres such as art-horror films simply point up the problems that have historically characterized all attempts at genre definition. As S. S. Prawer notes,

> (i) Every worthwhile work modifies the genre [horror] to some extent, brings something new to it, and therefore forces us to rethink definitions and delimitations.

(ii) There are borderline cases, works that belong to more than one genre—
the overlap between the "fantastic terror" film and the "science fiction"
film is particularly large.

(iii) Wide variations in quality are possible within a given genre . . .

(iv) There are works which as a whole clearly do not belong to the genre in
question but which embody references to that genre, or contain sequences
that derive from, allude to, or influence it. The first dream-sequence in
Bergman's *Wild Strawberries* . . . clearly . . . [belongs] in that category.[78]

While Prawer is speaking here mainly of horror films, his
remarks—as he points out—can be adapted to fit "genre studies in any
medium" (37). Certainly, they can be adapted to fit other film genres.
Film noir, the thriller, and melodrama have a great deal of overlap with
other genres. Avant-garde cinema is just as divergent in scope and quality as horror cinema. The European art film is so diverse that it is generally not represented as a genre at all. And as Jim Collins maintains in
Architectures of Excess, the 1980s and 1990s have been marked by the increasing number of "eclectic, hybrid genre films"; films such as *Road
Warrior* (1981), *Blade Runner* (1982), *Blue Velvet* (1986), *Near Dark* (1988),
and *Thelma and Louise* (1991), which "engage in specific transformations
across genres."[79] In fact, genre overlap and instability are so common
that Robin Wood maintains that the tendency to treat genres as discrete
has been one of the major obstacles to developing what he calls a syn-
thetic definition of the term.[80]

Not only is there slippage between genres, but there is slippage
between evaluative classifications, as well. As Eric Schaefer pointed out
to me, if *Dementia* (Daughter of Horror, 1955) or *Carnival of Souls* (1962)
had been made in Europe, the films would probably be considered art,
or at least art-horror, films, instead of drive-in classics. Similarly, if *Eyes
without a Face* (Les yeux sans visage, 1959) had been made in the United
States it would probably be considered a low-budget horror film. That
is, in evaluative terms, the films would occupy not only a different
generic niche but a different artistic category or "class." The instability
of film categorization (as high or low art) in all genres was illustrated
when the July–August 1997 issue of *Film Comment* published a list of
the top thirty unreleased foreign-language films of the nineties. Drawing
on a poll that queried film scholars and critics such as David Bordwell,
Roger Ebert, Jonathan Rosenbaum, and Robert Sklar, Gavin Smith
(writing for *Film Comment*) listed *Les Amants du Pont Neuf* (Léos Carax,
1991) as the second-best unreleased art house flick of the nineties.[81]
Thus the film was categorized as high art. In 1996, however, before the

Film Comment poll results were published, the film was listed in a special paracinema company mailing, *Video Vamp Presents Celebrity Skin Videos,* as a "French sleaze classic." Clearly, as Jameson suggests, we need to rethink the emphasis we have placed on evaluation and essentialized categorization and replace it with a mode of assessment that is a little more dynamic.

As I've suggested, horror is not the only genre or category that is hard to pin down, nor is it the only genre or category that continually flirts with the possibility of existing simultaneously as high and low art.[82] To some degree, as William Paul asserts, all film still has something disreputable about it; all film still has to struggle to be seen as art at all.[83] And yet we do, as he also notes, consistently make distinctions between good cinema and bad, between artistic films and films that are "just entertainment." Even within as democratic a medium as film, we worry about "taste," a phenomenon that, social critics from Pierre Bourdieu to V. Vale and Andrea Juno maintain, always already entails questions of class.[84]

But while it is not the only popular genre that continually flirts with a kind of high-art double—in this case, the European art film or prestige import cinema—horror is perhaps the best vantage point from which to study the cracks that seem to exist everywhere in late-twentieth-century "sacralized" film culture. Precisely because it plays so relentlessly on the body, horror's "low" elements are easy to see. As Joe Bob Briggs is fond of reminding us, fans of low horror are drawn by the body count ("We're talking two breasts, four quarts of blood, five dead bodies . . . Joe Bob says check it out").[85] And as catalogs from mail-order video companies remind us, prestigious films, too, can play relentlessly on the public's desire—or at least its willingness—to be physically affronted. Like the lowest of low horror, European art films can "leave audiences gagging."

Bourdieu and the Class Configurations of Taste

I mentioned earlier that for Pierre Bourdieu, V. Vale, and Andrea Juno, the issue of taste always involves issues of class. In fact, Bourdieu is recognized as the theorist largely responsible for dragging class issues into discussions of "taste," a term that he sees as representing "one of the most vital stakes in the struggles fought in the field of the dominant class and the field of cultural production" (11). Interviewing people from a variety of classes, with a varying degree of educational backgrounds, Bourdieu found that respondents from the upper class and bourgeoisie—who had generally had some higher education—were more likely than people from working-class backgrounds to correctly identify paintings or musical pieces by famous composers such as Mozart, Beethoven, and Handel. This was not surprising, since the French education system has traditionally taught art and music appreciation as part of its curriculum. The more formal education a person has had, the more likely she is to have been trained to appreciate "classical" art. What was surprising was that Bourdieu found that "the relationship with educational capital is just as strong in areas which the educational system does not teach" (12). Thus the same people who were most likely to recognize Mozart's *Magic Flute* or Manet's *Olympia* were also more likely than their working-class counterparts to recognize the names of jazz musicians and film directors. Whereas working-class respondents scored high in questions asking them to identify film stars, television personalities, and popular singers, they did not perform as well when asked about "highbrow" popular music stars such as jazz great Miles Davis, and for the most part, they didn't recognize the names of directors such as Antonioni, Fellini, and Bergman—important figures in the European auteur cinema of the time.

The survey, Bourdieu writes,

> sought to determine how the cultivated disposition and cultural competence that are revealed in the nature of the cultural goods consumed, and in the way they are consumed, vary according to the category of agents and the area to which they are applied, from the most legitimate areas such as painting or music, to the most personal ones such as clothing, furniture or cookery, and, within the legitimate domains, according to the markets—"academic" and "nonacademic"—in which they may be placed. Two basic facts were thus established: on the one hand the very close relationship linking cultural practices (or the corresponding opinions) to educational capital (measured by qualifications) and, secondarily, to social origin (measured by father's occupation); and, on the other hand, the fact that, at equivalent levels of educational capital, the weight of social origin in the practice-and-preference-explaining system increases as one moves away from the most legitimate areas of culture. (13)

Class (social origin) not only plays a major role, then, in determining who recognizes, appreciates, and consumes the legitimate culture taught in school (Mozart, Manet); in cases in which the amount of formal education is equal, class becomes a determining factor in "the practice-and-preference-explaining system" of less legitimate—or "popular"—culture. That is, in a situation in which people from different classes have the same amount and type of formal education, class plays an increasingly important role in determining the extracurricular tastes and preferences of the respondents. Bourgeois respondents are more likely than their working-class counterparts to recognize and like the music of Miles Davis, the films of Michelangelo Antonioni, *even if* the respondents have had the same amount and type of formal academic instruction in music and art.

Thus taste is never class neutral. Not only is it an important signifier of educational achievement and of class values, but it becomes the means through which class values are normalized and perpetuated within the larger society. In fact, this normalization of class values (Mozart, Manet) through the transmission of certain class-inflected tastes, Bourdieu tells us, remains "perhaps the best-hidden" effect of the educational system. That educational degrees and titles are themselves important traditional markers of class privilege in France (where individuals have traditionally been assigned to "hierarchically ordered classes" of achievement) indicates the very real stake that education has in perpetuating the existing class structure, with all its traditional markers of titles, degrees, and cultural preferences (23). And of course, as U.S. cultural critics have been quick to point out, education's investment in the existing class structure, the existing hierarchy of class values, is not restricted to Europe. Andrea Juno and V. Vale put it best: "The concepts of 'good taste' are intricately woven into society's control process and class structure. Aesthetics are not an objective body of laws suspended above us like Plato's supreme 'Ideas'; they are rooted in the fundamental mechanics of how to control the population and maintain the status quo."[86] Interestingly, it is in both "high" and "low" culture challenges to the status quo that an appreciation for paracinema—for what Vale and Juno call "incredibly strange films"—can be found.

Cutting Edge is largely about the politics of taste, about the stake that both avant-garde and low-body cultures have traditionally had in challenging the formally constructed notion of mainstream good taste. Most of the films and film movements discussed are drawn from the post–World War II era, not because that is the only historic period marked by such a shared interest in trash culture but because it is the era when many of the cultural debates that have traditionally peppered elite publications such as film journals have found their way into the popular press, and because it is an era when the political and social stakes involved in the regulation of culture have become "less subtle," "more direct."

The book is divided into three parts comprising eight chapters. Chapter 2 deals with spectator theory and collector culture and demonstrates that arguments concerning the way people watch and consume television and video often simply reinscribe the high/low culture debate onto technology itself. Here I argue that people do not *necessarily* watch television and video in a "distracted" manner, as has frequently been claimed, but can watch as attentively as they do in theaters. I also examine high and low collector cultures, looking at the similarities and differences (in economics, packaging, and constructed aesthetic taste) between paracinema collectors and Criterion laser disc collectors. In this chapter, as in the others that follow, I'm interested in constructions of fan culture and fan taste; as I mention in the chapter, real people often collect *both* Criterion discs and paracinema videos.

Chapter 3 considers Pauline Kael's "Zeitgeist and Poltergeist," an essay that unwittingly demonstrates many of the cultural tensions and assumptions of the early 1960s. This chapter is meant to be read in conjunction with chapter 4, an essay on Georges Franju's moody horror masterpiece *Les yeux sans visage* (Eyes without a Face, 1959). Here I discuss the way *Les yeux* engages residual French cultural concerns about World War II, and, aesthetically, the way it occupies two cultural sites— horror and art cinema—cultural sites that Kael links through audience response and reception.

Chapter 5 treats Jess Franco's two "low" European remakes of *Les yeux*. The chapter situates Franco within the larger context of Spanish film culture and attempts to demonstrate the revolutionary implications of making "body genre" films during the fascist era.

Chapters 6 through 8 deal with horror and the avant-garde. Chapter 6 discusses Yoko Ono's documentary *Rape* (1969), a cinema verité film in which a real woman is really stalked by Ono's film crew. In addition to raising ethical questions about the very existence of such a film, and of other avant-garde documentaries of the period, the chapter discusses the way that such issues entered mainstream discussion through press coverage of an alleged snuff film, and Yoko Ono's own relationship to "low" culture and exploitation cinema. Chapter 7 discusses the strange history of Tod Browning's *Freaks,* a film originally made as a mainstream horror film, then leased out as an exploitation film, and finally recuperated in the 1960s as an art film, in the mode of Buñuel. Chapter 8 analyzes Paul Morrissey's *Andy Warhol's Frankenstein* and discusses the way in which the film did and did not represent a radical shift in the Factory's production—away from avant-garde work to "commercial" cinema.

For the most part, the films I've chosen to discuss here all figure prominently in paracinema catalogs. The three that don't, interestingly enough, are the films discussed in Chapter 6, the "ethics" chapter (Yoko Ono's *Rape* and the Findlays' *Snuff*). I make a point of mentioning this not only to stress the way that paracinema culture informs and structures the book but also to stress that all the film art discussed here needs to be considered within the economic contexts that have regulated its production and control.[87]

2 Medium Cool: Video Culture, Video Aesthetics

The battle for the mind of North America will be fought in the video arena.
—Professor Brian O'Blivion, *Videodrome*

In many ways, paracinema catalogs are simply the newest, most technologically up-to-date manifestation of an already established mode of film and TV consumption. In the 1960s and 1970s, television programs like the San Francisco Bay Area's weekly psychotronic fest, *Creature Features,* purveyed paracinema to the public. Mainly the show featured what the host, John Stanley, called "less than classic" movies in the genres of "horror, science fiction, and fantasy."[1] But Stanley had a paracinephile's sense of humor and irony. In addition to showing films such as *Corpse Grinders* (1971), *Legacy of Satan* (1973), and *Return of the Vampire* (1943), Stanley showed his own minimovies, short compilation flicks that satirized the genres that made up most of *Creature Features'* fare; televised interviews with Ray Bradbury, Christopher Lee, and Leonard Wolf; and what could only be called weird flicks—government hygiene films, Nixon's famous *Checkers Speech* (1952), *Reefer Madness* (1937). He also showed art films: Fellini's *Juliet of the Spirits* (1965), René Clair's *The Crazy Ray* (1923), Julien Duvivier's *The Golem* (1937).

Similarly, the theatrical midnight screenings that J. Hoberman and Jonathan Rosenbaum discuss in *Midnight Movies* had a paracinematic dimension.[2] Before *The Rocky Horror Picture Show* (1975) began to corner the midnight market, theatrical midnight screenings traditionally featured an eclectic mix of art films and trash. In San Francisco, Philipe de Broca's *The King of Hearts* (1967) and Ken Russell's *The Music Lovers* (1971) regularly alternated with John Waters's *Pink Flamingoes* (1973). And in New York and Chicago, the cities that Hoberman and Rosenbaum know best, double features routinely mixed classic horror films like *Freaks* (1932)[3] with surrealist classics like *Un chien andalou* (1929). Old serials like the *Charlie Chan* series or *Flash Gordon* often preceded the feature presentation. These serials were read ironically; that is, the audience laughed itself silly.

But whereas the paracinema aesthetic has been with us for a long time, paracinema culture is heavily indebted to video technology. Not only has video collecting given rise to the catalogs I discussed in Chapter 1, but video culture itself has made possible a certain desacralization of cultural forms, a desacralization that theaters by their very nature simply cannot achieve.

By bringing both popular culture and high art into the home and giving audiences a greater measure of control over how and when they consume products, the VCR has unmoored both low culture and high art from public exhibition space. (It was the ghettoization of high

Figure 7. Plan 9 Video, a paracinema outlet in Bloomington, Indiana.

art in class-inflected spaces like the opera house that, Levine argues, led to the sacralization of high art in the first place.) Because people no longer have to go into neighborhoods or architectural spaces that make them uncomfortable (or that they simply can't afford) to view certain films, they are freer to experiment with both high- and low-culture titles they might not otherwise see. As Andrew Ross has suggested, the emergence of porn videos that specifically target a female or heterosexual "couples" audience is one manifestation of this.[4] The "New Arrivals" rack—a staple feature of many neighborhood video stores, where most newly arrived titles, regardless of genre or type, are temporarily shelved together—is another.

This unmooring of product from cultural space has sparked a debate about the comparative aesthetics of film and "other" (TV/video/ laserdisc/CD-ROM) viewing, a debate that has added still another dimension to the ongoing discussion of high and low culture. The technological capacity to control viewing, which the VCR and remote control give the spectator, *could* be seen as a manifestation of the viewing practices traditionally advocated by the historical avant-garde and what Peter Wollen has termed the postwar "European avant-garde."[5] Instead, critics such as Timothy Corrigan have linked video and laser viewing to a Baudrillardian postmodernism, an era—and, here, a mode of viewing—in which nothing is stable. And for critics such as Susan Sontag, home viewing is—by its very nature—low culture; that is, it's about as far from the avant-garde as you can possibly get and still be on the cultural continuum.

When a film is viewed on the VCR, the film becomes, as Timothy Corrigan notes, a more selective experience (than viewing it in the theater), "subject to the choices and decisions of the spectator."[6] Armed with a remote control, the viewer can replay selected bits of a film, fast-forward through unsettling sequences, watch the film in installments, watch parts of it frame by frame, or stop it altogether. She can also create composite cinematic texts by alternately viewing two films or by crosscutting between a movie on the VCR and the six o'clock news. That is, she can become a truly active viewer, one who creates her own texts, one who feels free to disrupt the narrative flow.

The technology of the VCR and remote control enables a mode of viewing potentially reminiscent of the Brechtian challenge that, Peter Wollen claims, Jean-Luc Godard leveled against "orthodox cinema." In his now famous essay "Godard and Counter-Cinema," Wollen identifies seven elements of countercinema, elements that he sees in Godard's

Figure 8. Ad for New Products home entertainment systems. Copyright 1998 Hachette Filipacchi Magazines, Inc. All rights reserved. Reprinted from *Video Magazine,* December 1998, with permission.

films: narrative intransitivity (gaps and interruptions in the story, episodic construction, undigested digression), estrangement (disturbance of the viewer's emotional involvement with characters through the use of direct address, multiple and divided characters, commentary), foregrounding (making the mechanics of film/text visible and explicit),

multiple diegesis (rupture between different codes and "different channels"), aperture (open-endedness, overspill, intertextuality), unpleasure
(aiming to dissatisfy and hence change the spectator), and reality (the
breakdown of representation, truth).[7]

Although not all of these elements necessarily inhere in televisual media, certainly the capacity for disrupting narrative flow, for
enforcing multiple diegesis and aperture, is a given component of channel surfing and of active video/disc viewing at home (fast-forwarding,
rewinding, watching the film frame by frame). In addition, the spectator has the *capacity* to use the other countercinematic elements, as well.
During the Gulf War, many viewers (myself included) continually and
nervously flipped from video to CNN, then back to video again, creating a viewing atmosphere in which displeasure, estrangement, and reality were literally built into the televisual experience (perhaps for that
very reason, during the Gulf War I tended to rewatch movies I'd already
seen, films I knew pretty well).[8]

Channel surfing itself (or flicking between video/disc and TV)
is the domestic version of a mode of viewing that, in an earlier time, was
decidedly surreal, that is, avant-garde. In his 1951 essay about film *Comme
dans un bois,* André Breton, the founding father of French surrealism,
describes a method of film spectatorship that bears a remarkable similarity to contemporary televisual viewing practices.

> Quand j'avais <<l'age du cinéma>> . . . je ne commençais pas par con-
> sulter le programme de la semaine pour savoir quel film avait chance
> d'être le meilleur et . . . je ne m'informais de l'heure à laquelle tel film
> commençait. Je m'entendais très spécialement avec Jacques Vaché pour
> n'apprécier rien tant que *l'irruption* dans une salle où l'on donnait ce que
> l'on donnait, où l'on en était n'importe où et d'où nous sortions à la pre-
> mière approche d'ennui—de satiété—pour nous porter précipitamment
> vers une autre salle où nous comportions de même, et ainsi de suite. . . .
> Je n'ai jamais rien connu de plus *magnétisant:* il va sans dire que le plus
> souvent nous quittions nos fauteuils sans même savoir le titre du film, qui
> ne nous importait d'aucune manière.[9] (first set of italics mine)

> [When I was "cinema age" . . . I never began by consulting the movie list-
> ings to find out what film might be the best, nor did I find out the time
> the film was to begin. I agreed completely with Jacques Vaché in appreci-
> ating nothing as much as *bursting into* the theater when whatever was
> playing was playing, at any point in the show, and leaving at the first sign
> of boredom—of surfeit—to take ourselves precipitously off to another

cinema where we behaved in the same way, and so on. I have never known anything more *magnetizing:* it goes without saying that more often than not we left our seats without even knowing the title of the film, which was of no importance to us anyway.]

Breton and Vaché's movie manners were not just a manifestation of normal pre-1954 filmgoing behavior.[10] Unlike their fellow patrons, they did not simply drop into a theater, "pick up" the thread of a film already in progress, stay until the end, and perhaps watch the beginning of the repeat screening (up to the part where they had come in). Instead they created a cinemagoing process that appears here as the geographic equivalent of television channel surfing with a remote control. They *burst into* the theater, stayed for a short time, burst out again, and moved on to the next theater, where they behaved in exactly the same way. They did not seek or even accept Hollywood's stock seamless narrative. In the face of such mainstream cinema, they were prepared to supply shocks and disruptions of their own.[11] They went from theater to theater, juxtaposing various film segments in their own surreal pattern, making—as it were—their own movie.

By disrupting the narrative flow of any particular film and by deliberately garbling film imagery, Breton and Vaché sought simultaneously to gain some control over the experience of spectatorship (they literally refused to be passive viewers) and to gain some mastery over the structure of the narrative itself. Even in later years, when the surrealists began to watch films in their entirety, they sought to maintain some control over their experience by having loud conversations and by eating entire meals in the theater. For them, cinema attendance required audience participation, and they were experts in turning audience participation into interactive performance art.

It's interesting to note here the value that the surrealists gave to "entertainment" or surrealist entrancement. Breton and Vaché left the theater "at the first sign of boredom—of surfeit" and charged off in search of another movie. The "magnetizing" experience that Breton describes consists in coming away with a head full of images that somehow pleased him, bits and pieces of films—whose names he did not even know—that seduced him into staying a few minutes longer in his chair.

Although the VCR and remote control make possible a mode of home viewing that, in other contexts, has been considered avantgarde (at the first sign of boredom or surfeit, home viewers can change the channel or eject the tape), film critics have been hesitant to read the televisual experience as either engaged or sophisticated. John Ellis and Timothy Corrigan identify video viewing not as a modernist or avant-garde practice but as a postmodern phenomenon, a spectatorial mode that presupposes not an informed, engaged viewer but a fragmented and distracted one.[12] Following Ellis, Corrigan writes,

> When any movie is watched as a television show . . . the domestic setting of the experience may create a kind of immediacy and complicity between the television image and the viewer, but that imagistic immediacy is very significantly redefined across the fragmentation that is either built into the television text (such as commercial interruptions and the cuttings or reductions of the image) or simply intrude upon and invade it as part of the distractions of a domestic environment (conversations or the ringing of a phone). The television spectator, according to John Ellis, "glances rather than gazes at the screen; attention is sporadic rather than sustained."[13] (27–28)

Because viewers watch and control video and televisual images "more extremely than ever before, as the narcissistic subject of their own active desires, distractions and domestic conditions," they are themselves, as Corrigan notes, reflected in the viewing experience "as always potentially a discontinuous or fragmented subjectivity without a centered or stable position, a discursively mobile identity" (28–29). They become both the subject and object of what Jameson has termed a fundamentally "schizophrenic" spectatorial address.[14]

This formulation, which some critics call "glance theory," has a number of obvious problems.[15] As John Thornton Caldwell points out, the home viewer does not always view in ways that can be alternately read as intellectual and avant-garde, or postmodern, fragmented and disaffected. She is not "always, nor inherently distracted."[16] Television continually addresses committed viewers and "asks" them to "start watching important televised events" (26). Premium cable movie channels, such as Showtime and HBO, show films and weekly television serials in their entirety, without commercial interruptions—a practice that seems to assume an audience committed to watching a program from beginning to end, to "gaze" at it. Furthermore, the increased investment in home theater systems that promise large screens and surround sound indicates that home viewers are far from being as distracted as Corrigan and Ellis claim.[17] In many homes, such systems occupy a separate room—a den or TV room, where the distractions of the home are literally shut out.

The emphasis that glance theory places on the potential distractions of the domestic sphere essentializes one possible set of domestic circumstances as the televisual viewing norm,[18] and it presumes what Caldwell calls "a *very* unmotivated viewer" (26), someone who is incapable of choosing a good viewing time (when the kids are in bed and the phone is unplugged), of turning off the lights, of focusing on the screen; someone who simply doesn't value the viewing experience (again, the large sums of money people are spending to create optimum viewing environments within the home would seem to refute this assumption).

But it also takes a set of viewing habits that had previously been regarded as intellectually viable, even desirable, ways of constructing what Barthes might call a "writerly" cinematic text[19]—the disruption of Hollywood narrative, lack of closure, multiple diegesis, the intrusion of the "real" into the spectacle—and reinvents them as components of low culture. This is most noticeable in Susan Sontag's radical formulation in "Decay of the Cinema," where she writes:

> To see a great film only on television isn't to have really seen that film. It's not only a question of the dimensions of the image: the disparity between a larger-than-you image in the theater and the little image on the box at home. The conditions of paying attention in a domestic space are *radically disrespectful of film.* Now that a film no longer has a standard size, home screens can be as big as living room or bedroom walls. But you are still in a living room or a bedroom. To be kidnapped [by the images] you have to be in a movie theater, seated in the dark among anonymous strangers. (60, italics mine)

Sontag's fetishization of traditional modes of exhibition and theatrical space is quite extraordinary. To remove a film from the sacralized space of the theater is to disrespect the film and—by extension—to demote what had previously been regarded as radical avant-garde and modernist viewing practices (outside the home) to the status of "distraction," or "lowbrow" culture (inside the home).

The emphasis that glance theory places on the potential distractions of the domestic sphere becomes, then, simply another way of constructing the divide between high art and low culture. The "discursive rules" of glance theory[20] essentialize performance and exhibition space, privileging and sacralizing certain spaces while expressing anxiety about others.[21] But they also serve to essentialize and fetishize media—where a certain value inheres in the medium itself (irrespective of content), such that one can somehow "disrespect" a film simply by consuming it within an unsacralized space, and where TV constructs not only the way we watch television programs but the way we watch *anything* (home movies, laser discs, soap operas) transmitted or projected via TV. In Cronenbergian fashion, TV takes on a kind of viral aspect here, such that not only TV programs but the apparatus itself seems empowered to infect and transform the viewer, to literally change the way the viewer looks (or doesn't look) at images.[22]

If such a division between public and private participates in a reification of both space and media, it also seems to continue what Andreas Huyssen has identified as a modernist tendency to identify mass culture with women. Here the domestic space, traditionally associated with women, becomes the unsacralized, vulgar zone that is somehow degrading to high culture. In its most extreme formulation, this view would connect TV (popular culture) with the feminine domestic space, and cinema (high art) with the public, masculine exhibition space. That cinema itself can be divided into high art and popular culture (into "film" and "movies") should be read here as the cinematic equivalent of painting, which encompasses both Van Gogh and Keene (high art and "kitsch").[23]

I've discussed this at length to emphasize the problems inherent in assuming that spectators who see films on TV, laser disc, video, or CD-ROM literally watch the screen differently than spectators in theaters do. Home viewers are not necessarily distracted viewers. In fact, video and laser collectors gaze just as fixedly at the screen as any cinephile. And home system collectors have their own "-philia," their own obsessions, which are just as aesthetically inflected as Sontag's elegistic celebration of celluloid.

Collection Culture, Collection Aesthetics

Before the advent of CD-ROMs and DVDs, Criterion's[24] laser discs, with their remastered images and sound, historically provided the best aesthetic quality available at a potentially affordable price for the home market.[25] The Criterion Collection has dominated the "serious" laser disc market in this country. And as anyone who has ever participated in a film listserv or chat group can tell you, Criterion collectors and fans are a staunchly loyal crew. Digital transfers are made from 35 or 70 mm prints minted from the original negative and from master sound and effects tracks. The colors are clean, the images are clear, and the original aspect ratio of the film is restored. Even the annoying lag time that accompanies the turning or changing of a disc isn't enough to spoil the pure enjoyment of the image. And if you have a home theater system, or simply the means of hooking your laser disc player to good home stereo speakers, Criterion's sound is phenomenal.

Certainly, the company capitalizes on the quality of its transfers. But the company also takes a strong auteurist stance, as evidenced by their promotional material, which tells us that Criterion is the only label committed to showing movies "as they were meant to be seen." "Whenever possible," the Web site proclaims, "we work with *directors and cinematographers* to assure that the look of our laserdisc does justice to their intentions."[26] And Criterion markets an entire line of discs designated as "director approved." In this way, Criterion aligns itself with auteurist "art" and independent cinema and distances itself from the mainstream Hollywood studio system. It constructs an "outsider" profile (outside and opposed to the studio system) for itself that aids in marketing to both home collectors and institutions (school libraries and offices). Chris McGowan writes that many of the directors who work directly with Criterion "are probably still in shock at finding their films so lovingly treated, after years of dealing with hostile or indifferent studio executives."[27]

What Criterion promises is the "restored" movie, the movie as it was originally made, but not necessarily as it was originally shown in the United States. The promotional material for the CAV version of *Blade Runner* (1982), for example, promises "the original European release, with footage cut from the American theatrical release."[28] The most highly valued product here is the director's cut, the version not previously seen.[29]

In addition, the company promotes what its literature calls the "annotated movie." As Chris McGowan describes it, Criterion

> took the special, but previously unused, features possible only in the laserdisc medium and utilized them in wildly imaginative ways. For example, every laserdisc has multiple audio tracks. On *King Kong*, . . . [Criterion] pulled off a neat trick and took full advantage of that capability: they included both the movie's regular soundtrack and a parallel audio commentary by film historian Ron Haver. The latter provided a shot-by-shot, scene by scene analysis as the movie played. This was an astounding innovation.[30]

In McGowan's terms, this innovation has allowed the Criterion Collection "to invent the annotated movie, replete with subtext, missing text, and might have been text."[31] *The Magnificent Ambersons* (1942) disc includes "story boards, the entire original shooting script, and the text of an earlier radio-play version." *Close Encounters of the Third Kind* (1977) enables us "to watch either of two versions of the movie(!)" *Ghostbusters* (1984) is "a primer in special effects technology." *The Fisher King* (1991) features "deleted scenes and costume tests." And *Akira* (1987) has "thousands of frames of original artwork and an in-depth study of the animation process."[32] Often the "annotated movie" attempts to package the entire cinematic event, including theatrical trailers, interviews with actors and actresses, and televised reviews of the film. It is the movie as complete experience.

The success of the "annotated movie," a format that combines film text with both criticism and fanzine material, has led to increasingly expanded and increasingly costly discs. John Carpenter's *Halloween* (1978), for example, has the following special features:

- new wide-screen digital transfer in the original aspect ratio of 2.35:1
- screen-specific audio commentary featuring writer-director-composer John Carpenter, writer-producer Debra Hill, and actress Jamie Lee Curtis on her big-screen debut
- Gene Siskel and Roger Ebert giving splatter movies two thumbs down while praising *Halloween* in a controversial 1980 *Sneak Previews* segment
- the original theatrical trailer
- separate music and effects track
- additional footage shot for the 1980 television release
- photo-essay on the making, marketing, and mimicking of *Halloween*
- illustrated filmographies of John Carpenter, Donald Pleasence, and Jamie Lee Curtis
- genre guide by John McCarty, author of *Splatter Movies: Breaking the Last Taboo of the Screen,* including capsule reviews of cold-blooded-killer movies from *The Bad Seed* to *Halloween 5.*

The package includes 58 chapters on two discs and, at the time of this writing, costs $100. The collector's edition of Terry Gilliam's *Brazil* (1985) has a whopping 104 chapters on five discs and costs $149.95. Criterion markets its CAV special edition of *Brazil* as "the world premiere of Terry Gilliam's 142 minute final cut."[33]

Unlike glance theory's construction of the home as an inherently distracting, profane (as opposed to sacralized) space, the special

edition of *Brazil* constructs the home viewing environment as a sacralized, theatrical space, the potential site of a major film's "world premiere."
It's curious that a word that traditionally refers to the first time a film is
screened—"premiere"—is here given a precise material existence and geographic location. Through an absence of linguistic modifiers, "the world
premiere" of Terry Gilliam's final cut seems to refer back to the disc itself. The collector's edition, then, becomes the marketing of an event—
the premiere—as well as a product, an experience that can be replayed
and looped.

The connection of "event" to mechanical reproduction here, the
notion that a "premiere" can be reexperienced and replayed, suggests an
odd link between the logic of the collector's edition and the logic of
home movies (through which we both capture and "relive" the baby's
first step and our trip to the Louvre). That such a link occurs precisely
in and through a text that is simultaneously coded as the most "authentic" version of a film text implies a very different reading of domestic
viewing than the one provided by Corrigan, Ellis, and Sontag. Here, the
appropriate way to view a film ("films as they were meant to be seen") is
to view it domestically—not only in the sense of viewing it in the home
but also in the sense of viewing it *as* you would view a domestic film (a
home movie). In other words, in the world of Criterion's promotional
material, it is from domestic norms of viewing that we learn to experience a movie appropriately.[34]

Like Criterion's promo Web site, paracinema's advertising promises to theatricalize the home environment. Here the references are
to "drive-in classics," bump-and-grind houses ("grindhouse follies"),
"underground" movies, and roadshow and working-class bar attractions
("mud-wrestling babes!"). And like Criterion's promotional materials,
there's a certain link to home-movie viewing culture here. Many of the
catalogs are steeped in nostalgia, invoking 1950s and early 1960s drive-
in culture in a way that has special resonance for people who actually
experienced the drive-in dating scene. Specific historical figures such as
Johnny Legend are mentioned, and the illustrations often refer the viewer
back to sexy "tramp" images of the time. That is, there's a definite way
in which the catalogs acknowledge middle-aged collectors, for whom
these tapes constitute a walk down memory lane ("Remember when we
saw that flick at the motor movies and then got a flat tire on the way
home, and your dad was so mad he wouldn't let me into the house?").

And like Criterion's discs, paracinema *products* also maintain
certain links with domestic viewing culture. Tapes are generally Sony or

TDK tapes, the kind any consumer can buy at the store. With the rise in PC use, side labels are beginning to look more professional, and some companies—most notably Luminous Film and Video Wurks—package tapes in attractive video boxes (complete with color photocopy or color scanned images and some kind of movie blurb on the back). Many smaller companies like Video Vamp, however, typewrite or scrawl a film's name on the side panel label, and most companies send a tape in the plain cardboard jacket in which it came (no picture, no blurb, just the TDK or Sony label identifying the brand name of the tape). The tapes not only have the possible function of unleashing memories (like a home video) but *look* like home videos, like domestic products.

But this is where the similarity ends. Paracinema companies form what Michael Atkinson, writing for the *Village Voice,* has called "a minor black market."[35] The tapes bear the stamp of an outlaw cottage industry. The viewer is not just seeing "the world premiere" of a famous film; often she is watching a tape that is, technically speaking, illegal.[36] And the illegality is emphasized in the tape's very mode of viewer address.[37] American films that aren't otherwise available in this country, for example, are frequently duped from European videos or laser discs. Films such as the unedited version of Samuel Fuller's *White Dog* (1981) often come with subtitles (*White Dog,* for example, is subtitled in Dutch, and the blurb on the box promises "een keiharde film van meesterregisseur Samuel Fuller");[38] Asian films frequently have multiple sets of subtitles: Japanese, French or German, English. Catalogs carry warnings, emphasizing the contraband nature of the tapes. Luminous Film and Video Wurks Catalog 2.0, for example, notifies the collector that "any tapes confiscated at the border to the country where you live is your concern. We make no claims that your government will allow any of these tapes in. ORDER AT YOUR OWN RISK."

In a way, then, the tapes (at least some of them) invoke a logic of estrangement or exoticism. Frequently, the viewer is addressed as though he were a tourist, going to see an American movie in the Netherlands or in France, an American movie with subtitles. Rather than inviting the viewer to read a film *domestically,* these tapes invite us to read American films through a foreign filter. That they're bootleg tapes underscores the notion that *only other cultures* know how to appreciate American cinema (or at least know *what* American cinema to appreciate). And because uncut, uncensored European horror, exploitation, and soft-core porn tapes are available only through bootleg companies,

European titles tend to be constructed (and consumed) as more sophisticated and daring, certainly more exotic, than domestic products.

For the most part, paracinema companies do not attempt to package an event or a complete film experience the way the Criterion collection does. They package the movie with very few frills attached. Sometimes the original theatrical trailer will be recorded as a kind of bonus. Sometimes trailers for other videos sold by the paracinema company will be included.[39] The "extras" that appear on a tape (traces of earlier recordings, which I will discuss later) generally have little or nothing to do with the title in question. This is not to say that paracinema tapes don't provide some textual acknowledgment of fan culture. As Jeffrey Sconce has pointed out, fans are able to use the stylistic excess of the films themselves "as a gateway to exploring profilmic and extratextual aspects of the filmic object itself" (Sconce, 387).[40] But this requires a special kind of work on the part of the spectator; actual elements of fan culture such as interviews with stars and directors, articles about the way certain films were made, and auteurist overviews of a director's collected works are primarily found in the 'zines and on the Net at certain Web sites. Some paracinema companies market 'zines in addition to tapes, and some market special fan tapes (Luminous sells *Dario Argento: Master of Horror* [1993], a documentary about the works of Italian horror director Dario Argento, for example), but these must be purchased as separate titles.[41]

The minimalist style of paracinema company tapes is dictated in part by cost. This is the low-budget end of collection culture. Whereas "regular" Criterion laser discs (not special editions or "collector's editions") usually cost $49.95 or $59.95, paracinema tapes run anywhere from $14.95 to $25.00 at the high end of the market. A special tape series like the four-tape package of Krzysztof Kieslowski's *Dekalog* (1988) can cost $40. Anything more than that is considered pricey.[42]

Similarly, fanzine prices are kept within a certain cost range. A year's subscription to *Fangoria* is $46.97; individual copies of *Eye* cost $3.95. Newsletters and newsprint 'zines often cost less than that or can be downloaded, free of charge, from the Net. If price is an accurate index of what the market will bear, paracinema really is low culture. The cost of tapes and fan publications reflects the relative incomes of the working-class people, intellectuals, and adolescents who are some of the most avid paracinema consumers.

If paracinema companies don't create the same kind of movie packages that Criterion does, they also fail to mimic Criterion's commitment to aesthetic quality. As the editors of *World Art* point out, "the aesthetics of bootlegs are in a realm of their own."[43] Kadrey echoes that sentiment as he describes his first paracinema experience.

> You always remember your first one. Mine was a blurry "director's cut" video of *Texas Chainsaw Massacre 2*. It must have been a ninth or tenth generation dub. The colors had been lost somewhere in the shuffling of electrons from tape to copper wire and back onto tape. The harshest reds had strained to a porn-zine labial pink, the blues and blacks had dulled to a bad-meat gray. And the whole look of the frame had changed; softened slightly with each generation—the images wavering in some liquid video purgatory—until the whole thing resembled a sort of vertiginous underwater snuff film. But it was enough. Like any true addict, it didn't matter that my first taste of forbidden fruit was some third-rate, stepped-on junk . . . I was hooked.[44]

This is the pulp version of video culture. Unlike Criterion fans who savor technology for the embellishments it can provide ("remastered," "digitalized sound," "extra footage"), paracinephiles most often use technology as a slave. VCRs and PAL system machines are simply there to do the work. And although some companies—most notably Luminous Film and Video Wurks—do strive to provide the best-possible image available for the money, many companies take a kind of pride in sending out dupes that look like the one Kadrey describes. Here, the very rawness of the image becomes both a signifier of the tape's outlaw status and a guarantor of its authenticity. You know this is the stuff you weren't meant to see simply because the image quality is so bad; you're constantly reminded that the tape was duped in somebody's Manhattan apartment (is an "outlaw" tape) because the image is so bad.

It's no accident that the language paracinephiles use is tinged with references to forbidden culture. Reds don't just wash out, they turn "labial-pink;" blues and blacks don't just dull, they rot into "bad-meat gray." The references are to porn, horror, exploitation ("vertiginous underwater snuff film"), drugs ("addict"), and the charnel house. And the tapes themselves often provide visual reminders of these associations. It's not unusual for companies to record over old tapes. So it's not unusual for bootleg tapes to contain "trailers," bits and pieces of old porn flicks and gothic videos copied from late-night New York cable television broadcasts. The casual attitude toward product here is aggressively enforced. Tapes are to be valued because they contain rare or hard-to-find material, not because of their quality or intrinsic value.[45] The low end

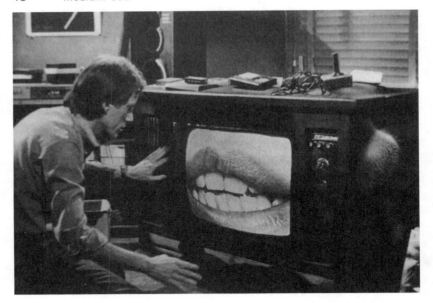

Figure 9. Video becomes monstrous for Max Renn (James Woods). *Videodrome,* by David Cronenberg.

of video culture is always interesting, but usually it's not pretty. And interestingly enough, it's this very absence of prettiness that grounds paracinema in what Ellis and Corrigan call "gaze" aesthetics.

While paracinema tapes can be watched "across the distractions . . . of [their] audiences" (Corrigan, 16), they do not support the aesthetics of the glance, which Corrigan sees as a defining element of video culture.[46] That is, a spectator can stop the video, go do something else, and then return to the tape. But he can't watch *while* cooking dinner or feeding a toddler. The images are too shaky to sustain the aesthetics of the glance. To see the movie, a spectator has to gaze at the screen, and often gaze hard, simply to make out what's happening.[47] In fact, paracinema is a good illustration of Marshall McLuhan's contention that low resolution necessarily fosters an engaged viewer response.[48]

In McLuhan's terms, paracinema tapes are a "cool" medium— in fact, since McLuhan designates TV as a "cool" medium, paracinema tapes could be considered "frigid." For McLuhan, "a hot medium is one that extends one single sense in 'high definition.' High definition is the state of being well filled with data."[49] A cool medium is the opposite; it provides relatively little data. A photograph is generally high definition and is, therefore, hot. A cartoon usually provides little information and is, therefore, cool. Because "hot media do not leave much to be filled in or completed by the audience," they are "low in participation." Cool media, on the other hand, are "high in participation or completion by the audience."[50]

McLuhan is speaking here only of the quality of the image—the amount of definition or information conveyed. But in a sense all collector culture could be said to be "cool." Collectors are connoisseurs and completists; that is, they collect different versions of the same title and compare them. A disc or tape may be valued simply because it has five minutes of footage not included in the original theatrical release. You have to watch the screen carefully to see all the differences, to know that you've gotten your money's worth. In McLuhan's terms, you have to participate to get all the data.

But in the world of collector culture, paracinema collection is the coolest of the McLuhanesque "cool." What's valued here is not just the director's cut, which both paracinema and Criterion Collection fans prize, but the *rough* director's cut—the working cut that is assembled before all the postproduction work is complete. As Richard Kadrey puts it, "the bootleg experience is shaped by the physical and legal constraints that define the bootlegged object's existence. When you watch or listen to a bootleg, you can't help but be aware that you're partaking of a kind of capitalist *samizdat,* indulging in a medium forbidden by the state. In that sense bootleg culture parallels drug culture, both in its word-of-mouth distribution system and in the kick of possessing, or simply being near the forbidden object."[51] As with drug culture, the closer you get to the source (in this case, the director), the purer and more unadulterated the goods, the better the high.[52]

At the Crossroads

Art Houses and Horrorshows; or, Pauline Kael Meets Georges Franju

We'd often go to the movies. We'd shiver as the screen lit up. But more often than not we'd be disappointed. . . . It wasn't the film we'd dreamed, the film we all carried in our hearts; the film we wanted to make and, undoubtedly, secretly wanted to live.

—Paul, *Masculin/féminin*

Pauline Kael's *I Lost It at the Movies* (1965) begins with "Zeitgeist and Poltergeist, or Are the Movies Going to Pieces," an essay on taste and film culture. It's a querulous, peevish essay in which Kael alternately mourns the death of well-crafted plot-driven cinema and lashes out against a younger generation of consumers, academics, and critics whose tastes are, she believes, draining the life out of movies. It's a curious read. The list of films that Kael sees as contributing to the "processes of structural disintegration" in 1960s cinema reads like a veritable compendium of the film canon—Michelangelo Antonioni's *La notte* (1960), Alain Resnais's *Last Year at Marienbad* (1961), Luis Buñuel's *Exterminating Angel* (1962), Jean-Luc Godard's *My Life to Live* (1962), the New American cinema of John Cassavetes and Shirley Clarke, the films of Ingmar Bergman.[1]

Some of what she says in the essay is interesting. The comparison of Resnais and Buñuel's "haunted house" films to classic ghost movies is perceptive, and her critique of art house audiences—that they often accept clumsiness and confusion as "ambiguity"—is well-taken. But her critical points are frequently undercut as she slips into a general complaint against the young. Her assessment of Susan Sontag (based on Sontag's review of Jack Smith's *Flaming Creatures*) is breathtakingly nasty (19),[2] and her irritation at an unnamed instructor in English— "the youngest person present" at a gathering in Kael's home—similarly betrays a real generational unease. His "neat little declaration"—that the scariest horror film ever made was *The Beast with Five Fingers* (1946)— upset her, both because it revealed "such shocking taste" and because it seemed to go unchallenged by the others present (6).[3]

The Beast with Five Fingers is one of many adaptations of Maurice Renard's *Les mains d'Orlac,* in which a pianist, who loses his hands in an accident, is given a murderer's hands, grafted onto the pianist's arms by a crazed surgeon. Here, it is the pianist's hand that becomes murderous, as it creeps around the chateau and molests anyone who threatens the pianist's beloved Julie. Luis Buñuel designed the creeping-hand sequences, which are marvelously surreal. The young English instructor at Kael's gathering found *The Beast with Five Fingers* to be scary because "it's completely irrational. It doesn't make any sense, and that's the true terror." And it was the young man's "existentialism in a nutshell" that leads Kael into her larger meditation on the waning relevance of plot in cinema (6).

If Kael found art and revival house audiences unsympathetic and, at times, incomprehensible, she found contemporary horror audiences—another young group—equally baffling. Like art house patrons, they always seemed to be reacting to a different film from the one she was seeing. While art house audiences were overly impressed by what she called "a kind of creeping Marienbadism" (21), horror audiences wanted "shock treatment, not diversion" (11). Her description of the horror audience at a screening of *The Haunting* (1963)—a film that Kael regards as better than Hitchcock's *The Birds* (1963)—demonstrates her confusion. *The Haunting* is, she tells us, "moderately elegant and literate and expensive. . . . it's basically a traditional ghost story" (12).

> It wasn't a great movie but I certainly wouldn't have thought that it could offend anyone. Yet part of the audience at *The Haunting* wasn't merely bored, it was hostile—as if the movie, by assuming interests they didn't have, made them feel resentful or inferior. I've never felt this audience hostility toward crude, bad movies. . . . But the few, scattered people at *The*

Figure 10. The "Greenwich Village Lesbian" (Claire Bloom) and the "repressed . . . virgin" (Julie Harris). *The Haunting.*

Haunting were restless and talkative, the couple sitting near me arguing— the man threatening to leave, the woman assuring him that something would happen. In their terms, they were cheated: nothing happened. And, of course, they missed what was happening all along, perhaps because of nervous impatience or a primitive notion that the real things are physical. (13)

Kael describes this audience in terms that one might use for her own reaction to art and avant-garde pictures, not "merely bored" but "hostile—as if the movie, by assuming interests . . . [she] didn't have, made . . . [her] feel resentful or inferior." And it's a sad commentary on the times that Kael doesn't think that a film in which only two women figure prominently—an unsympathetic "Greenwich Village lesbian" (Claire Bloom) and a "repressed, hysterical, insane" virgin (Julie Harris)— "could offend anyone." But I'm more interested here in the way that the film audience itself becomes fodder for her critique. A man and a woman arguing—perhaps because he really doesn't like arty horror flicks, perhaps because they were already irritated with each other when they arrived—lead Kael to fretfully grant the young English instructor's point (that true terror is always somehow bound up with the irrational, with stories that don't make any sense): "I am afraid . . . that there is no terror for modern audiences if a story is carefully worked out and follows a tradition, even though the tradition was developed and perfected precisely to frighten entertainingly" (14).

We all choose our examples to prove our points. Had Kael written about the audience for Hitchcock's *The Birds*—a film that delivers visceral shocks within the context of a well-crafted horror-romance with a relatively traditional plot structure (spoiled, beautiful rich girl meets good-looking middle-class man, irritates him, and finally overcomes his

Figure 11. Tippi Hedren as Melanie. *The Birds.*

irritation when she reveals her vulnerable side; in the meantime . . .)—
she probably could not have argued "that general audiences out for an
evening's entertainment . . . seem to have lost the narrative sense or become indifferent to narrative" (14). In fact, Kael would reverse much of
what she says in "Zeitgeist" in the seventies, when she would champion
Bernardo Bertolucci's *Last Tango in Paris* (1972)—a film whose end shooting sequence is as perplexing as the final shooting sequence of *My Life
to Live* (15)—and just about everything made by Brian De Palma, a horror director whose use of gore inspired concerned citizens to picket the
theaters where some of his films were shown. But by that time she had
a slightly different audience against which to measure her own reactions,
a slightly different group to construct oppositionally.

I mentioned earlier that "Zeitgeist" betrays a generational anxiety. The "bad" audience here—the Philistines, as Kael calls them (24)—
are younger, more intellectual. They seem to come from a different geographic and cultural zone. "In Los Angeles," Kael writes, "among the
independent film makers at their midnight screenings I was told that I
belonged to the older generation, that Agee-alcohol generation they
called it, who could not respond to the new films because I didn't take
pot or LSD and so couldn't learn just to *accept* everything" (19). It's hard
to imagine a group of filmmakers actually *saying* this to Kael, but I can
certainly imagine that she felt it—as a sort of implied message. As Janet
Staiger has pointed out, art house audiences comprised younger, better-
educated people.[4] Not only were art house and avant-garde audiences
more likely to attend lectures, the opera, theater, and ballet than "mass"
moviegoers,[5] they were also more likely to identify with the burgeoning
counterculture. As J. Hoberman and Jonathan Rosenbaum note, "the
pungent aroma of marijuana" frequently wafted through the Charles
Theater in New York (the theater where Sontag may have seen *Flaming
Creatures*), and

> mainstream critics who visited the Charles were as apt to review the au-
> dience as the movies: "Madison Avenue types mix among the beards,
> black leotards, and sloppy sweaters," wrote the correspondent for one
> Sunday supplement. "Half the audience juggles paper cups of coffee.
> Some pull sandwiches or chicken legs from pockets or bags." The screen-
> ings were social events—"a lot like a party," as Andy Warhol remembered
> them—and a *New York Times* reporter was as struck by the intensity of
> the discussion that erupted during intermission as he was nonplussed by
> the exhibit of "Easter Island monoliths" up in the mezzanine.[6]

David Skal paints a similar picture of the New Yorker Theatre, where Diane Arbus sat night after night in October 1961, watching Tod Browning's *Freaks* and smoking marijuana.[7] And Michael Brodsky was so taken with the cultural milieu at the Thalia Theater, a famous New York art house, that he wrote a novel about it.[8]

For Kael, this cultural milieu is as incomprehensible as the milieu surrounding the 1950s jazz clubs. It reminded her, she said, of her confusion "as a schoolgirl when a jazz musician who had been introduced to me during the break called out 'Dig you later' as he went back to the stand" (17). The example is telling. Like jazz, art house and avant-garde film culture seemed at once intellectual and primitive to Kael— who throughout this essay identifies herself with the plain folks who prefer films with "coherence and wit and feeling" (23). Like jazz lovers and musicians, art house fans and independent filmmakers seemed literally to speak a different language, one that Kael doesn't dig.

Not only is the young audience Kael describes constructed in terms of structural and spatial oppositions (Los Angeles, drugs, "swingers," couples, "bad taste," universities, youth), but they behave differently from other audiences. And this is where her description of the horror audience seems to connect most forcefully with descriptions of the art house crowd. In a passage reminiscent of Roger Ebert's later send-up of slasher film audiences,[9] Kael describes going to see *The Horror Chamber of Dr. Faustus*—a dubbed, mangled version of Georges Franju's *Les yeux sans visage* (1959)—at a theater on San Francisco's Market Street:

> But the audience seemed to be reacting to a different movie. They were so noisy the dialogue was inaudible; they talked until the screen gave promise of bloody ghastliness. Then the chatter subsided to rise again in noisy approval of the gory scenes. When a girl in the film seemed about to be mutilated, a young man behind me jumped up and down and shouted encouragement. "Somebody's going to *get* it," he sang out gleefully. The audience which was, I'd judge, predominantly between fifteen and twenty-five, and at least a third feminine, was as pleased and excited by the most revolting, obsessive images as that older, mostly male audience is when the nudes appear in *That Immoral Mr. Teas* or *Not Tonight Henry.* They'd gotten what they came for: they hadn't been cheated. But nobody seemed to care what the movie was about or be interested in the logic of the plot—the reasons for the gore. (8)

Kael here explicitly references the youth and predominant maleness (two-thirds) of the audience as she links horror to its sister body genres, exploitation and porn (*That Immoral Mr. Teas* and *Not Tonight Henry*).[10] As one might expect from such a crowd—the phrase "a third feminine" is telling, implying that girls somehow should know better—the audience is rowdy and loud. They talk during the slow part of the movie; they jump up and down and shout encouragement when someone on-screen is going "to *get* it." In a different context, with a younger group, for example, such a scenario can be constructed as innocent and charming; the puppet show scene in Truffaut's *Les quatre cent coups* (The Four Hundred Blows, 1959), in which a group of small children spontaneously reacts to a puppet show of *Little Red Riding Hood*—jumping up and down in excitement, yelling, gasping at the scary parts, and shouting instructions to the woodsman who has to kill the wolf—is one example of this. But here the audience is too old. Comprising mainly adolescents and young adults, its spontaneous reaction becomes immoral and threatening.[11]

By contrast, Hoberman and Rosenbaum's description of the scene at the Charles Theater is more tolerant. The *Midnight Movies* authors obviously feel some affinity with, some affection for, the audience they're describing. If they construct an oppositional Other, it is the mainstream press—the correspondents who aren't in the know—who take a gentle ribbing. "Out of discretion or ignorance," they write,

> no newspaper thought to mention the pungent aroma of marijuana that frequently wafted through the theater, but more than anything else, outside observers were impressed by the Charles's uninhibited patrons. AUDIENCE ADDS SOUND EFFECTS, *The New York Post* headlined a piece on the phenomenon, anticipating its coverage of the *Rocky Horror* cult by fifteen years. "Booing, hissing, and applause were all permitted equally," one habitué fondly recalled—a state of affairs that could prove quite traumatic. "After showing my rushes here I felt like committing suicide," the *Times* reporter overheard an unhappy NYU student complain.[12]

At the Thalia, too—"where the management talks so loud you can't hear the subtitles"—things could get noisy.[13]

The loud and unmediated carnival spirit that pervades these passages suggests one way in which art house, avant-garde, and horror audiences were linked in this period—through what Bakhtin might call the "language of the marketplace." As Bakhtin describes it, the marketplace of the Middle Ages and the Renaissance

> was a world in itself, a world which was one; all "performances" in this area, from loud cursing to the organized show, had something in common

and were imbued with the same atmosphere of freedom, frankness, and familiarity. Such elements of familiar speech as profanities, oaths and curses were fully legalized in the marketplace and were easily adopted by all the festive genres, even by Church drama. The marketplace was the center of all that is unofficial; it enjoyed a certain extraterritoriality in a world of official order and official ideology, it always remained "with the people."[14]

What Bakhtin calls "the unofficial folk culture of the Middle Ages" was an official part of the earliest manifestations of the historic avant-garde, as well. In their attempts to disrupt the institutionality of art and to scandalize ("épater") the bourgeoisie, the Parisian dadas staged matinees and manifestations designed to provoke the audience into active participation. Audience participants would arrive at avant-garde events well armed with tomatoes, raw meat, and insults, which they would proceed to hurl at the artists onstage. Like the punk rockers who came sixty years later, the performers would simply fling the projectiles (and epithets) back at the audience, delighted that the bourgeoisie found them so "sacrilegious, subversive, and altogether outrageous."[15] When the surrealists displaced the dadas as the reigning avant-garde group in Paris, they kept much of the old dada spirit. The first screenings of surrealist films provoked as violent an audience reaction as the dada matinees did. At a screening of Buñuel's films, for example, the theater was totally trashed, and the film screen itself was slashed. The surrealists also played the role of audience provocateurs themselves, attending events simply in order to disrupt the performance, and bursting in and out of movie theaters as whim or fancy struck them. Often they had loud conversations in theaters and were known to eat entire meals—complete with fold-up table and white tablecloth—while watching their favorite films (often "low" comedies or horror films).

The idea of the movie theater as a privileged populist site—one where people are free to act out their spontaneous responses to the entertainment, however rude such acting out might seem to be—is one that has roots, then, in both populist and avant-garde traditions. The jumping up and down to which Kael objected in the exploitation house, the yelling, and the smoking of pot in art house venues construct the movie theater (like the medieval marketplace) as "the center of all that is unofficial," a space that enjoys "a certain extraterritoriality" and seems to exists outside the "world of official order." It's a place where "official ideology" can be mocked, as audience members either avidly consume

Figure 12. Delphine Seyrig confronts "creeping Marienbadism." *Last Year at Marienbad.*

films meant to startle and confuse spectators (avant-garde films such as *Flaming Creatures* and art films such as *Last Year at Marienbad*) or react in ways that official ideology might regard as antisocial and downright frightening (cheering the slasher). At the same time, the booing and hissing at the Charles Theater, the spirited conversations during intermission at the Thalia, and the audience hostility at the theater where Kael saw *The Haunting* are part of a rigorous refusal of spectator passivity, a refusal that—in other contexts—has been lauded by Breton, Brecht, and Godard as avant-garde, even revolutionary.[16]

Kael is one of the few critics during this period who link—albeit elliptically—horror and art film audiences. Adopting what Dwight Macdonald might call an unabashedly "mid-cult" view,[17] she describes her uneasiness both with the art crowd and with the horror fans who were interested only in *Dr. Faustus*'s gore, not in "the reasons for the gore" (8). She argues that neither group knows how to look at a movie. The horror crowd is too interested in visceral response to pay attention to the real business of the picture, and the art crowd is too high-minded to ask the really tough questions—like "does this movie make sense?" But ultimately the art crowd's taste frightens her more than the horror fans' lack of taste ("bad taste"). More interested in "cinema" than in "movies," the art crowd represents a new intellectualization of film, an intellectualization that Kael believes will ultimately rob cinema of its lifeblood (25). Critics (like Dwight Macdonald and Susan Sontag) who write approvingly of the new "cinema" and the "academic bureaucracy" that nurtures them are considered vampires (26).

In many ways, "Zeitgeist" engages the aesthetic quarrels of the period. Kael's assessment of *The Birds,* a movie she considered to be "terrible" (10), can be read as a swipe at Andrew Sarris, who called *The Birds* a major work of "cinematic"—as opposed to literary and sociological—art, "the picture of the year."[18] The comments about Dwight Macdonald and Richard Roud overtly criticize the men's art house sensibilities:

> At the art-house level, critics and audiences haven't yet discovered the beauty of indiscriminateness, but there's a lot of talk about "purely visual content"—which might be called the principle of ineffability. *Time* calls Resnais's *Muriel* "another absorbing exercise in style." Dwight Macdonald calls *Marienbad* "'pure' cinema, a succession of images enjoyable in themselves." And Richard Roud, who was responsible (and thus guilty) for the film selection at the New York Film Festivals, goes all the way: films like *La Notte,* he says, provide an "experience in pure form." Once matters reach this plane, it seems almost unclean to raise issues about meaning and content and character, or to question the relevance of a sequence, the quality of a performance. (20)

Thus Kael sets herself against the formalism of Sarris, Macdonald, Roud, and others (Penelope Gilliatt, Susan Sontag, and *Time*), positing what she regards as a more authentic, more commonsensical approach. She wants to raise questions about "meaning and content and character . . . the relevance of a sequence, the quality of a performance." Of course, as Sarris's remarks about *Lawrence of Arabia* show, formalist critics also worried about "meaning" and the "relevance of a sequence"; they simply cast their comments differently.[19] And it is this casting—this dressing up of criticism in formalist, intellectual rhetoric—that Kael can't abide.

Furthermore, Kael is something of a formalist herself. Writing about *The Horror Chamber of Dr. Faustus,* she notes that "it's a horror film that takes itself very seriously, and even though I thought its intellectual pretensions silly, I couldn't shake off the exquisite, dread images" (7). This statement comes very close to Macdonald's and *Time*'s comments about Resnais's films (*Muriel* and *Marienbad*) and echoes what Roud says about *La Notte.* The difference, of course, is a matter of image-taste. The "exquisite, dread images" Franju created in *Dr. Faustus* moved Kael; the images of Resnais and Antonioni did not. As Hoberman and Rosenbaum might say, this is another case of "erotic preferences rationalized into esthetic manifestos, if not religious dogma" (37).

Kael wants to emerge as a mid-cult populist in "Zeitgeist." Whether aligning herself with "'sensible' people" against the "preposterous, unreal and fantastic side of life" in Los Angeles (5) or mourning the transformation of "movies, the only art which everyone felt free to enjoy" into "cinema . . . another object of academic study" (23), Kael invites us to see her as one of us—someone who enjoys "coherence and wit and feeling" and stories (22). But there's an element of audience phobia here that I find disturbing. As Kael makes abundantly clear in "Zeitgeist," she goes to the movies not only to gaze at the screen but to gaze at the audience, not only to critique the movie but to review the movie's patrons. She knows that roughly a third of an audience is female, knows the audience's age bracket, eavesdrops on lovers' quarrels. As Valerie Walkerdine notes in an article about television reception, this spying on, and study of, the audience might be called "the most perverse voyeurism." And while Kael does not attempt to hide her own reactions to the films from us—does not adopt the so-called "objective" stance that Walkerdine finds so objectionable in many social science reception studies—she does construct the audience as Other. And she does exhibit the "terror of the other who is watched," which, Walkerdine maintains, is a hallmark of the kind of academic scholarship that Kael purports to despise.[20]

Strong audience distrust runs throughout the piece. "Audience reaction" puzzles Kael as much as critical response here. Not only horror and art theater audiences, whose tastes are quirky and who don't seem to know how to behave, but "regular" audiences, too, baffle her. "The immense audience for *The Bridge on the River Kwai* . . . didn't express discomfort or outrage or even plain curiosity about what exactly happened at the end," she writes. "Was it possible that audiences no longer cared if a film was so untidily put together that information crucial to the plot or characterizations was obscure or omitted altogether?" (8). As uncertainty grows about what will draw audiences, she writes, "films in production may shift from one script to another or may be finally cut so that key sequences are omitted. And the oddity is that it doesn't seem to matter to the audience" (8). Audiences "can no longer be depended on to respond to conventional forms" (10). In fact, audience taste has become so baffling to Kael that it's not always clear in "Zeitgeist" when she believes she is speaking *for* those who enjoy "coherence and wit and feeling," and when she is trying to protect such audience members from themselves. It's not clear when she considers herself part of the audience and when she considers the undependable, capricious audience as one factor contributing to the demise of the movies she loves so much.

The reason for the change in audience is not easy for Kael to pinpoint. The emergence of intellectual, academic moviegoers seems to be part of the problem. The other part of the problem, however, is TV. Anticipating Ellis's elaboration of glance theory, Kael writes that "television viewing with all its breaks and cuts, and the inattention, except for action, and spinning the dial to find some action, is partly responsible for destruction of the narrative sense. . . . it may be that audiences don't have much more than a TV span of attention left" (9–10). Like the academic audiences who, Kael suggests, are more or less drugged into an artifically receptive state, "regular" audiences have been spoiled through their exposure to another form of mind-numbing popular culture. Not only is TV keeping people at home in the suburbs—away from the movie theaters in the city—but it's destroying their ability to enjoy movies (when they do get a chance to go out and see one) at all. Or rather, it's destroying their ability to enjoy the right movies, and to enjoy movies in the right way. As an arbiter of taste, Kael can only look at the enjoyment she does see going on all around her and shake her head. Too many people are enjoying films for the wrong reasons, she argues. So much so that it's destroying the medium.

4 The Scalpel's Edge: Georges Franju's
Les yeux sans visage

Let the wild rumpus begin.

—Maurice Sendak, *Where the Wild Things Are*

In this chapter, I look at one of the films that Kael analyzes in "Zeit-geist" and discuss the way it has occupied two cultural sites—horror and art cinema—that Kael links through audience response and reception. A lyrical film that has been claimed as an important link in the histories of both low cinematic culture (splatter films) and high cinematic art (art movies), *Les yeux sans visage* (Eyes without a Face, The Horror Chamber of Dr. Faustus, 1959) illustrates many of the cultural tensions and contradictions that Kael sometimes unwittingly lays out in her essay. In that sense, I think Kael is right. *Les yeux* is a key text for understanding the critical-cultural zeitgeist—the spirit (or should I say "poltergeist") of the times.

For many horror fans, *Les yeux* marks a turning point in the history of the genre, similar to the one marked by Michael Powell's *Peeping Tom* (1960) and Alfred Hitchcock's *Psycho* (1960). As *The Encyclopedia of Horror Movies* notes, "with the camera looking unblinkingly on as . . . a scalpel . . . [traces] a bloody line on a girl's face preparatory to the removal of facial tissue for a skin graft, *Les Yeux Sans Visage* has some claim along with *Psycho* (1960) to co-paternity of the splatter genre" (125). Cathal

Tohill and Pete Tombs cite *Eyes without a Face* as the film that paved the way for what they call the "kinky" European sex-horror films of the 1960s and 1970s (Tohill and Tombs, 17–25). Philippe Ross calls *Les yeux sans visage* one of only two French classics of the horror genre—the other being Henri-Georges Clouzot's *Les diaboliques* (Diabolique, 1954).[1]

But although *Les yeux sans visage* "merges with popular horror on some levels," it is still seen primarily as an art film.[2] That is, although the film is included as an important title in the history of the horror genre, many film scholars and critics have resisted analyses that define the film according to the expectations and formulas of fright films. For such diverse scholars and critics as Carlos Clarens, Raymond Durgnat, and Jonathan Rosenbaum,[3] the film seems to "rise above" the splatter aesthetic of low horror.[4] In mainstream critical discussion, as Jim Naremore notes, the film "remains within the formal/textual and critical/discursive realms of 'poetry' and 'art,'"[5] an example of sacralized cinematic culture and artistic—if disturbing—cinematic style. In this sense, it occupies a contested critical site similar to the one occupied by *Peeping Tom, Repulsion, Daughters of Darkness,* and *Un chien andalou*— a critical site in which the film's affective properties tend to be divorced from its "artistic" and "poetic" ones, so that it's difficult to find a critical language that allows us to speak about the film as a whole.

It is this dual status of the film as both poetic "art" film and affective horror movie that Kael references when she criticizes the primarily young audience of *The Horror Chamber of Dr. Faustus* for not caring "what the movie was about," for not being interested in "the reasons for the gore" (8). And it is the dual status of the film that marks or mars all early attempts at marketing the movie. "A horror film?" film reviewer Bruno Gay-Lussac rhetorically asked when the film opened in Paris. "No, a fabulous story of modern mythology" [une histoire fabuleuse de la mythologie moderne].[6] His review of the film as primarily an art film was undercut, however, by the thumbnail description that accompanied the theater listing of *Les yeux* in the same issue of *L'Express: "Les Yeux sans visage*—la poésie de l'horrible. Mais pas pour nerfs fragiles" [poetry of the horrible. But not for fragile nerves].[7] Furthermore, whereas the previous week's edition of the paper had claimed that "spectators dropped like flies" when the film was shown in England ("les spectateurs sont tombés comme des mouches"),[8] *Variety's* reviewer worried that the film might be too arty for American horror audiences. "Ambitious horror pic depends on clinical operation scenes and the showing of deformed faces for its effect," the *Variety* reviewer wrote after seeing the Paris preview.

"It has some queasy scenes, but unclear progression and plodding direction give this an old-fashioned air. . . . Director Georges Franju has given this some suspense and not spared any shock details. But the stilted acting, asides to explain characters and motivations, and a repetition of effects lose the initial impact. Lensing is excellent and technical effects okay. The editing is too leisurely and lacking in snap for this type of film." Main U.S. marketing possibilities for the movie, the reviewer advised, would be for "dualer and exploitation chances on its theme, with arty chances also possible if well sold."[9]

Director Georges Franju was no stranger to the sometimes restrictive function of critical and artistic categories such as the ones outlined. An acquaintance of André Breton, and an "enfant bâtard du surréalisme" [bastard child of surrealism],[10] he shared the surrealists' appreciation for the way in which the "'magical' could exist in bad films just as keenly as in good films."[11] At one point, he planned to join Breton for a lecture "on those fragments of bad films which correspond to surrealist notions, so that despite the intentions of directors, cinematographic poetry tends to rise up and come to the surface" (28). For Franju, as Raymond Durgnat notes, poetry—cinematographic or literary—"is the act of really seeing" (28), and if Franju shared a certain trash aesthetic with Breton, he also shared an important bond with the renegade surrealist Georges Bataille.[12]

For Franju, the only poetry that mattered was the poetry that cuts to the quick (Durgnat 1968, 28), poetry that holds to the romantic idea of the revolutionary power of violence.[13] As Durgnat notes, Franju's own pursuit of such an aggressive poetry brought him very near Bataille's view "that beauty's mainspring is the breaking of tabu" (28). It is not surprising, then, that he'd be drawn to the low, "tabu"-breaking genres that the surrealists admired: gothic, horror, fantasy. The first *ciné-club* program he organized with Henri Langlois[14] featured *The Cabinet of Dr. Caligari* (1919), *The Cat and the Canary* (1927), and *The Fall of the House of Usher* (1928)—all films praised by the surrealist group.[15] The program was called "Le Cinéma Fantastique."[16]

Franju's own contribution to horror cinema began with *Le sang des bétes* (1948), the documentary short that launched his career. For this film, Franju took his camera into a Paris slaughterhouse for what Gene Wright calls "an uncompromising look at conveyor belt death."[17] Brutal in its images, the film is indeed a clinical and unflinching examination of the activities of a charnel house; it is a horror show. But it is also an excellent early example of Franju's "poetic" style and antibourgeois politics.

As Gene Wright notes, "typical of his work, the film juxtaposes images of lyric beauty with blunt horror, and, typically, it outraged middle-class audiences who didn't want to know where their hotdogs and hamburgers came from" (70). In fact, one of the most unnerving aspects of the film is its interdiegetic representation of the blissfully ignorant, meat-eating bourgeoisie. Scenes of lovers kissing and women shopping are juxtaposed with images of bludgeoned, gutted animals, which sometimes howl with pain. That this torture takes place right on the outskirts of Paris only adds to the general creepiness of the film.

The image of a "House of Pain" on the outskirts of Paris—a place where animals are tortured and brutal scientific experiments are carried out—is also a central organizing feature of *Les yeux sans visage* (1959), Franju's second feature-length film and his first official horror title.[18] The film revolves around Christiane Génessier, a young woman who has been horribly disfigured in an automobile accident. She has no face, and she is forced to spend all her time in her father's house, wearing a white mask. Her father, a renowned surgeon who is obsessed with his daughter's "open wound," begins experimenting with skin-grafting techniques. With the help of a faithful female assistant, Louise (whose face he *was* able to restore), Dr. Génessier begins kidnapping young women who have Christiane's "genre de beauté" [kind of beauty]. Surgically removing their faces, he tries unsuccessfully to graft these *visages* onto his daughter. With each unsuccessful attempt, Dr. Génessier's despair and Christiane's depression grow worse. Finally, Christiane rebels. She frees her father's latest human victim; she releases the dogs that had been used in the doctor's preliminary experiments. In a final moment of poetic justice, the dogs turn on their tormentor and rip into Dr. Génessier's face.

The film clearly owes a lot to the mad-scientist formula of popular cinema. Although Franju had been warned by the film's producer, Jules Borkon, to avoid the theme of mad doctors (Tohill and Tombs, 23),[19] "the essence of *Eyes without a Face*," as Richard von Busack notes, "is the loathing of the God-like power of doctors. This hatred extends not just to their capacity for causing pain but also to their obscurity, their capacity for hiding behind a glass."[20] What von Busack calls "the bloody core" of Franju's horror film is its disturbing depiction of what Michel Foucault has dubbed the modern clinical gaze, a gaze that—in its zeal to see beyond medical symptoms into the very interior of the body—has "as its field of origin and of manifestation of truth the discursive space of the corpse."[21] Close-ups of the eyes of Dr. Génessier and his assistant Louise dominate the scenes in the operating theater and contrast with the close-ups of the eyes of potential victims in the Paris street scenes. Furthermore, the clinical eye is implicitly linked to Foucauldian notions of medical power and knowledge. Dr. Génessier literally cannot see women except as possible skin donors for his daughter. Under his clinical gaze, even the traditional Gallic male appreciation for different "genres" of female beauty (cited frequently by the police in the film) is linked to the "discursive space of the corpse" as Dr. Génessier kidnaps women whose beauty he admires, opens their bodies, and inadvertently kills them in the process. In this sense, Franju's film belongs to a subgenre of mainstream horror films concerned with medical ethics and the birth of the modern clinical method. Like Robert Wise's *The Body Snatcher* (1945), James Whale's *Frankenstein* (1931), and *The Bride of Frankenstein* (1935), *Les yeux* questions the morality of a science that must depend on "fresh bodies" as the major source of its knowledge.

Le Résistancialisme

Eyes without a Face gives the mad-scientist formula a historical relevance. Franju had been told to avoid the subject because, Borkon felt, it would "upset the Germans, who would see references to the experiments of the concentration camps" (Tohill and Tombs, 23). Indeed, it is difficult not to see such references in Franju's film. Doctor Génessier's painstaking removal of female skin is reminiscent of the horror stories about lampshades made from the bodies of concentration camp victims. And the chilling way in which the doctor is able to see his potential victims not as human beings but only as specimens, as laboratory animals, also brings the horrors of Nazi medical practice to mind.[22] The doctor is obsessed with "ordre" [order], and the factorylike precision of his movements both inside and outside his surgery (what *Variety* termed his "stilted acting") are reminiscent of Erich von Stroheim's Germanic figure expression in Renoir's *La grande illusion* (1937). Furthermore, the doctor himself has an oddly Germanic look. Actor Pierre Brasseur's squarish jaw, glittering glasses, low, rumbling voice, and somewhat ponderous delivery set him apart from the rest of the Gallic-looking, Gallic-sounding male cast.[23] Dr. Génessier may be "a normal man who does extraordinary things," as Tohill and Tombs assert (23), but he is normal in the way that Hannah Arendt asserted Eichmann was normal. His monstrously rational and chillingly inhumane code of ethics makes him a prime example of what Arendt has called "the banality of evil."[24]

If the film seems to reference German atrocities (the death camps), it also alludes to French collaboration and French anti-Semitism. Dr. Génessier mutilates women in order to restore to his daughter her true face, "ton vrai visage," he tells Christiane. But "vrai visage" is the term that French Nazi sympathizers used during the war to describe French racial and national purity. "Nous combattons le juif pour re-donner à la France son vrai visage" [We fight the Jew in order to restore to France her true face] read a 1941 sign at the Institut d'Etudes des Questions Juives (Institute for the Study of Jewish Questions).[25] And the question here, as in occupied France, is precisely how many people must be removed, how many people must be tortured and killed, to "restore" a true French face—a "vrai visage" that is always, it seems, con-structed from the skin of the Other.

Collaboration was a taboo topic in France after the war. Refer-ences to Vichy and to the French deportation of French Jews were largely downplayed in favor of what Guy Austin calls *le résistancialisme,* the the-ory that, during the Occupation, the entire nation had supported Charles de Gaulle and the Resistance rather than collaborating. Estab-lished during the postwar Fourth Republic, the myth was perpetuated with the founding of the Fifth Republic by de Gaulle in 1958.[26] In fact, one might argue that it was *le résistancialisme* that gave the Fifth Repub-lic, under de Gaulle's leadership, its legitimacy.[27]

In cinema, *résistancialisme* was promulgated through careful ed-iting and censorship of certain images. Alain Resnais's powerful docu-mentary of the Holocaust, *La nuit et le brouillard* (Night and Fog, 1955), was withdrawn from the Cannes Festival of 1956. The ostensible reason was that the French government did not want to offend the Germans. But as James Monaco argues,

> what really disturbed the censors was the challenge the film presented to the French to recognize their own complicity in the extraordinary crime of the death camps. They glossed over, for the most part, the inferences of the narrative to seize on one particular image, a shot of about five seconds which showed the Pithiviers assembly camp. In the control tower a French gendarme was clearly visible. This visual evidence of collaboration was in-tolerable to the authorities. After two months of negotiation, the produc-ers of the film agreed to alter the image (and the evidence of history) by covering the gendarme's uniform. It would be another fifteen years before Marcel Ophuls's *Le Chagrin et la pitié* [The Sorrow and the Pity, 1972] would bring the dirty secret of collaboration back into the light.[28]

Borkon may have wished to avoid *Les yeux*'s mad-doctor theme, then, not only because he felt it would "upset the Germans" but because he feared that—as in the case of *La nuit et le brouillard*—it would upset the French censors, who were touchy about references (however brief and tangential) to French involvement in crimes associated with the camps. In fact, as the case of *La nuit et le brouillard* shows, "upset the Germans" was often code for "upset French officialdom." And here Borkon's fear that *Les yeux* might upset the French censors makes a certain amount of sense. Not only are Génessier and his clinic French, but the terminology he uses to comfort his daughter and excuse his crimes (he kidnaps women and kills them in order to restore Christiane's "vrai visage") explicitly references French anti-Semitic slogans calling for racial purity.

Even the disfigurement of women in this film has an eerie postwar French resonance. In *Les yeux,* we are told that Christiane was injured in the course of an automobile accident caused by her father ("he was driving like a madman," she tells Louise). The main horror of the film involves kidnapping young women and destroying their looks to conceal the signs of this originary patriarchal crime and guilt. Women's faces are stolen so that Christiane's "vrai visage" might be restored, and the physical punishment for Dr. Génessier's crime—such as it is—is routinely played out on women's bodies. Women are disfigured because he was driving like "un fou."

In postwar France, as well, bad memories of the war and of patriarchal guilt were initially exercised by (temporarily) destroying the looks of women. While only the most egregious male collaborators and only some of the merchants who did extensive business with the Germans were tried for their crimes, women who had consorted with *les Boches*—for either sentimental or commercial reasons—were publicly humiliated and had their heads shaved. In a sense, French guilt over all French collaboration was intially mapped onto women's bodies, and it was women who bore the brunt of the punishment for most of the quotidian traffic in German commerce (prostitutes were punished for doing business with the Germans; bakers and butchers generally were not). In that sense, shaved postwar French women stood in for *all* French collaborators, and their temporary disfigurement served to cover over or mask some of the wider crimes and guilt of the patriarchal homeland (crimes that began to come to light only in the 1970s and 1980s).

The 1959 film that bears the most stylistic resemblance to *Les yeux,* and that treats memory in a similarly haunted way, deals explicitly with the way women's collaboration became the "official" postwar dirty secret of France. In Alain Resnais's *Hiroshima mon amour*, a woman known primarily as "elle" [she] and identified only by her birthplace, "Nevers en France" [Nevers in France], becomes involved with a Japanese architect while she is in Hiroshima making a film about peace. The love affair is continually refracted through the couple's memories and experience of the war: his of the bomb falling on Hiroshima, hers of a tragic love affair with a German soldier. In a sense, both individual stories become the official history of the war. In a memorable scene, she explains to him the way her German lover was killed, and she recounts the manner in which she was punished and confined in her parents' home. She went mad, she tells him. And the images of blood running down her fingers as she claws the walls in the flashback sequence are reminiscent of the moisture (sweat?) glistening on his skin in the first frames of the film—in which the couple makes love while discussing the museum at Hiroshima. "I saw everything," she tells him; "You saw nothing," he replies. And it is in the space between everything and nothing (Sartre's "être et néant") that the film—both the love story and the history of the world—takes place.

There is no evidence that either *Les yeux* or *Hiroshima mon amour* ran into trouble with the French censors. But the popular press did see the postwar-war connection binding the two films. When Bruno Gay-Lussac called *Les yeux* a fabulous "histoire" of modern mythology ("une histoire fabuleuse de la mythologie moderne"), he was to some extent referencing Michèle Manceaux's observation that the film treats "everyday" horror (as opposed to the fantastic horror of England's Hammer films, which specialized in vampires and "monstres aimables," or "lovable monsters"). But what is interesting is the way both reviewers for *L'Express* define "everyday" and "modern mythology." Not only is violent crime mentioned in this context, but the death camps ("les poteaux d'execution") and the bombing of Hiroshima are explicitly referenced as part of the "mythology" that provides impetus for the "everyday" horrors of the film.[29] In that sense, Gay-Lussac is playing with the dual meaning of "histoire," so that *Les yeux* becomes not only a "fabulous story" but a "fabulous history" as well.

Occupying a Double Niche

If the film can be read on one level as a sociopolitical allegory, it is also, as Philippe Ross points out, an ode to paternal love gone mad ("ode magnifique à l'amour paternel fou").[30] In fact, one of the most disturbing things about the film is the way in which it insistently and consistently conflates Nazi medicine with family politics and paternal devotion.[31] In that sense, *Les yeux sans visage* participates in the kind of psychosocial critique that Franju's earlier film *La tête contre les murs* (Head against the Wall, 1958) mounted against the patriarchal family. As in *La tête*—where a rebellious young man is committed to an insane asylum by a stern and unforgiving father—the medical establishment in *Les yeux* serves as an extension of absolute paternal power. It is there, the film insists, not so much to heal people as to exert social control.

For that reason, *Cahiers* critic Michel Delahaye calls *Les yeux* a "late gothic" work (literally, flamboyant gothic, "Gothique flamboyant").[32] Playing down the film's allusions to Nazi medicine, Delahaye concentrates on Franju's effective use of mise-en-scène, the family romance, and genre conventions. What is interesting here, though, is that Delahaye apparently can't make up his mind what *kind* of genre conventions the film employs. Uncomfortable with horror, "a genre so frequently decried, more frequently still abused" [si souvent décrié, plus souvent encore malmené] (48), Delahaye initially struggles to justify Franju's use of what he calls a minor genre ("Franju utilizes the real in order to transcend horror and horror in order to transcend the real")[33] and then introduces a subtle slippage of genre terms as "horror" ("l'épouvante") becomes "gothic," "late gothic," and finally "film noir" (54). In fact, the illustrations that accompany the piece—Louise in a dark raincoat pulling a body out of a car at night, and Christiane, wearing her mask and white robe, lying in a faint on a patterned carpet—invoke film noir and gothic much more than the low, "minor" genre of horror.[34]

The trajectory from horror to noir here makes a kind of sense. As James Naremore points out, noir can historically be linked to gothic fiction, and the overwhelming majority of films called "noir" are located somewhere between supernatural fiction and science fiction.[35] But Delahaye's use of the terms "gothic" and "noir" is also clearly meant to draw a cultural distinction between the kind of "sensational" horror put out by Hammer Studios and the kind of "serious" horror that both *Cahiers* and *L'Express* felt that *Les yeux* represented.[36] In fact, *Les yeux* became something of a watershed film for the French (and for Francophile critics), a film that permitted them both to reiterate (and perhaps reify) the high-low dichotomy that exists within the ranks of horror cinema itself and to demonstrate their contempt for British (film) culture. "Spectators dropped like flies" when the film was shown in England, *L'Express* crowed.[37] And Raymond Durgnat cited the film's reception in England as yet another sign that British (film) culture lacked taste. "In England," he wrote, "*Les Yeux sans visage* was greeted with a unanimously shocked or contemptuous press. . . . Almost the only reviewer in a national daily to give it a good review very nearly lost her job as a result. . . . Needless to say *Sight and Sound* bayed its utter scorn."[38]

In both the French popular press and the film journals, then, *Les yeux* always occupied a double niche. Horror but not Hammer horror, not low horror, not *horror* horror, Franju's film became a sort of cultural lightning rod, a property around which contradictory discourses about horror and art cinema could take place. But as the *L'Express* articles demonstrate, "horror" already had a deeper resonance in the popular imagination than the *Cahiers* writers were willing to admit. Delahaye's discussion of horror seems almost naive to fans of the genre. His comment that "Franju utilizes the real in order to transcend horror and horror in order to transcend the real" (50) is such a generic truism that one can say it about *any* horror film; Manceaux and Gay-Lussac's discussions seem much more nuanced. While the *L'Express* reviewers share *Cahiers*'s dim view of horror (particularly British horror) as a genre, they also share Jules Borkon's understanding that the common horror mad-doctor theme could have profound social and political resonance in countries still grappling with the horrific memories of World War II. For the popular press, *Les yeux* partook of a social mythology that derived from the death camps, the slaughterhouses, and Hiroshima. For *Cahiers* critics like Delahaye, it remained the story of individual psychological obsession, an unsettling work that spoke to the politics of the family more than to the politics of historical racism and war.

When the film came to the United States as *The Horror Chamber of Doctor Faustus,* the horrific operating-room sequence described earlier had been cut. Perhaps for this reason, the cultural and generic discourses surrounding the film and audience reception of the film appear even more mixed than they did in France, almost confused. In fact, a certain amount of confusion seems to have been built into the marketing of the film itself. Lopert released *Doctor Faustus* in the United States in 1962, on a double bill with a U.S-Japanese coproduction, *The Manster* (Kenneth Crane and George Breakston, 1959), a sort of postwar combo of *Frankenstein, Island of Lost Souls,* and *Dr. Jekyll and Mr. Hyde.* In *The Manster,* Larry Stanford, an American journalist working in Japan, is sent on one final interview assignment—with renegade scientist Dr. Suzuki—before returning home. During the interview, Suzuki, impressed with Stanford's physique, drugs him and injects him with serum. In the following weeks, Stanford undergoes a personality change and experiences a variety of odd symptoms—symptoms that are ultimately explained when one hand turns into a hairy paw and a second head emerges out of Larry's body. Now a two-headed manster, Larry runs around Tokyo killing people. Finally, his monstrous, mutant self splits off and becomes a separate being. After a struggle, Larry throws his ape-man double into a volcano and returns home, a sadder but wiser, less naive American reporter.

Posters and ads for the double bill stress both high- and low-culture connections. The copy for *The Manster*—"See the two-headed killer creature," "Half-Man–Half Monster," "Invasion from the Outer World by 2-Headed Creature-Killer"—links the "Master Suspense Show!" to carny freak shows, tabloid journalism, and B horror flicks. But the copy for *Horror Chamber of Dr. Faustus*—"worthy of the great horror classics of our time," "selected for special showings at the Edinburgh film festival," "a ghastly elegance that suggests Tennessee Williams"—stresses that film's connection to the sacralized world of legitimate theater and international film festivals, a connection that seems simultaneously to be undercut by the sensational title given to the film itself. As Eric Schaefer notes, "they're certainly trying to give *Eyes/Faustus* a bit of a class sell with the film festival line and 'classic' designation, but it's packaged with a film from a very different league and the lines for *Manster* on the poster are a more traditional pitch for a horror flick."[39] No wonder the audience who saw the movie with Pauline Kael in San Francisco seemed restless. They didn't know *what* to expect, except that occasionally someone would "get it" and they'd see "something good."

But they were also restless because U.S. horror film culture of the fifties and early sixties had literally taught them to be so. As Carlos Clarens points out, the success of 3-D horror films in the early fifties "pointed the way to the next step: an increased audience participation was in order if horror was to survive."[40] And so the master horror showmen of the era staged gimmicks. William Castle was the most notable, electrically wiring theater seats during the initial screenings of *The Tingler* (1959), so that selected members of the audience would feel a "tingle" during key scenes in the movie when the tingler is actually supposed to be loose in the theater. But other gimmicks—all with highly scientific, technical-sounding names—became staples of the horror experience of the period: percepto *(The Tingler)*, psychorama (*My World Dies Screaming, Terror in the Haunted House,* 1961), hypnovista (*Horrors of the Black Museum,* 1959), and Emergo (*The House on Haunted Hill,* 1959). Many of these gimmicks, particularly Emergo—which consisted of a luminous skeleton suspended on wires and swung over the heads of the spectators—are reminiscent of the "special effects" used in the original Grand Guignol Theater, a French theater that specialized in often hokey special effects and gratuitous displays of violence (this is the theater from which the adjectival use of the word "Guignol" derives).[41] Certainly, there was something theatrical about the presentation of the flicks. Often tables were set up in the lobby so that actresses dressed as nurses could check the patrons' blood pressure before they entered the theater; this was to ensure that the spectator's heart was "strong" enough to take the thrill promised by the show. Sometimes patrons were asked to sign waivers, swearing that if they did in fact have a cardiac crisis during the movie, they wouldn't sue the theater. Often Castle himself—accompanied by one or two buxom female assistants—introduced the film and helped to set the mood. And the mood, as *Matinee* (Joe Dante's 1993 tribute to Castle productions) shows, was carnivalesque. Patrons moved around the theater, yelled things at the characters on-screen, sneaked up behind their friends and tried to scare them, threw food at the screen, made out. In *Matinee,* tragedy nearly strikes when a poorly constructed theater balcony gives way under the rambunctious activities of the preteen crowd. In the film, as in real life, ushers are nowhere to be seen; having quickly despaired of ever controlling the kid mob, they're presumably out in back, enjoying a smoke.

Even when films weren't specifically geared to a carny show atmosphere, filmmakers of the period often assumed that a Bakhtinian marketplace mood would dominate audience reception of the show. So B horror films of this period are short on important dialogue, and what dialogue there is is often repeated. Films such as *Manster* and *The Brain That Wouldn't Die* (Joseph Green, 1959)—a film in which a scientist tries to bring his girlfriend back to life by keeping her head in suspended animation in his lab while he searches for a suitable body—feature a repetitious litany of moral qualms about the scientist's activity. In part this litany functions as the editor in chief's speech in *Scarface* (Howard Hawks, 1932) does, as a means of giving a "moral" patina to films that might otherwise be deemed too sensational and dark for public consumption. But it also ensures that the audience can talk, laugh, neck, and hoot and holler without missing anything essential. In fact, the period audience's historical response to horror dialogue and to what Kael calls "plot" seems to be one of the motivational factors behind Alfred

Figure 13. Publicity for *The Brain That Wouldn't Die,* starring Jason Evers and Virginia Leith. "A great absurd movie," writes Michael Weldon in *The Psychotronic Encyclopedia.*

Hitchcock's see-it-from-the-beginning rule for *Psycho* (1960). *Psycho,* a film that does rely heavily on plot articulation and dialogue to drive home its horror, needed a different theatrical treatment than the one horror flicks usually got. And Hitchcock, as great a showman as Castle ever was, took pains to ensure that *Psycho* got the treatment it needed.[42]

That is not to say that these films didn't have serious content. There were often pointed cultural messages buried in the repeated litany of moral misgivings. Certainly, at the purely visual level, the number of films featuring women—or women's body parts—contained in cages, jars, boxes, and vials says something about the larger cultural anxiety about the powers exerted by women relegated to (and imprisoned within) the home. In that sense, films like *Manster* and *The Brain That Wouldn't Die* can be read as horror's dark take on *The Ozzie and Harriet Show, Leave It to Beaver, Father Knows Best,* and all the mainstream situation comedies of the period. In horror of the fifties and early sixties, women are destroyed by the experience of giving everything to men, and their containment in the home/lab either renders them zombies or pushes them over the brink into primeval rage. An odd amalgam of both Philip Wylie's *Generation of Vipers* and Betty Friedan's *The Feminine Mystique,* low horror of this period marries a real awareness of the mental and physical toll that enforced housewifery took on women (Friedan) with a real fear of women's influence, power, and thirst for vengeance (Wylie).[43]

As many scholars have pointed out, horror—particularly sci-fi horror—of this period also reflected U.S. cultural anxiety about Communism, the Red Scare, and the Bomb.[44] In Japanese films and Japanese-U.S. coproductions, mutations caused by nuclear energy both invoked and reflected anxiety about the aftermath of the bombing of Hiroshima and Nagasaki during World War II and about the nature of future relations between the two countries. Certainly, *Manster*—with its two-headed (two-faced) American journalist and wicked Japanese doctor—managed to invoke both American fear, and mistrust, of the Japanese and American dis-ease over the way the war had ended. As one of my students said, the two-headed American journalist seems to represent the duality of America's relationship with Japan: "First we bombed the hell out of them, then we helped them rebuild."[45] And the sneaky Japanese doctor, who feigns friendship to gain access to the superior (if more primitive) Western body, is yet another popular culture example of America's continuing fear of the "inscrutable, vengeful" East (an East that in this instance may have real reasons for wishing us harm).

So although the *Manster/Faustus* double bill seems, at this remove, confused in terms of its cultural codes, it made a certain amount of thematic sense. Not only were both films concerned with mad scientists and the godlike power of an unscrupulous patriarchal male, but they both reflected lingering anxieties about the horrors unleashed during World War II. And both films share the concern that, once unleashed, these horrors—death camps, medical experimentation on unwilling subjects, Hiroshima, the atomic bomb—will continually return to haunt us; the fear that having once crossed a certain moral threshold, we will never be able to go back.

Reception of the "dualer" in San Francisco, the city where Kael saw *The Horror Chamber of Dr. Faustus,* was "good," according to *Variety.* The double bill opened at the Paramount Theater on 28 March 1962 and made an estimated $13,000 its first week. Because receipts did not fall off during the second week of the run, we can assume the audience was satisfied (at least audience members didn't race home and tell their friends not to bother with the show).[46] And the audience, as Kael's piece tells us, was a mixed group. Both horror fans and art film afficionados turned out for *Dr. Faustus,* a situation that was not unusual for the Paramount—which, like so many houses, ran horror and exploitation flicks, reissues and revivals, and art films. The theater clearly actively courted both the horror and art film crowd. Not only does the theater ad reference elements of both horror and sacralized film culture (film festivals, Tennessee Williams, etc.), but the newspaper announcement for the film maintains the same cultural duality. While the title—"U.S. Premiere of Horror Films"—is designed to attract the attention of horror fans, the article plays down *Dr. Faustus*'s horror associations completely. Here the film is called a "suspense and thrill show," and the synopsis of the movie's plot says only that a girl who had been disfigured in a car accident is "repaired by her father." The elimination of all references to the stalker/mad-doctor theme, combined with the reference to Georges Franju himself as a "new wave filmmaker," seems clearly designed to attract the same kind of audience that turned out for Chabrol.[47] More interesting still, the article makes no attempt to describe *The Manster*, referring to it only once—in the lead sentence of the article. "Today marks the premiere of *The Horror Chamber of Dr. Faustus* and *The Manster*."[48] Despite an ad campaign that appears to suggest that *Manster* is the main feature (with the copy and graphics for that film being given prominence in the poster and ads), both the *San Francisco Examiner* article and the *Variety* report feature *Dr. Faustus* as the main draw of the show. *Variety* gives Franju's film most of the credit for Paramount's box office receipts, singling out *The Horror Chamber of Dr. Faustus* in its lead paragraph on "Frisco" attractions and only mentioning *The Manster* in its later listing for the Paramount Theater itself. The body of the *Examiner*'s article does not mention *The Manster* at all.

Les yeux sans visage goes further in exploring both female subjectivity and male identification with the victim than most art-horror does. The restored version is also more direct, more blatantly gory, than most art-horror of the period. The scene I mentioned at the beginning of the chapter culminates with a shot of Dr. Génessier lifting the face of one of his victims into the air. As Adam Lowenstein points out,

> Franju . . . invokes the science film by dwelling on the clinical details of the procedure: the powerful surgical lamps, the adjustment of the gloves and masks, the metallic sheen of the operating tables, the sleek shape of the scalpel. The methodical execution of the sequence greatly accentuates its horror. Franju first details the preliminary tracing of the scalpel's path in marker, and then the actual slicing of the skin. He inserts many shots displaying the sweat on Génessier's brow, the exchange of instruments and glances between himself and Louise, and the orientation of characters around the operating table. By the time the scene climaxes with a

grisly close-up of the complete removal (in a single fleshy strip) of the facial skin, the spectator squirms from the sheer perceived duration of this ordeal. The cold, distant authority of clinical practice disintegrates when confronted with the audience's physical reaction to its tidy order.[49]

As Lowenstein points out, the very length of the scene has the audience squirming in their seats long before Génessier actually peels the skin away from his victim's face. For that very reason, the culminating sequence of shots seems gratuitous—not necessary to convey the horror of the procedure. The audience is already spooked; the final elevation of the victim's masklike face before the unflinching gaze of the camera is pure Guignol, a spectacle included simply for affect.

Apparently, it had quite an effect. Seven people reportedly fainted during the film's screening at the Edinburgh Film Festival in 1959, and the scene showing the surgical peeling away of skin was cut from many of the theatrical prints that still circulate in the United States. Despite the cut, however, the film was distributed in the United States under the alternative title of *The Horror Chamber of Dr. Faustus,* a title that—Jonathan Rosenbaum notes—invokes a certain "'psychotronic' treatment."[50]

As Rosenbaum points out, both the original U.S. title and the emphasis that the film places on affect, on what Judith Halberstam has called "skin shows,"[51] link it to low horror, specifically to the splatter genre. John McCarty defines the splatter film as a horror-film offshoot that aims "not to scare . . . [the] audience, nor to drive them to the edge of their seats in suspense, but to mortify them with explicit gore. In splatter movies, mutilation is the message."[52] Certainly, it is the message here. In *Les yeux sans visage,* female identity is a medical construction, as essential and fragile as the surgical "skin job" that creates it. Traditional binary oppositions between interior and exterior, Self and Other, literally break down as the skin of various women is peeled away, resutured, rejected, peeled away again. Identity and meaning are not, therefore, *dependent* on Freudian readings of the skin as representative of something else. Rather, meaning and the production of identity reside in the flesh, and power is precisely measured through literal incisions and markings on the skin. Like David Cronenberg, Franju can be seen as "a literalist of the body."[53]

He is also a superb craftsman, and much of the grisliness of the film derives directly from his ability to reinforce many of the film's most visceral moments with an analogous cinematic style. "This time I have to remove a much larger graft," the doctor tells Louise, at a key point in the film. "All in one piece. Without cuts [sans coupures]." For Franju, who seeks to find a cinematic equivalent to the doctor's "style," the main professional problem is how to deal with the long take—the unfurling of a scene in a single uninterrupted shot, without cuts ("sans coupures"). Long takes, deep focus, and lengthy scenes are the organizing cinematic technique of a film that is unrelentingly Bazinian in its emphasis on mise-en-scène and theatrical detail.[54] Montagelike juxtaposition is used to create meaning in certain key sequences, but more frequently Franju uses Hollywood's invisible style to mask cuts within lengthy scenes. In the operating-room sequence cited earlier, for example, cuts are masked so that the viewer's attention is drawn to the "longeur"—the sheer length—of the operation.

Obviously, this is done for affect. The spectator is much more likely to become uncomfortable, to feel the horror, if a scene is held just a tad too long. But it's interesting to note how much Franju's long takes and slow, methodical attention to detail mirror Dr. Génessier's own clinical practice. The long tracking shots, the close-ups (on objects, on the doctor's perspiration, on the painstaking removal of a long strip of skin), and the number of deep-focus shots all serve to create the impression of a cinematic eye that is not all that different from Dr. Génessier's probing clinical eye (his reading of symptoms and his prolonged investigation of physical details). Even the language here serves to reinforce the analogy. "Cuts," "takes," "masks," and "shots" take place within an operating theater, a medico-horror space where different body parts are spliced together (the medical equivalent of an editing room).[55]

More important, however, the power politics of medicine are shown here to be not all that different from the power politics of film. The clinical gaze is shown to be analogous to the cinematic gaze, which—as Laura Mulvey taught us—generally takes woman as its object.[56] Finally, the power politics of medicine and the power politics of the horror film are explicitly linked through the very notion of "body genres." Just as Dr. Génessier's clinical and patriarchal power plays itself out on and through the bodies of his female victims, so too Franju's cinematic power is played out—at least in part—on and through the body of the audience. In places, the film seems to literally assault the viewer. In this sense, *Les yeux sans visage* may be said to foreshadow *Psycho*. Although Dr. Génessier's knife might not seem to rip through the screen and actually cut the body of the spectator (Hitchcock's ambition for *Psycho*),[57] Franju does share with Hitchcock an uncanny and masterful ability to make the spectator *feel* the violence that seems (in both men's work) to be an implicit part of the filmmaking process itself.[58]

But if Franju—like Hitchcock—has his sadistic moments, he is also, as Carlos Clarens suggests, something of a poet. And it is his poetry that has made both film scholars and contemporary critics reluctant to classify *Les yeux sans visage* as a splatter film.[59] When a remastered 35 mm print of the film was released in 1995, U.S. critics praised Franju for his lyricism. Writing for the *Chicago Reader,* Jonathan Rosenbaum points out that the film is "as absurd and as beautiful as a fairy tale." He continues, "this chilling, nocturnal black-and-white masterpiece, possibly Franju's best feature, was originally released in this country dubbed and under the title *The Horror Chamber of Dr. Faustus,* but it's much too elegant and poetic to warrant the usual 'psychotronic' treatment."[60] Gene Wright agrees: "Georges Franju might have become France's premier splatter-chef if not for his formidable talent and his larger purpose."[61] And *The Encyclopedia of Horror Movies* is lyrical itself as it notes:

> Although the plot is as wildly fantastic as anything Hollywood ever dreamed up for Boris Karloff or Bela Lugosi, Franju invests it with a weird poetry in which the influence of Cocteau is unmistakable (scenes, for instance, in which Scob [Christiane] wafts through the house in a waxen mask of eerie beauty). "The more you touch on mystery, the more important it is to be realistic," Cocteau once said in discussing his hatred of poetic effects; and the mysterious breath of poetry which surges through *Les Yeux Sans Visage* comes precisely because Franju coaxes a hard, insistent realism out of his fantasy material. (125)

"Poetry" is a word that the surrealists applied to film, and its appearance in so many discussions of *Les yeux sans visage* is a way of paying homage to the surrealist elements in Franju's work: the dreamlike pacing; the juxtaposition of extraordinary realism (the clinical details of everyday life) to what Breton calls the *marvellous* (the final scene, where Christiane walks out into the night surrounded by doves, is just one example of this);[62] the antibourgeois morality that the film espouses; and Christiane's ethereal appearance, which, as Tohill and Tombs point out, reminds one of "coldly beautiful and ethereal female figures in the paintings of the Belgian surrealist, Paul Delvaux" (23). Even the expressionist mise-en-scène and cinematography seem surrealist here, as they invoke the silent German horror masterpieces that Breton, Franju, and the other surrealists loved.

But "poetry" is also a way of talking about some of the art cinema elements in a film that horror critics see as a precursor to the slasher flick. The long, slow tracking shots and long takes give the film a rhythm that one associates more with art cinema than with horror.[63] The lack of clear cause and effect, the absence of an easily identifiable hero, and the lack of closure all bring the film in line with David Bordwell's description of the art cinema mode.[64] And the film looks like an art film. The frame composition, as *The Encyclopedia of Horror Movies* notes, is often reminiscent of surrealist paintings, and the recurring contrast of white clothing seen against a black background is stunning. The cinematography is expressionistic—in the manner of Universal's classic 1930s horror masterpieces and of film noir—as shadows are used both to conceal details and to signal moral ambiguity and low-key lighting is used to design graphic chiaroscuro patterns as well as to create a mood.[65] The mise-en-scène is effective, often moving.

Still, at the time of the film's original release, all of its artistry was not enough to blunt the effect of its affect. As Carlos Clarens notes, "except in the French magazines circulated primarily among *cinéastes, Les Yeux sans Visage* was adversely criticized in just about every country it played. In America, it was dubbed, mangled, and . . . dismissed by those hardy reviewers who caught it at theaters specializing in nudist/sadist fare, as a nauseating piece of sensationalism."[66] But for filmgoers trained in the cruel aesthetics of European horror, the film marked a definitive turning point in the history of the genre. As Tohill and Tombs point out, *Les yeux sans visage* "was a widely seen and influential film. Its combination of unflinching gruesomeness, bizarre poetry, and pulp imagery was picked up by a host of imitators" (23).

It's clearly a film that occupied, and continues to occupy, several different cultural niches simultaneously. Both grisly horror film and lyrical-poetic art flick, it is celebrated in most paracinema and psychotronic catalogs as a "classic French horror film" (European Trash Cinema), a "masterfully told tale" (Sinister Cinema), and a "classic, poetic" film *(Psychotronic Encyclopedia of Film)* with "one extremely shocking scene" *(Psychotronic Encyclopedia),* "the infamous face removal scene missing from all U.S. prints" (European Trash Cinema), a scene that "will literally make your skin crawl" (Sinister Cinema).[67]

Jonathan Rosenbaum once said of the movies, "by the time the academics pick something up, it's the equivalent of being in fifth run."[68] In other words, once a film title makes it into academic discussion, you know it has lost its immediate importance as a cultural document; in many ways, it has lost its edge. In part, this is because it takes time for a film to attract academic attention. Partly it is because academic discussion—as rich as it can often be—has traditionally treated films as enduring, "universal" documents and thus has tended to collapse the historical and cultural specificity of each individual title. Certainly this has been a problem with psychoanalytic readings, which many argue tend "to reduce all cinema to a rather uniform series of themes, processes and effects on the spectator."[69] But rarely do we see academic, psychoanalytic, and aesthetic means of analysis used almost deliberately to tame a film, to ensure its place through an almost willful campaign to mute or subdue thematic elements that censors and distributors might find objectionable. Yet this seems to be the case with *Les yeux sans visage*. Michel Delahaye's review of the film in *Cahiers du cinéma* reifies the film as an art film both by mixing the terms of its generic discourse—linking horror to the more acceptable B genres of gothic and noir—and, more importantly, by simply avoiding discussion of disturbing allusions to World War II, allusions that sprang up quite spontaneously in the popular press. From the very beginning, then, academic—or at least specialized cinephile—reception of the film in France dovetailed with Borkon's desire not to upset the Germans, and not to upset the official French censors.

I don't mean to suggest here that *Cahiers* intentionally participated in some kind of plot designed to render the film less potentially subversive and disturbing. But I do believe that the reification of the movie as a noir art flick did ultimately distract from some of the larger cultural and sociopolitical issues that the film threatened to engage. Certainly, it tended to displace them onto some ongoing *aesthetic* quarrel with the British and with British film culture, rather than leaving them as uncomfortable reminders of the tremendous ideological and political challenges (eliminating, or at least controlling, anti-Semitic nationalism) confronting all the postwar Western European nations.

Of course, the reification of the film as an art film also helped to ensure its survival. Certainly in the United States, where *Les yeux* had a limited initial run and attracted very little attention in the mainstream press, it was the academic reputation of the film—its inclusion in course syllabi and in university archives—as well as its reception by important film critics such as Durgnat, Kael, and Sarris that helped to build a continuing audience for Franju's masterpiece and contributed to its rerelease in remastered form in 1995. But the other factor contributing to *Les yeux*'s continued life took place at what many regard as the opposite end of the cultural spectrum. In horror fanzines and video collectors' catalogs, *Les yeux* assumed a life of its own. And here the discourse surrounding the film has always emphasized both its lyricism—its art film status—and its gore. Presented as a "censored," edited consumer object, the film—with its taboo operating-room sequence—was restored for the video market years before its rerelease in theaters. Professors with psychotronic leanings regularly showed the "forbidden clip" to classes the day after students had seen the "official print," and class discussions often took on a more interesting—or at least far-ranging—tone as a result. In fact, for all her skepticism about what might happen once movies became "another object of academic study and 'appreciation'" (23), Kael would have been happy to note that in film classrooms, people finally did begin to talk about "the logic of the plot—the reasons for the gore," and the effect that removing the most grisly scene had had on what many believe to be Franju's greatest movie (8).

5 The Anxiety of Influence: Georges Franju and the Medical Horrorshows of Jess Franco

You're amazing, Doctor. And so *different.*
—Nathalie to Dr. Moser, *Faceless*

For Europe's "low" horror directors, *Les yeux sans visage* was an influential film. Its combination of traditional Sadeian motifs with what might be called the horror of postwar anatomical economy—too few faces to go around—appealed to continental filmmakers who were trying to create a niche for themselves in a market heavily dominated by American and British horror.[1] In addition, the film's invocation of death camp imagery seemed to lift a perhaps self-imposed political taboo. During the sixties and seventies, Italian horror directors made a string of low-budget SS sexploitation horror movies, frequently set in concentration camps. And the Nazi doctor—a figure of some anxiety in postwar Europe (just where exactly had all those sadistic physicians gone?)—showed up with increasing frequency in medico-horror tales.

In addition, the basic story of *Les yeux*—a father or other male relative kidnaps young women and surgically removes their faces to restore the face/beauty of his beloved daughter/sister/wife—became something of a stock tale in postwar European horror. Franju's movie was remade and reworked frequently, usually by directors who wanted to up the gore ratio. But at least one director—Spanish filmmaker Jess

87

Franco—seemed to use *Les yeux*'s story to push Eurohorror into a new, more overtly sexual arena, and in so doing, he changed the face of European horror.

Jésus (Jess) Franco is known primarily as the maker of what Mikita Brottman has called "cinéma vomitif,"[2] and despite Franco's second-unit work on Orson Welles's *Chimes at Midnight* (1965)[3] and his own later high-budget work, he generally receives attention only in publications devoted to body genres and low culture. Although the *BFI Companion to Horror* (1996) calls Franco (who has made more than 160 feature films) "a hyperactive presence" on the post-1959 European film scene and devotes a full page to his work, for example, another BFI publication, *The Encyclopedia of European Cinema* (1995), does not give him an entry at all.[4]

To some extent, Franco's categorization as a "low" director is understandable. As Jim Morton points out, Franco often "makes his films quickly and seemingly with little regard to production values,"[5] and his graphic depictions of sex and violence link him to the category of "body genre" directors. Most of his films, as Jim Morton notes, are horror films, "and several concern the exploits of women in prison. . . . Because of their 'sexism' and 'bad taste,' his films are sometimes loathed by even staunch fans of weird films."[6]

I've never seen Franco referred to as an "art" director, but he does have a following of fans who appreciate his films as much for their paracinema aesthetics as for their affective emphasis on sex and gore. As Morton points out, Franco's films have "a definite style and flavor,"[7] characterized by his "notorious" use of the zoom lens, his sometimes frantic dolly work, and what Tohill and Tombs call an underlying jazz rhythm or beat (79).[8] At his best, Franco is an accomplished cinematographer. Orson Welles hired him to direct the second-unit photography on *Chimes at Midnight*, and although some critics speculate that Welles's decision was influenced as much by the American director's vanity as it was by Franco's talent,[9] nobody underestimates the influence Welles had on the Spanish director.[10] Some of Franco's shot compositions are simply stunning. And his deep-focus black-and-white work often screens like a low-budget version of Welles's and cinematographer Gregg Toland's own.

At his worst, Franco can be sloppy. He makes his films quickly to give them a "different and spontaneous look"; and as Tohill and Tombs point out, "sometimes it works, sometimes it doesn't" (88). The editing can be erratic. At times this leads to the syncopated jazz rhythm

Figure 14. Falstaff (Orson Welles). *Chimes at Midnight.*

that critics praise in Franco's work. At others, it simply leads to confusion, as narrative continuity is totally jettisoned for the sake of affect or economy. And for the uninitiated, the slow pace of Franco's early films can be maddening. As Tim Lucas—writing for *Video Watchdog*—notes, Franco can be "clumsy" and "numbingly dull."[11]

For many paracinephiles, though, any new Franco film is a big event.[12] Franco himself is considered one of paracinema's important auteurs. And his work is frequently discussed in auteurist terms. "If I've learned anything from watching 90 Franco films," Tim Lucas writes in one *Video Watchdog* article about the Spanish director, "it's that these movies cannot be watched in the same way one might view any comparable English-language releases. With the films of Richard Donner or John Badham (to use examples of Franco's own favorite contemporary American filmmakers), if you've seen one of their films, you've seen them all. With Franco's films it's different: *You can't see one until you've seen them all.* A degree of immersion is essential."[13] Franco, Lucas writes, is "the Henry Jaglom of Horror—casting himself and his actor friends in anguished, blood-and-semen-scarred scenarios that tell you more about his inner life than you really want to know."[14] It isn't that these films are so exceptional in themselves, "indeed any one of them might seem just as disorienting or discouraging as any random selection to the

Figure 15. Cinematography. *Chimes at Midnight.*

Uninitiated—but rather that their maker's language at some indistinct moment begins to sink in, after one has seen a certain number of them, and this soft, persuasive language coalesces in some films more tangibly, more audibly, more obsessively, than in others."[15]

Here, as in Andrew Sarris's 1962 version of auteurist criticism, "the distinguishable personality of the director" is a "criterion of value." Part of the strength of Franco's work, Lucas argues, is that "over a group of films," he exhibits "certain recurrent characteristics of style, which serve as his signature." Indeed, Lucas argues, this is so much the case that it's impossible for a first-time viewer to watch one of Franco's films and "get it." Not only do the ways his films look and move "have some relationship to the way . . . [Franco] thinks and feels,"[16] Lucas maintains, but the way Franco thinks and feels is an essential component of the works themselves, constitutive of their idiosyncratic cinematic vocabulary. It's only through immersion in Franco's *complete* oeuvre—only through exposure to his total artistic and psychological development over time—that one can hope to understand the themes and language peculiar to the works.

The comparison Lucas draws between independent filmmaker Henry Jaglom and Jess Franco is telling. Like Franco, Jaglom makes films for a specialized audience, and like Franco's horror movies, his art house flicks are an aquired taste. Jaglom specializes in Cassavetes-style productions, in which actors are encouraged to reveal a kind of inner truth in front of the camera. The films strive for a "spontaneous," improvised look, and they often deal with the way men and women view sex, love, family life, and friendship differently. Hence Lucas's comment about "blood-and-semen-scarred scenarios that tell you more about his [Jaglom's/Franco's] inner life than you really want to know."[17] The difference, of course, is that Franco doesn't push his actors to reveal themselves on camera the way Jaglom does; and because Franco works in a genre with strict formulaic conventions, he is less interested in blurring the line between fiction and reality, more interested in simply telling a good story. To put it another way, Franco has fewer illusions than Jaglom has about fiction cinema's ability to get to the "truth."[18]

Whereas Lucas compares Franco to Henry Jaglom, Tohill and Tombs situate him firmly in the Spanish tradition, likening him to compatriot auteurs such as Luis Buñuel and Pedro Almodóvar. "There's something rigid and fossilized about the Spanish film industry," Tohill and Tombs write.

> Filmmakers like Almodóvar, Buñuel and Franco aren't exactly the norm inside Spain. They're outsiders and wild men, guys who have an unholy fascination with sex, excess, and the dreamlike potential of film. To these men, predictability means stagnation and death. Like Buñuel, Franco is a born rule breaker, a man driven to make his own brand of sex soaked cinema, a maverick trailblazer who personifies the untapped potential of film. . . . Almodóvar, Buñuel and Franco are creative bedfellows. Each follows a different trajectory, but they all curve inexorably towards sex. Of the three, Franco has followed its steamy siren-call further and longer, he's taken his flesh-filled interest to the very limits of human imagination. (78–79)

The rhetoric here is inflated and lionizing, but the authors are right to link Franco to the other bad boys of Spanish cinema. Like Buñuel, Franco brings a certain surrealist sensibility to his work. And like Almodóvar, Franco grew up in fascist Spain. That is, he came of filmmaking age in a political and social climate in which explicit depictions of sex and violence really were transgressive, revolutionary, and often illegal.

Jess Franco began making horror films in the 1960s, sometimes called *los felices 60* (the happy sixties), a time of some liberalization in Spain. In 1962 Manuel Fraga was appointed as minister of information and tourism. He was, as Tohill and Tombs note, "a cautious liberal" (63).

In cooperation with another government minister, Cinema Supremo José García Escudero, Fraga allowed the rigid censorship laws to relax a little. New laws were enacted to help Spanish producers, quota systems designed to help the Spanish film industry were put in place, and in 1967, a system of *salas* (special theaters) modeled on the French ciné-clubs allowed foreign films to be shown under "less rigid systems of control" (63).

This was "the Golden Age of Spanish cinema" under General Franco (63). Genre films were popular, and coproductions *(copros)* with other European countries gave Spanish directors a chance to work in the international arena, with American producers and directors as well as with European auteurs.[19] *Los felices 60* were, however, short-lived. At the end of the decade, social controls were tightened. The government was concerned by the rising number of cheap coproductions and tried to limit them by imposing high minimum budgets. "This was combined with a general tightening up of the political situation, resulting in the removal of Fraga and an attempt to return to the 'good old days' of the 1950s. The immensely popular film clubs also came under close scrutiny" (Tohill and Tombs, 64).

But once a country's borders are opened, it's extremely difficult to close them again. In the 1970s, Spanish middle-class audiences started going across the border to see forbidden films in France. "Special trips were arranged to Biarritz and Perpignan to see films like *Last Tango in Paris* or *Decameron*" (64). French distributors were quick to seize on what seemed like a golden opportunity. Special "Spanish weeks"—in which films subtitled in Spanish would be shown to a largely Spanish audience—were arranged in the French border towns and advertised in Spanish newspapers. As Tohill and Tombs describe it:

> Every weekend during 1973 and through 1974, a regular convoy of battered Seat cars would descend on these border towns, and for years it was impossible to get a hotel room in Perpignan on a Friday or Saturday night. In 1973 five new cinemas opened there and *Last Tango in Paris,* a particularly hot item at the time, was seen by more than 150,000 viewers in the town's cinemas. With a population of 200,000 this is an astonishing figure. The cinemas would open their doors at ten in the morning and show films right up until midnight. Often keen Spaniards would catch three or four films in a weekend.[20]

Spanish horror was born out of financial necessity (66). When the government tightened restrictions on cheap coproductions, the Spanish film industry needed to find films they could make cheaply and export (in order to recoup the costs of their bigger-budget productions). Horror seemed the perfect choice. The films were popular, and they sold well. Drawing on the formulas already established by England, Italy, and the United States, the Spanish film industry churned out a large number of Hammer takeoffs, psycho killer flicks, and gothic supernatural thrillers. Most of the films were European and Euro-American coproductions; some of them were filmed outside Spain. The government budgetary restrictions were met by simply making two versions of each movie— one for export, and a tamer version for domestic and, in some cases, U.S. and British distribution.

Spain didn't have the same literary tradition of horror that England, Germany, the United States, and even France had, and so it drew on different sources. Directors borrowed stories from other traditions and "nationalized" them with Spanish iconography. Drawing on the painting tradition of artists such as Goya and Velázquez, the industry stamped the films with what Tohill and Tombs call "a Spanish flavor." The best Spanish horror films of the period—films such as Amando de Ossorio's *Blind-Dead* series, Vicente Aranda's *La novia ensangretada* (The Blood-Spattered Bride, 1972), the films of Paul Naschy and Jess Franco—are "cruder" than their Anglo-American counterparts; "more violent and visceral, with a definite flavor of the grotesque. Audiences are more often led to identify with the monsters than their victims" (Tohill and Tombs, 66). Some of the films—de Ossorio's *Blind Dead* films, for example—even have a Goyaesque look. The scenes are washed in browns and reds, a palette that beautifully captures the feeling of the medieval church (the world from which the Blind Templars come).

The existence of these films is extraordinary, given the social and political climate of the time. Even the tame, domestic versions of Franco's films hint at illicit sexuality, lesbianism, and other activities officially designated as perversions by General Franco's government.[21] And de Ossorio's films link the church to sadoerotic rites of torture and mutilation that, even when not shown on-screen, rival Sade's. The fact that the Templars were originally blinded and killed because of their excesses, the movies tell us, does little to mitigate the truly anticlerical, sacrilegious tone of the *Blind Dead* films. Furthermore, even with censorship editing, the films are often quite violent.

Horror cinema had special resonance in a society in which, as Marsha Kinder tells us, "the graphic depiction of violence is primarily associated with an anti-Francoist perspective." In many horror films—

de Ossorio's being just one example—eroticized violence was used "to speak a political discourse, that is, to expose the legacy of brutality and torture that lay hidden behind the surface beauty of the Fascist and neo-Catholic aesthetics."[22] Even when horror films were not especially graphic, they served to make a strong political point. One of the most

Figure 16. The Knights Templar rise again. *Blind Dead*, by De Ossorio.

beautiful and emotionally moving art films of the period, Victor Erice's *El espíritu de la colmena* (Spirit of the Beehive, 1973), uses a child's response to James Whales's *Frankenstein* as a means of exploring political and social reality in the immediate post–civil war period. While not, strictly speaking, a horror film, Erice's masterpiece illustrates the way horror can be used to explore subversive cultural themes (John Hopewell, for example, sees the film as a demonstration of "the sadness and frustration attendant upon Franco's victory," clearly a forbidden topic under the dictatorship).[23] It is perhaps for that reason that *El espíritu de la colmena* is often mentioned in books treating the horror genre.

Spanish horror production began to decline after 1972. Government restrictions on the practice of making double versions of a film effectively undercut the industry's ability to export horror movies. And after General Franco's death in 1975, the industry no longer needed horror to finance mainstream production. But the lingering effect of horror's heyday is evident in the films of post-Franco Spain. Films such as Almodóvar's *Matador* (1988), which focuses on the relationship between love and death, eroticism and murder, explore the same troubling themes that horror does and perhaps demonstrate the degree to which eroticized horror became the very model of transgressive, revolutionary cinema for directors who grew up in fascist Spain. Interestingly, the images in the title sequence of *Matador,* Almodóvar tells us, come from films by Jess Franco.[24]

Franco's Status in the U.S. Market

Franco's cultural significance and status in the United States is difficult to track. Until the 1986 publication of Phil Hardy's *Encyclopedia of Horror Movies,* nothing of significance had been written about Franco in English. Until the advent of home video, Franco's movies were largely unavailable to U.S. consumers. Never picked up for distribution by either exploitation entrepreneurs or late-night television, Franco's films remain largely unseen in the United States. Currently, he is best known to American horror fans as the director of *Count Dracula* (1971), a Spanish, German, and Italian coproduction starring Christopher Lee as a strangely lethargic count; *The Castle of Fu Manchu* (1968), another multinational production starring Christopher Lee; and *Deadly Sanctuary* (1970), an English-language French production based on the writings of the Marquis de Sade. Franco is also well known as the director of *Succubus* (1968), the first mainstream horror film to receive an X rating.

Although these film titles are available through companies such as Facets Multimedia, which cater to a wide range of video collectors and movie buffs, most of Franco's movies are available only through paracinema and psychotronic video catalogs. Because different versions of Franco's films were often released simultaneously, publications like *Video Watchdog* try to keep track of which video releases contain the most complete (uncensored) footage, and which versions come closest to Franco's own vision of the movies. These are not always the most explicit versions available. Franco is one of the few European directors who have publicized the distribution practice of adding hard-core inserts to body genre films. In an interview with Harvey Fenton and William Lustig, Franco describes seeing a "hard-core" version of a Christopher Lee movie in Paris.

> Christopher Lee . . . is one of the most proud men in the world, he would say things like "I don't want to kiss her on the mouth." And I saw a film of his, directed by Terence Fisher, with porno inserts . . . I saw that film and I laughed in my guts! I told Christopher immediately. I called him and said "I didn't know you had made a porno film!" And he went completely out of control, so I explained to him about the process and how the producers and distributors who had the rights for France and Germany and some other countries in Europe made these versions. And you know they are made with that awful quality also, because if you try to make a similar light or similar sets. . . . No, it's just *shit*.[25]

The same thing had happened to his own films, he tells Fenton and Lustig. Producers added hard-core sequences to *La comtesse noire* (The Black Countess, 1973) to get what Franco called "a primitive porno film." "I have nothing against porno," he tells his interviewers, "but just that they do this normally very badly, because they are not real people of cinema."[26]

It is perhaps in response to the distribution practice of adding hard-core inserts to already completed films that Franco himself began making "erotic" versions of his own horror movies. *La comtesse noire*, for example, was made three times—as a vampire film *(La comtesse noire)*, as a horrific sex film (*La comtesse aux seins nus*, The Bare-Breasted Countess, 1973), and as what *Video Watchdog* calls a "non-supernatural hardcore picture" (*Les avaleuses*, The Swallowers, 1973).[27] Even this practice, however, has not kept distributors from modifying Franco's horror titles to reach a wider "horrotica" audience.

What brings paracinephiles to Franco's work is a mixture of

irritation at what *Video Watchdog* calls "the insultingly mild horror product tailored to fit the MPAA straightjacket" and curiosity about a director who has a kinky sex-horror reputation.[28] For many, as Tim Lucas writes, "Franco's defiantly uncommercial, acutely revealing taboo-breaking stance is like a breath of fresh scare, even when his movies are clumsy, which is (let's be honest) most of the time."[29] The implied connections between sex and death, blood and semen, cruelty and sexuality, that haunt all horror are laid bare in Franco's work.[30] In Franco's own version of *La comtesse noire,* for example, the countess sucks the semen of her male victims rather than their blood; in a parody of *Deep Throat* (1972), she fellates them to death. Similarly, it is an excess of sexual passion rather than the loss of essential bodily fluids that destroys her female partners. In *Gritos en la noche* (The Awful Dr. Orlof, 1962), Franco's first reworking of Franju's *Les yeux sans visage,* the doctor caresses his victims' breasts before beginning his horrific operation to remove their faces; after surgery, he chains his victims—in sadoerotic bondage fashion—in the tower. Tohill and Tombs call *The Awful Dr. Orlof* (Franco's first feature-length horror film) "a cinematic time bomb" and credit it with revolutionizing European horror (77). "Before *Orlof,*" they write, "horror films had opted for the poetic approach, playing down the sexual element, only hinting at the dark recesses of the human psyche. With *Orlof* sex sizzled into the foreground, changing the face of Euro horror for the next twenty years (77).

But if Franco's films are taboo breaking and sexy, they're also demanding in unexpected ways. Not only are they clumsy and thus "high in participation or completion by the audience" (in the way in which, McLuhan tells us, all "cool" media are high in audience participation),[31] but they self-consciously create an aural dissonance that Laurie Anderson once humorously called "difficult listening."[32] That is, the viewer not only must work hard to "complete the picture" but must listen through the music, which frequently serves as a counterpoint to what is happening on-screen. If Dario Argento is the acknowledged master of the creative use of sound to "layer" meanings in his work, Franco is the forerunner who laid the groundwork for the creative—and often extreme—use of aural montage in horror. Furthermore, the film seems to challenge many of the assumptions traditionally made about the position of women in low genres and self-consciously (and self-reflexively) explores the connections between the worlds of high art and low culture.

Figure 17. Morpho (Ricardo Valle) and Wanda (Diana Lorys) in *The Awful Dr. Orlof*.

The Awful Dr. Orlof

In many ways, *The Awful Dr. Orlof*[33] is more like a *giallo*—a graphically violent Italian thriller—than like a horror flick.[34] Oh, there are definite horror elements: the creepy Dr. Orlof stalking attractive women and kidnapping them, the laughably monstrous figure of Morpho, the amaz-

ing chateau with its winding candlelit passages, a beautifully shot opening abduction scene, and a restrained operating-room scene (the doctor
makes an incision in a woman's chest). But the main driving force behind the narrative is the story of police inspector Edgar Tanner and his
pretty fiancée, Wanda. Which is not to say the film adheres to all the
genre conventions of a police story. In fact, one of the interesting things
about the film is the way in which it continually raises genre expectations and then disappoints them: the police inspector doesn't solve the
mystery, his girlfriend does; Orlof is not killed or arrested at the end,
just momentarily halted in his nefarious operations; a woman in the
tower who might still be alive is forgotten as the lovers walk away from
the chateau. With the exception of Wanda and Tanner's survival, we
never get quite the denouement we expect.

The film is set in 1912. The video box copy stresses the mad-
doctor theme: "Franco fave Howard Vernon is an obsessed surgeon trying to restore his daughter's fire-scarred face by abducting buxom
young women and performing skin graft operations on them. Assisting
him is his sadistic slave Morpho, a 'sightless idiot' (in creepy bug-eyed
makeup), who occasionally BITES his victims (?) and keeps 'em chained
up afterwards."[35] But the story that actually drives the narrative is, as I
mentioned earlier, not the horror story but the story of the police investigation. When the film opens, five women have disappeared, all under
identical circumstances. Long sequences show Inspector Tanner trying
to make sense of conflicting eyewitness accounts of these abductions.
The sheer amount of time spent on police business in the film, as well
as the lengthy development of Tanner's relationship with his fiancée,
tends to give *Orlof* a curious rhythm. Horror sequences frequently bot-
tom out in farce or melodrama, so that the affect level of terror or shock
(or even suspense) is hard to maintain.

In addition, the film spends a lot of seemingly "dead" time investigating theatrical spectacle. There are extended sequences at both the
opera, where Wanda performs ballet, and the cabaret, where Orlof looks
for victims. While performance does not assume quite the central role
here that it does in later Franco films, it still takes up more screen time
than American audiences expect—so much screen time that we antici-
pate some important clue to derive from theatrical performance itself.
Whereas in later Franco films, nightclubs often become anarchic spaces
where subversive dramas are enacted and bourgeois morals are traves-
tied, in *Orlof* both the cabaret and the opera are connected to what Tim
Lucas sees as Franco's aesthetic of "ennui." Places where people kill time,

they represent the space in which "aberrant behavior begins."[36] It's interesting that at both the opera and the cabaret, characters are shown—dimly lit—sitting alone in boxes; wrapped, it would seem, in their thoughts and obsessions. The threat here is not that Orlof, like Dr. Orlac in *Mad Love* (1935), responds to the performance of the woman he watches onstage but rather that he doesn't. It is his inability to enjoy watching, to play the voyeur, that is immediately suspect. It is his inability to really enjoy looking at other women that makes us uneasy about the hours he spends staring at his comatose daughter.

Although *The Awful Dr. Orlof* is in many ways a curiously unaffective and tedious film, it also has a distinctly edgy feel. This derives largely from its use of music and sound to create dissonance and build tension. In fact, in *Orlof* Franco uses music in a way that's reminiscent of the dialectical potential that Eisenstein ascribed to sound. That is, Franco uses music as a form of "temporal counterpoint" that creates a sense of "collision" and enhances the dramatic potential of the film.[37] This is evident from the very first scene, in which the hard-driving (and very good) jazz score seems totally out of keeping with the 1912 "period piece" look of the film. And it continues throughout the movie as both the extradiegetic score and diegetic sound (echoes, reverberations) break in frequently as a marked juxtaposition to what is happening on-screen. Visually, canted framing, the occasional jump cut, and some inserted shots (shots of cats and an owl watching, for example) create a similar sense of conflict, but in terms of pure affect, this is a film that seems to be largely sound driven.

The score is not an easy-listening jazz score. This is bebop. The "background" music is characterized by unusual chord structures, accents on the upbeat, lengthened melodic line, and harmonic complexity and innovation. It's loud, and it demands attention. This is the kind of jazz that makes non–jazz lovers nervous, the kind of music that creates an aural distraction. And it's a heavy presence in the film. While some scenes include only diegetic sound, a surprising number are introduced with the clash of cymbals or a long, frantic drum riff that seems as though it should come at the end of a piece, not introduce it. The music gives the impression that we are always entering in medias res, joining a set that's already in progress.

The demanding nature of the jazz score in *The Awful Dr. Orlof* helps to situate the film within the same kind of liminal space occupied by Franju's *Les yeux sans visage*. Invoking both the cerebral work and reception associated with high culture and the physical affect and response associated with low sex-horror, the film seems permanently poised between high and low genres, belonging to both of them simultaneously.

Thematically, the film plays pointedly with parallel story lines, contrasting images, and twin motifs. Orlof's daughter Melissa, who spends all her time lying motionless in what appears to be a little chapel, has a Janus face. Half of her face, the half that remains hidden from the camera's and Orlof's view, is scarred; the half we see is lovely. Her visual twin in the film is Tanner's fiancée, Wanda (played by the same actress). Because Melissa seems to spend all her time in a supine, trancelike state, Wanda almost functions as her emissary out in the world. Certainly, Wanda provides the emotional center to a film that desperately needs one. She's the only character whose fate we even remotely care about. It is Wanda's resemblance to Melissa that first catches Orlof's eye, and it is Orlof's fascination with Wanda's good looks that, in part, links him to Tanner.

The connection between Orlof and Tanner is less physical (they don't look like twins, as Wanda and Melissa do), but it's more stylistically emphasized than the connection between the two women. The film moves frequently between Orlof's pursuits and Tanner's, and the cuts between scenes are masked often by a graphic Orlof-Tanner match. Orlof puts his head in his hands; cut to Tanner putting his head in his hands. Orlof strokes Melissa's hair; cut to Tanner stroking Wanda's hair. The men seem to mirror each other; they're paired or twinned in the way that criminals and crime fighters, monsters and exorcists, frequently are paired and twinned. And as in most crime and horror stories, the pairing here makes a certain amount of sense. Orlof started his career, the narrative tells us, as a prison doctor. It was in this capacity that he met and fell in love with a female convict named Armée and acquired the services of Morpho (incarcerated for raping and murdering his parents). Orlof helped Armée and Morpho to escape and then began the experiments that turned Morpho into the bug-eyed "sightless idiot" we see throughout the film.

If Orlof is a monster figure, then, his monstrosity predates his obsessive need to repair his daughter's damaged face. And it's interesting that his mad-science mania is linked in the film to the darker sides of law enforcement—incarceration, institutional medicine, experimentation on prisoners. The prison motif carries over into the chateau as well. If Dr. Génessier in Franju's *Eyes without a Face* embodies the modern clinical method (surgical mask, white coat, sterile environment), Orlof reminds one of a medieval torturer. He wears a day coat when he operates.

Nothing in his operating room seems hygienic, and after surgery he chains his victims—in sadoerotic bondage fashion—in the tower.

In some ways, then, he can be seen as the dark shadow figure, the primitive ancestral antecedent, to a modern detective like Tanner. While Tanner is initially linked to modern scientific method (he examines fingerprints, checks records, examines evidence), Orlof—like Dracula—seems permanently bound to barbaric rituals of the past. And Tanner must move from his well-lit (visually speaking, "enlightened") office and enter the dimly lit, low-key underworld if he wants to fight Orlof. He begins frequenting the dive—literally, the "cave"—where Janot, the town drunk, tells him about a mysterious chateau and a diamond necklace found at the site of an old boat launch. When a supposedly dead Morpho's fingerprints are found at one of the abduction scenes, Tanner even becomes a grave robber. He digs up Morpho's grave and finds an empty coffin.

Just as Franco emphasizes disturbing connections between the worlds of law enforcement and horrific crime (in this film, the monster-criminal seems to emerge from, and in some ways to represent, the dark side of the legal and penal system), so, too, he underscores the parallel links between high art and popular culture. Scenes at the opera segue into scenes at the cabaret. And here the points of similarity—men in darkened boxes watching women perform onstage—are markedly clear. Performance sequences at both the opera and the cabaret are framed and shot in identical fashion. Furthermore, the two worlds are linked through the figure of Wanda. A professional ballerina, Wanda performs at the opera, but determined to help Tanner solve his case, she also—unbeknownst to him—frequents the cabaret after hours. Dressed as a "shameless hussy" (English version) or "street girl" (French version)—another kind of gender performance—Wanda has absolutely no trouble passing as a club habitué. And the ease with which she migrates from the sacralized world of ballet opera to the eroticized popular milieu of the after-hours dance hall suggests that the difference between the two worlds is not so great as one might think.

There's a certain insistence on cultural transgressivity here, as high culture is emphatically paired with low culture. There's also a certain insistence on the way both high art and popular culture fetishize the female body, female performance. The dress Wanda is wearing the night that Orlof picks her up has the same heart-shaped bodice that her tutu has; and her pose, drinking cognac at the bar—upper body inclined slightly forward, head lifted, one leg stretched *en arrière,* slightly behind the other—resembles a dancer's attitude. Furthermore, she has come to the bar specifically to attract Orlof's gaze, and as she drinks her cognac she looks toward the balcony, searching for his face in the darkness—the same way that she had glanced earlier at the darkened opera balcony, looking for Tanner.

Wanda is, as I mentioned earlier, the most interesting and emotionally compelling character in the film. What I find particularly interesting, though, is the way she is given command of the gaze. Unlike the fetishized female Hollywood character described by Laura Mulvey, who is always the object—never the subject—of an active (male) gaze, Wanda becomes the chief investigator on the Orlof case. From the moment she first sees Orlof's eyes on her, she turns the tables and makes him the object of her active, inquiring, investigative gaze. She puts herself in danger, in the hope that he will invite her home. And when he does, she uses her time in the chateau to investigate Melissa's room and to search the tower. It is she who actually solves the case. And although she *almost* becomes Orlof's final victim, ultimately she is not punished for assuming the active male gaze and usurping police and patriarchal authority. She does not have to go through a protracted traumatizing battle at the end of the movie, the way final girls in slasher films do, and when Orlof is finally dispatched at the end, her role in solving the case is explicitly acknowledged by Tanner. "You're the best detective," he tells her. "My right hand from now on."

It's tempting to dismiss Tanner's final comments as another example of the patronizing "brave little woman" speech that screen detectives frequently make to their girl Fridays. But here Tanner's speech serves to codify, or formally acknowledge, a kind of validation that the film has already shown. Throughout *Orlof,* much of the camera movement and many of the camera angles are motivated by Wanda's gaze. Certainly, her point of view drives most of the narrative in the second half of the film. If classical Hollywood cinema can sometimes be seen, as Laura Mulvey argues, as being organized around the male gaze, here it is, at least occasionally, linked to an active female gaze. In a way, then, *Orlof* seems to foreshadow some of the remarkable Spanish art house films of the 1970s. Like Victor Erice's *El espíritu de la colmena* (1973) and Carlos Saura's *Cría cuervos* (1975), both of which use the gaze of a female child to destabilize the dominant militaristic male gaze, *The Awful Dr. Orlof* subtly challenges police hegemony and control through the measured use of a female's point of view.

Faceless

Les prédateurs de la nuit (Faceless, 1988) is both a reworking of *The Awful Dr. Orlof* and a sequel to it. Here, Dr. Flamand (Helmut Berger), aided by his trusted wife and assistant Nathalie (Brigitte Lahaie), runs an exclusive cosmetic clinic in St. Cloud, France (a little town on the out-

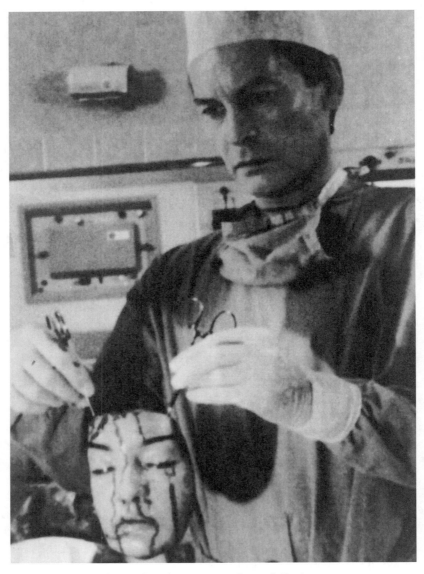

Figure 18. Dr. Flamand (Helmut Berger) prepares a new face graft. *Faceless*.

skirts of Paris). In this clinic, he not only performs cosmetic surgery but rejuvenates wealthy female clients by injecting them with a serum made from the blood and bone marrow of kidnapped women. One of his middle-aged clients, dissatisfied with the results of her cosmetic surgery, surprises Dr. Flamand in a Paris parking garage one evening and throws a vial of acid at him. The acid misses the doctor but hits his sister, Ingrid (Christiane Jean), in the face. The rest of the film revolves around Flamand's attempts to restore his sister's beauty. To that end, he visits his old professor, Dr. Orlof (Howard Vernon, the same actor who portrayed Orlof in the 1962 film). Orlof sends him to *his* old mentor, Karl Moser (Anton Diffring), a man who perfected his surgical methods in Dachau. It is Moser who finally performs the successful skin graft.

Interwoven with this story is the story of the criminal investigation. Here, however, the hero is not a police officer but a private detective, Sam Morgan (Chris Mitchum). Sam has been hired by a wealthy American, Mr. Hallen (Telly Savalas), to find his daughter, Barbara (Caroline Munro), a professional model who has disappeared in Paris. Barbara has a cocaine habit and a propensity for what Sam calls "whoring around." But she was once Sam's lover, and he's still crazy about her. Sentiment and Hallen's bankroll convince Sam that he's the man for the job. In an interesting reversal of genre convention, though, Sam doesn't save the girl. When he finds Barbara in Flamand's clinic, Sam stupidly leaves the key he used to open her cell door dangling in the lock. Nathalie sees the open door and the dangling key and imprisons them both in Barbara's cell. At Dr. Moser's urging, she walls them in with brick and mortar.[38] The film ends with the newly restored Ingrid, Dr. Flamand, Nathalie, and Dr. Moser drinking a champagne toast to the New Year, and Mr. Hallen booking a plane reservation to Paris.

As I mentioned, *Faceless* is heavily indebted to *The Awful Dr. Orlof.* Using the same basic plot and one of the same characters/actors, the film seems both to rework the story in eighties terms and to provide a kind of sequel. Flamand is, after all, Orlof's protégé, and repairing women's looks is his trade. But whereas *The Awful Dr. Orlof* seems—at this remove, anyway—curiously restrained, *Faceless* revels at times in special effects and excess. A woman is stabbed through the eye—an operation that is delineated with great precision and shown from almost every conceivable camera angle. A face donor's head is removed with a chainsaw. A male prostitute is stabbed in the neck. A nosy hospital worker is drilled through the forehead, with a power drill, as she cowers in a closet. One operating-room scene shows Dr. Moser's failed attempt to remove the face of a still-living victim. Under the effects of sodium pentothal, the donor's skin is too elastic; it clumps and crumbles like cookie dough under Moser's fingers. A subsequent sequence shows a successful face removal, this time from a pharmaceutically paralyzed but fully conscious victim.

Here the famous face-lifting scene from *Les yeux sans visage* is repeated almost shot for shot, but stretched out, elongated. Dr. Moser removes the face from the conscious victim on the table, displays it to the camera, and then, in a supreme act of sadism, shows it to the woman to whom it once belonged. "See how beautiful she will be," he purrs. Then he hands the face to Dr. Flamand, who exhibits it again to the camera before dipping it in some kind of solution and placing it over his sister's acid-scarred face. The effect is reminiscent of the shot repetition Eisenstein uses in *Strike* and *Battleship Potemkin* to slow down time. But because the shot (displaying the face to the unflinching gaze of the camera) is duplicated using another actor, the sense of historical continuity, of one surgeon literally passing the results of his nefarious experimentation to another, is also highlighted. The scene plays like an homage to one of the central tropes of horror—what Robin Wood, in one famous essay, has called the continual "return of the repressed."[39] Monsters may be temporarily laid to rest at the end of any given film, Wood notes, but the terror they represent always rises again. In Franco's films, as in *The Nightmare on Elm Street* series, every horror title contains the seeds of a sequel; closure is always illusory.

But although *Faceless* shows more graphic violence than *The Awful Dr. Orlof* does and is, in some ways, more visually transgressive, it also strikes me as a more conservative, less edgy film than Franco's earlier work. Partly this is due to the crude quality of the makeup and special effects. Even *Video Watchdog*, which usually promotes graphic display over implied danger, doesn't quite know what to make of the gore in this film. "The Watchdog was able to screen an uncut copy of *Faceless*, along with Malofilm's edited version," *Video Watchdog* reported in its July–September 1990 issue, "and while it's always better to see the unedited version of anything, I must say that the movie's special makeup effects are pretty crude, and the loss of some of them actually enhances the impact of certain scenes (particularly the first operating room mishap)."[40]

In addition, the choice of a pop music score and the overall glossy look of the film can be disappointing to fans hooked on Franco's jazz beat. As *Video Watchdog* points out, *Faceless* is the first movie the ultraprolific Franco had made with a complete production crew in nearly twenty years, and the result is a "slick, sick, All-Star production that unreels like a 'That's Entertainment' of Eurotrash."[41] But although *Video Watchdog* celebrates the film as one of Franco's best, I find the slickness a little off-putting; I miss the raw edges and bebop rhythm of the earlier low-budget work.

Still, the film exhibits the political and historical commentary of more "highbrow" art cinema. The allusions to Nazism, World War II, and the death camps, which are implicit in *Les yeux sans visage,* are foregrounded here. Not only is Dr. Flamand played by Helmut Berger, a German actor, but Dachau and Auschwitz are explicitly mentioned as the laboratories where Moser's famed skin-grafting technique originated. And the character of Karl Moser, the Nazi surgeon who appreciates fine wines, good art, and "unusual" women, allows Franco to explore social and political contradictions more pointedly than he does in his earlier films. "You French are a strange people," Moser tells Flamand and Nathalie when they balk at the idea of operating on living flesh. "You're really sentimental over trivial things. On the one hand you protect the baby seals. And, on the other, France, the country of human rights, has become the third largest arms dealer in the world, behind Russia and the United States. This industry of death earns your country, a land of refuge, 4,000 billion dollars a year. A votre santé."

There's a certain irrefutable logic to Moser's position that allows him, like the snake in the Garden of Eden, to persuade Flamand and Nathalie to do what they had wanted to do all along. Actor Anton Diffring, who had played nefarious plastic surgeons in a number of Hammer films, brings just the right amount of seductive appeal to Moser; and the fact that he does his own postdubbing ensures that Moser's character is one of the best acted in the film. Lines are delivered with a fluency and consistency of style that's refreshing after some of the clumsy dubbing we see elsewhere in the movie. And Diffring plays his role with a passion and a zest for life that's completely missing in the other characters.

The choice of Helmut Berger for Flamand links *Faceless* to other films about decadence, moral ambiguity, and the Third Reich. His previous roles—in Visconti's *La caduta degli dei* (The Damned, 1969) and Massimo Dallamano's *Il dio chiamato Dorian* (The Evils of Dorian Gray, The Picture of Dorian Gray, 1970)—have created a star persona for Berger that exudes both seductive charm and moral instability, characteristics that are perfect for Flamand. While this film does not insist on the connection between homosexuality and fascism, as *The Damned* does, it does stress the connection between medical moral depravity (Nazism) and sexual perversion in Flamand's character. Here we get more than a hint of incestuous longing as Flamand watches his sister sexually humiliate Gordon (this film's equivalent of Morpho). In fact, the film suggests that the only sexual pleasure Flamand might enjoy is the onanistic pleasure that comes from watching. Lesbian love scenes between Nathalie and prospective skin graft donors are periodically staged for Flamand's—and the film audience's—enjoyment (it's interesting that Flamand watches these on the television monitors used to safeguard the patients' "stability" in the clinic); and Nathalie, a kleptomaniac, tells Flamand that she would steal less if he "loved" her more.

Certainly, here, as in both *The Damned* and *The Picture of Dorian Gray*, we see Berger portraying what Peter Bondanella once described as a "pathological case history bordering on the Grand Guignol."[42] And here, as in his earlier films, the depravity of Berger's character seems to extend to all facets of his life. Like Dr. Orlof, Flamand does not become monstrous *after* his sister's accident. The secret prison cells of his clinic contain not only potential skin donors but women who are systematically drained of their blood and bone marrow to "feed" the clinic's regular clientele. Flamand, we are given to understand, always was something of an opportunist and a ghoul, a medical and corporate vampire. Ingrid's accident simply leads him into further excesses and abuses. And Berger—who plays Flamand as seductive but rather preternaturally subdued—captures, I think, the overall creepiness that constitutes the doctor's moral makeup.

If the film links medical procedures to death camp experiments, it also emphasizes an uncomfortable connection between the "skin jobs" at Dachau and the beauty industry, of which Flamand's clinic is a part. Not only does he cater to wealthy middle-aged women who wish to look young again, but he repairs the faces of women who depend on their beauty for their livelihood. Barbara Hallen had come to the clinic for nose repair after excessive use of cocaine a year or so before the film opens. Melissa, a high-priced call girl, had similarly come to the clinic for face repairs, after her pimp-boyfriend Rashid had beaten her up. That most of Flamand's potential skin donors are former clients gives the film something of a closed-world, hothouse feel. Flamand fingers the glamour photos in his files like a fashion designer choosing the models for his next runway show, before eventually selecting the famous face that will be right for his beloved sister. Once the choice is made, he knows exactly where to go to find the victim. And neither he nor Nathalie has any problem persuading the victim to come with them; the promise of drugs or sex is usually all that's required.

As in many Spanish horror films, the emphasis here is on the monsters' point of view, not the victim's. We rarely get a shot of the victim outside the mediating gaze of one of the monster figures.[43] Even camera movement and distance reflect the monsters' point of view—particularly that of Dr. Flamand and Ingrid—as the film moves from a relatively free, liquid camera style (in the credit sequence) to a claustrophobic and cramped series of long still takes and static shots. Most of the action takes place within the confines of the clinic—and confinement is indeed the main feeling that the shot composition and editing convey. Tight framing and the excessive use of close-ups give the clinic scenes a cramped and oddly static feel. If Franco's early work is characterized by his notorious use of the zoom lens, *Faceless* tends rather to mimic fashion still photography, emphasizing glamour head and shoulder poses. Cutting tends to follow the classic shot-countershot Hollywood formation. And camera movement is subtle and slow. To some extent, it could be argued that the film plunges us into the same narrow cinematic space inhabited by its victims, but since we develop so little feeling for the victims, I think we tend to read the claustrophobia more in terms of Flamand and Ingrid's own growing sense of confinement and desperation.

More provocative—although less easy to read—is the way that claustrophobia and claustrophobic filming attach to what the movie establishes as a distinct cinematic mode and (inter)national style. In fact, one of the most interesting aspects of the film is the way it more or less neatly divides into two genres or modes with two very different sets of aesthetic conventions.[44] There are the Eurohorror segments, which are dominated by actors from European cinema.[45] Here, the defining formal element seems to be the Antonioni-like claustrophobia and stylization mentioned earlier. The pacing is leisurely, even slow. Cuts are masked, and emphasis appears to be on the mise-en-scène. Scenes are framed to convey a sense of confinement. Even the sex scenes are so tightly framed that it's hard to tell where exactly the players are. One memorable scene, which takes place in Ingrid's bedroom, is shot through a fish tank—heightening the sense that poor Ingrid is contained, not only because she is humiliated by the state of her face but because she is the Flamands' domestic pet. Her sexual relationships—the few she's able to have—are carefully monitored by Flamand and Nathalie on the clinic's surveillance monitors. Furthermore, they seem to be shot with a long lens that compresses space, so that instead of appearing as acts of liberation, they function as still more examples of the claustrophobia that Ingrid increasingly feels. In the horror sequences, the only place where space regularly tends to open up and out (so that we get a sense of depth) is the Parisian club where Flamand and Nathalie cruise their former clients. But even these scenes, which do provide dynamic interludes in the European section, rely more on camera distance and mise-en-scène (strobe lights, dancing) than on camera movement or editing to achieve their effect.

Contrasting with this is the criminal investigation part of the film, which is dominated by American actors Chris Mitchum (who bears a remarkable physical resemblance to his father, Robert) and Telly Savalas. The criminal investigation sequences rely heavily on what the film references as American "action" codes.[46] In his role as Sam Morgan, American private eye, Chris Mitchum pummels his way through Paris's high-fashion industry, looking for clues about his girlfriend's disappearance. In these scenes, tightly framed close-up shots of Mitchum's face and his opponent's body alternate with high-angle shots that have the curious visual effect of compressing the violence, holding it close to the ground. This compression tends to be shattered, though, as punches erupt up out of the center of the frame and push bodies out toward the edges. The signature move here is Morgan's fist jutting quickly upward and sideways, shattering the constraints and tight holds of fashion world thugs. The editing rhythm is fast paced, full of quick cuts, and the framing gives a fairly accurate sense of space. While bodies and space are frequently fragmented, these (fragmenting) shots are almost always followed by an establishing or reestablishing shot, so that viewers generally know where the men are and have a sense of the amount of space (the surrounding space) they could conceivably occupy (where they could go).

Not only do these action sequences put the male body on display (providing a kind of male analogue to the punishing mechanisms of female fashion), but they also shatter the constrained feel of the rest of the film. The scenes are beautiful to watch. The fights are well choreographed. The violence itself is stylized. Here, as in the action films that Yvonne Tasker analyzes, "suffering—torture, in particular—operates as both a narrative set of hurdles to be overcome, tests that the hero must survive, and as a set of aestheticized images to be lovingly dwelt on."[47] This contrasts with the clumsy gore shown in the horror sequences, whose function seems to be more one of gross-out comedy—

the kind of images that leave you "laughing, screaming," in front of the television set.

It's tempting to read the action sequences metaphorically, as a celebration of the way European directors have increasingly used American movie conventions to break or challenge some of the constraints of European art cinema. Certainly the date of the film (1988) is right for such a move. The French *cinéma du look* films that, beginning with Jean-Jacques Beneix's *Diva* (1980), rose to prominence in the 1980s,[48] as well as Pedro Almodóvar's films of the late 1980s and early 1990s— *Mujeres al borde de un ataque de nervios* (Women on the Verge of a Nervous Breakdown, 1988), *Tacones lejanos* (High Heels, 1991), and *Kika* (1993)—often irritated critics precisely because they seemed to push continental cinema closer to a peculiarly Anglo-American, pop-culture, postmodern aesthetic.[49] So reading the action scenes as a kind of homage to American action films—and as a kind of jab at European critical response to the "new" European cinema—makes sense in terms of an increasingly Americanized, or American-fixated, continental film culture. And certainly Franco's own love of American film, which he tends to analyze in opposition to European art cinema, makes such a reading of the American action scenes feasible.[50]

But the film's diegetic construction of two different cinematic codes inevitably reinscribes binary oppositions into the text and seems to undercut the central thematic thrust of the film. Like *Les yeux sans visage* and *The Awful Dr. Orlof*, *Faceless* seems to be about the disruption of polarized categories. Traditional binary oppositions between interior and exterior, Self and Other, literally crumble as the skin of various women is cut, mangled, peeled away, sutured, and resutured. And here, as in the slasher films that Carol J. Clover analyzes, fascination with both the opened body and the destruction of the permeable membrane— which protects the corporeal inside from the outside world—is highlighted as the camera closes in for a variety of gore shots. But this fascination with the destruction of essential physical boundaries seems to exist at the level of plot—and skin—alone. Stylistically and generically, the film insists on maintaining the cinematic distinctions between action and horror, American and European, fluid and static (camera), open and closed (narrative), high and low (art and culture).[51]

While the American action sequences continually threaten to shatter the confines of the film text, they never really affect the (European, claustrophobic) clinic scenes. When Sam Morgan finds Barbara Hallen, he is simply locked in her cell with her. The two lovers are contained, walled in together, to suffocate and die. Even the dual ending enforces the essential difference between American action codes and European art-horror codes. The film ends where an episode of *Kojak* might begin—with Telly Savalas standing in his office, making plans to take on a case. What's interesting here is the suggestion that the successful closure of a European art-horror film (the Flamands and Dr. Moser toasting the New Year) might open up into the beginning of an American action film sequel (Mr. Hallen, in his Kojak mode, coming in to save the day). But a real mixing up of codes, a real contamination of polarized genre conventions (in which elements of the horror film would bleed into the action film and vice versa), a real challenge to cinematic binaries, seems outside *Faceless*'s scope. For that reason, the film seems less interesting and less truly subversive than *The Awful Dr. Orlof*, which really does destabilize traditional cinematic binaries and the hegemonic male gaze.

Cultural Capital

Within dominant cultural codes, both *The Awful Dr. Orlof* and *Faceless* qualify as "bad art," as works that often look sloppy, that privilege affect over meaning and story, and that resist cohesion. But both works also enact an aesthetic shared by fans of low Eurohorror—a tendency toward excess, syncopated rhythms, and surreal frame compositions. They draw on what Bourdieu would call a "cultural accumulation"[52] that is shared by paracinephiles and Eurohorror afficionados, a "cultural accumulation" that accrues from both "high" and "low" culture. To really appreciate Franco's films, it helps to know something about—or at least like—jazz (which Bourdieu links to "aristocratic" culture, the cultural elite), the works of the Marquis de Sade, European art films, other horror movies, porn flicks (Brigitte LaHaie, one of the stars of *Faceless,* made her name as an actress in adult movies), Nazi/SS exploitation films, American action movies, cop shows, and fascist history and culture. In fact, without such cultural accumulation, it's difficult, as Tim Lucas points out, to "get" or even like the films.[53] There's simply not enough *affect* to help the viewer over the slow parts.

  The idea that viewers have to learn to like Franco's style, have to learn how to watch his movies, removes the director's work from the arena of what Adorno would call true "mass culture."[54] Here, as in Bourdieu's descriptions of mainstream elite culture, the viewer has to be educated into the system. The more Eurohorror experience one has, the more one is likely to be willing to immerse oneself in Franco's work, to put in the time that's necessary for a complete understanding of the director's "soft persuasive language."[55] And because the cultural codes that Franco draws on derive both from a classical European education and from the "low" culture world of body genre movies, his films occupy a liminal cultural site much like the one occupied by Franju's *Les yeux sans visage*. Despite the raw visual quality of most of the films, they can still be situated at the intersection of high and mass culture, the place where traditional distinctions between high and mass culture become unhelpful, if not completely meaningless.

That Franco's images are raw, too raw and grainy for most mainstream film buffs and too gory for many mainstream viewers, links them to a certain "classed" and politicized taste. Within Spain, it links them historically to an antifascist aesthetic, a subversive tradition of controlled resistance that has a certain cultural resonance inside contemporary American paracinema circles as well. American low-horror fans turn to European cinema when their irritation at the "MPAA straightjacket"[56] begins to outweigh their impatience with a set of film codes they have to learn to decipher. As Lester Bangs puts it, "we got our own good tastes."[57] And those "good tastes" often encompass works that are difficult, that require cultural experience to properly decode. That is, the "good tastes" of low culture are every bit as complex, nuanced, and acculturated as is the elite taste for classical music, European art movies, and modern art.

Pauline Kael was right to link art house and horror audiences—both of which are characterized by a high degree of audience participation, a strong appreciation of both affect and formalist style, a tendency to privilege auteurs, a tendency to create long, hypertext narratives (Truffaut's Antoine Doinel films being a case in point), and a tendency to speak what Bakhtin has called the "language of the marketplace." But whereas Kael lumps both avant-garde and art film audiences together under the rubric of "art-house patrons," my discussion of *Les yeux sans visage* and the horrorshows of Jess Franco has focused mainly on the connections between European art cinema and low horror. In part 3, I look at three films that show the connections between horror cinema and avant-garde aesthetics and culture: Yoko Ono's *Rape* (1969), Tod Browning's *Freaks* (1932), and Paul Morrissey's *Andy Warhol's Frankenstein* (1973).

When Horror Meets the Avant-garde

6 Exploitation Meets Direct Cinema: Yoko Ono's *Rape* and the Trash Cinema of Michael and Roberta Findlay

> I'm making a film . . . it's a documentary.
> —**Mark Lewis, *Peeping Tom***

"The simplest Surrealist act," André Breton once wrote, "consists of dashing down into the street, pistol in hand, and firing blindly, as fast as you can pull the trigger, into the crowd."[1] In addition to highlighting the way surrealism frequently collapsed art and political action, Breton's statement illustrates (or perhaps enacts) three of the prevailing features of twentieth-century avant-garde aesthetics: the breaking of taboos surrounding the depiction (and performance) of sex and violence, the desire to shock *(épater)* the bourgeoisie, and the willful blurring of the boundary lines traditionally separating life and art. Unfortunately, Breton's statement also demonstrates a certain willingness to sacrifice bystanders (shoot into the crowd); it demonstrates a certain stated need for victims. And it is this last feature—the avant-garde's apparent willingness to hurt real people for the sake of art—that has created the most stunning ethical dilemmas for both the practitioners and consumers of experimental work. It is also this feature that has aligned the politics of experimental art with those of documentary, low horror, and pornography.

I've chosen to discuss Yoko Ono's documentary *Rape* (1969) in

117

part because it clearly demonstrates the generic and ethical issues I have described, and in part because it is such an affecting film. Because of Ono's participation in both the avant-garde art scene of the sixties and exploitation cinema, *Rape* is a particularly rich text for demonstrating the kind of dialectic that operates between high and low Anglo-American cinematic culture during the sixties and early seventies. But I don't want to give the impression that Yoko Ono is the only filmmaker whose avant-garde praxis invokes (or should invoke) the ethical concerns of both documentary and body genre cinema. Roman Polanski's *Break Up the Dance* (1957), in which the director hired real-life thugs to disrupt a school dance and then filmed the brawl,[2] Andy Warhol's *The Chelsea Girls* (1966), in which Ondine shot up on-screen and repeatedly slapped an actress, Shirley Clarke's *Portrait of Jason* (1967), in which Clarke and her husband Carl Lee staged a kind of psychodrama that effectively undercut Jason's subjectivity, and Mitchell Block's *No Lies* (1973), in which a filmmaker appears to psychologically brutalize the survivor of a violent rape, similarly interrogate the boundaries between fiction and nonfiction (documentary and staged event), art film and exploitation. Ono's film should be seen, then, as one example of a disturbing cinematic tradition, not as an isolated phenomenon or uniquely perverse artifact of cinematic culture.

Yoko Ono's *Rape*

Yoko Ono has consistently violated the separation between fiction and reality, the separation between representation and incitement that informs traditional theatrical and cinematic work. She entered the avant-garde art world, as Barbara Haskell and John G. Hanhardt point out, during the crucial period of the early 1960s and joined with other artists, dancers, poets, and filmmakers in challenging the limits of traditional aesthetic boundaries.[3] Influenced by John Cage and by the early Fluxus group (of which she was a member), Ono believed that "the boundaries between art and life should be eliminated" (2). For Ono, as well as Cage, "the world itself was a work of art," and making art was simply "a means of revealing to people the beauty around them" (2). It was, as Cage said, "an affirmation of life" (2).

Certainly much of Ono's early work was affirmative. In fact, it was the affirmative, positive nature of her art that first attracted John Lennon. "It was in 1966 in England," Lennon told David Sheff in an interview that is worth quoting at length.

I'd been told about this "event," a Japanese avant-garde artist coming from America. She was red-hot. There was going to be something about black-bags,[4] and I thought it was all gonna be sex. . . . Well, it was far out, but it was not the way I thought it was going to be. . . .

I did the breathing [Ono had given Lennon a card with "BREATHE" written on it], but I wanted more than . . . putting my consciousness on my breathing . . . I saw the nails . . . I thought . . . I can make that. I can put an apple on a stand. I want more. But then I saw this ladder on a painting leading up to the ceiling where there was a little spyglass hanging down. It's what made me stay. I went up to the ladder and I got the spyglass and there was tiny little writing there . . . and it just says "YES." . . .

Well, all the so-called avant-garde art at the time and everything that was supposedly interesting was all negative, this smash-the-piano-with-a-hammer, break-the-sculpture boring, negative crap! It was all anti-, anti-, anti-. Anti-art, anti-establishment. And just that "YES" made me stay in a gallery full of apples and nails instead of just walking out.[5]

While much of Ono's work was positive, drawing attention either to the simple beauty of things or to the wonder of life and nature itself,[6] some of her early pieces come remarkably close to the "break-the-sculpture" genre that Lennon found objectionable. *Painting to Be Stepped On* (1961) was a finished painting, lying on the floor. Spectators were instructed to walk on the painting and mar its surface. Similarly, *Painting to Hammer a Nail* (1961) was a white board with a hammer attached to it. Once again, spectators were invited to ruin the surface of the piece by pounding nails into it. More disturbing than the anti-art paintings, however, were the performance pieces that seemed to be directed against the artist herself. In *Cut-Piece* (1964), for example, Ono came out onstage wearing an expensive suit and carrying a pair of scissors. Kneeling on the stage, hara-kiri fashion, she placed the scissors in front of her and invited people to come up and snip away fragments of her clothing. And in *Wall Piece for Orchestra* (1962), she knelt on the stage and repeatedly banged her head against the floor.[7]

Ono's art provides a good illustration of the Fluxus movement's tendency to privilege social goals over aesthetic ones.[8] "The main aim" of the movement, Robert Atkins writes, "was to upset the bourgeois routines of art and life."[9] Both Ono's positive, affirmative pieces and her negative anti-art, antiestablishment works appear to accomplish just

that. But the vulnerable posture that Ono assumes during the performance pieces, the posture that, Barbara Haskell and John Hanhardt argue,
give the pieces such psychological effect (91), does more than simply
upset certain bourgeois "routines" of art and life. It forces the spectators
to participate in a ritual of real (the head banging) or potential (the scissors) violence and to make certain moral choices about their own role(s)
in the process.

The crucial questions for the audience (aside from the question
of sheer boredom) is the degree to which an audience member is willing
to cooperate in a piece that might prove dangerous to the artist. At what
point should one disrupt the piece to stop actual damage from taking
place? At what point should one step outside the role (spectator) that
one has been assigned? These are not simply hypothetical, intellectual
questions. The issue of spectator responsibility and complicity was explicitly raised during the first Kyoto performance of *Cut Piece*. During
that performance, Haskell and Hanhardt report, "latent violence nearly
erupted" when a man came onstage and "made a motion to stab" Ono
(91). And when—later in her career—Ono released her first disturbing
recordings, audience anxiety about the violence implicit in her work was
overtly expressed. Irritated by the music, people joked that the artist had
literally knocked something loose during her repeated performances of
Wall Piece for Orchestra.[10]

The discomfort that audience members felt during both *Cut
Piece* and *Wall Piece for Orchestra* did not arise, then, merely from
thwarted expectations about the theatrical experience (i.e., that a theatrical piece is supposed to entertain or, in lieu of that, inspire the audience). Rather, it arose, in part, from the feeling the audience had of
being "put on the spot," of being somehow implicated in the violence—
real or potential—taking place onstage. And this feeling of implication
was, according to some critics, an integral (as opposed to tangential) aspect of the works. The point of *Cut Piece* and *Wall Piece for Orchestra*,
Haskell and Hanhardt argue, was to raise questions about "the nature
of . . . personal violation" and violence against women (6). In *Cut Piece*
especially, Haskell and Hanhardt continue, Ono forced the spectators
to "confront their own attitudes toward sexual aggression, voyeurism,
and gender subordination," and she did this precisely by forcing them
to identify with (and, in some cases, to carry out) explicitly aggressive
behavior (91).

The active involvement of the audience in any given artistic
piece quickly became a trademark of Ono's work. Her gallery shows

often featured pieces that the viewer was instructed to "complete."[11] And her book *Grapefruit* is full of suggestions for ways of transforming everyday tasks into pieces of conceptual or performance art.[12] But Ono's instruction for making art out of life increasingly involved methods for "raising consciousness" about the patriarchal nature of everyday life itself. "Stir inside of your brains with a penis," she wrote, "until things are mixed well. Take a walk" (quoted in Haskell and Hanhardt, 34). This need to raise the audience's "consciousness" about patriarchal hegemony and its concomitant victimization of women led her into increasingly aggressive, increasingly controversial projects.

In the late sixties, Yoko Ono and John Lennon hired a cameraman, Nic Knowland, to "chase a girl on the street with a camera persistently until he corner[ed] her . . . and, if possible, until she [was] in a falling position" (*Film Script No. 5,* quoted in Haskell and Hanhardt, 94). *Rape* (1969) is the appropriately named cinematic realization of the project. In the film, Knowland and his crew encounter a woman in the Highgate cemetery and begin to film her, tracking her relentlessly through London's streets and finally forcing their way into the flat she shares with her sister. Unable to speak English, the woman, as the Pacific Film Archive program notes, "can neither understand why she is being filmed [her German and Italian inquiries elicit no response from the crew], nor make her stalkers go away."[13] By the end of the film, she is huddled in one corner of the flat and appears completely victimized and frantic.

As a documentary film, *Rape* simultaneously engages what Bill Nichols calls the "observational mode" (which "stresses the nonintervention of the filmmaker") and the "interactive mode" (in which the filmmaker intervenes and interacts).[14] Here Knowland uses the camera as a weapon, a device that forces Eva Majlata—the subject-victim of the film—to help him make a movie, create a narrative. The style invokes the style of both direct cinema and cinema verité; the camera apparently "objectively" records in observational fashion the action before it—an action that the filmmakers have always already initiated (interactive).[15] Like Jim McBride's quirky *David Holzman's Diary* (1967), *Rape* challenges the existence of the observational and interactive as discrete modes and—to borrow Nichols's words—"gives a particular inflection to [the] ethical considerations" of documentary filmmaking.[16] Or, to put it less generously, "ethical considerations" become the structuring absence in a film that appears to purposely ignore and confuse categories such as observational and interactive, life and art, public and private.[17]

The point of making *Rape* was, L. Marsland Gander of the

Daily Telegraph maintains, "to indict the over-exposure to which some people [notably Beatles and their wives] are subjected by the modern mass media of communication."[18] But while the film is "usually interpreted as a realization in the extreme of the paparazzi syndrome," as the Pacific Film Archive program notes, "*Rape* speaks (rather screams) to the cinema as well. And specifically of woman as she is captured in the cinema."[19] Certainly, the film does seem to illustrate Laura Mulvey's argument that visual pleasure in the cinema derives, to some degree, from the victimization of women.[20] And this metacinematic aspect of the film has led some scholars to read it as a feminist work.[21] But *Rape* goes far beyond the self-reflexive cinematic posture we are used to seeing. Unlike *Peeping Tom* (1960), a fiction horror film that mounts a similar critique against the apparatus of filmmaking and viewing, *Rape* actively participates in the victimization of the woman on-screen.[22] As Vivian Sobchack notes in her discussion of Mitchell Block's disturbing film *No Lies* (1973), cinematically the film "demonstrates and commits rape."[23] Unlike Block's film, however, where the female protagonist within the diegesis is revealed by the end credits to be an actress, *Rape* enacts a double outrage. The camera "demonstrates" rape to us, the viewers, and cinematically commits it, by brutalizing a real woman within the diegesis. As Rosemary in *Rosemary's Baby* (1968) says, "This is no dream. This is really happening."

The seventy-seven-minute, black-and-white film opens with a long shot of Eva Majlata walking toward the camera (there are no titles or credits).[24] As the cameraman, Nic Knowland, begins to follow her, Majlata is calm. She asks Knowland if he speaks German or Italian ("Sprechen Sie Deutsch?" "Parla italiano?").[25] When he does not reply, she tells him—in carefully rehearsed English—"I'm so sorry, I don't speak English." She smiles. She seems open, friendly, and charming. As the camera continues to follow her, she tries several times to engage Knowland in some kind of interaction, and one of the most poignant aspects of the film is the way in which she continues to address him in German and Italian, obviously hoping for some kind of response. Knowland, in return, never speaks to her.

"I'm sorry you don't understand German," she tells him early in the film, and then asks (for the second time) if he speaks Italian. When he continues to film her, she explains very slowly, patiently, in German that she wants to be left alone ("Ich möchte gerne allein werden"); "really alone." This entire exchange is filmed in medium range, and dur-

Figure 19. Majlata looking up at the camera in *Rape*.

ing the exchange, Majlata respects the physical boundaries established by Knowland. Although he is blocking the narrow cemetery path in front of her, she does not try to get around him. Neither does she turn away from him. She seems to be waiting for him either to make his purpose clear to her or to let her pass. When she realizes that he plans to continue silently filming her, she becomes impatient. "Mein Gott!" she exclaims, before explaining for the third time that she wants to be alone. When he still fails to respond, she darts away. Knowland has to run to corner her a second time. "End tape one," he says.[26]

At this point she begins rummaging in her handbag. She finds a cigarette, but no match. She asks for a light, and when he doesn't respond, she signs to him—with her cigarette—that she'd like a match. When he still doesn't respond, she tries to move past him, but he forcibly blocks her path. At this point, another man passes by. She asks him for a match ("feuer") and lights her cigarette. She does not try to get help from him. Turning back toward Knowland (who moved slightly to let the man pass and then rapidly resumed his place), she blows smoke at the camera lens. Moving a short distance away from the camera (medium long shot), she sits down and smokes her cigarette. "Four, take one," Knowland says.

While smoking her cigarette, Majlata seems to have come to some kind of decision. "Basta, veramente!" she says, switching to Italian ("Really, enough!"); "voglio restare sola!" ("I want to be alone"). "Eight, take one," says Knowland. Suddenly he's walking by the Strand, following Majlata, who has become visibly upset. She tells him in German that she's had enough, that he's making her nervous ("das macht mir so nervös"). She is clearly distressed that—if he keeps following her—he'll know where she's staying. She paces back and forth for a while (medium to medium long shot), speaking to herself (low tones and very rapidly) in German. Then a new thought occurs to her. "What are you going to do with this film?" she asks him in German, and then, switching to Italian, "Why are you making this film? For whom?" ("Perché sta facendo questo film? Per chi?"). Again, Knowland fails to respond. "I've had enough," she tells him, switching back to German. "I've really had enough!" She runs into the street and stops a passing taxi. Knowland follows her.

When she arrives at the building where her sister lives and finds that Knowland is still following her, Majlata explodes in frustration.

Figure 20. Majlata looking angry in *Rape*.

"Why can't I be alone," she says. "I only have three days here, and I haven't been allowed to enjoy anything. I want to look at the flowers, the sea." She turns and enters the building; the screen goes black.[27] The camera seems to be going down a long corridor, and then into an apartment. We hear someone banging on a door or wall. We don't see Majlata at first. Then we hear more banging and dimly see Majlata standing by the door, pounding on it with her fist. Knowland has apparently locked the door from the inside and pocketed the key. Majlata is a prisoner in her own—or, rather, her sister's—home.

She asks Knowland several times to open the door. "One-oh-one, take three," he replies. When he refuses to let her out, she buries her face in her arm. Knowland stalks behind her and tries to get a shot of her face. She pushes the camera away, and several crazy lateral traveling shots seem to indicate a physical struggle. "One-oh-one, take 4," says Knowland. Once again, Majlata covers her face, and we hear her sobbing. Throughout the rest of the film, she tries to shield her face from the camera. Periodically she runs to the door and bangs on it, trying to attract someone's attention. Most of the time her face is shadowed; Knowland contents himself with shooting close-ups of her hair and arms.

After a while the phone rings. Majlata begs the person on the other end to come at once. Later, she phones her sister. She asks her how to tell Knowland in English that her passport has expired and that she has to go to the Austrian Embassy. Looking bewildered,[28] she finally hangs up the phone and slumps to the floor. She curls up; she hides her face (medium shot). The only sounds come from outside the flat. The screen blackens. The credits come up:

> RAPE
> Directed by John and Yoko
> Eva Majlata
> Nic Knowland[29]

Rape was read, as L. Marsland Gander points out, as an indictment of mass media. Majlata's complaint that the ever present camera has ruined her enjoyment of the day echoes the statements of celebrities who wish—however temporarily—to be left alone.[30] Certainly, Knowland's attempt to film a close-up of Majlata's face, as she is sobbing in her sister's apartment, is reminiscent of the worst excesses of broadcast journalism. But *Rape* is not a film about celebrity.[31] And it is, I think, Majlata's status as a noncelebrity, as an "ordinary" woman, that gives the film such a sinister atmosphere. Anyone, the film implies, can suddenly become the unwitting object of media fascination and persecution. But women, because of their "objectified" status and their socialization, are unusually vulnerable, the film insists, to the camera's predatory gaze.[32]

The project relies heavily on the female gender of the camera's victim. "Chase a girl . . . with a camera," *Film Script No. 5* specifies, and the script's insistence that the victim be female makes cinematic sense.[33] There is, as Laura Mulvey points out, a long cinematic tradition of positioning women as the object of the cinematic gaze.[34] And it is because of that tradition that we, as viewers, accept the basic premise of the film. We accept that the camera is chasing Majlata simply because she is an attractive woman. No motivation other than that of pleasure in looking at the female object need be ascribed to the cameraman. Trained by years of cinema viewing, we even accept, to some extent, the camera's obsession with Majlata as "normal."

But Ono and Lennon's insistence that *Rape*'s victim be female was dictated, I believe, by certain social conventions as well. At the press conference that followed the film's screening at Montreux, journalists (mostly males) wondered at Majlata's passive acceptance of her terrorization. "Why didn't Miss Majlata break the camera?" one reporter asked the two filmmakers. "Because people have a basic respect for machinery," John Lennon replied.[35] Lennon's response evades the central point, the crucial issue, that I believe the journalist's question—perhaps unwittingly—raised. The reason Majlata did not break the camera is because women in Western society have been socialized differently from men. After all, male celebrities from Frank Sinatra to Sean Penn have been notoriously disrespectful of both photographic "machinery" and of the physical welfare of the photographers behind it.[36] Had a man been chosen for the victim's role, it is quite possible that Knowland's camera would have been broken. But women, for the most part, have been trained to use their wits and their words to resolve situations. In the film, Majlata does not give physical expression to her anger until quite late in the "story" when she is trapped in her sister's apartment. Instead, she persistently attempts to reason with the cameraman, telling him again and again—in two languages, which he appears not to understand—that she "really" ("wirklich," "veramente") would like to be alone. The reason, I would argue, that Majlata did not break Knowland's camera is simply that it did not even occur to her to do so. And it was this very fact—her socialization as a woman—that Lennon and Ono were counting on.[37]

Lennon's reply to the reporter's question points up, then, one of the troubling aspects about the way the film was made. In an uncharacteristic act of what Jean-Paul Sartre would have called "bad faith," Lennon seems reluctant to admit that he and Ono knew it would be safe (camera equipment is expensive) to terrorize someone on the street only if that someone was female. If one of the main points of the film is that women are easily victimized by the camera's incessant gaze, the easy terrorization of women was also a necessary social precondition for the filmmaking process itself. Like Lennon, however, Ono too seems uncharacteristically reticent to discuss the moral implications of the film. When reporters at the press conference asked the couple if they had "the right to put this girl through this ordeal," Ono told the reporters to "leave our morals alone."

Like *Cut Piece* and *Wall Piece for Orchestra*, *Rape* insists that women, under the patriarchal system, are positioned as victims of the spectacle. And like *Cut Piece* and *Wall Piece for Orchestra*, *Rape* seems to encourage the audience to feel complicitous in the violence that is taking place in the performance space. Relying completely on I-camera shots, the film encourages spectators to identify with the brutalizing medium, to feel as though Majlata is simultaneously trying to shrink away from and (through the use of language) to make contact with us.[38]

As in Ono's earlier performance pieces, there is a certain culpability associated with looking at the spectacle here. That guilt seems to persist even during the moments when the cinematic illusion is broken. "End tape one," Knowland says; "Four, take one"; "One-oh-one, take three." Throughout the film he provides a kind of verbal clapboard, reminding us that *Rape* is a constructed piece.[39] But unlike other films whose self-reflexive posture provides a kind of emotional release for the audience ("it's only a movie"), *Rape*'s metacinematic moments simply plunge the audience into another kind of discomfort. The advance publicity that preceded the film's premiere (and that has continued to precede and accompany successive screenings) ensured (and continues to ensure) that audiences would be aware of the "nonfiction" nature of the film; it guaranteed that audiences would know that Majlata's suffering was real. While Knowland's verbal notations temporarily rupture audience identification with the I-camera, then, they simultaneously draw the audience's attention back to itself. Like some hideously sadistic

Candid Camera episode, *Rape* insists we remember that it is really torturing Majlata, and that it is doing so just for us.

So far, I've been emphasizing the painful aspects of viewing *Rape*. Of course, the film has its pleasurable moments, too. Like any good stalker film, it is thrilling to watch. And a stalker film is what *Rape* most closely resembles—in terms of both its content and its style. Like *Halloween* (1978), the film that Vera Dika designates as the prototypical stalker film, *Rape* "functions to envelop its viewers in a precisely orchestrated system of gratification and shock."[40] Like *Halloween*, "perhaps the most striking characteristic" of *Rape* "is the . . . [stalker's] lurking point-of-view shot" (53). And like *Halloween*, *Rape* uses this steady camera gaze "focused on a character" to "[mark] the character as a victim" (54). Furthermore, as a low-budget film, *Rape* suffers from the low production values generally attributed to "body genres" (horror and porn), documentary, and New Wave/neorealist films. Improper lighting and poor-quality film stock give the film a grainy look. At times, the screen images are completely washed out; at others, they're completely obscured by shadows. And the use of a handheld camera makes for very rough traveling shots.

Unlike a formulaic stalker film, however, *Rape* ultimately thwarts viewer pleasure and expectation.[41] It does not, in the mode of stalker films, provide any kind of dramatic resolution or allow for any kind of catharsis. Although we hear the stalker's voice ("end tape one") and occasionally get a glimpse of his hand or shoe, there is no interdiegetic unmasking of the stalker. And although Majlata does seem to fight with her attacker when she is trapped in her sister's apartment, she never rises to the Final Girl behavior that—as Carol J. Clover points out—resolves the tension at the end of a good stalker movie.[42] Not only does she fail to temporarily vanquish her attacker, she fails to assume "the active investigating gaze," which—Clover argues—the Final Girl always manages to assume (60). Slumped on the floor, her head buried in her hands, Majlata remains the passive object of a sadistic, male-gendered gaze. Unlike the Final Girl in stalker films, she does not convince us that she has (psychologically speaking) survived.[43]

If *Rape* resembles the stalker films that Dika discusses, it has close links with 1960s exploitation cinema, as well. Four years before making *Rape*, Yoko Ono starred in a low-budget exploitation film, whose story shares some notable features with Ono's own avant-garde production. *Satan's Bed* (1965) was made by Michael and Roberta Findlay, the husband-wife team who later became (in)famous for their role

Figure 21. Publicity art for *Satan's Bed*. "Starring Yoko Ono."

in making the controversial *Snuff* (1976), a film in which an actress was supposedly killed on-screen.[44] As the 1995–1996 Something Weird Video Catalogue admiringly notes, "Michael and Roberta Findlay win the award for making the most sick and bizarre sexploitation features ever put on celluloid."[45] But they also, the catalog tells us, make films that play "like . . . demented, utterly out of control 'art film[s]'" (37). That is, they make films that are violent, erotic, and sensational but often privilege style over content. In fact, because of the Findlays' tendency to salvage old films by simply editing in new footage, their movies have an oddly surreal, "exquisite corpse" look and narrative structure,[46] a look and structure that seems equally indebted to Buñuel and Godard and shares attributes with Paul Sharits's and Yoko Ono's Fluxfilms.[47]

Certainly, *Satan's Bed* is an exquisite corpse of a film. As the blurb on the back of the video box informs us, *Satan's Bed* is

> Yoko Ono's film debut—in a sleazy, adults-only S&M drug movie, partially made by Roberta and Michael Findlay (SNUFF).[48] Michael was the photographer and editer *[sic]* and Roberta acted and did the lighting. SATAN'S BED is really an earlier "unfinished" feature called JUDAS CITY by "Tamijian" with new footage and characters edited in. Yoko (in a kimono) shows up in New York to marry Paulie who wants out of the drug business. She can't speak English and he's preoccupied, so she's taken to a filthy, cheap hotel room. A gangster (in the concrete business) rapes her on the floor (offscreen). He takes her to his penthouse and rapes her again. Interwoven with this (JUDAS CITY) footage is the sick tale of Snake, Dip, and Angel, addicts in black clothes, who look like part of Andy Warhol's Exploding Plastic Inevitable show. The first line heard is "I'd like to take his needle and shove it in his greedy mouth." They roam around tying up women (Angel helps) and raping them. Finally a Long Island housewife with a gun escapes from the hoped *[sic]* up trio and footage of Yoko escaping is intercut. SATAN'S BED was released about the same time as HELP![49]

With the appearance of Yoko and three characters "who look like part of Andy Warhol's Exploding Plastic Inevitable show," the film has a certain arty appeal, an appeal that is underscored by Findlay's sometimes-beautiful camera work, the discontinuous editing, and the cobbled-together narrative. The references to drugs, to lesbianism, and to S/M link the film as much to Andy Warhol's films as to exploitation; and the image of suburbia as a place where people stay locked inside their antiseptic dwellings, ignoring the real world outside (in this film, violence often explodes on suburban lawns, and even though the victimized woman yells for help, nobody seems to hear or see), is as much a feature of avant-garde art as it is of exploitation.[50] Interestingly, what the film doesn't seem to do (or at least doesn't do as aggressively as other exploitation films of the period) is the very thing that Gene Ross notes makes a "sexploitation film so endearingly successful." It doesn't go "straight for the [male audience's] crotch." [51]

As the video box notes inform us, two pivotal scenes of sexual violence in the film take place off-screen. And as Gene Ross observes in a different context, "unlike most sexploitation films . . . [Satan's Bed] offers us very little in skin."[52] Although there are quite a few "undraped females" in the film,[53] they are undraped in the manner of Janet Leigh in *Psycho* (1960) or *Touch of Evil* (1958)—at the edges of, but still within, the norms established by mainstream cinema of the period. Even women whom—the narrative suggests—have already been abused appear chastely clad in bras and panties. And the most direct representation of sexual desire is Angel's fidgety, lip-smacking, lascivious attitude as she helps the boys hold screaming housewives down (in this film, hopped-up lesbians just look, they rarely touch).[54] When the film played the Fine Arts Theatre in New Jersey as the main feature during the week of 6 July 1966, it only had—the projectionist's notes inform us—"a fair week." "I feel," he continues, "(co-fea) [Russ Meyers's *Motor Psycho*] didn't help." The "mixed-up story with a little of everything in it" could be brought back, he wrote, "with a good nudie or a very good nudist picture," but theater records do not list any return engagements. And it is Yoko Ono's role in the film that seems largely responsible for its cult status now.

While the similarities between the Yoko Ono character in *Satan's Bed* and Eva Majlata in *Rape* are mainly superficial—both are non-English-speaking women, whose foreign status makes them vulnerable to the thugs who are stalking them—one scene in *Satan's Bed* bears a striking resemblance to the final sequence in *Rape*.[55] Near the end of the film, one of the gangsters who is trying to convince Paulie to continue dealing drugs takes Ono to a penthouse. Shoving her into the living room, he locks the door from the inside. "Sit down and relax," he tells her. "We'll be here for awhile, until I get that Paul-san of yours straightened out." Then he goes upstairs. Ono runs to the windows and tries to open them. The film cuts to a high-angle point-of-view shot of Ono, taken from the stair landing. Framed by the vertical slats of the banister, Ono is clearly marked as a prisoner. "Go ahead," her captor tells her. "It's twelve stories. Straight down." The film cuts to a point-of-view shot—representing Ono's point of view—out the window. The man descends the stairs. Showing Ono the key, he tells her the door locks both ways. Then he leaves. Ono tries to make two phone calls. Slumping to the floor, she picks up a piece of paper and folds it into an origami bird. The camera cuts to a shot of a picture hanging on the wall, then to a reverse shot of Ono looking thoughtful. Going into the kitchen, she rummages through the cupboards and tiny refrigerator and puts food and wine on a tray. Then she changes into a kimono. When her captor returns, she serves him. He drinks some wine and eats some crackers. Then he rapes her.

As noted, the scene bears a striking resemblance to the end of *Rape*. The apartment door locked from the inside, the image of a frantic woman trying to attract attention by pounding on windows and walls, and the futile attempts to make a telephone call are all reminiscent of Ono's (later) film. What's different is the point of view. As a fictional exploitation film, *Satan's Bed* inscribes the female victim's point of view into the diegesis. While she may not ever acquire an "active investigating gaze," neither does she remain solely the observed object of an increasingly sadistic camera. For all its sensationalism and silliness, *Satan's Bed* has a poignancy that is missing from *Rape,* an interdiegetic way of acknowledging the subject status of the objectified Other.

Speaking about, Speaking Nearby

In *Rape,* none of Majlata's lines are translated; the film is not subtitled. In some ways, this decision on the part of the filmmakers makes perfect sense. Viewers who do not understand Italian or German will be plunged into exactly the same position that Majlata herself and, perhaps, Nic Knowland occupy—the position of being a stranger in a strange land, of literally not understanding what the Other is saying (I say "perhaps Nic Knowland" because it is not clear in the film whether or not he understands what she says; that is, it isn't clear in the diegesis to what degree his refusal to respond is a power ploy and to what degree it is ignorance).

You could even argue that the absence of translation appears here as a subject-affirming act. That is, Majlata's words—incomprehensible as they may be—are not mediated by a translator. She speaks directly to us, and if we don't understand what she says, at least we don't find ourselves relying on the interpretation (the interpretation that translation always entails) of her tormentors. If she is physically harassed, at least she is not "spoken for." In a way, this is reminiscent of Trinh T. Minh-ha's *Reassemblage* (1982), an ethnographic documentary in which the filmmaker attempts to "speak nearby" rather than "speak about" Africa. To this end, she leaves many of the African voices we hear in the film untranslated. In *Reassemblage,* to translate the subjects' words—to speak for Africans—becomes another way of colonizing them, of asserting cultural hegemony. The best one can do, Trinh suggests, is to put oneself in the work, to make one's own stake in the profilmic enterprise clear, to be resolutely—and sometimes irritatingly—self-reflexive.[56]

That, however, is not the case in *Rape.* Here Nic Knowland never explains what he is doing; he certainly does not worry on the sound track about the political or moral implications of his filming—as Trinh does.[57] And I cannot help but feel that the film loses something for audiences who don't understand what Majlata is saying. In the absence of translation, Majlata's speech becomes the inarticulate cries of a woman in frustration and anguish, the cries of the star victim in a horror film. And while these cries may be very affecting, they do not give the viewer an accurate sense of the ways in which Majlata attempts to negotiate the situation, a full account of the way her civility and charm continually fail her.

If the physical and visual dynamic of *Rape* is a "rape with camera"[58]—a rape in production—as Ono maintains, then the spoken and aural dynamic of the film is, similarly, a kind of rape in postproduction, a refusal (even at the level of postdubbing) of Majlata's subjectivity, of her right to represent herself through speech. This is, interestingly enough, not the case in *Satan's Bed,* where Ono's character's inability to speak English is not highlighted so dramatically. The Ono character says very little in *Satan's Bed* (she does not try to negotiate with or understand her abductor, as Majlata does), and given that she ultimately gets away from her rapist, her silence here can be read as a means of closing up within herself, of keeping her own counsel. Like Nic Knowland's silence in *Rape,* Ono's silence in *Satan's Bed* becomes a locus of strength and the means to escape.[59]

What I find troubling in *Rape,* then, is not only its *real* sensationalism (which is very troubling) but also the way it enacts a kind of double violation, a double erasure of the female subject. While the film chillingly portrays the ways in which power often "works through physical bodies,"[60] first by showing the cameraman stalking Majlata and finally by showing him holding her physically captive, it also demonstrates that—as Foucault taught us—power works through discourse. Here, the one who asserts physical dominance is also the one who is understood by the English-speaking audience. That he chooses (or has been instructed) not to speak, chooses (or has been instructed) not to understand or render comprehensible Majlata's words, chillingly illustrates the degree to which, under the right conditions, silence can become an instrument of power, a colonizing force.[61] It also illustrates the degree to which mechanisms of power are often consolidated through the regulation of language, of speech.[62]

The choice of a non-English-speaking foreign woman as the subject of *Rape* illustrates what E. Ann Kaplan calls "the parallels between the structures of the male gaze as feminist film theorists, following Mulvey, have thoroughly examined it, and the structures of the 'imperial gaze.'"[63] To a foreign woman whose papers had expired, Knowland's camera might well have conveyed an "air of authority" that it would not have conveyed to a native Brit. That is, Majlata may have been intimidated—and intimidatable—by the camera partly because she knew that strictly speaking, she wasn't currently "legally" in Britain. Certainly the gaze of the camera goes a long way toward emphasizing (for the audience) her status as foreign, "exotic" Other. To borrow Ella Shohat's phrase, it demonstrates the way the patriarchal gaze is intimately linked to the "disciplinary gaze of empire."[64] It demonstrates the degree to which state power (the surveillance gaze of the Law) can be articulated with personal power (the colonizing male gaze that Kaplan, following Mulvey, discusses).[65]

But it also establishes the logic of the film as clearly a logic of violence. As Majlata becomes increasingly desperate in the face of an impossibly nonverbal situation, she has no other recourse than to physically struggle with the cameraman, no other recourse than to construct a (physically) defensive posture for herself. And it is this end goal toward which the "camera" seems to be working during the entire film. In fact, it is this end goal that Ono seems to have had in mind all along. Speaking to Scott MacDonald, Ono remarked,

> Nic Knowland did the actual shooting. I wasn't there. Everything was candid, but I kept pushing him to bring back better material. The type of material he brought back at first was something like he would be standing on the street, and when a group of girls passed by, he would direct the camera to them. The girls would just giggle and run away, and he wouldn't follow. I kept saying he could do better than that, but he actually had a personal problem doing the film because he was a Buddhist and a peacenik: he didn't want to intrude on people's privacy.[66]

If Scott MacDonald asked any follow-up questions about the ethics of forcing a cameraman to violate "people's privacy," they aren't documented in the interview. In part, this is a generic convention. Academic interviewers are not in the business of writing exposés, and MacDonald would have a difficult time recording the impressions of avant-garde artists if he were perceived as unfriendly—or even hostile— to the artistic community. But the absence of a follow-up question confers a certain legitimacy on the *Rape* project, a legitimacy that I find troubling. Affect here—both the real effect that Knowland's actions had on Majlata and the cinematic affect that the film continues to produce in spectators—is ignored in favor of what Ono sees as the intellectual and artistic function of the film. In that sense, MacDonald's interview with Ono reinforces what I read as the dominant ideology of the [avant-garde] art world, an ideology that privileges an artwork's message over at least some of its content and sometimes ruthlessly privileges art and the avant-garde over the quotidian and the banal (the artist herself over the poor schmuck on the street).[67]

To some extent, the moral and ethical problems posed by *Rape* are, as Alan Rosenthal points out, emblematic of the moral and ethical problems faced by all cinema verité filmmakers: "The relationship of ethical considerations to film practice is one of the most important yet at the same time one of the most neglected topics in the documentary field. . . . [T]he question of ethics was not ignored by the early vérité filmmakers; rather such questions simply weren't taken seriously."[68] In that sense, *Rape* can be read as a self-reflexive exercise, a documentary that lays bare the ethical issues that, as Rosenthal suggests, haunt all vérité filmmakers. To borrow again from Sobchack's observations about *No Lies*, *Rape* makes "the experience of being the unwary unprepared victim of an aggressive assault on one's person, on one's pride and on one's expectations of a security in familiar surroundings a very real experience accessible to anyone of either sex who views the film."[69] Unfortunately, it does so at the expense of a real woman, and in so doing, it gives new meaning to the term "exploitation cinema."

Snuff

Many of the ethical issues raised by *Rape* became the topic of intense media debate in the United States during the mid-seventies, partly because of a fictional film in which Yoko Ono also participated: the Shackleton-Findlay production *Snuff* (1976). As David Kerekes and David Slater note:

Early in February of 1976, following rumours on the possible existence of "snuff" films, and reports circulating that one such film had been smuggled into the United States from South America, a one-sheet poster was displayed in the Times Square area of New York, outside the National Theatre, 1500 Broadway, 45th Street. The poster was for a motion picture called *Snuff*. X for violence. The artwork was that of a bloodied, cut-up photograph of a naked woman and it bore the legend, "The film that could only be made in South America where Life is CHEAP!" It also promised "The *Bloodiest* thing that *ever* happened in front of a camera!"[70]

The film in question was *Snuff,* another exquisite corpse exercise in exploitation cinema. Most of *Snuff* was taken from a Findlay film called *Slaughter* (1971), a movie about a murderous hippie cult, based on the Tate-LaBianca murders. *Slaughter* was shot in Argentina over a period of four weeks, on a budget of $30,000. Because the cast largely comprised Argentinian actors who spoke very little English, the film was shot silent; when shooting was completed, it was taken to the United States for postdubbing. As Kerekes and Slater note, the Findlays tried to arrange a distribution deal with Joe Solomon of Fanfare Films. When he declined, they screened the film for Allan Shackleton of Monarch Releasing. Shackleton took the film and shelved it; it sat, gathering dust, for four years.[71]

When press reports of snuff films began to surface in 1975, Shackleton decided to bring the Findlays' film out of storage. Removing all references to the original film, he shot a coda. At the end of the hippie cult footage from *Slaughter,* in which a female cult member menaces a pregnant woman with a knife, a voice yells "cut." The scene shifts to a soundstage. The "director" tells one of his production assistants that the gory scene just filmed turned him on. When she confesses that it turned her on as well, he suggests they have sex. He takes her to the bed on the set and begins to fondle her. When she protests that the crew and actors are watching, that the cameraman is actually filming the scene, he hits her. Then he asks the cameraman if he'd like to get some *really* good footage. With the assistance of a crew member, the "director" holds the woman down and tortures her—first with a knife, then with pliers. Finally he slices her open with a ripsaw and holds her entrails up in front of the camera. The screen goes black. Someone says that they've run out of film. Another voice on the sound track asks if the cameraman got it all.

Shackleton retitled the film *Snuff* and released it on the exploitation circuit. Before opening in New York, the film had already had brief runs in Philadelphia and Indianapolis, where the police forced it to close. By the time it reached Times Square, its reputation preceded it. And rumors surrounding the film convinced the public that the coda sequence, the scene in which a director tortures and kills a production assistant in front of the camera, was documentary footage—that the murder was real.

As Linda Williams points out,

> The sequence is as heavily edited and replete with "medical FX" as any other instance of mutilation in this (or any other horror) film. Nevertheless, its added signals of documentary evidence—the director's speech to and "look" at the camera, the indication of film "run out," the shocking transition from sex scene to violence—all operated to convince critics that if what they had seen before was fake violence belonging to the genre of horror, what they were seeing now was real (hardcore) violence belonging to the genre of pornography. The particular obscenity of this last sequence thus resided in a perverse displacement of pornographic hardcore sexual activities, which typically end in penetration onto the penetrating violation of the body's very flesh.[72]

In retrospect, it seems amazing that anyone mistook *Snuff*'s violence for cinema verité. As Richard Eder, writing for the *New York Times,* noted, "everything about the film is suspect: the contents, the promotion and possibly even some of the protest that is conducted each evening outside the box office."[73] Still, the rumors persisted, and finally, "prompted by complaints and petitions from well-known writers, including Eric Bentley and Susan Brownmiller, and legislators," Manhattan District Attorney Robert Morgenthau investigated the circumstances surrounding the film's production.[74] On 10 March 1976, the *New York Times* ran an article revealing that the famous snuff sequence was a hoax. At Morgenthau's urging, the police tracked down the actress who had supposedly been murdered on-screen and interviewed her. "It is nothing more than conventional trick photography," Morgenthau said after the interview. "The actress is alive and well."[75]

As Linda Williams notes, though, "even after the hoax was revealed . . . the idea of snuff continued to haunt the imagination."[76] Certainly, it marked a major turning point in the public debate over pornography. Beverly LaBelle credits *Snuff* with making "the misogyny of pornography a major feminist concern."[77] When the fictional status of the film was revealed, the parameters of the debate simply shifted—

away from the real physical dangers that the film (had) posed to an actress in the diegesis to the real physical dangers that the film might pose to *all* women. Following *Snuff,* feminist antiporn writing increasingly focused on the way in which graphic cinematic depictions of violence against women (even when such depictions are staged or fictional) create a climate that encourages (or at least appears to condone) real violence committed against real women in the extradiegetic world.[78] It increasingly equated the consumption of violent porn with violence against women, particularly rape.

Snuff, then, ultimately focused attention on the social and moral implications of watching and enjoying—as well as of filming—gross violence against women, even when such violence was clearly fictional. Of course this increased concern and scrutiny had implications for exploitation cinema as well as for porn. It became harder to find exploitation cinema outside paracinema catalogs and venues that catered to hard-core porn fans. Paracinema television programs, such as *Creature Features* and Vampira's *Midnight Madness,* restricted exploitation horror offerings to films that had a politically correct ending (unlike the films of the Findlays, which often have no ending at all), or (for laughs) some kind of pointed antidrug message.

The documentary that ran the risk of brutalizing a real woman—*Rape*—did not inspire the same kind of far-reaching reconsideration of what was appropriate or inappropriate cinematic pleasure. Partly this is because the film enjoyed much less of a succès de scandale than *Snuff* did. Distributed largely through museums and other art venues, the film was coded as serious in intent; disturbing but not titillating.[79] Partly, it's because the film's disturbing implications for film spectatorship and pleasure are less easy to see than *Snuff*'s are. But if *Snuff* erroneously focused public attention on the sexual politics of watching porn, *Rape* should have focused more attention than it did on the sexual politics of what Mulvey calls the camera's sadistic gaze. When *Rape* was theatrically released, Willi Frischauer of the *Evening Standard* reports, it made a star of its victim-protagonist. According to Frischauer, Eva Majlata "won a contract as a star model as a result . . . of her appearance in *Rape.*"[80] Partly, that may have been due to her association—however minimal—with a Beatle (Lennon). But partly it's due, I think, to a certain cultural (or, as Mulvey—following Freud—would argue, psychosexual) investment we have in watching women suffer on-screen. As Hitchcock, the director whose work Mulvey most associated with the sadistic gaze, said during the filming of *The Birds* (1963), "I always believe in following the advice of the playwright Sardou. He said, 'Torture the women!' The trouble is that today we don't torture women enough."[81] *Rape*—a film that clearly tortures a woman "enough"—apparently takes Hitchcock's advice to heart.

It is never easy to speak about "morality" or "ethics" in connection with art. Particularly in the current cultural climate, such discussions inevitably seem to lead to attempts at public censorship and regulation, attempts that are, as Steven C. Dubin rightly points out, at least as shocking and scandalous as the "immoral" art works themselves.[82] But to avoid speaking of the "morality" and "ethics" of avant-garde art is to avoid theorizing much of what is truly disturbing and revolutionary in post–World War II experimental work. It also leaves unchallenged the central binary opposition structuring many of the cultural debates taking place in the current fin de siècle period. The idea that low culture can sometimes be more ethical than high art, that high art is as willing as low culture to exploit its stars and audience, is a hard notion to swallow. And yet they are notions we have to swallow (and begin to talk about) if we're ever going to understand our cultural investment and stake in watching women suffer on-screen.

From Horror to Avant-garde: Tod Browning's *Freaks*

Freaks was one thing I photographed a lot. It was one of the first things I photographed and it had a terrific kind of excitement for me. I just used to adore them. I still do adore some of them. I don't quite mean they're my best friends but they made me feel a mixture of shame and awe. There's a quality of legend about freaks. Like a person in a fairy tale who stops you and demands that you answer a riddle. Most people go through life dreading they'll have a traumatic experience. Freaks were born with their trauma. They've already passed their test in life. They're aristocrats.

—Diane Arbus, *Diane Arbus: An Aperture Monograph*

We accept her, one of us. We accept her, one of us. Gooba gobba, gooba gobba, we accept her; we accept her. Gooba gobba, gooba gobba, one of us; one of us.

—Wedding banquet toast, *Freaks*

If avant-garde films have at times encroached vigorously on horror, at least one horror film seems to have "crossed over" into the avant-garde. That film is Tod Browning's 1932 classic *Freaks*. Removed from distribution by MGM shortly after its release and banned outright in Great Britain, the film—as *The Encyclopedia of Horror Movies* points out—immediately "acquired an unsavoury reputation which lingers on even though denied by the film itself."[1]

Freaks tells the story of a circus midget's impossible love for a

"big woman," the circus trapeze artist Cleopatra.[2] When she becomes
aware of Hans's love for her, Cleopatra contrives to marry the midget for
his money (Hans, we learn, has a fortune). Shortly after the wedding,
she and her strongman lover, Hercules, begin administering poison to
Hans. But when Hans falls ill, the other freaks in the circus become suspicious. Following "the code of the freaks," they kill the strongman and
mutilate Cleopatra, turning her into a chicken-woman, the star of the
freak show.

Critical reception of the film was mixed. "*Freaks,*" the *New
Yorker* reports, "is a little gem."

> I don't think everyone should see it. It's certainly not for susceptible
> young people. . . . As a very special case, though, as a little venture into
> the grisly and the gruesome, it has its remarkable qualities, and leads our
> guileless fancy into curious fields of speculation—curious if not exactly
> wholesome.[3]

The reviewer for the *New York Times* echoes the *New Yorker*'s
warning that *Freaks* "is not for children." That is, in fact, the only thing—
according to the reviewer—"that can be said definitely" for the film.
"Metro-Goldwyn-Mayer," he writes, "has on its hands a picture that is
out of the ordinary. The difficulty is in telling whether it should be
shown at the Rialto—where it opened yesterday—or in, say, the Medical Centre."[4] While the reviewer does have some complimentary things
to say about the film, particularly about Browning's direction, he hesi-
tates to give it a firm recommendation. "The picture is excellent at times
and horrible, in the street meaning of the word, at others . . . whether
it deserves the title abnormal is a matter of personal opinion."[5]

If the critics could not quite make up their minds about *Freaks,*
neither, it seems, could the public. "In spots," *Variety* reports, "it has
been a cleanup. In others it was merely misery."[6] The audience that the
New York Times critic observed "patently could not decide" what it
thought of the film, "although there was a good deal of applause."[7] And
at least one reviewer speculated that certain audience members would
find the film "too mild."[8]

Confusion about the film seems to have stemmed largely from
the use of real freaks to play the parts.[9] Critics worried that the film
merely replicated the most unsavory aspects of the "Freak Show." The
New York Times reviewer talks about "the underlying sense of horror . . .
that fills the circus sideshows."[10] *Variety* faults the film for its "too fantastic romance," claiming that "it is impossible for the normal man or

woman to sympathize with the aspiring midget."[11] And *Time* refuses to evaluate the picture at all, detailing instead all "the misfits of humanity" it numbers among its cast.

> A man without legs walks on his hands.
> A woman without hands eats with her feet.
> A Negro with no limbs at all lights a cigaret *[sic]* with his teeth.
> Siamese twins have courtships.[12]

Certainly publicity for the film points up its relationship to the carny culture it so poignantly depicts. "Unlike anything you've ever seen," the Rialto Theater's 1932 ad for the film proclaims. "The *strange* and *startling* love-drama of a *midget,* a lovely *siren,* and a *giant!*" In addition to Leila Hyams, Baclanova, Wallace Ford, and Rosco Ates, the ad lists "a horde of caricatures of creation—not actors in make-up—but *living, breathing* creatures as they are and as they were born!" The base of the ad carries a warning: "Children will not be permitted to see this picture! Adults not in normal health are urged not to!"[13]

Although both critical reaction and box office success appear to have been mixed, mass public reaction was not. A few favorable statements buried in otherwise ambivalent reviews were not enough to counter the markedly negative reviews that appeared in the local press. One reviewer worried that the film's "unwholesome shockery creates morbid audience reactions."[14] Another described it as "so loathsome I am nauseated thinking about it" and solemnly declared that "it is not fit to be shown anywhere."[15] Apparently, both theater owners and parents agreed with the latter reviewer's final point. Although the film had shown good box office receipts in some venues, theater owners—particularly those in rural areas—refused to handle the film. At the same time, PTAs and what Leslie Fiedler calls "other organizations specializing in moral indignation" lobbied against the film (296). Even some of the freaks who had played in the movie, Fiedler notes, "most notably the Bearded Lady, were convinced in retrospect that Browning had vilified their kind and said so in public" (296). In the face of so much opposition, MGM withdrew the film from circulation after it completed its New York run.[16]

At this remove, it seems remarkable that MGM—a studio noted for its high-gloss, evenly lit family films—should have made a dark little horror show like *Freaks.* Or even that it hired Tod Browning. While Browning is best known for his popular horror hit *Dracula* (1931), he had a reputation in the industry for making bizarre films that reflected his experience with sideshow culture. His collaboration with Lon Chaney led to a remarkable series of movies in which Chaney literally "gave body to the macabre figments of Browning's carnival background" (*Encyclopedia of Horror Movies*, 35) In *The Unholy Three* (1925), a ventriloquist, a dwarf, and a strongman carry out a series of bizarre crimes that end in murder. *The Road to Mandalay* (1926) revolves around a man who is so crippled and scarred that he is ashamed to reveal himself to his daughter. And *The Unknown* (1927) stars Chaney as a con artist who has his arms surgically removed in order to better woo the woman he loves, a

Figure 22. "The man with a thousand faces." Lon Chaney in *London after Midnight*.

woman who has a pathological fear of being touched. "When I am working on a story for Chaney," Browning said in a 1928 interview, "I never think of the plot. That follows by itself after the characterization. *The Unknown* began merely with an armless man. I asked myself what would be the most startling situation in which a man so deformed could be involved. The plot about a circus performer who uses his feet as he would his hands, who loves and loses the girl, and eventually attempts a terrible crime with his toes, grew out of my speculations."[17]

What Browning valued in Chaney was the actor's mutability, his willingness to "take on guises and disguises of the more grotesque nature. He will do anything," Browning said, "and permit almost anything to be done to him for the sake of his pictures."[18] And it was this aspect of Chaney's star persona that the public valued, as well. In a period still dominated by a kind of heady Horatio Algerism, the idea of success through metamorphosis went over well with film audiences. "There is not a screen performer who so illustrates the fascination for audiences of the idea, promise, and threat of metamorphosis," wrote film historian David Thomson.[19] And as David Skal notes, Chaney so captured the popular imagination "that a familiar saying of the time, referring to spiders, lizards, or other crawling things was 'Don't step on it—it might be Lon Chaney.'"[20]

But Chaney was only acting the role of a freak. In real life, as pictures in the fanzines stressed, Chaney was a handsome, "normal" bodied man. And in one of the more bizarre slippages in movie fan history, audiences seemed almost to associate Chaney's real-life good looks with the torturous contraptions he wore to change his appearance on-screen. As Skal points out:

> A glimpse at the back pages of the fan magazines that published studio-canned features on the Man of a Thousand Faces is revealing; up front, you could discover Chaney's latest grueling disguise and the agony he was enduring, Christ-like, on your behalf; and when you finished reading about the actor's latest hunchback harness, you could peruse innumerable back-of-the-book advertisements for products to straighten your own spine, reduce or enlarge your body, or give yourself a "round, pretty" face instead of "unsightly hollows."[21]

Fanzine ads from the period show harnesses that could be strapped to the face "to obtain a perfect looking nose." And Youth-Ami Liquid Skin Peel promised movie magazine readers that if you didn't like the skin you had, you could simply peel it off and find a new beautiful layer underneath.[22]

But that was the Roaring Twenties, when prosperity seemed endless and anyone, so the myth went, could transform himself from a paperboy into an oil tycoon—if he was willing to put up with a little hard work and temporary discomfort. *Freaks,* however, was made in 1932, the time of the Great Depression—when the mood of the country had shifted radically. As Jonathan Rosenbaum notes in *Midnight Movies,* "the interesting thing about *Freaks* as a film of 1932 is that it's dealing almost literally with the same things that the *Gold Diggers* musicals deal with, but more directly—because the end product isn't just putting on a show, but slaves breaking their chains and triumphing over their masters."[23] Unlike the *Gold Digger* musicals, however, J. Hoberman replies, "*Freaks* is asking a Depression audience to identify not with the Beautiful People who are going to make it in Hollywood, but with sideshow mutations, a total underclass. As a reflection of the time, it's almost revolutionary. But Depression audiences were not prepared for this kind of thing."[24]

Furthermore, unlike Tod Browning's earlier freak shows, in which Chaney wore painful "enfreaking" contraptions in order, it seemed, to emerge (at least in real life) more handsome, more virile, and, certainly, a greater star at the end of the picture, *Freaks* describes metamorphosis as a downward spiral. Cleopatra is transformed through her hard labors into a chicken-woman, the chief attraction of the freak show. She represents the dark underside of the "idea, promise, and threat of metamorphosis" that Chaney had so vigorously embodied. Interestingly, the general public anxiety over freakishness that the film unleashed seemed to prompt reevaluations of Browning's earlier "grotesque" work as well. When Tod Browning died in 1962, most of his obituaries omitted both *Freaks* and the Lon Chaney films from his list of accomplishments. Clearly, the American press preferred to remember him as the director of *Dracula,* a more safely traditional kind of horror flick.

When MGM shelved *Freaks,* it gave a twenty-five-year license on the film to Dwain Esper, "the father of modern exploitation."[25] According to David J. Skal and Elias Savada, it was Esper who added the awkward preamble to *Freaks,* a preamble that was retained even after film rights reverted back to MGM and that still appears on show prints and video copies (223). "As a result," Skal and Savada note, "audiences and critics have assumed it is some kind of position statement by Tod Browning himself, instead of a distributor's cynical attempt to position the picture with a moralistic, 'educational' defense—just like the pictures about sex and drugs" (223).

> Before proceeding with the showing of this HIGHLY UNUSUAL ATTRACTION, a few words should be said about the amazing subject matter. BELIEVE IT OR NOT . . . STRANGE AS IT SEEMS . . . In ancient times anything that deviated from the normal was considered an omen of ill luck or representative of evil. Gods of misfortune and adversity were invariably cast in the forms of monstrosities . . . The revulsion with which we view the abnormal, the malformed and the mutilated is the result of long conditioning by our forefathers. The majority of freaks themselves are endowed with normal thoughts and emotions. Their lot is truly a heartbreaking one . . . With humility for the many injustices done (they have no power to control their lot) we present the most startling story of the ABNORMAL and the UNWANTED.

As Skal and Savada note, the preamble links *Freaks* to the drug and sex education films that were staples of the exploitation circuit. And *Freaks*—minus the MGM logo—played the exploitation circuit under a variety of titles for almost thirty years. But while this recasting of *Freaks* as exploitation film removed the movie from the mainstream theater circuit, it also underscored the difficulty of classifying the film.[26] As David J. Friedman notes in his memoir *Hollywood Babylon,* the film sometimes bombed on the exploitation circuit simply because it wasn't exploitative enough. As an example, Friedman describes a disastrous screening of the film, under the title *Forbidden Love,* at a North Carolina drive-in.[27]

> The Charlotte drive-in audience sat through the feature as it unreeled in torrents of rain. But by the time the "End" title came on, they began blowing their car horns, flashing their headlights at the screen, yelling and screaming out rolled-down windows, and yanking car speakers off the posts. Although they had seen a film now classified as one of the great screen shockers ever, they hadn't seen any skin. A real "hey rube" was imminent.[28]

As Friedman describes it, Dwain Esper pacified the irate audience by projecting a "scratched fourth or fifth-generation duped black-and-white nudist colony one reeler" that he had pulled from his car. "The rowdy Tarheels," as Friedman calls the unruly North Carolina audience, "quickly quieted down." Friedman cites this story as an example of the "massive boredom" of running the Paramount branch in Charlotte, North Carolina,[29] but the story itself points up the difficulty of marketing *Freaks*. Too disturbing for a mainstream audience, *Freaks* was simply not disturbing (or sexy) enough for an audience lured into buying tickets for a movie called *Forbidden Love*.

But although Freaks was not distributed on the mainstream circuit in either the United States or Britain until after its 1962 revival, the film quickly achieved a sort of cult status in France. As Leslie Fiedler points out in his book *Freaks,* a small group of cinephiles especially admired the film, and it continued to be shown in the tiny movie houses of the Latin Quarter long after it had closed in New York.

> Moreover, no American critic had up to the year of his death [1962] written such praise of Browning's *chef d'oeuvre* as had appeared in 1951 in Paul Gilson's *Ciné Magic*. Speaking of the "magic" which redeems "the black images of this cruel film" and the "grandeur of its terror," Gilson is led to evoke Edgar Allan Poe's *Tales of the Grotesque,* especially, of course, "Hop-Frog." (298)

Browning, it is clear, *had* achieved a certain Poe-esque stature among French intellectuals. In 1951 the French Surrealist Group (champions of Poe) urged its followers to go see *all* of Tod Browning's films.[30] And in the 1960s, as both Leslie Fiedler and John Thomas point out, Browning's *Freaks*—like Poe's work a century before—"returned to the United States . . . as an export of French avant-garde culture" (Fiedler, 298).[31]

The Return of the Repressed

In 1962, the year of Tod Browning's death, *Freaks* played at the Venice Film Festival.[32] This major revival, as Skal and Savada point out, "followed a summer of horrific headlines about the consequences of a morning sickness drug called thalidomide, which triggered gross birth defects. Images of limbless, flippered babies turned tabloids in America and Europe into newsprint sideshows—an uneasy media stew of pity and morbid voyeurism" (223). In the face of such everyday horror, *Freaks*—with its emphasis on a closed, self-contained world of "monstrosities"—lost a great deal of its earlier shock value. In fact, Skal and Savada argue, its depiction of a family-like freak culture and its initially positive representation of the freaks themselves may have seemed somewhat reassuring to parents who fretted about their childrens' future in such a freak-phobic society. The year of Tod Browning's death, the film was released—for the first time—in Great Britain (home of the thalidomide tragedy), and in 1964, the U.S. critic John Thomas hailed the film as a "minor masterpiece."[33]

I'm not convinced that the appeal of *Freaks*—in the wake of the thalidomide scare—was primarily one of reassurance to parents who worried over the fate of their children (what parents, after all, want to think of their children as safe only within the confines of a circus side-show?). The fact that the freaks in the film turn on the "normal-bodied" woman in the film and turn her into one of them ("one of us") hints at a much darker, deeper guilt and anxiety that the film perhaps unwittingly addressed. The thalidomide scare threw into sharp relief not only public anxieties about a medical establishment that seemed to be willing to use patients as "guinea pigs" (giving drugs before the full side-effects of the chemicals are known) but also the sometimes disastrous effects of a continuing medical tendency to view pregnancy—and the female body—as always already pathologized. Women took thalidomide to prevent miscarriages. That is, women took thalidomide within a context of medical scrutiny that represented the "normal" looking female body as always potentially lethal—a body that could not carry a child to term without outside "help." Within this context, what I later posit as the latent misogyny in this film makes absolute social sense. The thalidomide scare engaged two different images of female monstrosity, both of which had roots in ancient belief systems and teratology—that the female body is itself always potentially in need of a fix, and that monsters are born because of some monstrous trauma in the womb, a trauma occasioned by either the vision or sexual (mis)behavior of the mother.

The revival of *Freaks* coincides, then, with a time period in which the perhaps unconscious guilt of women who had "thalidomide babies" ("if only I hadn't taken the drug") dovetailed with deeper, more long-standing folkloric traditions that read mothers as always somehow responsible for the physical shape of their children, a time when maternal guilt dovetailed with deeper currents of gynophobia just barely submerged in the society.[34] Within this context, the punishment visited on Cleopatra by the freaks in the film both speaks to the real fears of women (that their children would hate and resent them, and would especially resent them for being able-bodied) and provides a cathartic, if extremely cruel, way of working through some of that guilt—by watching the punishment of the maternal body on-screen.

Whatever catharsis it offered to parents struggling with their own guilt and resentment, the revival did not necessarily reestablish the film as a stunning example of *popular* cinema. Situated as it was between the real-life horror stories of thalidomide births, on one hand, and the rise of the art film, on the other, the rereleased film was reevaluated as both documentary and art house product.[35] Its art house revival in the United States during the sixties unleashed a whole new generic debate about the movie; namely, should it be considered a horror film at all.

Writing for *Film Quarterly*, John Thomas makes it clear that *Freaks* is not a film for the average horror audience. *Freaks,* he writes, "will disappoint no one but the mindless children who consume most horror films. . . . Certainly it is macabre, and the final sequence in which the freaks stalk and mutilate their victim is enough to scare the hell out of anybody. *But the point is that* Freaks *is not really a horror film at all, though it contains some horrifying sequences.*"[36]

Raymond Durgnat agrees with Thomas's assessment. Comparing the film to the surreal masterpieces of Luis Buñuel, Durgnat cautions that the film should really be seen more than once: "*Freaks* is one of those films which, like so many of Buñuel's, grows at each viewing. At first its very real shock-value seems to mingle with moments which seem shallow, but by the end of the film one begins to catch their mood, a calm, cold combination of guignol and eerily matter-of-fact *[sic]*."[37] For Durgnat, as for Thomas, the film—while horrifying—is not really horror. Even the stalking sequence, which Durgnat qualifies as "really obscene," seems more avant-garde than anything else. "The 'blackness'" of the film's "moral," he writes, "is one more Buñuelesque trait in a film which at every turn evokes the name of Buñuel, in haunting subtlety as well as in downright shock."[38]

Even the film's new distribution seemed to give it avant-garde credentials. Anthony (Antony) Balch—who was largely responsible for the screening of *Freaks* in London—also took charge of U.S. distribution of the film. Before picking up the distribution rights to *Freaks,* Balch had been known to the general public mainly for the experimental films he programmed for the Times Baker Street Theater in London.[39] But to a select group of cognoscenti, he was also known as the maker of a series of experimental Beat films, featuring Brion Gysin and William S. Burroughs. In fact, when *Freaks* opened in London (at the Paris-Pulleman Theater), it shared a double bill with Balch's avant-garde piece *Towers Open Fire.*[40] And *Freaks* figured prominently in Balch's later avant-garde works, as well. In his film *Bill and Tony,* for example, the filmmaker and William Burroughs take turns reciting the barker's opening speech from *Freaks.*

We didn't lie to you, folks. We told you we had living, breathing mon-strosities. You laughed at them, shuddered at them; and yet, but for the accident of birth, *you* might be even as they are. They did not ask to be brought into the world, but into the world they came. Their code is a law unto themselves. Offend one and you offend them all. And now, folks, if you'll just step this way. You are about to witness the *most* amazing, the *most* astounding living monstrosity of all time. Friends, she was once a beautiful woman.[41]

Mutatis Mutandi

Watching *Freaks* today is an unnerving experience, although not for the reasons implied by the 1932 reviews of the film. It is not seeing the freaks lead normal lives ("Siamese twins have courtships") that is unsettling. On the contrary, the film's apparent thesis—namely, that "freakishness is only skin deep, and that differently formed people have all the feelings, intelligence and humor of 'normal' folks"[42]—is one that most contemporary audiences find appealing. "What keeps *Freaks* 'freakish,'" as the Pacific Film Archive program notes for the film point out, "is rather the duality of Browning's own intentions. Despite being one of the few films that, *mutatis mutandi,* treats the Other as 'one of us'; and despite purporting in the original prologue to be an exposé of the exploitation of 'nature's mutants,' *Freaks* is guilty of the crime it denounces."[43] "By virtue of its bizarre revenge plot" and its periodic insistence on "the code of the freaks," the film, as the PFA program notes point out, "traps its characters in a horror mode." It reinscribes physical difference as a thing to be feared.

The first half of the film goes to great lengths to "normalize" the freaks. We see differently formed people going about the usual everyday business of life. Frances, the armless woman, eats; Randion, the "living torso," lights a cigarette; Frieda, a midget, hangs out the laundry. And while it is tempting to read these actions—as the *Time* review of the film does—as a series of sideshow acts, the presence of sympathetic "big people" in nearly all these scenes helps to mitigate the performative aspect. Randion is in the middle of a conversation with one of the Rollo brothers when he lights his cigarette. Similarly, Frances, the armless woman, is listening to one of the Rollos brag as she eats her evening meal. Frieda, as she hangs out her laundry, exchanges confidences with Venus. The film clearly brackets these exchanges as everyday conversation ("You're not singing this morning, Frieda," Venus observes as she sits on her wagon step to sew and chat). It also uses the "big people" as audience stand-ins: much like the screaming victims in traditional horror films, they "cue" us to the appropriate audience response.

Furthermore, there seems to be something odd about most of the "normal" people in the film.[44] The Rollo brothers' excessive bragging appears here as far more quirky than Randion's dignified cigarette routine. Rosco, the man who works with Hercules, stutters. The sword swallower and the fire-eater are lumped with the freaks in the circus attractions. And Phroso the clown, the most sympathetic "big man" in the film, refers ominously to his "operation" and appears a little slow in his dealings with the street-smart Venus.

Even Cleopatra, the "queen of the trapeze" and the "most beautiful big woman" Hans has ever seen, appears as somehow too large. Seen in Hans's wagon after her marriage to him, Cleopatra must hunch over in order to move around. And Venus, Phroso's sympathetic, conventionally formed lover, calls Cleo a "big horse" when she learns—from Frieda—about the trapeze performer's designs on the midget. But it is Cleo's perverse nature that most establishes her as the "living monstrosity" of the circus. Initially flirting with Hans as a nasty joke, Cleo turns deadly serious when she learns he has money. "Midgets are not strong," she tells her lover Hercules. "He could get sick . . . It could be done." And the hunched position she must assume to give Hans his poisoned medicine once he does, in fact, become ill is simply the visible sign of the predatory nature that Cleo has nurtured all along. "In this extraordinary film," Ivan Butler writes,

> Browning has turned the popular convention of horror topsy-turvy. It is the ordinary, the apparently normal, the beautiful which horrify—the monstrous and distorted which compel our respect, our sympathy, ultimately our affection. The visible beauty conceals the unseen evil, the visible horror is the real goodness.[45]

Just in case the audience somehow fails to get the point that it is the "freaks" in this film who deserve our allegiance and sympathy, Browning includes at least two scenes that make the film's thesis quite explicit. When Hans falls ill, Venus confronts Hercules and makes it clear that she does not regard herself as one of his "kind." "You better get Cleo to tell the doctor what she put in the wine last night," Venus tells Hercules, "or I'll tell the coppers." "So," he replies, "you'd tell on your own people." "My people," Venus says, pulling herself up, "are decent circus folks, not dirty rats what would kill a freak to get his money."

Early in the film, Mme Tetralini makes an impassioned speech for tolerance of the freaks' difference. The scene here shifts away from the cloistered world of the circus to the surrounding countryside. We see a gentleman walking with his groundsperson, Jean (medium shot), who is struggling to describe the horrors he has just seen. "Horrible, twisted things," he says, "crawling and gliding." Laughing, the gentleman asks what he had been drinking the previous night. But Jean insists that he saw "things" that should have been "smothered at birth." The gentleman assures the distraught man that he'll clear his grounds of any "things" or persons who do not belong. We then see—in long shot—Mme Tetralini, the owner of the circus, and a group of circus freaks that she has brought out for exercise. The human skeleton is lying on his back, playing a reed pipe. The pinheads, Schlitze, Elvira, and Jennie Lee, and some of the midgets are dancing in a circle, singing and giggling. Johnny Eck, "the half-boy," leaps from his perch and scampers along on his hands. Randion, the "living torso," rocks and slides to the music. A little way away from this strange pastoral, Mme Tetralini sits reading. As the disgruntled Jean moves in to chase the strange band away ("Dépêchez-vous," he cries, waving his walking stick), the camera comes in for a medium to medium-close shot. Mme Tetralini rises; Schlitze and Elvira run to her for protection. The others, too, gather closely around.

Figure 23. "Have I not told you that God looks after all his children?" Schlitze and Jenny Lee with Madame Tetralini in *Freaks*.

Clinging to her skirts, they—especially Schlitze and Elvira—look like frightened children. And children, Mme Tetralini explains, is exactly what they are.

> These are children from my circus . . . when I get the chance I like to take them into the sunshine and let them play like—children. That is what most of them are—children.

When the gentleman gives them permission to stay and calls the still-sputtering Jean away, Mme Tetralini scolds her charges for being frightened.

> Shame . . . How many times have I told you not to be frightened. Have I not told you that God looks after *all* His children.

Mme Tetralini's speech, like Venus's, is clearly meant to remind the audience that physical difference is an accident of birth. Her gentle insistence that we are *all* God's children functions here as a reproach to any Philistines in the audience who might believe—as Jean and Hercules clearly do—that differently formed people are "little apes" or "monsters."[46] But Mme Tetralini's speech points up one of the subtler aspects of the film. While it is certainly true that the freaks are all God's children, that is, his offspring, it is not so clear that all the freaks—or even "most of them"—are literally "children" (i.e., innocent and helpless beings), as Mme Tetralini claims.

Although some of the freaks—most notably the pinheads—*are* portrayed as childlike throughout most of the film,[47] the male freaks included in the pastoral scene are all explicitly linked to the adult world. The human skeleton playing the reed pipe appears in a later sequence as the proud father of the bearded lady's baby. Randion, the "living torso," has a mature, weather-lined face and sports several tattoos. And the midget who leads the band in thanking the gentleman for allowing them to stay is obviously mature. It is he who proposes and leads the "one of us" toast at the wedding banquet, he who seems to organize and orchestrate the surveillance of Cleo when Hans gets sick, and he who first calls the audience's attention back to the freaks' "code." Enjoying a glass of wine with Frances, the armless lady, he angrily predicts that Cleo will have problems if she tries "doing *anything* to one of us."

If it is wrong to judge people as "monsters" simply because they are differently formed, it is equally wrong (and potentially dangerous)—the film seems to be saying—to attribute childlike qualities (like help-

Figure 24. "What are you? A man or a baby?" Cleo (Olga Baclanova) with Hans (Harry Earles) in *Freaks*.

lessness and innocence) to adult people who happen to be diminutive in size. And this is a mistake that many of the "normal" people in the circus make. Even Cleo, who plays on Hans's adult sexual feelings throughout the first half of the film, periodically confounds his appearance and behavior with that of a child. She laughs at his courtly manners behind his back and teases him when he shows signs of jealousy. At the wedding banquet, she accuses him of acting like "a baby" when he does not join in her outburst, and she further humiliates him by taking him on a horsey-back ride around the deserted table. Even in her gentle moments, Cleo tends to infantilize Hans. She calls him "my little," in a vain attempt to convince him of her affection, and tells his friends to go home so that she can tuck him in for the night. But Hans is not "a baby." He is—as he tells her early in the film—"a man," who has the same feelings "big people" have. And these feelings turn quite nasty when he begins to suspect that Cleo is trying to poison him.

The blend of gender and genre codes is interesting here. As the victim of Cleo's murder plot, Hans bears a striking resemblance to the female protagonists of gothic romance.[48] Suffering from a suspicious illness (the doctor says it is food poisoning) from which he seems unable to recover, Hans is completely dependent on Cleo. She carries him to bed, takes care of him, and administers his medicine. But as he continues to languish, Hans—like any gothic victim—begins suspecting that his spouse is trying to kill him. He starts to spit out the medicine that Cleo so lovingly prepares, and when he is finally strong enough to sit on the edge of his bed, he surprises her in the act of contaminating his medicine with poison.

But while Hans's illness seems to code him for femininity and for melodrama,[49] his position in the circus community works to undermine such coding and to establish *Freaks* as a horror film. Unlike the traditional victim-heroine of gothic romance, Hans is part of a large community, a community that clearly shares his suspicions of Cleo. From the moment that Hans is humiliated at the wedding banquet, an elaborate spy network of freaks is set up. Peering in at the windows, skulking under Cleo and Hans's wagons, hovering by the door, circus freaks seem suddenly to be everywhere. In fact, it is quite possible that Hans's growing suspicion of Cleo derives not so much from his own deduction and paranoia—as Mary Ann Doane argues the traditional gothic heroine's does—but rather from the intelligence gathered by his friends.[50]

Hans is not alone, then, as so many gothic heroines are.[51] Most important, he is not alone when he confronts Cleo with his suspicions. Unlike the gothic heroine whose "exercise of an active investigating gaze can only be simultaneous with her own victimization,"[52] Hans scrutinizes Cleo from a position of power. Hunched in the wagon kitchen's doorway, Cleo is quite literally trapped by Hans's accusation. A knife-wielding midget guarding the door guarantees there is no escape.

If Hans's situation seems to place him—across gender lines—in the female gothic position, so too does Cleo's. In one of those interesting twists that so often mark horror, Cleo emerges as the potential victim of the freaks at the same time that she emerges as the victimizer of Hans. And Cleo's position seems to conform much more closely to the one that Doane describes. Alienated from the rest of the circus, Cleo has no community of friends to protect her or to keep an eye on the freaks' activities. Like the classic gothic victim, she is reduced to interpreting surfaces. And like the classic gothic victim, she is convinced that she is being watched.[53] When Cleo is confronted by Hans in the wagon, she does "exercise . . . an active investigating gaze" that "can only be simultaneous with her own victimization." Scanning the faces of her husband's friends and finally staring fixedly at the knife that menaces her, Cleo realizes too late that her paranoid delusions of being watched and menaced were not delusions at all. She drops the spoon she is holding and hands her bottle of poison to her husband.

I mentioned earlier that it is Hans's position in the circus community that sets the film apart from the gothic thriller genre and that helps to establish *Freaks* as a horror film. Certainly, the freaks' revenge against Cleo is terrifying in a way that suspense can never be. But if the freaks' revenge inscribes the film as part of the horror genre, it also reinscribes the freaks as monsters within that genre. In fact, the entire revenge sequence can be read as a systematic reversal of the pastoral scene (the scene that attempted to establish the freaks as harmless children) earlier in the film. Whereas the pastoral takes place in a contained, sunlit space, the revenge sequence unfolds at night during a rainstorm, and its overt sense of menace derives precisely from the fact that the freaks can *not* be contained. Anywhere that Cleo runs, she is vulnerable. Furthermore, whereas the pastoral sequence expounds antifreak prejudice (in the form of Jean's tirade to his employer) so that Mme Tetralini might refute it, here Jean's anxieties about the freaks are given literal expression. Pursuing Cleo through the mud and rain, the freaks *do* crawl and glide; and given the fact that it is night, they *do* resemble "horrible twisted things," rather than differently formed people. Finally, whereas the pastoral scene attempts (somewhat unsuccessfully, as I have argued) to represent the freaks as "children," the revenge sequence shows clearly that the most childlike freaks can be quite vicious. Even Schlitze—perhaps the most childlike pinhead—appears monstrous here as she gambols through the mud clutching a knife.

If the pastoral scene shows a group of vulnerable freaks who cling to a big woman, Mme Tetralini, for protection, the revenge sequence depicts a big woman who desperately needs protection from a band of marauding freaks. It is clear that Cleo occupies the star-victim position here. From the moment she runs screaming into the night with the band of vengeful freaks behind her, Cleo begins attracting audience sympathy.[54] And it is this very shift in audience sympathy—*away* from the freaks and *toward* their intended victim—that tends to undermine what Robin Wood would call the earlier "progressive" nature of the film.[55]

Furthermore there are indications that the freaks have done this sort of thing before. The barker's ominous references to "the code of the freaks," as well as the prologue's invocation of such a code, sensitizes the viewer from the very beginning to the possibility of freak violence. Even the "progressive" sequences of the film—those that show the freaks behaving "normally" at home—hint at a dark side of freak culture. Relaxing over a glass of wine, Frances, the armless woman, and her friend, the midget who played a leadership role in the earlier pastoral scene, gossip about the budding romance between Cleo and Hans.

> SHE: Cleopatra ain't one of us. Why, we're just filthy *things* to her. She'd *spit* on Hans if he wasn't giving her presents.
>
> HE: Let her try it. Let her try doing *anything* to one of us.
>
> SHE: You're right. She don't *know* us; but she'll find out.

Frances's observation that Cleo doesn't really "know" the freaks serves in part to remind us that the freaks are a marginalized, maltreated group. Like any such group, they have been forced to adopt an inscrutable, "unknowable" public demeanor to survive. But the reminder comes at a very odd moment in the film. At the very moment that the film appears to be downplaying difference (by showing that the freaks' domestic lives are not very different from those of "big people"), it explicitly connects the idea of difference to an implicit threat ("She don't know us; but she'll find out"). It is this threat that is, of course, realized in the revenge scene.

Although there is a certain poetic justice to Cleo's final transformation, her emergence as a chicken-woman further complicates the depiction of physical difference in *Freaks*. Cleo is constructed, not born, as a freak, and this construction seems to have two implications for the film. On the one hand, it works as a nice metaphor for the way that freaks are shown as "social constructs" throughout the film (i.e., the film shows that there is nothing inherently freakish about differently formed people and that in the freaks' world, it is "big people" who seem abnormal and odd). On the other hand, however, it directly contradicts the argument for tolerance that we are given at the beginning of the film. Having been initially reminded by the barker that physical difference is an "accident of birth," not the visible sign of some inner monstrosity, we are ultimately presented with a woman who has been turned into a freak as punishment for her immorality and greed (i.e., a woman whose physical difference *is* the tangible sign of her inner monstrosity). That Cleo—the true "living monstrosity" in the circus—is transformed into a physical "monstrosity" raises the possibility that physical difference can be the tangible sign of inner depravity. And it is this possibility that serves to partially blunt the progressive edge of the film.

Blurred Boundaries

If, as Raymond Durgnat argues, *Freaks* partakes in some of the best traditions of avant-garde cinema (cf. Durgnat's comparison of the film to
those of Buñuel), it also shares one of the avant-garde's major failings.
Like Yoko Ono's *Rape,* the film ultimately perpetrates the very behavior
it purports to critique.[56] And like Yoko Ono's *Rape,* it tends to blur the
line between cinematic representation and reality to a disturbing degree.
The fact that the freaks are—for the most part—played by themselves
(i.e., that the fictional characters have the same names and perform the
same circus acts as the actors who portray them)[57] encourages the audience to read the freaks' story as a semidocumentary of circus life. And a
semidocumentary is precisely what the film purports itself to be. The
film's "apologetic foreword"[58]—added by the distributor—informs the
audience that no story like *Freaks* will ever be told again, "as modern science and teratology is rapidly eliminating such blunders of nature [the
freaks] from the world." Like *Wild Kingdom,* then, *Freaks* is presented as
a final opportunity to see an endangered species in its protected habitat.
Even sophisticated reviewers such as Dilys Powell seem at least partly
ready to accept the film's self-proclaimed semidocumentary status. The
freaks' revenge is seen by Powell as a lifelike portrayal of circus life, since
"in those days [the 1930s] something revolting was always going on in
the circus."[59]

The actual appearance of Cleo as chicken-woman does—as
Leslie Fiedler argues—help to undermine the documentary quality of
the film.[60] The chicken-woman is so obviously a makeup department
coup that contemporary audiences frequently laugh in relief when the
camera finally reveals Cleo's mutilated condition. But while the appearance of the chicken-woman seems to signal an interdiegetic shift from
"documentary" to "Grand Guignol," it does not completely mitigate the
horrific quality of the revenge plot. It seems all too plausible that the
downtrodden of society should "have built up among themselves a code
of ethics to protect them from the barbs of normal people."[61] And this
very plausibility, coupled with the strong cinematic portrayal of the
freaks' revenge, plays on the very audience prejudices and fears that the
early part of the film attempts to challenge.[62]

The film seems to acknowledge the fact that it comes perilously
close to completely undermining audience sympathy for the freaks. Although Cleo's appearance as a chicken-woman seems to be the logical
conclusion to the film,[63] *Freaks* has a brief coda whose only purpose

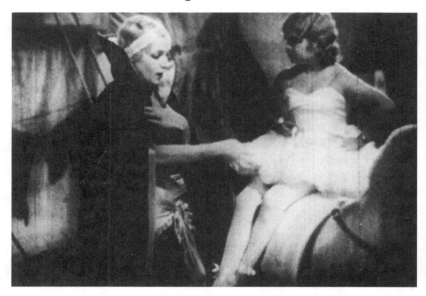

Figure 25. "Nice. Nice." Cleo with Frieda (Daisy Earles) in *Freaks*.

seems to be the recuperation of audience sympathy for Hans.[64] In the coda, Phroso and Venus bring Frieda to see Hans. Hans, who has been a recluse since leaving the circus, does not wish to see his old friends, but Phroso and Venus contrive to enter and to leave Frieda with him. "Please go away," Hans tells them, "I can see no one." "But Hans," Frieda tells the now-sobbing midget, "You tried to stop them. It was only the poison you wanted. It wasn't your fault."

Besides providing a romantic ending (Hans and Frieda are together again) to an otherwise grim film, the coda serves to remove responsibility for Cleo's condition from Hans. But it also serves to establish Hans as another victim of the freaks' revenge. Completely broken by the events he seems to have unleashed, Hans can now bring himself to see no one. Hidden away, he is even more isolated from the "normal" world than he was in the circus. And it is hard not to see this all as somehow Cleo's fault. She's the one—after all—who encouraged his attentions, she's the one who gave him "ideas," first to send her gifts and later to marry her, and she's the one who tried to poison him.

In fact, the film's ending can be read as the logical conclusion to Hans's relationship with Cleo. For in true horror-victim fashion, Hans seems to be completely feminized in this scene. Whereas Phroso and Venus's tiptoed exit—complete with pokes in the side and broad winks to each other—leads the audience to expect to see the midgets in a passionate embrace, the final shot of the film shows a completely un-manned Hans sobbing in Frieda's arms. And it is the unmanning of Hans—the divestment of both his money and his sexual pride—that Cleo seems to have had in mind all along. Early in the film she coaxes Hans to massage her bare shoulder, for the amusement of Hercules and the other "big" men who are watching. At the wedding feast, she bursts into laughter as she tells the assembly that "my husband is jealous." And the horsey-back ride she gives Hans around the wedding banquet table shows that Cleo's idea of the wedding night is radically different from her husband's. From the beginning of their relationship, Cleo seems to have mounted a campaign of sexual humiliation against Hans. "Are you laughing at me?" Hans asks Cleo when she first attracts his attention. And it is Hans's sexual humiliation that Frieda tries to prevent when she goes to see Cleo in her wagon. "Everybody's laughing," she tells Cleo, "because he's in love mit you. . . . I know you just make fun, but Hans, he does not know this. If he finds out, never again will he be happy."

Despite Frieda's attempts to comfort Hans with the thought that Cleo's tragedy was not his fault, one has the impression that the *real* cause of Hans's depression at the end of the film is the collapse of the marriage itself. Hans finally did find out that Cleo was just making fun. "I don't blame you, Cleo," he tells her on their wedding night. "I should have known you would only laugh at me." And having found out, Hans—as Frieda predicted—can never again be happy.

The coda, then, attempts to undo some of the revenge sequence's impact. Having been forced—almost against its desire—to see the freaks as monsters, the audience can return at the end to its earlier vision of Hans as Cleo's victim. It is significant, though, that such a return can be effected only through the complete feminization and infantilization of Hans. As the camera rests on Frieda and Hans at the film's end, Cleo's earlier taunt (that Hans was a "baby," not a man) seems to have been re-alized. Having failed in his efforts "to be a man" (i.e., to win Cleo's re-spect and to control her punishment), Hans is recast at the end as Frieda's "baby." Sobbing in his fiancée's arms, he seems to be destined for maternal rather than sexual love.[65]

"The Most Astounding Monstrosity"—*Freaks*' Misogyny

I have argued that *Freaks* remains a troubling film to watch largely be-cause of its own internal demonization of the freaks and because of the demands it makes on the audience (first we sympathize with the freaks, then with their victims, then with the freaks again). But equally troubling, I believe, is the misogyny and gynophobia that run throughout the film. From the opening barker's speech—"Friends, she was once a beautiful woman"—to the revelation of the chicken-woman, the film's real topic seems to be "dames" who "squeal when [they] . . . get what's coming to [them]."[66] And it is the punishment of one such "dame," Cleopatra, that I wish to reconsider here.

On one level, there is an element of poetic justice in Cleo's final transformation. Having previously refused to symbolically become "one of us" during the wedding banquet scene, Cleo is literally transformed into a freak as punishment for her arrogance and her betrayal of one of the freaks. But there is also a strong sexual component here. Not only did Cleo plot to kill her husband, but she sexually humiliated him in front of all his friends. Kissing Hercules passionately at the wedding banquet, insulting the wedding guests, and finally unmanning Hans symbolically (with the piggyback ride around the table), Cleo emerges as the quintessential transgressive woman. And her mutilation appears as an atavistic enactment of the punitive scarring visited upon adulteresses in certain preindustrial tribes.[67] The goal is to ruin her looks so that she cannot attract other men, and as in any ritual designed to bring female sexuality under control, the rape imagery in the revenge sequence is strong. When Hans demands—in the wagon—that Cleo turn over her little black bottle of poison, one of his friends dramatically opens a switchblade. In the hands of the midget, the knife looks enormous, and the spring action of the weapon combined with its piercing, penetrating function seems a perhaps too obvious phallic symbol for Hans's assumption of authority over his wife. Later, in the chase scene, everyone—even the pinheads—is armed with some kind of phallic weapon.

Interestingly, Cleo alone is mutilated in *Freaks*. As J. Hoberman and Jonathan Rosenbaum point out, the story's original ending called for the castration of Hercules, as well as for Cleopatra's mutilation.[68] Originally, then, both lovers were to be treated with sexual brutality; both lovers were to be essentially "neutered." The transformation of Hercules' punishment from castration to swift capital punishment (one of the midgets throws a knife into Hercules' back) is just one of the elements that is troubling here. For it is not really certain that Hercules is being "punished" at all. When the midget throws his knife into the strongman's back, Hercules is in the process of strangling Phroso. The knife attack is, then, as much an expedient means of saving Phroso's life as it is punishment for the crimes that Hercules committed against the freaks.

If—as the original ending for *Freaks* would suggest—mutilation and castration are the appropriate penalties for sexual transgression, then Cleo takes the punishment for both herself and Hercules. Her mutilation stands in for *two* violent and disfiguring acts: her own symbolic rape and Hercules' castration as well. In that way, Cleo may be said to serve the same symbolic function that Carol J. Clover maintains the female victim in contemporary slasher films always serves. As her body symbolically becomes the site for Hercules' punishment as well as her own, Cleo becomes the figure onto which the male experience of castration may be quite literally displaced.[69]

But Cleo's punishment symbolizes a kind of female castration, as well. For if Cleo is, as I argued earlier, a monstrous figure, much of her monstrosity derives from her assumption of male prerogatives and roles. It is Cleo who takes the sexual initiative with both Hans and Hercules ("So that's how it is," she tells the strongman after she calls him to her wagon, "You have to be called"). It is Cleo who devises the plan to kill Hans and avail herself of his money. And it is Cleo who takes responsibility for carrying the plan out. Physically stronger than anyone in the circus except Hercules,[70] Cleo's very physiognomy establishes her as an androgynous creature. As Ivan Butler describes her, she is

> tall, blonde, almost aggressively vital. . . . One critic described her performance as "voracious," and there is indeed at times a nasty feeling that at the back of her mind is an obscene desire to sink her teeth into the midget and gobble him up.[71]

Certainly, she physically dominates Hans. Carrying him piggyback around the banquet table, she asserts her physical strength and humiliates him in front of his friends. Carrying him to his own wagon when he is ill, she reinforces his position as feminized victim.

Cleo's sexual criminality is compounded, then, by the masculine codes she so readily assumes. Not only does she betray Hans in standard femme fatale fashion,[72] she also overtly usurps his position of physical and emotional dominance. Demonstrating that she is a better man than Hans will ever be, Cleo becomes what Susan Lurie would designate a "phallic woman."[73] And as such, she must literally be "cut down to size" by her husband and his friends.

Cleo's mutilation—her punishment for transgressing certain sexual and gender limits—is the culminating event in a film obsessed with the meaning of physical difference. In fact, its presence here serves to highlight the degree to which *Freaks'* obsession with physical difference can be read as an obsession with gender difference as well. For the film does repeatedly raise gender issues; it does repeatedly question the basis of gender assignment and identity. The silence that falls over the performers whenever Josephine/Joseph—half woman, half man—walks by, the accouchement of the bearded lady, and Hans's struggle to be recognized as a "man" are all indications of the way in which "freakishness" in this film seems inevitably to involve gender duality or confusion.[74] Even the performers associated with the freaks are often cast in sexually ambiguous roles. Rosco, the stutterer who performs with Hercules, dresses as a Roman lady for his act. And Phroso the clown refers to an unspecified "operation" in one of his early conversations with Venus.

But if Cleo's mutilation is the culminating event in a film obsessed with gender confusion and duality, it is also the culminating event in a film haunted by misogyny. Punished for betraying Hans and for transgressing her gender and sexual role, Cleo emerges as the "*most* amazing, the *most* astounding living monstrosity of all time." She emerges as the quintessential example of what Phroso would call essential femininity. At the hands of the freaks, she becomes one of those "dames" who "squeal when [they] . . . get what's coming to [them]."[75]

One of Us

Freaks, as Leslie Fiedler notes, "has become part of the canon of the counterculture."[76] Admired by 1960s youth—people who frequently referred to themselves as "freaks"—the film has continued to appeal to viewers who identify with the "fringe" or "marginal." The Ramones traditionally led a "gooba-gobba" cheer (taken from the movie) before their rock concerts in the 1970s and 1980s, and the interest in body modification—piercing, tattoos, brandings, earlobe extensions—that has marked the 1990s counterculture aesthetic shows the same radical refusal of the standards of "normal" beauty that the freak culture represented in *Freaks* does. Marilyn Manson's video *The Beautiful People* (Dir. Floria Sigismundi) appears to invoke *Triumph of the Will, Metropolis,* and *Freaks* as it invites viewers to identify with the tortured and the maimed, who are depicted in the video both as victims of on-screen fascist cruelty and as personification(s) of resistance to the totalitarian normatizing trends of protofascist culture. Furthermore, the popularity of Browning's film itself has not diminished. In a recent Halloween screening of *Freaks* at the university where I teach, the auditorium was packed, and when I introduced the movie, students began chanting the "gooba gobba, one of us" Ramones cheer.

But while I agree with Jonathan Rosenbaum that *Freaks* is perhaps the most "militant counterculture film,"[77] that it is truly subversive in its depiction of freak culture, I also believe that its popular reception by art and avant-garde audiences points up a disturbing trend in avant-garde culture itself. As Susan Rubin Suleiman points out, in its pursuit of the radically transgressive, avant-garde culture has often displayed a disturbingly misogynist cast.[78] In such diverse films as Buñuel's *Chien andalou* (1928), Buñuel's *Viridiana* (1961), and Alain Robbe-Grillet's *La belle captive* (1983), rebellion against social and sexual constraint is played out—violently—on a woman's body. And as I mentioned earlier, at least one gynophobic avant-garde film—Anthony Balch's *Bill and Tony*—plays explicit homage to *Freaks,* as Anthony Balch and William S. Burroughs take turns reciting the misogynist prologue from Browning's movie. The barker's speech takes on special significance coming out of Burroughs's mouth. Legendary for both his homosexuality and his drug addiction, Burroughs has frequently been attacked for his "nature" and the "freakish" things he chose to write about. Furthermore, Burroughs—as his biographer Ted Morgan points out—long identified the avant-garde with the marginal world of outlaws and drug pushers, social "freaks" who operate according to a special "code." (Burroughs himself was a great believer in both vengeance and the occult; he claimed that he successfully placed curses on a number of people who offended him.) Finally, despite his marriage to Joan Vollmer Burroughs, whom he appears to have genuinely loved, and his friendship with certain exceptional women—most notably Jane Bowles—Burroughs was a noted misogynist. His intonation of the last lines of the barker's speech, "the *most* amazing, the *most* astounding living monstrosity of all time. Friends, she was once a beautiful woman," points up the latent gynophobia of the text.[79] Like horror movies, then, avant-garde cinema is often "spectacularly nasty toward women."[80] And as the films of Balch and Burroughs show, it is *Freaks'* nastiness toward women—as much as its celebration of freak counterculture—that has been cited (and mimicked) in avant-garde cinema.

The revival of *Freaks* has also been cited—indirectly—as one of the founding moments in the antihumanist trend of postmodern art and photography. As I mentioned in Chapter 1, when *Freaks* was re-released on the art house circuit, one of its most avid fans was Diane

Arbus. For three successive evenings, Arbus went to the New Yorker Theater to watch *Freaks*. She'd been told about the film by her friend, documentary filmmaker Emilio de Antonio (*McCarthy: Death of a Witch-hunter,* 1964; *Millhouse,* 1971), who admired the movie for its cinema verité aspects (Skal, 16).[81] Arbus admired it, too. A fashion photographer with an impressive portfolio, Arbus was ready to try something new, and—as one biographer describes it—her viewing of *Freaks* marked something of an epiphany. "She was enthralled because the freaks in the film were not imaginary monsters, but *real.*" Differently formed people "had always excited, challenged and terrified her because they defied so many conventions. Sometimes she thought her terror was linked to something deep in her subconscious. Gazing at the human skeleton or the bearded lady, she was reminded of a dark, unnatural hidden self."[82]

Arbus had already taken some photographs of twins and midgets, but after viewing Browning's film, she began a more systematic exploration of freak culture. As Skal notes, she started frequenting one of the last remaining freak shows in North America, Hubert's Museum on Forty-second Street. The freaks were initially aloof but gradually accepted her presence and began to act more "naturally" around her. Finally, they allowed her to photograph them. Skal writes, "Arbus shot her subjects with a square-format Rollei and fine-grain black-and-white film, striving for and achieving an unflinching catalog of images previously forbidden or deliberately overlooked in modern photography. The deformed. The retarded. The sexually ambiguous. The dying and the dead. All the things people wanted to look at but had been taught they must not" (Skal, 18). Arbus was well aware that these photos were often unforgiving and brutally matter-of-fact. "The process itself has a kind of exactitude," she once wrote, "a kind of scrutiny we're not normally subject to. I mean that we don't subject each other to. We're nicer to each other than the intervention of the camera is going to make us. It's a little bit cold. A little bit harsh."[83]

But if Arbus's pictures of freaks and freak culture appear "a little bit cold, a little bit harsh," her pictures of "normal" people often appear downright freakish. In that sense, as Skal rightly observes:

> Arbus understood Tod Browning's America better than anyone. She saw that "monsters" were everywhere, that the whole of modern life could be viewed as a tawdry sideshow, driven by dreams and terrors of alienation, mutilation, actual death and its everyday variations. Working class families, through Arbus' unforgiving lens, emerged as denizens of an existential suburban sideshow. Society dowagers were close cousins to Times

Square transvestites. Caught at the right moment, almost anyone could look retarded. America, it seemed, was nothing but a monster show. (18)

Arbus's "monster-show" photos were displayed, as part of a major retrospective of the photographer's work, at New York's Museum of Modern Art in 1972. Susan Sontag wrote about the exhibit—which she compared to Edward Steichen's 1955 exhibit *Family of Man*—in her book *On Photography*, a book about the politics of looking and taking pictures. Not surprisingly, Sontag felt that Arbus's photos "imposed a feeling exactly contrary to the reassuring warmth of Steichen's material. Instead of people whose appearance pleases, representative folk doing their human thing, the Arbus show lined up assorted monsters and borderline cases—most of them ugly, wearing grotesque or unflattering clothing; in dismal or barren surroundings—who have paused to pose and, often, to gaze frankly, confidentially at the viewer. Arbus's work does not invite viewers to identify with the pariahs and miserable-looking people she photographed. Humanity is not 'one.'"[84]

Sontag sees Arbus's documentation of Tod Browning's America as "anti-humanist." The photos—many of which appear to have been indirectly inspired by the photographer's initial viewings of *Freaks*—are troubling precisely because they seem to participate in one of art photography's oldest projects, "concentrating on victims, on the unfortunate—but without the compassionate purpose that such a project is expected to serve" (33). Without such a compassionate purpose, Sontag argues, Arbus's photos become something of a horror show. They "undercut politics . . . by suggesting a world in which everybody is an alien, hopelessly isolated, immobilized in mechanical, crippled identities and relationships" (33). They "render history and politics irrelevant . . . by atomizing . . . [the world] into horror" (33).

The use of the word "horror" here seems to bring us full circle. Tod Browning's *Freaks* started as a mainstream horror film that migrated into the exploitation arena before being finally recuperated as an avant-garde or art project. And although the title is traditionally shelved in the horror section of video stores, it has retained a reputation for being something more. At the Halloween screening I described earlier, I saw not only counterculture students and horror fans but colleagues who generally see only European and independent "art" films. They knew the film by reputation and were curious to see if it was as "moving" as people said it was. "I've heard it's not really a horror film," a friend from the French Department told me.

If the film has retained a dual ("not really a horror film") art-horror/avant-garde status within the world of cinephile culture, it's also responsible (at least in Sontag's view) for introducing "horror"—the low generic kind—into the world of high art. Functioning as a kind of subtext behind Arbus's photographs, *Freaks* becomes indirectly responsible for bringing Tod Browning's view of America to the Museum of Modern Art. Through Diane Arbus's work, it's reinscribed—at least for Sontag—as something that's not really art at all, or perhaps as too near art for comfort. "Much of modern art," Sontag writes, "is devoted to lowering the threshold of what is terrible. By getting us used to what, formerly, we could not bear to see or hear, because it was too shocking, painful, or embarrassing, art changes morals—that body of psychic customs and public sanctions that draws a vague boundary between what is emotionally and spontaneously intolerable and what is not" (41). Sontag's description of the moral "dangers" of modern art comes remarkably close to similar descriptions of the moral dangers ascribed to body genre cinema and low culture. It lowers the threshold for what is terrible in art and perhaps in so doing makes us more willing to tolerate—or at least look at—the terrible in real life. It desensitizes us. It might change our moral values. The overlap of moral discourses here in both the art world and the public arena point up one of the central theses of this book. As Arbus's work demonstrates, "high art" often violates the same taboos that horror violates; it participates in the very same kind of freak show. And as *Freaks* shows us, the line between what is generally regarded as low culture and what is regarded as high art can be very difficult to see.

As a coda, I'd like to add that a recent museum exhibit explored the "resurgence of a Gothic sensibility" in art, fashion, music, and cinema.[85] Aptly named *Gothic,* the exhibit took place at the Institute of Contemporary Art in Boston, 24 April to 6 July 1997.[86] It included the work of twenty-three artists "who produce horror as well as amazement through often repulsive, fragmented and contorted forms. Some employ a detached and reductive formal language to evoke discomfort and claustrophobia or to transmute images of gruesome violence, achieving an equally disconcerting impact."[87] The catalog includes reproductions of work by Julie Becker, Monica Carocci, Gregory Crewdson, and Jackson Pollock, as well as photographs of fashion designs by Thierry Mugler and musical performances by Marilyn Manson and Bauhaus. The catalog also lists the films that were shown in conjunction with the show. According to the published list, the second art film "exhibit" was Tod Browning's *Freaks.*

8 Monsters in the Art World:
Andy Warhol and Paul Morrissey

To know Death . . . you have to fuck life in the gallbladder.
—Frankenstein, *Andy Warhol's Frankenstein*

Paul Morrissey's *Carne per Frankenstein* (Flesh for Frankenstein, Andy Warhol's Frankenstein, 1973) engages most of the issues raised in the previous chapters. Made by a member of Andy Warhol's Factory, the film invokes frequent comparisons both to Warhol's own experimental films and to other gross horror movies made during the 1970s. In that sense, it can be said to occupy a liminal space between the conventional categories of high art and low culture, much like the liminal generic-cultural space occupied by Georges Franju's *Eyes without a Face,* Tod Browning's *Freaks,* and Yoko Ono's *Rape.* The confusion over the identity of the film's director—a confusion ensured by at least two of the film's American titles, *Andy Warhol's Frankenstein* and *Andy Warhol Presents Frankenstein*— highlights and problematizes the auteurism that, I have argued, characterizes the reception of both art films and paracinema in this country. Finally, the film engages the discursive strategies surrounding avant-garde, art, and body genre cinema of the time and illustrates the dialectical relationship between what was considered to be high and low culture. For these reasons, *Andy Warhol's Frankenstein* seems like the perfect monster text with which to conclude this composite body-text of horrors.

169

Auteur/Auteurs

One of the first questions that inevitably arises in any discussion of this film is the question of authorship. Released in the United States as *Andy Warhol's Frankenstein* and *Andy Warhol Presents Frankenstein,* the film is often mistakenly attributed to Warhol, a mistake that the English language titles seem to encourage.[1] Compounding this orchestrated error, however, the Italian prints of the film credit Antonio Margheriti (under his pseudonym of Anthony Dawson), an Italian Euro-trash and *gialli* director, with direction of the movie.[2] The *BFI Companion to Horror* explains that Margheriti/Dawson was given directorial credit for both *Carne per Frankenstein* (Andy Warhol's Frankenstein) and *Dracula vuole vivere: Cerca sanguine di vergine!* (Andy Warhol's Dracula, 1973), "the Italian versions of Paul Morrissey's films . . . for union reasons."[3] And Michael Ferguson writes that the films bore Margheriti's name "to oblige financial subsidy by the Italian government."[4]

Unfortunately, however, American fans of European horror have picked up the Margheriti/Dawson credit from "Italian sources" and have used it. For example, *The Encyclopedia of Horror Movies,* one of the major reference sources for the horror genre, lists Margheriti/Dawson as the *real* director of the films and credits Morrissey only with "providing scripts and a 'supervisory' role" (279).[5] In the entry under *Dracula cerca sanguine di vergine,* even this credit is attenuated; Morrissey is cited as providing only a "vague 'supervisory' function" (274). Furthermore, the decision to privilege Italian sources over "Anglo-Saxon" sources (279) leads the encyclopedia authors into a sometimes convoluted discussion. In a dizzying demonstration of the shortcomings of auteur theory, they use the films themselves as proof that the Italian sources must be correct. "Judging by the Warhol factory's cavalier attitude towards directing and the use of Warhol's name as a publicity gimmick," the encyclopedia notes, "the Italian version of the credits, with their clear implication that Morrissey's presence may have animated the picture but that it was directed by Margheriti, seems the most likely one" (279). Why "the use of Warhol's name as a publicity gimmick" would lead the authors to assume that *Frankenstein* was *not* directed by someone still close to Warhol's Factory is not clear. What is clear is that "Italian sources" have introduced a degree of misinformation that exceeds the parodic confusion fostered by the film's English-language titles.

As for Warhol's role in making the films, it's not clear what, if anything, he provided besides funding and inspiration. Warhol is credited (listed in the credits) as the "producer" of other Morrissey films such as *Flesh* (1968), *Trash* (1970), and *Heat* (1971), but his name does not appear in the credits for *Andy Warhol's Frankenstein.* And yet the film is his—not only in the sense that everything produced by members of the Factory[6] was somehow Warhol's but also because there's some indication that Morrissey made the film "for Andy." According to *New York Times* film critic Paul Gardner, Morrissey made *Andy Warhol's Frankenstein,* in part, to comfort Warhol after he was shot by Valerie Solanas.[7] "Andy once told me that he felt as if he would pop open one day," Morrissey said. "When I filmed *Frankenstein* I thought it might be a kind of exorcism for Andy and all the people who are crippled and haunted by some nut-case. And then I added laughter, because that's the only way we survive."[8] And in *The Philosophy of Andy Warhol,* Andy's alter ego, "B," claims that Warhol "produced" *Frankenstein* so that he could put his scars in the ad.[9]

For some scholars, the degree of credit that Warhol has been given for Morrissey's films is galling. Maurice Yacowar, the author of one of the few serious auteurist studies of Morrissey, complains that "although Morrissey was solely responsible for *Flesh, Heat,* and *Trash,* they still are often called Warhol films. Films Warhol financed, but otherwise had nothing to do with, either creatively or consultorily, remain lumped into the Warhol canon."[10] *Andy Warhol's Frankenstein* and *Andy Warhol's Dracula* are examples of this.

Certainly, the inclusion of Morrissey's films in Warhol's film canon has affected the amount (and kind) of credit that Morrissey *himself* has received for his work. A major presence in documentaries and retrospectives about Warhol, Morrissey has received very little recognition for developing his own aesthetic, independent of Andy's. This is striking, because at the time Morrissey filmed *Andy Warhol's Frankenstein* at Cinecittà—a time when it appeared he might be breaking away from the Factory—the American press seemed ready to embrace Morrissey as an independent genius.[11] Writing for the *New York Times,* Melton S. Dawes called Morrissey "the most important directorial talent to emerge from the underground."[12] But Morrissey's moment in the sun was short-lived. Although he made a number of European and commercial American films after completing *Andy Warhol's Dracula,*[13] he is best known for the films he made at the Factory—the films that, as Yacowar claims, are "lumped into the Warhol canon."[14]

Of course, Morrissey himself has been complicit in the erasure of his own "auteur" status. In interviews and documentaries, he has

stressed the collaborative and evolving nature of his work with Warhol.[15] In 1973 he told Dawes that his films "derive from Andy's." And
while "he objects to living in Warhol's shadow," he uses "we" throughout the interview—sometimes concretely to refer to his collaboration
with Carlo Ponti, Jean-Pierre Rassam, and Andrew Braunsberg (on *Carne
per Frankenstein*), sometimes in an ambiguous way that seems to refer to
his ongoing relationship with Warhol.[16] Even Yacowar, who believes it's
"probably inaccurate to speak . . . of 'collaboration' in the Warhol-
Morrissey films," finds it difficult not to do so.[17] "To Warhol's nonnar-
rative cinema," Yacowar writes, "Morrissey introduced a quietly coher-
ent succession of picaresque incidents that might be taken as a plot; he
also brought elements of technical sophistication, camera strategies,
eruptions of black humor and a penchant for letting his characters
talk."[18] The implication here is that the two men were working *together*
on films (Morrissey was bringing something to Warhol's movies), not
that Morrissey was setting himself up as an independent filmmaker.
Thus Morrissey himself and Morrissey scholars have contributed to the
impression that Warhol continued making films long after he ceased to
do so, and that Warhol was at least a codirector of the films Morrissey
made at the Factory. In this sense, both the filmmaker and his support-
ers appear to accept the underground film community's view of Morrisey's role at the Factory. He has become the man who taught Andy to
move the camera, the man who "changed Warhol."

Or destroyed him. Morrisey's role at the Factory has been be-
moaned and vilified in more than one underground account. In *Underground Film: A Critical History*, Parker Tyler notes that "Paul Morrissey
is now the production manager of Warhol's films and his presence is obviously what has given the conventionalizing turn of 'entertainment' to
Warhol's absorption with the groovy scene." As a result, Warhol's movies
"are headed as fast and as far as possible toward more commercial success."[19] Tony Rayms credits Morrissey with "abandoning the formal integrity of Warhol's cinema and deliberately setting out to make films
which would catch and hold an audience's interest." He also "introduced a transparent vein of moralism" into Factory productions, "or did
he take the blank sheet of Warhol's moral silence and fill it with
Republican bigotry?"[20] And for Stephen Koch, "Morrissey's ambition"
changed Warhol. Under Morrissey's tutelage, Koch argues, "something
absolutely grotesque happened to Warhol's two finest gifts: his visual intelligence and his taste."[21]

Morrissey was, as Koch claims, "a kind of anomaly in the Factory."

> He was in no way a member of that street culture that it had assimilated in the years before. He was another, far more familiar kind of person: Somebody who very much wanted to be somebody, a very typical young man in a hurry. That was not really the Factory style: Pushiness was out. Morrissey liked most of what he saw in the Warholvian world he had hurried into, but he didn't like all that fooling around, didn't like arty movies for small chic audiences who arrived late and left early, who made jokes among themselves about ennui, who "just *loved* your movie, Andy." And he wasn't so sure about the lingering ambience of the art world either. His attitude toward such things was simple—that is if Viva's accounts of them in her *roman à clef, Superstar,* can be believed. All this high-culture stuff is just a lot of self-indulgent fooling around, and nobody really gave a damn, they were just a bunch of people sitting around waiting for the end. The end of a boring movie. The end of high culture. There were only two kinds of *real* artists in America. . . . There were the "Pop" singers. And there were the high commercial film directors, the biggies of Hollywood. As for the rest, they were a bunch of freaks and losers trying to talk themselves into thinking they cared. That's putting it bluntly, but then Morrissey is a blunt man. "There's an English word for the people who think [Warhol's eight-hour movie] *Empire* is the height," he once told a German interviewer. "It is snob."[22]

The tone here is nasty, as Koch obviously dislikes Morrissey's influence on Warhol. But the details about Morrissey's politics and artistic agenda appear to be true. Even Yacowar, who believes that "Paul Morrissey may be America's most undervalued and least shown filmmaker" (1), writes that Morrissey "is a reactionary conservative" (1). And Yacowar cites the same quote that Koch cites ("there's an English word . . .") to demonstrate Morrissey's "integrity" (11).

If Morrissey was regarded with something like suspicion outside the Factory, inside the Factory, he was often resented. As Yacowar notes, "remnants of Andy's entourage have not forgiven Morrissey for refusing to work with anyone using drugs or for otherwise introducing efficiency and order into the Factory" (1). Artists such as Viva disliked his openly anti-art stance.[23] And members of the original group (Gerard Malanga, Viva, Ultraviolet, Brigid Polk, et al.) reacted strongly against both his apparent coldness and what they saw as his attempts to erase every trace of what the Factory had been—its history. When Edie

Sedgwick—the poor little rich girl who was once Warhol's fastest-rising superstar and one of his closest confidantes—died of a drug overdose at age twenty-eight, someone called the Factory to give Warhol the news. Morrissey's reaction to the death of someone he knew—affected ignorance—was considered "typically" insensitive by Factory regulars. As Gerard Malanga describes it, "I remember Paul Morrissey saying something to the effect of—when the news came to the Factory that Edie had died . . . 'Edie *Who?*' "[24]

High Art/Pop Culture

In a now famous quote, Andy Warhol said that he started making movies because it was easier than painting. "The camera has a motor," he told an interviewer. "You just turn the camera on, and walk away."[25] Certainly, Warhol's early films were like that. The camera never moved. Warhol would set up the shot, turn the camera on, and that was that. In fact, after setting up the shot, Warhol often did walk away, leaving it to his assistants to change the film cannisters and keep the celluloid running, and leaving it to the stars to improvise as best they could.[26] In a sense, he didn't direct his films at all. "Warhol defines his art anti-romantically," P. Adams Sitney wrote in *Visionary Film.* And his earliest films showed "how similar," how romantic, "most other avant-garde films were."[27]

Warhol pioneered what Sitney has called "structural" films, "in which the shape of the whole film is predetermined and simplified, and it is that shape which is the primal impression of the film" (369). The four defining characteristics of the structural film, as Sitney delimits them, are fixed camera position (fixed frame from the viewer's perspective), the flicker effect, loop printing, and rephotography off the screen (370).Very few structural films have all four characteristics, and many structural films modify the characteristics considerably. But they all "attempt to divorce the cinematic metaphor of consciousness from that of eyesight and body movement" (370). Instead of treating perception "as a special condition of vision, most often represented as an interruption of the retinal continuity (e.g. the white flashes of early lyric films)" as someone like Stan Brakhage does, the structural filmmaker brings "apperceptive strategies" to the fore. "It is cinema of the mind," Sitney explains, "rather than the eye" (370).

As Sitney sees it, "the roots of three of the four defining characteristics of the structural film can be found in Warhol's early works."

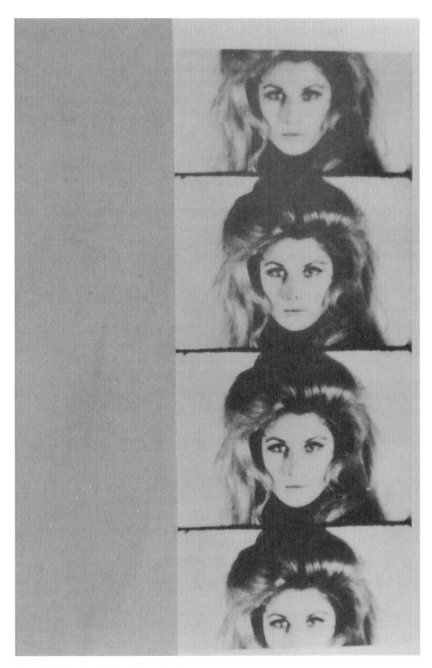

Figure 26. Baby Jane Holzer, *Screen Test.*

He made famous the fixed-frame in *Sleep* (1963), in which half a dozen shots are seen for over six hours. In order to attain that elongation, he used both loop printing of whole hundred foot takes (2 ¾ minutes) and, in the end, the freezing of a still image of the sleeper's head. That freeze process emphasizes the grain and flattens the image precisely as rephotography off the screen does. The films he made afterward cling even more fiercely to the single unbudging perspective. (372–73)

If Warhol's early films were static (fixed-frame single unbudging perspective) and structural, they were also, as the foregoing quote illustrates, *long*. *Eat* (1963) shows a man nibbling a mushroom for forty-five minutes; *Kiss* (1963) shows close-up after close-up of people kissing and lasts fifty minutes. *Sleep* (1963) is six hours of a man sleeping. And the infamous *Empire* (1964) is eight uninterrupted hours of the Empire State Building. Even Jonas Mekas, who was noted for his generosity to the up-and-coming avant-garde, didn't know how to take these films. When he first mentioned Andy Warhol in his *Village Voice* column on 5 December 1963, Mekas was honest about his bewilderment. "Is Andy Warhol making movies," he asked, "or is he playing a joke on us?"[28]

In a way, time (both duration and speed) is the real focus of

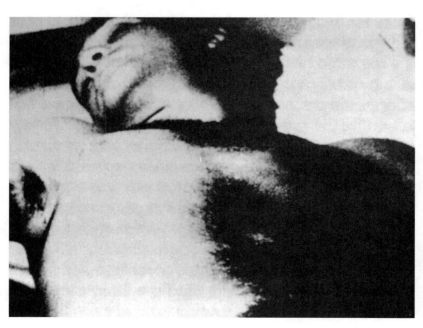

Figure 27. John Giorno sleeping. Still from *Sleep*.

Warhol's early silent films. Not only are the films long, but they are meant to be projected at silent speed (sixteen frames per second, as opposed to twenty-four frames per second for sound film), so that each frame stays on-screen just a little longer than an audience who has grown up seeing sound films expects. Sometimes the silent speed corresponds to the speed at which the film was shot. But often it does not. *Kiss,* for example, was shot at sound speed (24 fps) but is projected at 16 fps; that is, it's artificially slowed down during screening. For critics such as Peter Gidal, this manipulation of screen time is one of the most important aspects of Warhol's early work. "With one flick of the switch," Gidal writes, "the sense of time is changed. An action, although 'real' . . . becomes an event even more minutely watchable, clinically observable, with the slowing down of time."[29]

Parker Tyler describes the "inner slow motion" in Warhol's films as "drug time."[30] As Gidal defines Tyler's term, "drug-time" or "the stoned concentration on the supposedly negligible" in Warhol's films "is precisely a re-creation of being smashed out of one's mind; one's head lets go, there's a certain amount of ego-dissolution, and one can float. . . . Concentration on nuances of movement (in time) not only makes the slightest change of position (even breathing) important but also is involved with silence in *visual terms.* It is not stasis, but a silence *filled.*"[31] Warhol's use of time, Gidal argues, *deconditions* the spectator, awakens him to his bad viewing habits, and helps him see both cinema and the world around him in a new, pared-down way, in much the same way that Philip Glass's music sensitizes the audience to the slightest variation in a musical theme, the slightest change in a sequence or chord.

But whereas Glass seems to intentionally use time (tempo), rhythm, and repetition to achieve the effects that music critics attribute to his work, Warhol's expressed aesthetic—indeed, his notion of time— differs markedly from the discussions I have cited. When Warhol himself spoke of the length and slowness of his early films, he did so in terms of "dead time," or "killing time"; he invoked boredom rather than the intense attention to minutiae that one associates with drugs. "I like boring things," he said once. "When you just sit and look out a window, that's enjoyable. It takes up time."[32] The sense here is not that perception is heightened when you are forced to slow down and really notice things but rather that noticing things becomes a way of "taking up" a time that already hangs a little too heavy. The difference is subtle, but— as I hope to show—characteristic of Warhol's approach to film.

I don't mean to suggest that Sitney, Tyler, and Gidal are wrong in their assessment of the importance that fixed perspective, static camera, and "drug-time" play both in Warhol's work and in the underground film movement. As film professors tell beginning students, directors often don't intend the meanings we see in their films. That doesn't mean those meanings are not there, just that the directors themselves don't always intend *or even perceive* the full richness of their work (if we limited our discussion of Hitchcock's work to his stated intentions, for example, most of the existing books on Hitch would have to be destroyed, and our class sessions would suddenly become too long instead of too painfully short). My purpose in discussing Warhol's own statements about his work, then, is not to say that existing criticism is wrong but rather to demonstrate that there's an additional aspect of even Warhol's earliest work that few writers on avant-garde cinema have taken seriously—namely, the degree to which he conceived his cinema as existing alongside of, and in a sense interacting with, popular culture.[33] Warhol was, as Sitney reminds us, a "pop artist" who remained "spiritually at the opposite pole from the structural film-makers" (373). And it's that opposite pole that I'd like to explore.

Just like TV: Warhol's Glance Aesthetics

The discussions of Warhol's early cinema cited in the previous section share the assumption that viewers of underground film, by definition, embrace what we might call the gaze aesthetic of cinema.[34] That is, Sitney, Tyler, and Gidal assume that viewers will sit and quietly watch the screen in something like rapt attention. While this may certainly be the case—indeed, the degree to which many early viewers in New York were angered by Warhol's films demonstrates that a large number of people did try to gaze at the screen—it isn't the only way to watch a Warhol movie. When I saw part of *Sleep* in San Francisco in the late sixties, only a few diehards actually planned to sit through the whole thing. Most of us (my friends and I) planned a more irreverent approach to the film. We picked a time that was convenient, dropped in for a while, and then, when we got bored, went out and did something else, came back to the movie for a while, and so on. From what I could tell, most of the movie patrons were getting their hands stamped so that they could drift in and out in this way. In addition, people talked to each other throughout the film and sometimes talked to the screen or the audience at large ("Doesn't this cat ever turn over?").[35]

This particular form of spectator response seems to be exactly what Warhol had in mind when he made the movie. For Warhol, the idea was not to stare fixedly at an image on-screen until you noticed subtle changes and shifts and patterns. The idea—according to Warhol—was to watch the movie while doing something else. "You could do more things watching my movies than with other kinds of movies," he said, "you could eat and drink and smoke and cough and look away and then look back and they'd still be there. It's not the ideal movie, it's just my kind of movie."[36]

What Warhol wanted to do was make a film you could watch the way glance theorists say you watch TV, to make a film you could watch "across the distractions" of everyday life.[37] In fact, there's an indication that Warhol both saw his films as being like TV and believed that TV had more radical potential for audience engagement than cinema did. "I like commercials cutting in on television every few minutes," he said once, "because it really makes everything more entertaining. I can't figure out what's happening in those shows anyway. They're so abstract. I can't understand how ordinary people like them. They don't have many plots. They don't do anything. It's just a lot of pictures, cowboys, cops, cigarettes, kids, war all cutting in and out of each other without stopping . . . like the pictures we make."[38] It's unclear how much this abject speech owes to the self-effacing role that Warhol often adopted before the public, or even how much he might have been putting on the reviewer.[39] Certainly it's hard to believe that *Mod Squad* (1968–1973) was too complex for Warhol to follow, even with commercial breaks. But he's right to argue that the interruption of television programs by ads and public service announcements lends TV an "abstract" quality, which brings it remarkably close to Sitney's description of the cinematic avant-garde. Like the films of Stan Brakhage, TV treats perception "as a special condition of vision, most often represented as an interruption of the retinal continuity (e.g. the white flashes . . .)" (Sitney, 370). And one has only to look at episodes of Rowan and Martin's *Laugh-In* (1968–1973)—a TV show that really was incomprehensible to the uninitiated—to appreciate the degree to which television of the period was willing and able to incorporate and exploit the avant-garde or "experimental" elements of youth culture (rapid cutting, strobe light effects, abstract light and color patterns).

For Warhol, television lent itself to the kinds of distanciation devices advocated by Brecht and Godard and actually had more radicalizing potential than film, more innate ability to disrupt the passivity of the audience that mainstream cinema (at least according to Brecht and

Godard) enforces. "My first films using the stationary objects were also made to help the audiences get more acquainted with themselves," Warhol said. "Usually when you go to the movies, you sit in a fantasy world, but when you see something that disturbs you, you get involved with the people next to you. Movies are doing a little more than you can do with plays and concerts where you just have to sit there and I think television will do more than the movies."[40]

Rainer Crone correctly argues that Warhol's early films are Brechtian or Godardian in their use of distanciation techniques and their encouragement of active audience participation.[41] But—at least if we're to take even some of the director's statements seriously—Warhol's use of distanciation and alienation devices to break the audience's passive involvement in a movie is as indebted to "popular culture" as it is to "high art." Even a later Warhol film such as *Chelsea Girls* (1966), which makes use of simultaneous dual-projection (two projectors working simultaneously side by side), wild zooms, pans, and tilts, is as indebted to pop culture (in this case, melodrama and the light shows that accompanied rock band performances) as it is to experimental cinematic art. The simultaneous use of dual projectors for screening *Chelsea Girls,* so that disconnected film scenes—some in black-and-white and some in color—were projected side by side, for example, was reminiscent of the wall projections that were a given part of rock concerts at the Fillmore Auditorium and San Francisco's Winterland, and reminiscent of the special effects Warhol used with his own rock group, the Velvet Underground, during their "Exploding Plastic Inevitable" show.

Given Warhol's interest in rock and roll culture, it's perhaps not surprising that Warhol's "signature" film cut became what Rainer Crone has dubbed "the strobe cut." Here, Warhol lets the camera produce "a fully exposed frame each time the filming stops,"[42] so that instead of the "action" being broken up by sequences of black screen—as it is in Godard's films of the same period—the screen periodically goes white, creating a strobe effect. As its name suggests, the "strobe cut" owes as much to the light show aesthetics that dominated acid rock concerts during the sixties as it does to the lyrical practices of avant-garde filmmakers like Stan Brakhage.

I don't mean to suggest that Warhol had no knowledge of, or interest in, experimental cinema, or that he never stated that making experimental films was his intent. Before making his first film, Warhol was a regular at the Filmmakers' Co-operative and the Filmmakers' Cinematheque, underground theaters where filmmakers often staged impromptu screenings, not only of completed works but of rushes just back from the lab. Like many filmmakers, Warhol felt compelled to immerse himself in cinema, to get a sense of (underground) film history, before picking up the camera himself. And he certainly was aware of the degree to which his films did and did not participate in the dominant underground aesthetic. When asked by a reviewer about the "look" of some of his sound films, Warhol replied that he wanted the scratches and dirt on the film to show, "so that everybody knows that you're watching a film."[43] This is a sentiment that brings him more closely in line with the American cinematic underground than with commercial television.

But perhaps more than most experimental filmmakers of the period, Warhol was aware of the links connecting experimental cinema to popular culture.[44] In addition to making underground films, Warhol managed a rock band, the Velvet Underground. And unlike most experimental filmmakers of the period, Warhol made his avant-garde movies within a milieu that was designed to operate like the old Hollywood studios. Thus, at the same time that he was "capturing ordinary everyday occurrences that seemed too small for Hollywood pictures" (making coffee, eating, sleeping)—an enterprise that, as Juan Suárez has noted, brought him perfectly in line with the stated goals of the American cinematic avant-garde—he was also creating a studio that "took as its main points of reference the notion of stardom and the discourses of fashion and advertisement."[45]

The films Warhol made at the Factory were star vehicles. Every one of his superstars was "given" a reel of film, in which s/he could do whatever s/he wanted. And while many of the feature-length films are organized around improvised scenarios or vignettes, others like *Poor Little Rich Girl* (1965, 70 minutes) feature one superstar—or a series of superstars—drinking coffee, ordering orange juice, talking on the phone; being superstars, being magical. In fact, Warhol's interest in a star-driven, personality-driven cinema was one of the things he shared with Paul Morrissey. "Andy and I really try not to direct a film at all," Morrissey told Paul Gardner in 1972. "We both feel the stars should be the center of the film."[46]

The degree to which Warhol felt that stars "should be the center of the film" is clearly illustrated by the issue of *Film Culture* devoted to his film work (summer 1967).[47] "Despite [its] being 'his' issue," Warhol is, as Juan Suárez notes, "hardly present at all."[48] Instead, the issue is given over largely to the superstars. There are articles about Edie

Figure 28. Edie Sedgwick gets dressed. *Poor Little Rich Girl.*

Sedgwick, Fredie Herko, and Ondine, and interviews with Jack Smith and Mario Montez. The illustrations consist mainly of film stills, photos of Factory stars, and glamour shots of Hollywood stars like Greta Garbo.[49] In fact, the look and tone of the Warhol issue resembles nothing so much as a fan magazine, in which the filmmaker himself becomes the gushing admirer of his own star creations.

Suárez compares this issue of *Film Culture* to a previous one devoted to the writings of Stan Brakhage. The differences between the two issues, Suárez notes, "suggests the gap between Warhol and the more transcendent sector of the underground.[50] Brakhage's issue is printed on dark sepia paper and sparsely illustrated with abstract stills from his films. It includes numerous pages of scratched, heavily edited typescript and facsimiles of handwritten notes and sketches. Overall, the issue breathes seriousness and emphasizes Brakhage's subjective inscription in his work, an attitude that appears the photographic negative of Warhol's self-erasure and seemingly frivolous plunge into Hollywood glitz."[51]

Warhol's tendency to present his cinema as a star-driven enterprise extends beyond this one episode. When Jonas Mekas offered him several nights at the Filmmakers' Cinematheque in the summer of 1965,

Warhol did not—as Mekas might have expected—propose choosing key films that would demonstrate the evolution of his already prolific movie-making career. Instead, he immediately suggested a retrospective of Edie Sedgwick films, implying, as Suárez notes, "that he conceived his productions as star vehicles rather than as subjective expressions of his personality."[52] Everyone who came to the Factory was given a screen test, because everyone and anyone might be a superstar. It is perhaps a fitting testimonial to Warhol's own perception of his cinema that some writers consider the screen tests to be among the most interesting and truly innovative films that Warhol made.[53]

Given Warhol's infatuation with both Hollywood glamour and star making, it seems odd to credit Paul Morrissey with "commercializing" Warhol's films, with giving them "the conventionalizing turn of 'entertainment.'" Warhol's cinema, at least as Warhol conceived it, always was a commercial cinema waiting to happen. Part of the dominant mythology of the Factory was that someday soon, Hollywood would call.[54] And Hollywood—not the historic avant-garde—was the shadow image haunting Warhol's cinema apparatus (if not his early production). The Factory was organized according to the old studio guidelines; it guaranteed everyone a certain amount of work and maintained strict control over the glamour images and publicity of its stars. Morrissey did impose a degree of discipline and efficiency on the Factory regulars. But in terms of film artistry, he didn't take Warhol anywhere that Warhol didn't already want to go. "As if Andy could be corrupted," he told Paul Gardner. "When Andy started making movies, he went all the way back to Edison. The only thing he could do was move forward."[55]

As Morrissey himself has noted, the charges that critics leveled against him—"abandoning the formal integrity of Warhol's cinema," "deliberately setting out to make films which would catch and hold an audience's interest," heading "as fast and as far as possible toward more commercial success"—smack of elitism. The assumption that runs throughout such critiques is that film artistry and commercial success are mutually exclusive; that "art" is the sole provenance of the cognoscenti and should preferably be housed in museums, away from the riffraff; and that any film made to appeal to a wide market is by its very nature pandering to the lowest common denominator. This indeed is snobbery, and whatever Morrissey's private views about art, his irascibility in the face of an art establishment that seemingly wanted to imprison his work in small Cinematheque venues is understandable.

But the criticisms leveled against Morrissey by the underground establishment also reveal the degree to which the New York avant-garde (or at least, the critics and writers studying them) ignored important aspects of their own culture. As Suárez has demonstrated, Warhol's cinema was not the only avant-garde cinema that was imbricated with pop culture. Theoretically and historically, he argues, there has always been a dialogue between "avant-garde and mass culture." But the 1960s, with their "irruption of pop forms into . . . experimental American film," highlighted the dialectical relationship that has always existed between the avant-garde and popular "entertainment"(high/low).[56] This irruption "presented an interpretive problem for reviewers schooled in the ideologies of postwar modernism, which stressed clear-cut cultural divisions such as [Clement] Greenberg's distinction between kitsch and avant-garde, or [Dwight] Macdonald's parallel distinction between mass-cult, midcult, and high culture. Being such an intractable cultural object, the underground drew negative reviews from such modernist intellectuals as Macdonald, Parker Tyler, and Amos Vogel."[57]

Certainly, the critics who denounced Morrissey's work were caught in just such an interpretive trap. Not only did their criticisms misrepresent Morrissey's own production (someone who's really motivated *only* by mainstream commercial success does not make black comedies about homosexual cowboys, drug addiction, or transvestism), but they also seriously misrepresent Warhol's "avant-garde" production. As P. Adams Sitney has perceptively pointed out, "on one level at least" Warhol's early films can be read as parodies of experimental cinema. As Sitney puts it, "Warhol turned his genius for parody and reduction against the American avant-garde film itself."[58] In a sense, he really was—as Jonas Mekas suspected—"playing a joke on us." Or at least forcing us to look at experimental cinema the way he'd forced us to look at death and Mao Tse-tung, as just another commodity—just another mass-produced, and reproduceable, set of images.

Monsters in the Art World

Ironically, the charge of "commercialization" is another point that Morrissey and Warhol have in common. Warhol is both praised and vilified for introducing images and techniques that "commercialized" the fine arts. Using silk screen techniques (a technique of mass reproduction) to create his famous series of Marilyns, Elvises, Brandos, Maos, and electric chairs, Warhol—as Benjamin predicted—challenged the artistic "aura" that was presumed to characterize "original" work.[59] With the exception of Factory members (who were there), nobody who buys a Warhol silk screen knows who exactly did the labor. Who photographed the newspaper image, who poured the paint on the silk screen, who chose the colors? Warhol may have had the idea for the piece, but it's highly likely that Gerard Malanga or someone else actually made the silk screen. In addition, since so many of the images were tabloid images, some members of the art world felt that Warhol was not an "artist" at all. Just an ad man. Maybe a technician. Certainly no De Kooning.

Warhol himself was aware of the low regard in which he was held by some members of the art establishment. In *POPism*, he wrote:

> The painting style that everybody accepted and that dominated the art scene was still Abstract Expressionism. The post–Abstract Expressionist painters had come along afterward and the Hard Edge geometrics, too, but the last thing to happen in art that was completely accepted was Abstract Expressionism. So when Pop appeared, not even the style it followed had been fully accepted yet! The resentment against Pop artists was something fierce, and it wasn't coming from just art critics or buyers, it was coming from a lot of the older Abstract Expressionist painters themselves.[60]

This resentment was "brought home" to Warhol, he says, "in a very dramatic way" at a party given by abstract expressionist painter Yvonne Thomas, mainly for other abstract expressionist painters. One of Warhol's friends was invited to the party, and she insisted on taking Warhol and Robert Indiana with her. "When we walked into that room," Warhol writes, "I looked around and saw that it was chock full of anguished, heavy intellects."

> Suddenly the noise level dropped and everyone turned to look at us. (It was like the moment when the little girl in *The Exorcist* walks into her mother's party and pees on the rug.) I saw Mark Rothko take the hostess aside and I heard him accuse her of treachery: "How could you let *them* in?" She apologized. "But what can I *do?*" she told Rothko. "They came with Marisol."[61]

Warhol's allusion to himself as a monster here is telling. Like Regan, the little girl who peed on the rug, Warhol describes himself as a possessed or satanic "innocent," a naïf, through whom the twin demons of commercialization and kitsch would enter the art world. But while Warhol constructs himself here as a monster only within the context of an abstract expressionist party (that is, he doesn't really see himself as a monster—it's just the way he imagines the abstract expressionists see him), his monster identity extended well beyond the stuffy world of the art establishment. Within the Factory, too, his connections to the world of commercialized glitz and glamour were occasionally demonized. Only there Warhol was not considered naive or innocent. As Suárez points out, Warhol's in-house Factory nickname "Drella"—a combination of Cinderella and Dracula—"expresses the vampirism attached to his activity as image producer and stargazer, the notion that his touch had the effect of draining away the life of his 'found personalities.'"[62]

My point in discussing Warhol's monster image here is to show how much like Morrissey's image—both in the world of high art and in the Factory—it was. If Warhol was suspect within the art establishment because he "popped" high art, Morrissey was suspect within the film art community for much the same reason. He "popped" avant-garde cinema. And if Morrissey was seen as something of a leech or bloodsucker, attaching himself to Warhol in a crass bid for recognition and fame, Warhol himself was "affectionately" tagged by some of his close associates as a vampire.[63]

Toward a Paracinema Aesthetics

While some members of the avant-garde establishment felt that Morrissey's participation in Factory productions threatened to commercialize "Warhol's" films, it was, ironically, Warhol's name that eased the entry of Morrissey films such as *Lonesome Cowboys* (1967), *Flesh, Trash,* and *Heat* into mainstream culture, both in the United States and in parts of Europe. Remembering the success of *Trash* in Germany, for example, actor Udo Kier remarks that, had the film been made in Germany, it wouldn't have been shown in mainstream venues at all. It was Warhol's name, he said, that gave the film legitimacy and helped to classify it as "art" (and therefore as acceptable provocation).[64]

In the United States, all the Warhol-Morrissey films were "crossover" films.[65] They played in commercial art houses (rather than noncommercial venues like the Filmmakers' Co-operative and the Filmmakers' Cinematheque) or in mainstream commercial theaters (rather than in bump-and-grind houses). In part, the films' commercial distribution was related to the popularity—at least among young people—of Warhol himself. In part it was due to the popularity of the counterculture and counterculture themes. And in part, it was related to a real public desire to see things that were "provocative" or slightly scandalous

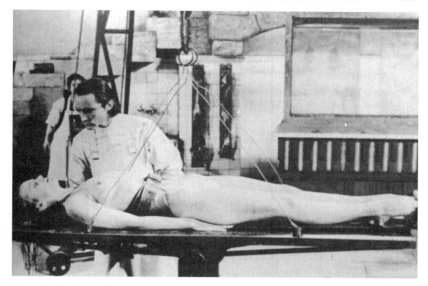

Figure 29. The Baron (Udo Kier) regards his female zombie (Dalila Di Lazzaro). *Andy Warhol's Frankenstein.*

(whether they were "counterculture" or not). This was a time when a film could get an X rating and still play the local theaters. *Midnight Cowboy* (1969) and *Last Tango in Paris* (1972), for example, were widely distributed despite their X ratings.[66] And as the ads for *Andy Warhol's Frankenstein* demonstrate, this was a time when X meant something like the current NC-17 rating. The New York City theater ads for *Frankenstein* stipulate "no one under 17 admitted."[67]

"Commercial" in this context, then, does not necessarily mean "uncontroversial," "safe," or "mainstream." It simply refers to the mode of distribution and to the size of audience that the film hoped to attract. As Amos Vogel points out, all of the early Warhol-Morrissey films can be considered "subversive" because of their subject matter. *Trash,* for example, is "a high camp 'love story' of an outrageously handsome heroin junkie and his trash-scavenging girlfriend (played by a female impersonator).[68] . . . [It] skips from fellatio to seduction to foot fetishism in its attacks on soap opera myths and Hollywood myths. . . . Drug-fixes or penises casually displayed . . . [and] the mounting intrusions upon the viewers' value system mark this as a truly seditious work."[69]

Elsewhere Vogel uses Morrissey's films to describe the collapse of traditional boundaries between avant-garde film, commercial cinema, and hard-core pornography. Stating that sexual permissiveness—destructive of traditional mores—has been "an aspect of the ideology of the avant-garde from its inception," Vogel notes that "this is why 'serious' homosexual cinema begins with the underground, forever ahead of the commercial cinema and setting it goals which though initially viewed as outrageous are later partly absorbed by it." Citing Kenneth Anger, Warhol, and Morrissey as some of the avant-garde pioneers in this area, Vogel goes on to note the increasing emergence of "serious" homosexual themes in commercial cinema (equivalent here to the increasing "absorption of avant-garde ideology" by commercial movies). "Not only are homosexuals more freely portrayed in commercial films," he writes, "but a large number of explicit homosexual films are made for public showings, some by hacks, some by artists. In 1973, there existed in New York at least a dozen hard-core homosexual cinemas."[70]

The curious conflation in this passage between avant-garde, commercial, and hard-core films shows how difficult it was becoming—even for a modernist critic like Vogel—to make the kinds of distinctions on which the high-low cultural divide has traditionally relied. Even the distinction he does draw—between "hacks" and "artists"—becomes in this context difficult to read. We don't know if he means that "hacks" make porn and "artists" make avant-garde and commercial art films, or if he means that "hacks" and "artists" operate across the spectrum, making films in all three areas. What *is* clear is that he includes Morrissey in his lineup of avant-garde directors. Instead of depicting Morrissey as the man who commercialized Warhol, Vogel describes him as one of the avant-garde pioneers whose ideas were absorbed by commercial movies. Despite the commercial distribution of Morrissey's films and their obvious attempt to appeal to a broader audience (they had story lines; they were normal feature-length films, two hours long instead of six), *Lonesome Cowboys* and the *Flesh* trilogy remain, for Vogel, avant-garde productions. In fact, they mark the incursion of avant-garde ideology into commercial cinema.

While I believe there are a lot of problems with the "top-down" model of liberalization that Vogel delineates (in which increased sexual tolerance begins with the avant-garde and then filters down to the plebes), I think he's right in pointing out the degree to which commercial cinema and theaters of the period were willing to take risks on daring material.[71] In fact, commercial cinema often relied on exactly the same material that fed Warhol's avant-garde productions at the Factory. Warhol's *Vinyl* (1965), for example, is an S/M treatment of Anthony

Burgess's *A Clockwork Orange,* the novel that in turn became the basis for Stanley Kubrick's 1971 art film *(A Clockwork Orange). My Hustler* (1965) treats much of the same material as *Midnight Cowboy* (1969), and *Flesh,* the first film with Paul Morrissey's name on it, indirectly grew out of the Factory's experience with the making of *Midnight Cowboy.* As Yacowar describes it, the idea for the film "originated in a telephone conversation with Warhol, hospitalized from his near-fatal shooting by Valerie Solanas. Morrissey told Warhol that [John] Schlesinger [*Cowboy's* director] was ignoring the entourage Morrissey had provided for the first party scene in *Midnight Cowboy.* Warhol suggested Morrissey make a film on the same subject, featuring the people Schlesinger left in the background" (23). And when Warhol's sexually explicit *Blue Movie* (1968) was seized by the New York police, an incensed Paul Morrissey challenged the presiding officer to explain the difference between Warhol's movie and the commercially successful art film *I Am Curious Yellow* (Sjöman, 1967), then playing in New York.[72]

At the same time that commercial cinema was becoming more daring, exhibition spaces became somewhat more democratic (or, in some cases, gentrified). Art films increasingly moved out of museums and into neighborhood theaters, where they often played with Hollywood classics.[73] Crossover porn films like *Deep Throat* contributed to the rise of gentrified neighborhood "adult" theaters that weren't heavily coded as male domains.[74] And in towns too small to have "special" theaters just for art house and crossover porn films, the commercially successful crossover movies of the period played at the local Bijou.[75]

If the incursion of avant-garde ideology into commercial cinema during this period signaled the public's desire for (or at least its willingness to sample) more daring material, it also signaled the public's willingness to experiment with different reading strategies.[76] One of the things that characterizes both the Warhol-Morrissey films and the crossover porn films (like *Deep Throat,* 1972) of the period is an ironic mode of enunciation, a mode that aligns films such as *Trash* with the paracinema aesthetic. As I mentioned in chapter 1, paracinema is best represented as a strategy of reading—one that is often highly ironic. And one of the most noticeable aspects of Morrissey's commercial films is the degree to which they seem to demand a similarly ironic strategy of reading. This is a break from Warhol's early experimental work—which, I argued earlier, *could* (but didn't necessarily have to) be read in a more or less ironic fashion. In Morrissey's films, the humor is so broad that it's virtually impossible to appreciate them on a nonironic or "straight" level. In *Flesh,* for example, two people sit on a couch and read a magazine while an act of fellatio takes place about eighteen inches away in the same room. They are uninterested in the sex taking place and, in fact, don't even seem to notice that it's occurring. That they are transvestites makes the domestic scene just that much more parodic. In a similarly overdetermined scene in *Trash,* Morrissey plays with the increased anxiety over male performance and female orgasm that can be traced in magazines and self-help books of the period.[77] Here, the heroin addict (described earlier) solicitously attempts to help his girlfriend reach a climax. Since he is impotent, he suggests that she masturbate with a beer bottle. He holds her hand as she does so, periodically asking if she's come yet. At the end of the scene, he promises to do better next time. And in *Andy Warhol's Frankenstein,* Frankenstein brings his female zombie to life in one of the most bizarre copulation scenes in the history of cinema. "To know Death, Otto," he tells his assistant when he's finished penetrating the zombie's "digestive parts," "you have to fuck life in the gallbladder."

Clearly these are all distanciation devices, which interrupt and interfere with our ability to identify with the characters on-screen and "lose ourselves" in the story. In fact, as I argued earlier, if you try to identify with the characters or lose yourself in the story, you probably won't like the films at all. The story lines are preposterous; spectator pleasure to some degree turns on remaining distanced from (and probably above) the action you see unfolding on the screen (in the same way that paracinema fans "enjoy" *Reefer Madness* by laughing at its absurd assertions about the dangers of smoking marijuana—which, the movie insists, always leads to prostitution, IV drug use, and an uncontrollable urge to lounge around the house in soiled lingerie).

The mode of enunciation that Morrissey's films employ encourages the spectator to identify not with one of the characters on-screen (who are usually too silly to take seriously) but with the filmmaker or with some "implied" savvy spectator who's in the know.[78] Such a mode of enunciation is generally seen as a defining feature of what Peter Wollen has called countercinema (the cinema of Godard, for example).[79] But in this period, at least in the American market, it's also a defining feature of crossover porn and exploitation films (a different kind of countercinema). *Deep Throat,* for example, continually asks the viewer to laugh at depictions of sex while simultaneously becoming aroused by them. In a humorous cunnilingus scene, for example, the woman reaches for her cigarettes. "Do you mind if I smoke while you eat?" she asks her partner. Apparently he doesn't, so she lights up. And the entire premise of *Deep Throat*—that the Linda Lovelace character can reach orgasm only while performing exceptionally "deep" fellatio, because her clitoris is in her throat—encourages us to laugh at a standard trope of phallocentric porn (a woman's insatiable desire for fellatio) while simultaneously using that trope to gratify (or arouse) the spectator.[80]

While it's tempting to read such scenes as "avant-garde" or at least subversive (in the case of *Deep Throat,* they do frequently break traditional genre patterns of phallic spectator identification), I think we have to be careful about investing certain formal cinematic techniques (distanciation) with an essential aesthetic identity (avant-garde) irrespective of their context or function. As Jeffrey Sconce has shown, the same distanciation device can be used in different films and contexts to engage radically different audiences. Thus critics were able to receive *Henry: Portrait of a Serial Killer* (1990) as a "spare, intelligent, and thought-provoking film" in part because of the *way* it employed standard distanciation devices.[81] And they were unable to receive *Freddy's Dead: The Final Nightmare* (A Nightmare on Elm Street 6, 1991) as a film meriting serious consideration, at least in part because of the way it employed the *same* devices. Put another way, *Henry* constructed a distanced relationship between the viewer and the protagonist that the critics understood and appreciated, and *Freddy's Dead* constructed a relationship (using the same techniques) in a way that literally did not speak to them.[82]

The point here is that it's a mistake to equate distanciation devices necessarily with avant-garde strategies (that is, with strategies that speak only—or even primarily—to an avant-garde audience). As I've tried to show, Morrissey's films were received differently by different avant-garde audiences, and perhaps differently still by "mainstream" audiences. That crossover porn films of the same period employed the same distancing strategies that Morrissey's films employed shows the degree to which films at both ends of the cultural spectrum (avant-garde and body genres) had a vested interest in disrupting traditional generic modes of spectator identification and thereby (perhaps) enlarging their potential audience.[83]

A Film for Drella

If "low" genres of the period sometimes employed devices that we tend to associate with high cinematic culture, art and avant-garde films also increasingly engaged the spectator's body in a way traditionally associated with body flicks. Nowhere is that more evident than in *Andy Warhol's Frankenstein,* a film that still sends my horror students into "laughing-screaming" fits. The movie breaks the decorum usually associated with "classroom" screenings and frees the students to yell things like "gross" at the screen. In a way that undergraduates quickly understand, the film positions itself as a body genre flick, and that is how the students receive it.

The film is a takeoff of the traditional Frankenstein story. Here Baron Frankenstein (Udo Kier) is married to his sister and lives in the ancestral castle with his wife-sibling and their two offspring. Because he is interested only in science and in animating his female "zombie," his wife is left bored and sexually frustrated. To remedy this situation, she regularly acquires male servants who work in her bedroom by day and serve dinner at night. Her newest acquisition is Nicholas (Joe Dallesandro), a lusty field hand who is—the baroness tells him—"remarkable" at his new in-house job.

When the film opens, the baron is working against the clock to create two creatures who will breed him a race of perfect Serbs. The beautiful female zombie has been completed and tested in the field by the baron himself. The only remaining problem is to find a head for his male zombie. The two requirements are that it must have the perfect Serbian nose ("the nasum," as the baron keeps reminding his assistant, Otto, is the seat and sign of the Serbian ideal) and that it must come from a man with strong sexual appetites. In search of such a head, the baron goes to the town brothel. But in a scene reminiscent of the bungled brain theft in James Whales's *Frankenstein* (in which Fritz accidentally chooses a "criminal brain" for the creature), the baron and Otto mistake which of the two brothel patrons would best suit their plans. Instead of the lusty Nicholas (Joe Dallesandro), the baron selects Nicholas's celibate, monkish friend Sasha (Srdjan Zelenovic) to be the unwilling donor. As a result, once the head is in place, the baron's male zombie has a beautiful Serbian nose and absolutely no libidinal drive, a state of affairs that drives the baron nearly mad with frustration.

Finally, there are the children. Effectively abandoned by both their parents, they creep around the castle, spying on their mother as she entertains her male "help" and stealing things from the laboratory—a hand, a few instruments—with which they play charming childish dissection games. Since the baron's children are played by (non-English-speaking) Italians, they rarely speak in the film—and their silence gives them an added sinister air. They seem almost telepathic as they play silently together or exchange nods and glances over their scalpels. At the end of the movie, they prepare to take over their father's work as they threaten the only remaining living adult—Nicholas—with vivisection.

The movie thus touches (often humorously) on serious themes: the family, racial purity, class. In addition, it lays bare and satirizes what Gilbert and Gubar have called "the barely disguised incest at the heart" of Mary Shelley's novel—in which Victor Frankenstein is slated to marry his "more than sister" Elizabeth, for whom he seems to feel little sexual passion.[84] And as Yacowar points out, Morrissey "develops the central psychological aspects of his legend. From the *Frankenstein* lore, Morrissey singles out the idea of sexual displacement . . . the unnatural urge to find an alternative to sex," which Walter Evans maintains is the central theme of the novel (76–77).[85]

But while the film touches on all these issues, it doesn't really engage them in any meaningful or sustained way. In that sense, the very inclusion of them is a kind of parody—Morrissey's way of letting us know that *he* knows the kind of material art cinema is supposed to address and that he is deliberately choosing not to address it. If *Frankenstein* embodies a paracinema aesthetic, Morrissey himself is the paracinema brat director par excellence. He hates important themes.[86] What he tries to do in his filmmaking, he told one interviewer, is to avoid the "latter-day horrors of filmmaking that have deteriorated and hurt it so much—the emphasis on directors and important themes and statements. All that garbage, which has alienated films from a popular audience."[87]

In *Frankenstein,* Morrissey not only refuses to develop any of the "themes" the story somewhat tantalizingly raises—the "garbage," as he calls it—but uses the film to make fun of art movies, which he feels are portentously mired in themes. Chief among these is Bernardo Bertolucci's *Last Tango in Paris,* which became—during this period—Morrissey's chief cinematic bête noire. "Today, New Yorkers are much more impressed by European films or a big picture from the never-never land of Hollywood," he told Melton S. Dawes. "Take what I would call a very un–New York, old-fashioned film like *Last Tango in Paris,* which has a big man running around emotionally wrought through the whole film and then a girl gets all upset toward the end and shoots him. We did the same thing in *Heat,* a May-December romance about a man and a woman, only the woman is older and she pulls a gun out in the end, but it doesn't go off. In *Tango* it does . . . [Here Morrissey clasps a hand to his chest and falls back]. This is supposed to purge your emotions.

Figure 30. Jeanne (Maria Schneider) and Paul's (Marlon Brando) last tango. *Last Tango in Paris*.

That kind of silly, old-fashioned melodrama had a great success but *Heat* had practically none."[88]

Morrissey's comments here sound like sour grapes, the sort of rude things you say about a film that got better press than yours did. It's interesting, however, that he didn't mention his chief objection to Bertolucci's film in the interview with Dawes. What drove Morrissey crazy about *Last Tango*'s success was not that Bertolucci's film was, in his opinion, old-fashioned or melodramatic. It was that it took itself so seriously. He was particularly offended by the two anal sex scenes in the film and the spoken lines that accompanied them. In both scenes, Paul (Marlon Brando) makes a speech to Jeanne (Maria Schneider), a speech designed to let the audience know that these scenes are not *about* anal sex; rather, they're really about existential angst, social hypocrisy, and the family. The infamous gallbladder scene in *Andy Warhol's Frankenstein* is a pastiche of the pedagogically motivated anal intercourse scene in *Last Tango*.[89] And in case anyone fails to get the allusion, Morrissey, Yacowar, and Joe Dallesandro have publicized the fact that the goofy line "to know death, Otto, you have to fuck life in the gallbladder" was consciously meant as a parody of Paul's lines (in *Last Tango*) "you won't be able to be free of that feeling of being alone until you look death right in the face . . . Until you go right up into the ass of death—right up his ass—till you find a womb of fear."[90]

The use of anality as a metaphor has a long tradition in European intellectual culture. Sade's use of sodomy is read in philosophical terms by most academic critics.[91] Georges Bataille discusses sodomy and sadoeroticism in the largely economic terms of "appropriation" and "expenditure" and reads sadistic sex as both an irruption in bourgeois morality and a relatively unadorned model for the way power relations in Western society actually work.[92] Intellectual filmmakers such as Godard and Bertolucci, then, were simply following an already established avant-garde philosophical tradition when they introduced anality as a metaphorical device in their films. For both men, Yosefa Loshitzky writes, "anality is a metaphor of the capitalist system of oppression/repression— or in Godard's language of the 'society of the ass.'"[93]

But if anal sex has a certain analogical function in Western intellectual tradition, its appearance in films by art directors such as Godard and Bertolucci still raises disturbing questions about taste and about the assignment of cultural value to on-screen sexual acts. One of the curious cultural contradictions of the 1970s is that while women's bodies (and the violence visited upon them) were increasingly read as metaphors for *something else* (capitalism, patriarchal power, etc.) in art cinema, they were simultaneously denied metaphoric status in (noncrossover) body genre films. Hence, in the porn debates that followed the scandal surrounding *Snuff,* the viewer pleasure associated with watching violence against women was itself problematized in very tricky ways.[94] In the writings of Andrea Dworkin, Catherine MacKinnon, and others, on-screen violence against women was increasingly linked to the *real* violence perpetrated against women in their daily lives. Here on-screen rape was seen not as incisive political analysis of the power structures that dominate and oppress women (as it often was in Godard's films, for example) but rather as incitement to the male viewer to go out and perpetrate violence against women (to dominate and oppress them). Although female bodies and brutal rape could be seen as having a metaphorical or even educational function in art cinema, in "low culture," bodies and violence were meant to be (could only be) taken literally.[95]

Whereas Carol J. Clover and Linda Williams have written convincingly about the complicated signifying uses of the female body (including the brutalized female body) in body genres, in the political arena, the liminal space between fantasy and reality continues to be a contested site.[96] Certainly it was beginning to be a contested site in the 1970s. Not only violent porn but horror too came under attack. Brian De Palma's *Dressed to Kill* (1980) and *Body Double* (1984) were both picketed by Women against Violence against Women and by Women against Violence in Pornography and the Media when the films first opened in theaters. And the rape-revenge movie *I Spit on Your Grave* (1977) is often included in discussions and documentaries about violent pornography.[97]

The reason I have been discussing this at such length is not only to demonstrate the basis for Morrissey's extreme dislike of films like Bertolucci's *Last Tango* but also to point out the way in which aesthetic critical decisions can have politico-cultural ramifications. As Sconce points out in "Spectacles of Death," "what is at stake in valuing one film over another, or even in attempting to define systematically a group of films, is a struggle over cultural meaning and power."[98] In this instance, the larger cultural issues at stake may be said to be the following: How do we determine the number of readings a given cultural text can legitimately generate? Who determines when anal rape is a metaphor and when it is not? Who decides which sexual and violent metaphors are allowed to have cultural currency? In other words, where is the dividing line between high art and low culture? Where do Bertolucci's fantasies and allusions leave off, and porn director Michael Ninn's begin?[99]

In *Andy Warhol's Frankenstein,* as in other crossover films of the period, the filmmaker begs these unanswerable questions by mixing up the terms of their articulation. As Joe Dallesandro tells Michael Ferguson, the Italians' criteria for *Frankenstein* was simple. "The deal was that they would make these movies [*Frankenstein* and *Dracula*], that they'd back them for nearly a million dollars, but that they had to star Joe Dallesandro, they had to be directed by Paul Morrissey, and Andy had to lend his name, because that was the combination they saw as a success with *Flesh, Trash* and *Heat*."[100] Put another way, the Italians wanted a good low-budget European sex-horror flick that could be marketed as a racy art film. And that's precisely what they got.

Crossover Appeal

Andy Warhol's Frankenstein opened in New York City on Wednesday 15 May 1974 at the Trans-Lux East and Trans-Lux West, theaters primarily known as art houses. The film had already been previewed by some American critics in Paris (where it played in February 1974). Commenting that Joe Dallesandro was "in fine stud form," *Variety* predicted that the film and its companion piece, *Andy Warhol's Dracula*, "could find some playoff on regular horror and even sex circuits" and speculated that "some cult usage may develop for this pair of elegant horror pix."[101] What *Variety* failed to predict was the enormous crossover success that the film would have. Playing in art cinemas and regular commercial houses across the United States, the movie ranked sixteenth on *Variety*'s August list of the fifty top-grossing films.[102] By the end of the year, the film had grossed more than $5 million.

Partly, the film's success was due to the lure of Warhol's name and the scandalous reputation of the by now famous Factory. As mentioned earlier, outside avant-garde fan-cult circles, not much distinction was made between Morrissey's productions and Warhol's. So seeing the Warhol-Morrissey films gave mainstream moviegoers the sense that they were participating in the underground cinema, even though the films themselves were quite different from Warhol's earlier underground work. "I don't think . . . *[Frankenstein]* is sick," one Columbia University student told *New York Times* reviewer Paul Gardner during a July screening of the movie. "Some of it is funny, some of it is boring—like the other Warhol films."[103]

Partly *Frankenstein*'s success was due to the cult status of its star, Joe Dallesandro, whose physique, Vincent Canby once wrote, "is so magnificently shaped that men as well as women become disconnected at the sight of him."[104] Dallesandro, as *Variety* noted, is "in fine stud form" in *Andy Warhol's Frankenstein,* a fact that was emphasized—or exploited for the German market at least—with several full frontal nude shots of the actor.[105] In addition to Dallesandro's status as a cult star, the reputation of the Warhol-Morrissey films—which had previously used transvestites in the lead female roles—as well as *Frankenstein*'s campy tone helped the film garner a large gay audience.[106]

The film appealed to the increased public taste for interesting new and sensational material. Its X rating put it in the same category as *Clockwork Orange, Last Tango in Paris,* and *Midnight Cowboy* and in many places helped the film to cash in on the general liberal mood of the times.[107] Certainly, the gore factor didn't hurt. Besides attracting "regular horror" patrons, the film was able to exploit the crossover success of *The Exorcist,* another (for the times) supergross horror film that had opened earlier that year.[108]

Frankenstein is nothing if not visceral. As noted, Morrissey decided to make the film because Warhol was depressed about his scars. "Andy once told me that he felt as if he would pop open one day," Morrissey said.[109] And indeed "popping open" would be a good alternate title for the film. "Everyone [in the movie] spills their guts," Morrissey tells us on the analog audio track to the laser disc.[110] And practically everyone who "spills their guts" does so in a close-up (CU) shot, because a scar has popped open.

In the infamous gallbladder scene, the baron painstakingly cuts open (CU) the female zombie's incision, stitch by stitch, creating a vaginal slit that he can penetrate. Later Otto tries to open the same incision with his tongue (CU), so that he too can "know death." His attempt to follow the baron's example is disastrous. The female zombie's guts spill out and cannot be reinserted. She's ruined. In the meantime, a maid who wanders into the laboratory is disemboweled by Otto. Frankenstein is stabbed by his male zombie—an act that leaves his liver dangling on the tip of the spear that still penetrates his body. After murdering the baron, the male zombie commits suicide by ripping open the incision crisscrossing his chest cavity. As he bids his friend Nicholas farewell, the camera zooms in for a close-up of the intestines dangling out of his open wound. And a pair of lungs (attached to a mini-respirator), which the baron keeps closed up in a cabinet, functions as the Frankensteins' version of the Addams Family's Thing—a pet organ, which the children periodically visit for reassurance.

If this sounds gross, it is. Because the film was made in 3-D, not only do we see disembowelments and incision-openings in detailed close-up shots, but the spilled guts themselves come whizzing out of the screen to dangle, literally, above our heads, in our laps, or (depending on our height) under our very noses. When guts aren't being spilled, they're being stirred inside laboratory jars or stuffed back into lab containers. And when old incisions aren't being opened, new scars are being created and old scars are being highlighted. In fact, the poster and ad for the film show a torso with a scar, the word "Frankenstein" printed in black boldface type across the sutures.

In addition to guts and scars, there's plenty of plain old bloodletting. Sasha's head is removed with a huge pair of shears and dangled above the audience. Baron Frankenstein loses a hand before being gouged to death. Here we get a close-up of the baron's stump as blood seemingly spurts out of the screen into the audience. "While one suspects that the tales about upchuck at *The Exorcist* were eagerly exaggerated," Nora Sayre comments, "*Andy Warhol's Frankenstein . . .* almost begs the gorge to rise."[111]

Many patrons came, in part, just to see the novel technological gimmick of 3-D used well.[112] And some patrons who would never be caught dead at a horror movie came because the film successfully positioned itself as an outrageous comedy. "The afternoon I saw the film

Figure 31. Sutures advertisement for *Andy Warhol's Frankenstein.*

at the Trans-Lux West," Vincent Canby writes, "the packed audience roared with laughter at this sight [the decapitation scene] and others like it—which is Grand Guignol of a more or less competent order. . . . The audience also found it hilarious when, later in the film, the doctor gets his own hand chopped off and staggers around the lab, spouting blood and words. 'All I had was a labwatowy and a dweam,' says the doctor."[113]

"Movies were a form of circus spectacle," *New York Times* critic Stephen Farber writes, "before they began to tell stories—and long before they were considered an art."[114] And one of the unfortunate aspects of filmgoing in the mid-seventies, for Farber at least, was the degree to which movies were renouncing their hard-won intellectual status and returning to the realm of "pure spectacle." Films like *The Exorcist* and *Andy Warhol's Frankenstein* garnered good box office receipts in 1974 while "subtler, quieter films like . . . [Coppola's] *The Conversation*" had a hard time attracting an audience. "When the public is in the mood for carnival thrills," Farber mourns, "criticism is virtually irrelevant."[115]

Farber's use of the word "carnival" in this context is telling. In *Rabelais and His World,* Mikhail Bakhtin describes a tradition of "grotesque realism" that he believes derives from the medieval carnival—a "gay parody of truth" in which traditional power hierarchies are overturned and the world is "turned inside out." This grotesque realism finds its fullest literary expression in the works of Rabelais. "However, the tradition of the grotesque is not entirely extinct," Bakhtin writes, "it continues to live and to struggle for its existence in the lower canonical genres (comedy, satire, fable) and especially in noncanonical genres (in the novel, in a special form of popular dialogue, in burlesque). Humor also goes on living on the popular stage."[116] As William Paul asserts, one can add "almost the whole of movies" to Bakhtin's list of genres in which the grotesque continues (45). Certainly one can add gross-out movies, which, as Paul points out, are particularly illustrative of Bakhtin's notion of "grotesque realism" (46).[117] As Bakhtin writes:

> The essential principle of grotesque realism is degradation, that is, the lowering of all that is high, spiritual, ideal, abstract; it is a transfer to the material level, to the sphere of earth and body in their indissoluble unity . . . all . . . forms of grotesque realism degrade, bring down to earth, turn their subject into flesh. . . . The people's laughter which characterizes all forms of grotesque realism from immemorial times was linked with the bodily lower stratum. Laughter degrades and materializes.[118]

Gross-out horror films—with their emphasis on the physical and their tendency to linger over shots of various bodily parts, fluids, and products—reduce everything to blood and guts and gore. In *Frankenstein* even the "erotic" scenes are grotesque, as the Baroness noisily slurps Nicholas's armpit and the Baron penetrates his female zombie's "digestive parts." There is no room for idealized love here—erotic or otherwise—as marriage becomes a business relationship between brother and sister, and almost all sexuality (inside and outside the brothel) is conducted on a commercial basis (Nicholas's line just before he kisses the Baroness for the first time emphasizes this—"Do you want me to start work now?"). Furthermore, the grotesque character of the erotic scenes is explicitly linked to the grossness of the "opened body" shots. The baron's penetration of his female zombie is directly preceded by one of the goriest scenes in the film—the slow, painstaking slicing open of the zombie's stitches. And that both the Baron's "foreplay"—slicing open the female zombie and massaging her gall bladder, liver, and intestines—and his actual coitus are intercut with the Baroness's first romp with Nicholas serves to connect the scenes rather than contrast them. That is, rather than seeing the Baroness's "normal" sex as a counterpoint to her husband's kinky behavior in the laboratory, we see it as merely an alternate version of the same thing: sex reduced to an oddly cold desire for power over biology (it's interesting that real sexual desire remains completely unrepresented in a film in which so much sex takes place). In Morrissey's words, the sexuality in the film is "an absurd sexuality," and sex itself is "quite intentionally reduced to something that in effect has no meaning."[119]

Whereas Bakhtin and Paul stress the link of grotesque realism and the carnivalesque to popular culture, Bakhtin's analysis works equally well for transgressive avant-garde art culture. Certainly, the dadas took the challenge to degrade, to bring down to earth, and to turn their subjects into flesh seriously. Hence their outrageous programs, in which Hugo Ball would degrade "art" by dressing up as a bishop and reciting loud (often jarring) nonsense syllables that were passed off as "poems."[120] The surrealists simply continued this tradition by defacing pictures of the *Mona Lisa* and by making films in which the physical was privileged in often grotesque ways. One of the first shots of *Un chien andalou* shows the slitting of a woman's eye; a later shot gives us the close-up of a wound out of which ants are crawling. And many post–World War II American avant-garde productions emphasize the physical in often brutal fashion. In Kenneth Anger's *Fireworks* (1947), for example, the protagonist cruises in public lavatories and is badly beaten by a gang of sailors. Even an uneventful, placid film such as Warhol's *Sleep* can be seen as a form of "grotesque realism," as it brings what some might regard as the pretensions of avant-garde culture "down to earth," degrades cinematic expectations and forms, and materializes (in a very direct, corporeal way) boredom. In fact, P. Adams Sitney's definition of Warhol's avant-garde cinema, as a challenge to the "romantic" cinema of the existing avant-garde, can be read in this context as the reintroduction of "grotesque realism" into an art form that was starting to become too idealized, too abstract, too spiritual.

As I've tried to show, even art cinema encroached vigorously on the grotesque in this period. The long murder sequence near the end of *The Conformist* (1969)—in which Anna runs through the woods screaming, is shot, falls, rises, and is shot again—has the same texture and some of the same horror as the shower sequence in *Psycho*. And *Clockwork Orange* (1971) may be said to be the film that forcefully pushed art-horror into the art-splatter arena.[121] In fact, as Carol J. Clover notes in *Men, Women, and Chainsaws*, if *Clockwork Orange* and *Straw Dogs* (1971) "were less well and expensively made by less famous men, . . . [they] would surely qualify as sensationalistic exploitation" (116).

Bakhtin's discussion of "grotesque realism" provides a way, as Paul demonstrates, for us to consider gross-out films seriously—as films that intentionally challenge "the high and the spiritual" (46). But as I've tried to show in this chapter, avant-garde cinema and art cinema of this period also drew on "noncanonical traditions" to challenge "commonplace modes of thought" (46). In fact, it became very difficult during the early seventies to talk about "canonical traditions" in cinema, as crossover films became increasingly the norm and as consumers turned to genres they'd previously ignored for both entertainment and provocation.

Furthermore, as both Warhol's and Morrissey's films show, artistic and aesthetic categories—the discursive strategies on which distinctions between high cinematic art and popular cinematic culture rely—became increasingly problematic in an era that had as its social agenda a radical restructuring of evaluative judgments and a radical realignment of cultural and political power. Categories such as "structural" and "lyrical"—the categories critics such as Parker Tyler and P. Adams Sitney use to characterize different kind of avant-garde films in this period—essentialize structural or formal elements. But such categories are only helpful in distinguishing films in an already-finite and predetermined set of avant-garde texts. If you try to use them to determine whether a text is avant-garde or commercial, you immediately run into problems. All commercial television meets at least some of Sitney's criteria for "lyrical" avant-garde cinema. In fact, using Sitney's criteria, one would be forced to see all television as an avant-garde or experimental cinematic "mode" (hardly a view that the avant-garde establish-ment of this period would have embraced).

Finally, the continuing confusion over the authorship of Mor-rissey's films—that is, whether *Heat, Frankenstein,* and so forth should be considered as part of the same auteurist sensibility that gave us *Sleep* or as part of an oeuvre that includes *Hound of the Baskervilles* (1977) and *Beethoven's Nephew* (1985)—shows how difficult it is both to codify artis-tic sensibility and to determine where avant-garde production leaves off and "commercial" cinema begins. It shows how fragile and arbitrary the cult of the artist and auteur—such an important component of both avant-garde and art cinema reception during this period—really was. As Paul Zimmerman, writing for *Newsweek,* puts it, Morrissey acted "as a sort of alter-ego for Warhol" and in so doing demonstrated both the es-sential role that collaboration played in all the Factory productions (not only the Warhol-Morrissey films but also the ones in which Warhol turned on the camera and walked away) and the degree to which so much commercial cinema of this period functioned as another aspect of the avant-garde.[122] As Warhol once said, "I wanted to be an Art Business-man or Business Artist . . . [because] making money is art and working is art, and good business is the best art."[123] According to these criteria, *Andy Warhol's Frankenstein* and *Andy Warhol's Dracula* are the best movies that avant-garde filmmaker Andy Warhol (n)ever made.

Conclusion
Mainstreaming Trash Aesthetics

Any honest account of human experience must be shocking. For it is the function of art to make the reader or viewer aware of what he knows and in most cases doesn't know that he knows and doesn't want to know.

—William S. Burroughs, reviewing John Waters's *Shock Value*

I've never had any pretensions about what I do. I'm proud of *Hustler*. I'm proud of everything that I've done. I would like to be remembered for making a contribution to Free Speech but I'm by no means looking for respectability.

—Larry Flynt

Throughout this book I've discussed the way that consumers of both low and high culture, during the postwar period, attempted to define themselves in opposition to a dominant mainstream taste aesthetic, and the interest that both mainstream and, occasionally, high culture have had in policing taste. But I've also tried to draw distinctions between actual mainstream moviegoers—who, I argue, are frequently much more resilient and eclectic in their tastes than mainstream critics give them credit for being—and the mainstream, middlebrow critical establishment, the arbiters of taste, who have a certain vested interest in what the public does and does not consume.

In the 1990s, the eclecticism of the mainstream audience became evident as two cycles of films—one about Andy Warhol and one about trash aesthetics—reintroduced both high and low culture back into more or less mainstream cinema. The Warhol films were perhaps the most curious. Starting with Chuck Workman's *Superstar: The Life and Times of Andy Warhol* (1991), the cycle went on to include Susanne Ofteringer's *Nico Icon* (1995), Mary Harron's *I Shot Andy Warhol* (1996), and Julian Schnabel's *Basquiat* (1996). Although these films were hardly designed to unproblematically celebrate fringe art culture—and seem, in many ways, to be troublingly conservative movies—they still reserve their most spectacular visual moments for the heyday of the Factory. This is particularly true of the documentaries, which typically include a montage sequence of still photographs and movie footage of beautiful and engaged people doing what they did best, performing their "star" status. As Sconce argues in a completely different context, these elaborately staged, beautifully edited sequences—which unfold inevitably as a continuous party scene—encourage (through direct spectatorial address) a kind of identification with the characters Warhol's Factory attracted. Perhaps more importantly, they celebrate the kind of on-the-edge lifestyle that Factory regulars lived.[1] Although all the films inevitably end in tragedy, the postfilm memory that lingers is of a life that's more intense and certainly more interesting than what Lena Lamont in *Singin' in the Rain* calls our "humdrum lives." Furthermore, although the films initially played in art theaters and specialty houses, they showed up later on videotape and did well enough in rental receipts to encourage even mainstream video stores like Blockbuster to begin carrying other titles associated with Warhol. Paul Morrissey's *Andy Warhol's Dracula, Andy Warhol's Frankenstein, Flesh, Trash,* and *Heat* all showed up at the Blockbuster and Video World stores in the Midwest university town where I live, along with John Palmer and David Weisman's *Ciao! Manhattan* (1971), a non-Factory tribute to Edie Sedgwick, Warhol's favorite star. Hardly a bastion of avant-garde culture, the stores were apparently convinced to carry the titles by the number of "regular customers" renting Workman and Harron's films. It was the popularity of Workman and Harron's movies, one employee told me, rather than the proximity of the university, that convinced the store managers that "Warhol was a popular item."

In a similar vein, the same stores began carrying Ed Wood titles, *Bride of the Monster* (*Bride of the Atom,* 1956), *Glen or Glenda* (*I Changed My Sex,* 1953), *Jailbait* (1955), *Plan 9 from Outer Space* (1959), and *The Violent Years* (1956), after Tim Burton's *Ed Wood* (1994) became a popular video success. Which brings us to the trash movie cycle. Whereas the films about Warhol stressed the Otherness of Warhol's world, the films about trash culture—*Ed Wood*, *The People vs. Larry Flynt* (Milos Forman, 1997), *Boogie Nights* (1997)—sought rather to depict the assortment of characters surrounding Ed Wood, Larry Flynt, and 1970s porn culture as a kind of family. In this sense, the films unfold—as the beginning of

Figure 32. Larry (Woody Harrelson) in front of the U.S. flag. *The People vs. Larry Flynt*.

Freaks does—as vehicles for normatizing "freak" culture. *The People vs. Larry Flynt,* David E. Williams observes, could easily be seen as "a Frank Capra–style movie with pornography." A similar argument could be made for *Boogie Nights* and *Ed Wood* (Capra with exploitation).[2]

Of the three trash films, *The People vs. Larry Flynt* interests me the most because, like *Hustler* magazine and Flynt himself, the movie is quite explicit about the class locations of taste. In the film, Larry is driven to create *Hustler* because he simply doesn't understand *Playboy,* with its "fuzzy pictures" of breasts that "don't look real," articles about the upper-middle-class bachelor lifestyle, and ads for expensive consumer goods. "Do you guys read *Playboy*?" he asks a group of working-class friends assembled at his house to watch TV. The men nod. "Did you enjoy this month's article on how to hook up your quadrophonic stereo system? . . . And did you follow their advice on how to make a perfect martini? . . . Who is this magazine for, anyway? I mean, you know it's like if you don't make $20,000-plus a year, you don't jerk off. Seven million people buying it and *nobody's* reading it. Gentlemen, *Playboy* is mocking you." Cut from a series of close-ups showing startled male faces looking up at Larry Flynt (who is standing while they're sitting on a cushion couch on the floor) to the windows of *Hustler* magazine.

Hustler, the film argues, sought to provide sexy images that engaged working-class culture. Segments of the film show Larry overriding the "taste" proscriptions of a photographer and telling a model to open her legs *wide,* the startled responses of store proprietors opening the magazine for the first time, and covers of actual issues of the publication. In addition, the film demonstrates the fierce brand of humor that *Hustler* leveled against the sacred cows of the middle class. Examples mentioned in the film: the mock Campari ad in which the Reverend Jerry Falwell describes his "first time" with his mother in an outhouse, a cartoon showing the Tin Woodsman, the Scarecrow, the Lion, and Toto "gang-banging" Dorothy *(Wizard of Oz)* "in Kansas," and a cartoon of Santa holding a large erect penis and telling Mrs. Claus that this is what he has to "ho-ho-ho about." The images themselves, of course, aren't clearly shown, and the examples are chosen judiciously. None of the cruel *Hustler* jokes about Betty Ford's mastectomy are cited; neither does the film describe—much less represent—the brazenly tasteless magazine images of the detritus of aborted fetuses, jokes about amputees, and cartoons about how and where the homeless relieve themselves. Still, the film manages to show that class and taste were always twinned issues for Flynt. As Laura Kipnis puts it:

As a feminist (not to mention a petit bourgeois and denizen of the academic classes), I too find myself often disgusted by *Hustler*. This is *Hustler* hitting its target, like some heat-seeking offense missile, because it's someone like me who's precisely *Hustler*'s ideal sitting duck. *Hustler* pits itself against not just the proper body, that holdover from the bourgeois revolution, but against all the current paraphernalia of yuppie professionalism. At its most obvious *Hustler* is simply allergic to any form of social or intellectual affectation, squaring off like some maddened pit bull against the pretensions and the earning power of the professional classes: doctors, optometrists, dentists and lawyers are favored targets. It's pissed off by liberals and particularly nasty to academics, who are invariably prissy and uptight. . . . It rants against the power of government, which is by definition corrupt. . . . It smears the rich against the wall . . . and devotes many, many pages to the hypocrisy of organized religion.[3]

But these are just the magazine's "more manifest targets." Reading deeper, Kipnis claims, "its offenses create a detailed blueprint of the national cultural psyche." *Hustler*'s favorite tactic is to "zero in on a subject, an issue, an 'unsaid' that the bourgeois imagination prefers to be unknowing about—those very problematic materials a tight-assed culture has founded itself upon suppressing, and prohibits irreverent speech about. Things we would call 'tasteless'" (141–42). These cover everything from the list of offensive items mentioned earlier to AIDS to the problems of disposing the fat extracted during liposuction. In fact, one of the unsettling questions that *Hustler* continually poses is "which subjects are taboo even for sick humor?" What are we *really* uneasy about? (142).

As Kipnis points out, this question becomes doubly disconcerting when viewed within the historical context of various cultural coincidences: the negative response to *Hustler*'s jokes about Betty Ford's mastectomy, for example, compared to the number of popular sick jokes about dispersed body parts following the *Challenger* explosion. "Apparently, a mastectomy" is considered to be "more of a tragedy than the deaths of seven astronauts," Kipnis writes (142). Perhaps. But perhaps it's just a more taboo tragedy, one so disturbingly private we can't even make "sick" jokes about it. Within the film, historical coincidence is given a pointedly political edge when, shortly after his release from prison (the first time), Flynt gives a news conference at which he presents a slide show of "possibly" tasteless images. "Is this in bad taste?" he asks, showing a picture of a naked woman. "Or this?" Cut to a photograph of the My Lai massacre. The sequence is reminiscent of a famous

Lenny Bruce routine, in which the comedian asks the audience to consider why it's obscene to show sex but not violence, obscene to show breasts but not mutilated body parts. But it's also reminiscent of Oliver Stone films that are haunted by the imagery and legacy of Vietnam, and the photograph's inclusion is perhaps one nod to Oliver Stone's role as producer of the movie.

Working-class taste and culture in *Larry Flynt* is iconically encoded into the mise-en-scène. The strip club where Larry first meets Althea, the diners and bars where he initially hangs out, the low-rent house he occupies (complete with makeshift cushion-couch on the floor, inexpensive wood paneling, and pictures of naked women on the wall), and the clothes that Larry, Althea, and their friends wear are all visible reminders that these aren't your average Hollywood yuppie consumers. The character of Althea is particularly interesting in this regard. Althea is outspoken and has a wicked sense of humor, and she refuses to understand that there are times when it simply isn't appropriate to initiate sex (when Larry is on the phone with Ruth Carter Stapleton, for example). The story of Althea's descent into addiction and disease would, in most Hollywood films, signal an impending crisis in her relationship with her husband, but here we accept that Larry is just crazy about her; we accept that her behavior, which perhaps seems outrageous to us, doesn't seem outrageous to him at all. When she yells, "Bon appétit!" in the courtroom, Larry just smiles. "I love you, Baby!" he calls back. And when both her addiction and her illness make it increasingly difficult for her to stand up or maneuver, he simply props her up or sits her on his lap and gives her a ride in his wheelchair.

Throughout the film, Althea—even more than Larry himself—becomes the living symbol of a certain vulgarity and class identification.[4] The audience is clearly meant to root for her as much as it's meant to root for Larry. After Larry is shot and—during an emotional hospital room scene—repudiates Ruth Carter Stapleton and his own temporary conversion to Christianity, Althea returns to Larry Flynt Publications. "Take this thing down," she says, pointing to a Christian icon on the wall. "I want all this Christian stuff outta here, now!" Taking off her jacket, she begins climbing the stairs. "Uh, Ladies! Gentlemen!" she says, turning. "The reign of Christian terror at the magazine is now over. We're smut peddlers again. We're going back to our roots. We are porn again!" Althea had never really liked Larry's conversion, and she certainly hadn't liked the disastrous business decisions that, she felt, it had caused him to make. So this announcement is a triumphant one.

And the camera emphasizes Althea's triumph with a high-angle point-of-view shot that shows the *Hustler* staff, gathered together, looking up at her. When I saw the film in Chicago, the audience cheered.

One of the most subversive things about *The People vs. Larry Flynt* is the way it manages to get its mainstream audience on Althea and Flynt's side, the way it manages to turn "Hugh Hefner's low-brow doppelgänger" and his wife into icons of a quintessentially "American story" (Williams, 24). Largely it does this through the rags-to-riches Horatio Alger story of Larry's success as an entrepreneur, and through the sentimentalized story of Flynt's romance with his wife. Whereas the real Larry Flynt claims that he loved Althea largely because she was the "only woman he ever found who was sicker than himself," the film largely suppresses the couples' idiosyncracies in favor of a story most moviegoers can recognize. The film allows Althea to mention her bisexuality ("You aren't the only person in this club who's fucked every woman in this club," she tells Larry the first time they make love), and it permits one tastefully filmed orgy scene in a Jacuzzi. But once Larry and Althea marry, the images and dialogue are resolutely monogamous ("Our bed is so empty," Althea tells Larry when he's in jail). The couple is always shown together, and after the wedding, they are always shown to be *alone* together in their bedroom. If Larry is pursuing a "variety of vaginas" after their marriage, as he warned Althea he would, he keeps it a secret from us, as well as from her. Of course, much of Larry and Althea's story is the stuff from which romance is spun. Althea cares for her husband and loves him, even after he is shot and paralyzed from the waist down (reassuring us that this relationship really *was* about more than sex). He, in turn, loves and cares for her even after she becomes addicted to opiates and contracts AIDS. But the depiction of Althea appears to be one of the areas in the story over which Flynt himself had relatively little control. "We treated Althea with respect," screenplay cowriter Larry Karaszewski said, "Larry didn't have a lot to say about it" (Williams, 29).[5]

The other thing Larry didn't "have a lot to say about" was the actual aesthetic look of the movie. While *The People vs. Larry Flynt* represents trash aesthetics, the aesthetics of the film itself—the way in which it was shot, lit, and edited—conform to the dominant middle-class film aesthetic (an aesthetic that the real Larry Flynt has made a career of lampooning).[6] In fact, it has the visuals of an art film. Directed by Milos Forman, the Czech director who previously made *Fireman's Ball* (1967), a hallmark of the Czech New Wave, and *One Flew over the*

Cuckoo's Nest (1975) and *Amadeus* (1984), the film is beautiful and suggests, through its own use of visual style, an image of Flynt rather like the image of Mozart in *Amadeus,* an immature genius whose "art" isn't really as disreputable as it seems. Here Flynt talks about God creating vaginas so that they may be seen, and the diegetic *Hustler* photo spreads featuring Althea are as much about theatrical costumes and backdrops (complete with music) as anything in *Playboy.*

Furthermore, the conversion scene that Flynt himself wished to include in the film was vetoed by Forman. Scott Alexander described the scene for David Williams. "As Larry described it, there were lights, fog and all kinds of special effects. Then the ghosts of Jesus, Paul and Lenny Bruce appeared in this 'Born-Again moment'" (28). This has all the earmarks of what Sconce calls "excess" in paracinematic style—special effects designed to draw the viewer's attention away from the diegesis to style for its own sake, plus the kitschy visual representation of Flynt's personal pantheon, Jesus, Paul, and Lenny Bruce, "in a cloud" (28). "'It was a Ken Russell moment,' says Alexander, recalling the director of *The Devils* and *Altered States.* 'But Milos basically said, *Not in my movie'*" (28).

What ultimately makes Larry Flynt sympathetic in the film, then, is the erasure of all the things that made him offensive in real life. That is, while the film's script celebrates the rights of a resolutely working-class aesthetic, one that often makes tasteless jokes at the expense of the middle-class, the aesthetic it enacts is a bourgeois one. In that way, it more or less inscribes Flynt within a frame of mainstream, middle-class taste, a frame that Flynt has spent his entire life trying to explode; and contains working-class aesthetics within a homogenizing and harmonic universe of bourgeois visual culture.

I should say here that as a middle-class viewer, I like the way the film looks, and I certainly like the way it explicitly—if, aesthetically, problematically—foregrounds class cultural issues that rarely receive any acknowledgment in a mainstream, big-budget film. But that doesn't make me any less curious about the current cultural need to recuperate Larry Flynt as the poster boy for First Amendment rights or the cinematic trend to "normalize" fringe groups of trash culture producers and purveyors as exploiters of "quirky" variants on bourgeois normative taste. While making someone like Larry Flynt seem less offensive than he is in real life makes good box office sense, it also runs the risk of denying what made Flynt dangerous, interesting, and controversial.[7]

For some critics, this means it runs the risk of denying us access to the best that art can do. In a curious article about the continuing debate over NEA and NEH funding, Mark Edmundson (author of *Nightmare on Main Street*) elaborates the distinctions between the popular culture he sees everywhere around us and the art that, he feels, we so desperately need in this period of late capitalism.[8] Starting from the premise that the United States is an empire, he begins his article with the provocative question "what kind of art do the citizens of an empire crave?" Americans, he writes, "need to lean forward and face the truth that we are citizens of an imperium. . . . We are the world's most powerful military combine, armed to the teeth, able to defend ourselves and wage two wars at once anywhere on earth. Our coffers are filling, our economy is in streamlined forward fling and, maybe most important, our culture—by which I mean not just our culture of . . . movies, overprocessed rock and caramel-laden caffeined fizz but our culture of incessant acquisition, where get and grab are king—rules the Internetted earth."[9]

What this means to us, artistically, is that we tend to want art that follows the Roman imperial model rather than the Greek model. "Where the Greeks rendered their gods in exquisite statuary, exuding bittersweet eros and haughty everlasting life, the Romans declared their emperors gods and cast them in stolid, dead-eyed busts. Where the Greeks had the Olympic Games, the Romans had the bloody riot of the Colosseum" (25). What the Romans wanted from their culture, Edmundson tells us, bears an uncanny resemblance to what Americans want from culture. "The emperors," he writes, "required constant assurance that they were unsurpassed in power and would rule forever. For this, they turned to their artists. The people wished to believe, if only in passing, that they themselves were emperors . . . what the Romans wanted from their art, and from their culture overall was to be flattered" (26).

It's always dangerous to draw analogous links between historical periods, and here the comparison seems doubly unfair. Much of what Edmundson sees as U.S. cultural imperialism—"quick-cut, dumb and dumber movies," rock music, and Coca-Cola—are products of popular (read "democratic") rather than "official" culture. And his laudatory prose, elevating Greek art over Roman art, runs the risk not only of essentializing long periods of art and political history into nationalist "schools" but also of reinscribing something like a religious purpose into art (the only good art being that which elevates humanity and serves the greater purpose of the cultural deity or deities). In addition, Edmundson's imperial analogy runs the risk of somehow "naturalizing" cultural imperialism ("where get and grab are king") by removing it from a specific Marxist analytic context and reinscribing it as part of a long historical continuum, a continuum that makes it seem normal to want to dominate other peoples—the Romans did it, the French did it, the Brits did it, et cetera.

That said, it's curious that once he moves past the unfortunate imperialist analogy, Edmundson elaborates a notion of real art—the art we need—that bears a striking resemblance to both avant-garde art and to the kind of popular culture that Larry Flynt promulgated.

> In our stolidity, our cringing pride, our sense of entitlement, *what we need most is the shock of art,* its power to tell us that this world is not all there is. Rather than leave it to the politicians, the social scientists and the now beloved market forces to shape the future, we need the visions of our artists to give form to our hopes and terrors. (28, italics mine)

Edmundson is speaking of artists like Jane Austen and Charles Dickens, great writers who have the power to move the reader beyond the immediate, the continuous present, into the future; artists with visionary power. These are not necessarily artists who will operate within the confines of good taste, however. In fact, it would be better for us, Edmundson argues, if they didn't. "The citizens of an empire need real artists—whom they're prone to detest a great deal. We need to fight, oddly enough, to be offended" (28).

Such a prescription for art—the right and duty of art *to offend*—sounds remarkably like the Supreme Court decision that Larry Flynt's lawyer reads to his client at the end of Forman's movie. Upholding the rights of citizens to express themselves, by poking fun at public figures, and upholding the greater social need to tolerate a wide range of speech (even offensive speech), the Supreme Court sided with Flynt against Jerry Falwell (who had charged Flynt with libel after the Campari ad parody). The prominence given to the Supreme Court decision in the film reinforces the movie's self-positioning as a "serious" film about a fundamental constitutional right. But it also invites us to reconsider what exactly this consists of—the right to be offended, to run the risk of giving offense, and to tweak our noses at those whom we believe, rightly or wrongly, to be members of a dominant class.

Edmundson's prescription for the art we need, then, can be read as a call for an honest movie about Larry Flynt, a Jess Franco–style extravaganza that would run the risk of offending people, of grossing them out, of not making much money. Such a film would go further than

Dickens and Austen in reminding people that privilege and entitlement should never be taken for granted. And it would have a market. If this book has taught me anything, it's that there is a large group of consumers always on the alert for "something different," something tough, something that will, as *Videodrome*'s Max Renn says, "break through." And these consumers are frequently drawn to both high and low ends of the market.

I've ended this book about taste and horror with *Larry Flynt* and the Edmundson article for two reasons. As an attempt to market a working-class counteraesthetic to middle-class mainstream audiences, *The People vs. Larry Flynt* demonstrates the degree to which film representations can be *both* subversive and hegemonically contained. But this art film about a porn king also illustrates the degree to which low and high culture are always linked, always dialectically paired. Both high "art" and low culture have the capacity to deliver what Edmundson calls a "whack," to rattle the cage (28).

Both have the capacity either to reify culturally hegemonic norms or to run the risk of giving serious offense. Both traffic in images that frequently seem to violate "community standards of decency" and cultural values. So I'd like to end this book with a class and cultural corrective to Edmundson's prescription for a healthier nation. If what we, as "citizens of an empire," need is "real artists" who will deflate our egos, challenge our assumptions, and run the risk of giving offense, then we also—as I hope this book has demonstrated—need real goremeisters, offensive people whom we're "prone to detest."[10]

Notes

1. Sleaze-Mania, Euro-trash, and High Art

1. See Jeffrey Sconce, "'Trashing' the Academy: Taste, Excess, and an Emerging Politics of Cinematic Style," *Screen* 36, no. 4 (winter 1995): 372. Hereafter cited in text. Michael Weldon calls this cinema "psychotronic." See Michael Weldon, *The Psychotronic Encyclopedia of Film* (New York: Ballantine Books, 1983); Weldon, *The Psychotronic Video Guide* (New York: St. Martin's Griffin, 1996); and Michael Weldon, ed., *Psychotronic Video,* serial (Narrowsburg, N.Y.). For a good theoretical introduction to trash cinema, see Eric Schaefer, ed., *Trash Cinema Reader* (Austin: University of Texas Press, forthcoming).

Note that for fans of trash cinema, the word "trash" is not negative. Fans have appropriated the term in much the same way that queer theorists have appropriated the term "queer." Obsidian Video (at Newspeak in Providence, R.I.), for example, advertises "Trash and art from around the world."

2. Remarkably little has been written about the low end of the mail-order video business. Fanzines and mass-market horror publications periodically publish addresses and lists. But since they're preaching to the converted, they provide very little analysis of the phenomenon. At the time of this writing, Jeffrey Sconce's "'Trashing' the Academy" remains the only article that attempts to theorize the phenomenon and the aesthetic it represents. The best general-interest articles about mail-order video were published in the July–August 1991 issue of *Film Comment.* See Elliot Forbes, "The 'Lost' World," Maitland McDonagh, "The House by the Cemetery," and Peter Hogue, "Riders of the Dawn," *Film Comment* 27 (July–August 1991): 41–48. See also Richard Kadrey, "Director's Cuts," *World Art* 3 (1996): 64–68,

which discusses the aesthetic of bootlegs; and Tony Williams, "Resource Guide: Video Sales and Rentals," *Jump Cut* 37 (1992): 99–109, and "Mail Order and Video Companies II," *Jump Cut* 41 (1997): 110–18.

3. For years, scholars have been challenging the binary opposition of high art and popular culture and have been problematizing the uninflected use of the two terms. But the 1993 General Agreement on Tariffs and Trade (GATT) discussions over audiovisual products illustrated the degree to which the North American mainstream press continues to reproduce and valorize a dichotomy that cultural scholars and fans of paracinema find problematic. Throughout the debate, the press consistently associated French cinema with high art and American movies with popular culture. Often this polarization was framed in terms of the two big blockbuster movies of 1993—*Germinal* and *Jurassic Park*. European films such as *Diva* (1981), *La femme Nikita* (1991), and *The Crying Game* (1992) were, for the most part, conveniently left out of a discussion that alternately characterized European cinema as artsy or boring—the antithesis of popular. See Matthew Fraser, "A Question of Culture: The Canadian Solution Resolves a GATT Standoff," *MacLean's* (Canada), 27 December 1993, 50; and David Lawday, "France Guns for Clint Eastwood," *U.S. News and World Report*, 13 December 1993, 72. Even the alternative press tended to replicate the European film–high art versus American movies–popular culture polarization in its discussion. See Daniel Singer, "GATT and the Shape of Our Dreams," *Nation*, 17 January 1994, 54.

4. Carol J. Clover, "Her Body, Himself: Gender in the Slasher Film," *Representations* 20 (fall 1987): 187.

5. Most art cinema mail-order companies separate films into generic categories, but Home Film Festival simply lists titles alphabetically—to similarly startling effect. In *Program Guide* no. 12, for example, George Romero's *Night of the Living Dead* (1968) comes between Charles Laughton's *Night of the Hunter* (1955) and Paolo and Vittorio Taviani's *Night of Shooting Stars* (1982) (*Home Film Festival Program Guide* no. 12, 140).

6. The 1996–1997 Sinister Cinema Catalog does list "Mexican Horr/Sci-fi" and "Spaghetti Westerns" as separate categories.

7. Ginette Vincendeau, *Encyclopedia of European Cinema* (New York: Facts on File, 1995), 327.

8. *Mondo Video Catalog*, Mondo Video, Cookeville, Tenn., n.d., n.p. One scholarly treatment that does emphasize the horror in Pasolini's films, albeit not as brutally as Mondo's catalog, is Leo Bersani and Ulysse Dutoit, "Merde Alors: Pasolini's *Salo*," *October*, no. 13 (summer 1980): 23–35.

9. See Carol J. Clover, *Men, Women, and Chainsaws: Gender in the Modern Horror Film* (Princeton, N.J.: Princeton University Press, 1992); and Linda J. Williams, "Film Bodies: Gender, Genre, and Excess," in *Film Genre Reader II*, ed. Barry Keith Grant (Austin: University of Texas Press, 1995), 142. Williams article hereafter cited in text.

10. Internal quote taken from Mary Ann Doane, *The Desire to Desire: The Woman's Film of the 1940s* (Bloomington: Indiana University Press, 1987), 95.

11. Amos Vogel, *Film as a Subversive Art* (New York: Random House, 1974), 277; hereafter cited in text.

12. See, for example, Angela Carter, *The Sadeian Woman and the Ideology of Pornography* (New York: Pantheon Books, 1978); Gilles Deleuze, "Coldness and Cruelty," in *Masochism,* trans. Jean McNeil (New York: Zone Books, 1989); Jane Gallop, *Thinking through the Body* (New York: Columbia University Press, 1988); and Gallop, *Intersections: A Reading of Sade with Bataille, Blanchot, and Klossowski* (Lincoln: University of Nebraska Press, 1981).

For related discussions on the cultural meaning of sadistic representations, see Georges Bataille, *Visions of Excess: Selected Writings, 1927–1939,* trans. Allan Stoekl with Carl R. Lovitt and Donald M. Leslie Jr. (Minneapolis: University of Minnesota Press, 1985); and Linda Williams, "Power, Pleasure, and Perversion: Sadomasochistic Film Pornography," in *Hardcore* (Berkeley and Los Angeles: University of California Press, 1989), 184–229.

13. Gallop, *Thinking through the Body,* 18.

14. Laura Kipnis, "(Male) Desire and (Female) Disgust: Reading *Hustler,*" in *Bound and Gagged: Pornography and the Politics of Fantasy in America* (New York: Grove Press, 1996), 139. The essay is also printed in Kipnis, *Ecstasy Unlimited: On Sex, Gender, Capital, and Aesthetics* (Minneapolis: University of Minnesota Press, 1993).

15. See Carol J. Clover, *Men, Women, and Chainsaws;* Linda Williams, "Film Bodies," and *Hardcore;* and Robin Wood, "Return of the Repressed," *Film Comment,* July–August 1978, 25–32, "Gods and Monsters," *Film Comment,* September–October 1978, 19–25, and the horror chapters in *Hollywood from Reagan to Vietnam* (New York: Columbia University Press, 1986).

16. Carlos Clarens, *An Illustrated History of the Horror Film* (New York: Capricorn Books, 1967), 147–48.

17. Eric Schaefer, "Resisting Refinement: The Exploitation Film and Self-Censorship," *Film History* 6, no. 3 (1994): 293–313.

18. André Balazs, ed., *Hollywood Handbook* (New York: Universe Publishing, 1996), 85.

19. See Amos Vogel, *Film as a Subversive Art.*

20. A. S. Hamrah and Joshua Glenn, "Monsters, Sex, Sci-Fi, and Kung Fu," *Utne Reader,* July–August 1995, 30.

21. Bernard Weinraub, "Directors Fight for GATT's Final Cuts and Print," *New York Times,* 12 December 1993, 14.

22. Fredric Jameson, *Signatures of the Visible* (New York: Routledge, 1992), 14; hereafter cited in text.

23. As Jeffrey Sconce has noted, however, paracinema culture does construct itself in opposition to cineast or high-cinema culture. Thus it is often in the odd position of both challenging/destroying and upholding binary oppositions.

24. Lawrence W. Levine, *Highbrow/Lowbrow: The Emergence of Cultural Hierarchy in America* (Cambridge: Harvard University Press, 1988), 86. Hereafter cited in text.

25. Michael J. Weldon, *Psychotronic Video Guide,* vii.

26. Elliot Forbes, "The 'Lost' World," 41. As Eric Schaefer pointed out to me, the name "Elliot Forbes" is most likely a pseudonym. Elliot Forbes was the fictitious name of hygiene lecturers who spoke at showings of Kroger Babb's sex hygiene blockbuster *Mom and Dad* (1944), which played for decades. There were as many as twenty-four different "Elliot Forbeses" traveling around the country at any given point in the late forties as roadshow units of *Mom and Dad* moved from town to town. This author's use of the Forbes name reinforces the irony and playfulness of trash fans. I'm indebted to Eric Schaefer for this information.

For an interesting article on mainstream video collecting, see Charles Tashiro, "The Contradictions of Video Collecting," *Film Quarterly* 50, no. 2 (winter 1996–1997): 11–18.

27. The U.S. version of Andrzej Zulawski's terrifying *Possession* (France and West Germany, 1981), for example, was cut from its original running time of 120 minutes to 81 minutes. The cutting rendered the film virtually incomprehensible.

28. The other place this happens, of course, is the World Wide Web, where independent film and video companies engage in direct marketing and sales. Browsing the Web, consumers can find everything from *Burnin' Love* (1996), a direct-to-video rockabilly vampire flick featuring several Elvis impersonators, to a subtitled VHS version of Guy Debord's Situationist film masterpiece, *Society of the Spectacle.* Levine describes sacralization—the division of culture into high and low culture—as a historical process that took place during the latter half of the nineteenth century. Before then, he says, no art form—opera, painting, theater—was "elevated above other forms of expressive culture . . . they were part of the general culture and were experienced in the midst of a broad range of other cultural genres by a catholic audience that cut through class and social lines" (Lawrence W. Levine, *Highbrow/Lowbrow,* 149).

29. This is the Spanish-language version of *Dracula* that Universal Studios made at the same time that Tod Browning was shooting *Dracula.* Directed by George Melford, the film uses essentially the same script and sets. The film stars Carlos Villarias in the role of the count; Lupita Tovar plays Eva.

30. The Home Film Festival (HFF) list doesn't carry many low-culture titles. Interestingly, *Texas Chainsaw Massacre* (1974), which is part of the Museum of Modern Art's film collection, is not part of the list, but *Night of the Living Dead* is. Whereas HFF carries mainly art-horror titles, Facets handles an extensive list of slasher, cult, and horror films. Here, the interesting thing is not so much which titles aren't carried as which titles are specifically listed as horror and which aren't. David Cronenberg's films, for example, are all listed under the heading "Canadian Cinema," with the following catalog note: "David Cronenberg has matured from his early B-movie period into a filmmaker whose films transcend the horror genre."

Joseph Ruben's *The Stepfather* (1987) is listed under "Recent American Cinema." *Facets Catalog* no. 12, 72, 216.

31. While upscale mail-order video companies do tend to carry some low-genre titles, the sense that they *are* low-genre titles is clearly part of the marketing ploy. *Facets Multimedia Catalog No. 14,* for example, contains a "Guilty Pleasures section." Here consumers can find some of the staples of the paracinema trade: low-budget sci-fi flicks, cult films, Elvis Presley movies, trailers and commercials. That they are marketed as "guilty pleasures," however, inscribes a value hierarchy into the Facets catalog, one that is completely missing from the paracinema catalogs described earlier.

32. Peter M. Nichols, "A Hard Sell, Those Little French Films," *New York Times,* 26 June 1996, H29.

33. Ibid.

34. In part, this may be because of a heavy reliance on sales to institutions like university libraries and media centers and other specialized video rental stores.

35. Here I'm including the work of directors such as Dario Argento, Jess Franco, Lucio Fulci, Jean Rollin, and Andrzej Zulawski.

36. Susan Sontag, "The Decay of Cinema," *New York Times Magazine,* 25 February 1996, 60–61; hereafter cited in text.

37. See Timothy Corrigan, *A Cinema without Walls: Movies and Culture after Vietnam*; Thomas Elsaesser, *New German Cinema: A History* (New Brunswick, N.J.: Rutgers University Press, 1989); and Jill Forbes, *The Cinema in France after the New Wave* (Bloomington: Indiana University Press, 1992).

38. Peter Greenaway, Rainer Werner Fassbinder, and Bertrand Blier are some notable exceptions to this. I should also mention that post-1970 films by the "classic" directors are usually included—Godard's *Every Man for Himself* (1980), Fellini's *Intervista* (1988). It's also interesting to note that not all the films have subtitles. Luminous Film and Video Wurks provides a wider selection of contemporary European art films than most other companies do.

39. Dick Hebdige, *Subculture: The Meaning of Style* (1979; reprint, New York: Routledge, 1987).

40. Richard Kadrey treats the paracinema subculture as part of a larger consumer (subculture) group that he identifies as "covert" or "fringe." See Richard Kadrey, *Covert Culture Sourcebook* (New York: St. Martin's Press, 1993); and Kadrey, *Covert Culture Sourcebook 2.0* (New York: St. Martin's Press, 1994).

41. European Trash Cinema, Luminous Film and Video and Wurks, and Video Search of Miami all carry some hard-core titles.

42. This is the only qualitative distinction that the catalogs make—films that require ironized strategies of reading and films that don't. It's important to note, however, that films that don't are not considered better (or worse) than the ones that do—just different.

43. *Sinister Cinema* catalog, 12.

44. The reviewer does admit that "Harvey's direction has a weird flair,

sometimes suggesting a throwback to the silent days and drawing a kind of awkward honesty out of the actors." Phil Hardy, Tom Milne and Paul Willemen, eds., *The Encyclopedia of Horror Movies* (New York: Harper and Row, 1986), 147; hereafter cited in text.

45. *Sinister Cinema* catalog, 21.

46. Kyrou wrote: "Je vous en conjure apprenez à voir les 'mauvais' films, ils sont parfois sublimes" [I beg you, learn to see "bad" films; they are sometimes sublime]. Ado Kyrou, *Le surréalisme au cinéma*, 276; translation mine.

47. In an article that originally appeared in *L'Avant-scène du cinéma* 70 (May 1967), Godard confessed his desire to put everything into his films. "If I have a secret ambition," he said, "it is to be put in charge of the French newsreel services. All my films have been reports on the state of the nation; they are newsreel documents, treated in a personal manner perhaps, but in terms of contemporary actuality." Later in the same piece, he said, "everything should be put into a film. When people ask why I talk—or have my characters talk—about Vietnam . . . I refer the questioner to his own newspaper. It's all there. And it's all mixed-up. This is why I'm so attracted by television." Quoted in Tom Milne, ed. and trans., *Godard on Godard* (New York: Da Capo Press, 1972), 239.

48. That is, Godard's films reflect, interact with, and frequently advocate action on specific political issues of the 1960s—the Algerian and Vietnam wars, for example—and his social critique of commercial consumer culture is more pointed and philosophically oriented than the subversive analyses practiced by paracinema culture. But paracinema culture's circulation of banned and censored films and its devotion to what David Sanjek calls "uniqueness of vision" gives it a political edge not unlike Godard's own. Paracinema fanzines, as Sanjek notes, "value most works which bear the mark of an uninhibited visionary sensibility, one which pushes the boundaries of social, sexual, and aesthetic assumptions." David Sanjek, "Fan's Notes: The Horror Film Fanzine," *Literature/Film Quarterly* 18, no. 3 (1990): 153.

49. Monogram (1930–1953) was "the king of Hollywood's poverty row studios." It changed its name to Allied Artists in 1953 and continued making low-budget "youth-oriented features" and exploitation films and releasing foreign horror films until the 1970s. See Michael Weldon, *The Psychotronic Encyclopedia*, xv.

50. James Naremore, "Authorship and the Cultural Politics of Film Criticism," *Film Quarterly* 44, no. 1 (fall 1990): 18–19.

51. J. Hoberman and Jonathan Rosenbaum, *Midnight Movies* (New York: Da Capo Press, 1983), 25; hereafter cited in text.

52. "Sa présence dans un film, quel qu'il soit, suffit à provoquer la beauté. La violence contenue dont témoignent la sombre phosphorescence des yeux, le profil d'aigle, l'arc orgueilleux des sourcils, le saillant des pommettes, le courbe amère et dure de la bouche, la fabuleuse puissance du torse, voilà ce qui est donné, et que le pire metteur en scène ne peut avilir." Michel Mourlet, "Apologie de la violence," *Cahiers du cinéma* 18, no. 107 (May 1960): 24–25; translation mine. Also quoted by Hoberman and Rosenbaum, 26.

53. "Charlton Heston, par son existence seule *en dehors de tout film,* donne au cinéma une définition plus juste que des films comme *Hiroshima* ou *Citizen Kane* dont l'esthétique ignore oe récuse Charlton Heston." Mourlet, 25; translation and italics mine. Also quoted by Hoberman and Rosenbaum, 26.

54. On the other side of the Atlantic, avant-garde filmmaker Jack Smith launched a Maria Montez cult that shared many characteristics with the Mac-Mahon cult but that also—as J. Hoberman and Jonathan Rosenbaum point out—can be read as a "feminine counterweight to the macho persuasions of the French." See Hoberman and Rosenbaum, *Midnight Movies,* 31–34.

55. Michel Mourlet, "Apologie de la violence," *Cahiers du cinéma* 18, no. 107 (May 1960): 24–27.

56. Steven Shaviro, *The Cinematic Body* (Minneapolis: University of Minnesota Press, 1993), vii.

57. A special article that appeared in the spring 1993 *TLA Film and Video Quarterly* demonstrates the degree to which the scandalous aspects of art and avant-garde cinema, on the one hand, and horror, on the other, appear—to the commercial eye, at least—inseparable. In "Guess Who's Coming *as* Dinner," Eric Moore gives a quick rundown of films that treat the theme of cannibalism. Here such films as *Delicatessen; The Cook, the Thief, His Wife, and Her Lover;* and *Sweeney Todd* are listed beside *Night of the Living Dead, The Texas Chainsaw Massacre* Parts 1 and 2, and *Bloodsucking Pharaohs of Pittsburgh* (also *Bloodsucking Pharaohs in Pittsburgh*) as classics of the "cannibal-flick" genre. Eric Moore, "Guess Who's Coming *as* Dinner?" *TLA Film and Video Quarterly* (spring 1993): 23. The *TLA Film and Video Quarterly* is published by TLA Video Management Inc., 332 South Street, Philadelphia, PA 19147–9923.

58. This is part of the "exploitation" definition given by Thomas Doherty. Thomas Doherty, *Teenagers and Teenpics: the Juvenilization of American Movies in the 1950s* (Boston: Unwin Hyman, 1988), 8. As Eric Schaefer points out, the links between exploitation and European cinema in the United States date from the 1920s when the Hays Office mounted a campaign both to enforce the MPPDA code and to rid the screen of exploitation films. As Schaefer demonstrates, "exploitation films played a significant role in the formulation and maintenance of self-regulatory policy." That is, enforcement of the code was often dictated by what were perceived as the excesses of exploitation cinema. Because exploitation films often failed to obtain the desirable seal of approval, they were released in unaffiliated theaters that became known as bump-and-grind houses, or the exploitation circuit. Foreign films that were refused a seal were also distributed through the same unaffiliated venues. Hedy Lamarr's film *Ecstasy* (1933), which was originally refused the seal of approval, was one film that was, temporarily at least, distributed through the exploitation circuit. See Eric Schaefer, "Resisting Refinement: The Exploitation Film and Self-Censorship," 239–313.

59. Peter Lev, *The Euro-American Cinema* (Austin: University of Texas Press, 1993), 8.

60. That impression persists to this day. "People see 'French video' in the phone book," Donna Sayada, the owner of Video France, said in a 1996 interview, "and they think it's either highbrow cultural stuff or it's porno. . . . You should hear some of the calls we get." Peter M. Nichols, "A Hard Sell, Those Little French Films," H29.

61. "*Last Tango in Paris* has the same kind of hypnotic excitement as the . . . *[Rite of Spring]*," Kael writes, "the same primitive force, and the same thrusting, jabbing eroticism. The movie breakthrough has finally come. Exploitation films have been supplying mechanized sex—sex as physical stimulant but without any passion or emotional violence. The sex in *Last Tango in Paris* expresses the characters' drives." Pauline Kael, "Last Tango in Paris," in Pauline Kael, *For Keeps* (New York: Dutton, 1994), 450; reprinted from Kael, *Reeling* (1976).

62. Michael F. Mayer, *Foreign Films on American Screens* (New York: Arco, 1965), 1–3.

63. Kristin Thompson and David Bordwell, *Film History: An Introduction* (New York: McGraw-Hill, 1994), 386.

64. For a good account of the relationship between the Production Code, exploitation films, and European art cinema of the 1930s and 1940s—the period that set the stage for the 1950s and 1960s—see Eric Schaefer, "Resisting Refinement: The Exploitation Film and Self-Censorship."

65. "Parochial Uproar in Ft. Lee: Panics before Foreign Art Films," *Variety*, 24 February 1960, p. 24, col. 3.

66. In fact, Hollywood's attempt to compete for art film audiences has much to do with the fact that the traditional moviegoing base had been eroded. As Staiger points out, younger, better-educated people were more likely to go to the movies than older, less-educated people. These people had different tastes from the "masses." As Staiger notes, "while the 'masses' were not especially attracted to 'realism' or 'message' pictures, art-house audiences were typified as preferring those films." Janet Staiger, *Interpreting Films: Studies in the Historical Reception of American Cinema* (Princeton, N.J.: Princeton University Press, 1992), 185, chap. 9. Douglas Gomery concurs, noting that audience studies "found that art theatres attracted persons of above-average education, more men than women and many solitary movie-goers. This was the crowd who attended the opera, theatre, lectures and ballet." Douglas Gomery, *Shared Pleasures: A History of Movie Presentation in the United States* (Madison: University of Wisconsin Press, 1992), 189.

67. Staiger, *Interpreting Films,* 184.

68. Kadrey, *Covert Culture Sourcebook,* 1.

69. A few minutes into *Un chien andalou,* a man—played by Luis Buñuel—slices open a woman's eye with a razor. To gauge from student responses when I show the film in class, the segment has lost none of its power to shock and horrify the spectator, to act directly on the spectator's body.

70. Some of these defy all attempts to categorize. Mondo describes *Salome* (Neon Vampires), for example, as "one of the most truly bizarre films of all-time . . .

this all-vampire filming of the classic play, *Salome*. Nearly all the actors wear vampire fangs and glow-in-the-dark costumes." There are also films that could probably be unproblematically classified as horror or exploitation if they weren't produced by art film directors. Mondo describes *Tenderness of the Wolves* "as a German *Henry: Portrait of Serial Killer*" and calls it "an incredibly slick film produced by Rainer Werner Fassbinder." The film apparently "depicts the life of an infamous German serial killer who drank the blood of his victims." Mondo warns that patrons must be over eighteen years old to purchase a video of the movie.

71. Clover, *Men, Women, and Chainsaws*, 21.

72. William Paul, *Laughing Screaming: Modern Hollywood Horror and Comedy* (New York: Columbia University Press, 1994), 32; hereafter cited in text. Paul's analysis owes a great deal to Bakhtin's formulation of carnival, which posits that carnival temporarily empowers the lower orders (in both the individual body and society at large) and affirms "the possibility of alternative relations in the midst of order and control; it is the model for a society that is not slavishly determined by any one structure or conceived in terms of any one model or theory. . . . The carnivalesque is an unreal, fictive, theatrical element within history and society (within discourse) that serves to give critical perspectives on social reality, on 'things as they are.'" David Carroll, "Narrative, Heterogeneity, and the Question of the Political: Bakhtin and Lyotard," in *The Aims of Representation: Subject/Text/History*, ed. Murray Krieger (New York: Columbia University Press, 1987), 91, 95. See also Mikhail Bakhtin, *Rabelais and His World*, trans. Hélène Iswolsky (Bloomington: Indiana University Press, 1984). It should be noted that carnival can also be read as a means not of transgression but of containment, a tool for maintaining social hierarchical structures. See Arthur Kroker, *The Possessed Individual: Technology and the French Postmodern* (New York: St. Martin's Press, 1992); and Michael André Bernstein, *Bitter Carnival: Ressentiment and the Abject Hero* (Princeton, N.J.: Princeton University Press, 1992).

73. Lack of cause and effect and strategic use of discontinuous editing also link these films with exploitation cinema, which, as Eric Schaefer points out, can use similar techniques because of their reliance on forbidden spectacle. And it's a key feature of almost all European horror films made from 1956 to 1984. As Cathal Tohill and Pete Tombs point out, "linear narrative and logic are always ignored in a *fantastique* [horror] film." Cathal Tohill and Pete Tombs, *Immoral Tales: European Sex and Horror Movies, 1956–1984* (New York: St. Martin's Griffin, 1994), 5.

74. See Raymond Durgnat, "*Freaks,*" *Films and Filming* 9, no. 1 (August 1963): 23.

75. See David F. Friedman (with Don DeNevi), *A Youth in Babylon: Confessions of a Trash-Film King* (Buffalo, N.Y.: Prometheus Books, 1990).

76. See David J. Skal, *The Monster Show: A Cultural History of Horror* (New York: W. W. Norton, 1993) (hereafter cited in text); and Patricia Bosworth, *Diane Arbus* (New York: Alfred A. Knopf, 1984). I have written at greater length on the film elsewhere. See "*One of Us*: Tod Browning's *Freaks*," in *Freakery: Cultural*

Spectacles of the Extraordinary Body, ed. Rosemarie Garland Thomson (New York: New York University Press, 1996), 265–76; and David J. Skal and Elias Savada, "Offend One and You Offend Them All," in *Dark Carnival: The Secret World of Tod Browning* (New York: Anchor Books, 1995), 159–82.

77. Derek Hill, "Cheap Thrills," *Tribune* (London), 29 April 1960, 11.

78. S. S. Prawer, *Caligari's Children: The Film as Tale of Terror* (New York: Da Capo Press, 1980), 37–38.

79. Jim Collins, *Architectures of Excess: Cultural Life in the Information Age* (New York: Routledge, 1995), 131.

80. Robin Wood, "Ideology, Genre, Auteur," in *Film Theory and Criticism,* ed. Gerald Mast, Marshall Cohen, and Leo Braudy, 4th ed. (New York: Oxford University Press, 1992), 478.

81. Gavin Smith, "Foreign Affairs: Which Foreign Films Must Be Seen at All Costs," *Film Comment* 33, no. 4 (July–August 1997): 40–41.

82. Comedy, thrillers, sci-fi, and melodrama all have this ability. Jim Collins has done an excellent job of analyzing the way "the eclecticism of the contemporary genre films involves a hybridity of conventions that works at cross-purposes with the traditional notion of genre as a stable, integrated set of narrative and stylistic conventions." Jim Collins, *Architectures of Excess,* 126.

83. See Paul, *Laughing Screaming.*

84. See Pierre Bourdieu, *Distinction: A Social Critique of the Judgement of Taste,* trans. Richard Nice (Cambridge: Harvard University Press, 1984) (hereafter cited in text); William Paul, *Laughing Screaming;* and V. Vale and Andrea Juno, "Introduction," in Jim Morton (guest editor), *Incredibly Strange Films, RE/Search* no. 10 (San Francisco: *RE/Search,* 1986), 4–6.

85. Quoted in Clover, *Men, Women, and Chainsaws,* 21. See also Clover, 22 n.

86. Vale and Juno, *Incredibly Strange Films,* 4.

87. I'm grateful to Mark Jancovich for reminding me that economics are always a crucial issue. Mark Jancovich, "Cult Fictions: Cult Movies, Subcultural Capital, and the Production of Cultural Distinctions," manuscript, 1998.

2. Medium Cool

1. John Stanley, *The Creature Features Movie Guide* (Pacifica, Calif.: Creatures at Large Publishing, 1981), 11.

2. See Hoberman and Rosenbaum, *Midnight Movies.*

3. This particular double bill was also further evidence of *Freaks'* recuperation as an art house film.

4. Andrew Ross, *No Respect: Intellectuals and Popular Culture* (New York: Routledge, 1989), chap. 6.

5. See Peter Wollen, "The Two Avant-Gardes," in *Readings and Writings: Semiotic Counter-Strategies* (London: New Left Books, 1982).

6. Timothy Corrigan, *A Cinema without Walls,* 28; hereafter cited in text.

7. Peter Wollen, "Godard and Counter-Cinema: *Vent d'Est*," in *Narrative, Apparatus, Ideology,* ed. Philip Rosen (New York: Columbia University Press: 1986), 120–29.

8. John Fiske makes a similar argument in *Television Culture* to demonstrate that conventions of the classic Hollywood text don't apply to TV. See John Fiske, *Television Culture* (New York: Methuen, 1987). I am indebted to Chris Anderson for this reference.

9. André Breton, *Comme dans un bois,* in Alain et Odette Virmaux, *Les Surréalistes et le cinéma,* 278. Originally printed in *L'age du cinéma,* numéro spécial surréaliste, août-novembre, 1951, 26–30. Translation mine.

10. In France, Henri-Georges Clouzot's 1954 film *Les diaboliques* (Diabolique) experimented with the see-it-from-the-beginning policy. Newspaper ads for the film "discouraged moviegoers from seeing the picture except from the beginning. Theater doors were closed at the start of each performance." Clouzot's success with the policy, both in France and later in the United States, inspired Hitchcock to try it with *Psycho* (1960). Stephen Rebello, *Alfred Hitchcock and the Making of Psycho* (New York: Dembner Books, 1990), 21.

11. And it is clear that they were prepared to supply shocks and disruptions to the rest of the audience as well. Pity the poor spectator who went to the cinema on his one free afternoon during the week, only to have Breton and Vaché come bursting in. It is interesting to note also that Christian Metz views *any* viewer outburst, including those that result from a total immersion in the diegesis, as disruptive of the spectatorial identification, or passive viewing, that Hollywood films try to foster. "The outburst itself, once it has been set in motion (an outburst, moreover, which is most often collective) works to dissipate the budding confusion by returning the subjects to their rightful activity, which is not that of the protagonists as it is evolving on the screen. . . . The spectator lets himself be carried away—perhaps deceived for the space of a second—by the anagogic powers belonging to a diegetic film and he begins to act; but it is precisely this action that awakens him, pulls him back from his brief lapse into a kind of sleep, where the action had its root and ends up by restoring the distance between the film and him." See Christian Metz, *The Imaginary Signifier: Psychoanalysis and the Cinema,* trans. Celia Britton, Anwyl Williams, Ben Brewster, and Alfred Guzzetti (Bloomington: Indiana University Press, 1977), 102.

12. "Modernist" and "avant-garde" are vexed terms in cultural studies. As James Naremore and Patrick Brantlinger describe the difference, "modernist art develops of high-culture values. . . . Artistically, the early modernists were proponents of a media-specific formalism." What Peter Bürger calls the "historical avant-garde," on the other hand, "was a radicalized and largely political movement of the 1920s that used technology as a weapon against the institution of high art." In writings on the cinema, "avant-garde" is generally used to refer to abstract or highly experimental works that foreground artistic innovation and privilege a certain radical poetics of cinema over narrative or even philosphical content. The films of Stan

Brakhage, Maya Deren, Man Ray, Dziga Vertov, and Andy Warhol are examples. "Modernist" cinema tends to refer to European auteurist or American independent cinema, which may be experimental on a formal (and narrative level) but is still accessible to the untrained film viewer. As always, the distinction often seems to be made at the level of exhibition space. Modernist cinema is shown in art house theaters and on television, as well as in museums and universities. Avant-garde cinema is rarely screened outside sacralized art spaces—museums, the university, and special exhibition spaces like Millenium in New York. James Naremore and Patrick Brantlinger, eds., *Modernity and Mass Culture* (Bloomington: Indiana University Press, 1991), 9, 10. See also Peter Bürger, *Theory of the Avant-garde,* trans. Michael Shaw (Minneapolis: University of Minnesota, 1987); Greil Marcus, *Lipstick Traces: A Secret History of the Twentieth Century* (Cambridge: Harvard University Press, 1989); and Susan Rubin Suleiman, *Subversive Intent: Gender, Politics, and the Avant-Garde* (Cambridge: Harvard University Press, 1990). For a good discussion of the terms as they apply specifically to film, see Scott MacDonald, *Avant-garde Film: Motion Studies* (New York: Cambridge University Press, 1993); John Orr, *Cinema and Modernity* (Cambridge, England: Polity Press, 1993); Lauren Rabinovitz, *Points of Resistance: Women, Power, and Politics in the New York Avant-garde* (Urbana and Chicago: University of Illinois Press, 1991); P. Adams Sitney, *Visionary Film: The American Avant-garde, 1943–1971* (New York: Oxford University Press, 1979); Juan A. Suárez, *Bike Boys, Drag Queens, and Superstars: Avant-garde, Mass Culture, and Gay Identities in the 1960s Underground Cinema* (Bloomington: Indiana University Press, 1996).

13. The John Ellis quote is taken from John Ellis, *Visible Fictions: Cinema, Television, Video* (London: Routledge and Kegan Paul, 1982), 24.

14. In writing on postmodernism, Jameson uses Lacan's description of schizophrenia as "a suggestive aesthetic model." See Fredric Jameson, *Postmodernism, or The Cultural Logic of Late Capitalism* (Durham, N.C.: Duke University Press, 1991), 26–27. Jameson's book is exhaustive and far-reaching, and the Lacanian model is not the only one he uses.

15. I have stressed the binary gaze/glance theoretical split because of its connection with the high/low opposition that I'm questioning here. There are other ways of theorizing video culture, though. See, for example, Anne Friedberg's discussion of the *mobilized "virtual" gaze* in Friedberg, *Window Shopping: Cinema and the Postmodern* (Berkeley and Los Angeles: University of California Press, 1993).

16. John Thornton Caldwell, *Televisuality: Style, Crisis, and Authority in American Television* (New Brunswick, N.J.: Rutgers University Press, 1995), 27; hereafter cited in text.

17. For more on this, see Barbara Klinger, "The Media Aristocrats: Home Theater and the Domestic Film Experience," *Velvet Light Trap,* no. 42 (fall 1998): 4–19.

18. Similarly, it essentializes one mode of theatrical cinema viewing as the norm. We know that not every patron in a darkened theater is completely absorbed in the on-screen event. After all, people go to the movies for a lot of different rea-

sons: to get warm or to be in an air-conditioned environment, to do something nice for the family, to do something. Once inside the theater, some members of the audience eat, talk, think about business problems, make love, fall asleep, mourn. On the day that John Kennedy was shot, a good friend of mine went to the movies, because, as he put it, he couldn't think of anyplace else to go. He wound up in a theater showing an Elvis Presley film, along with about ten other patrons. Throughout the film, he told me, he heard people sobbing. The sobbing clearly had nothing to do with the film. If any people were distracted viewers, glancing at the screen from time to time instead of gazing at it in rapt attention, these spectators-in-shock-and-mourning were.

19. See Roland Barthes, *S/Z*, trans. Richard Miller (New York: Hill and Wang, 1974). I don't mean to invoke Astruc's conception of the *caméra-stylo* here. Rather, I'd like to suggest a similarity between Barthes's notion that a reader can become the producer of a text and the style of cinema spectatorship fostered or enabled by home viewing systems. For more on Astruc, see Alexandre Astruc, "The Birth of a New Avant-garde: La Caméra Stylo," in *The New Wave: Critical Landmarks*, ed. Peter Graham (New York: Doubleday, 1968), 17–23. Originally published in *L'Ecran français* 144 (March 1948), and in David A. Cook, *A History of Narrative Film*, 3rd ed. (New York: W. W. Norton, 1996), 528–29.

20. I'm borrowing the term "discursive rules" from Lynn Spigel to indicate that "glance theory" is part of a wider cultural debate both about television and about the division between high art and low culture. See Lynn Spigel, "Television in the Family Circle: The Popular Reception of a New Medium," in *Logics of Television: Essays in Cultural Criticism*, ed. Patricia Mellencamp (Bloomington: Indiana University Press, 1990; London: BFI Publishing, 1990), 73–97.

21. It's interesting that only performance and exhibition art seems to be contaminated by the home environment here. After all, nobody claims that you can't lose yourself in a good book (be "kidnapped" by the images) at home, despite the distractions of the domestic environment. Certainly, nobody suggests that it would be somehow disrespectful of *Anna Karenina* to read it at home, with your cat curled up on your lap and your four year old asleep on the couch beside you.

22. In *Videodrome* (1982), an addictive TV transmission opens receptors in the brain that allow the Videodrome signal to take hold. The signal causes a brain tumor that causes hallucinations; these can be recorded and fed back to the viewer via Videodrome. Not only does the signal alter the way the protagonist literally sees the world, but it can be used to program his actions and literally turn him into a machine. In one memorable sequence, Max Renn's body literally opens up to receive a video cassette; his body becomes a VCR.

As Caldwell notes, glance theory tends to ignore industry history. In constructing the way that TV and the home contaminate cinema reception, glance theorists have ignored the way that Hollywood and film colonized television. This is evident in the way the films began appearing on TV, then began to be made for TV, and finally became the primary product sold on specialized subscription cable channels. Similarly, as Christopher Anderson notes, in the late 1950s, Hollywood studios moved into TV production. And now, large "film" corporations such as Disney are buying both TV channels and independent film distribution companies (Disney, for example, bought Miramax). In terms of industry history, the two media giants were always more imbricated than glance theory would allow.

I'm indebted to Jim Naremore for the observation on the colonization of TV space by cinema. For more on the studio system's involvement in TV production, see Christopher Anderson, *Hollywood TV: The Studio System in the Fifties* (Austin: University of Texas Press, 1994).

23. See Andreas Huyssen, *After the Great Divide: Modernism, Mass Culture, Postmodernism* (Bloomington: Indiana University Press, 1986).

24. The Criterion Collection is produced by the Voyager Company, as a joint venture with Janus Films. To save confusion, I will be using "Criterion" here as both an industry and label name. In official literature and on the Criterion Collection Web site, the reference here would be to "Voyager's laser discs." Note: I didn't list 16 mm prints in the text because so many 16 mm prints are terribly dirty, badly spliced, and no longer available. As more and more institutions have begun using laser discs, the 16 mm situation has only gotten worse.

25. CD-ROM, digital video discs (DVD), and other advanced digital technology are in the process of changing viewing and buying patterns yet again.

26. "A Note to the Viewer," http:///www.voyagerco.com/criterion/about/note.html (accessed 8 August 1997).

27. Chris McGowan, "An Appreciation of the *Criterion Collection*," http://www.organa.com/Outerspace/Cargo/Lasers/criterion.html, 1994, page 1 of 2 (accessed 8 May 1997).

Upscale video companies have followed the Criterion Collection's lead in making "restored" versions of films available to the public. Although they don't attempt to package the entire cinema event, videotapes increasingly advertise "extra footage," "director's cut," and "remastered" images and sound. Special collector's versions of *The Wizard of Oz* and *Casablanca* include nondiegetic material at the end of the tape (*The Wizard of Oz*, for example, includes home movie footage of a musical number that never appeared in the film). Restored videos of *Frankenstein* (1931) and *King Kong* (1933) include scenes that were cut from the theatrical releases. In the restored *Frankenstein*, for example, we see the monster throw Maria in the water; in *Kong* we see graphic scenes of the giant ape trampling and killing people as he scours New York looking for "the golden woman," Ann.

While the director's cut is fetishized in this market, too, the competition of auteurist and nonauteurist impulses sometimes creates confusing or disturbing products. The drive to add extra footage is indulged even when it's not clear that such an addition restores original authorial intent (director's cut), and the drive to "remaster" images and sound sometimes results in terrible mistakes. Connoisseur's remastered VHS version of Jean-Luc Godard's revolutionary *Breathless*, for example, corrects the lighting of the original film. No longer are certain frames flooded by dazzling bursts of light or washed out through overexposure. The end result is a film that looks much more like other films of the period than the original *Breathless* did, a film that is perhaps easier to read than the original was, but one that is much less experimental and visually challenging.

28. "The Criterion Collection: Blade Runner," http://www.voyagerco.com/criterion/catalogpage.cgi?bladerunner, n.d., page 1 of 2 (accessed 8 August 1997).

29. In the case of *Blade Runner,* the Criterion Collection's Deluxe letter-boxed laser disc presentation of the international cut was followed by a number of director's workprint theatrical releases and, finally, by the theatrical release of what came to be known as the director's cut in 1992. This is definitely a case of the laser disc and videotape versions of the film creating a fan (or even cult) fan base. See Paul M. Sammon, *Future Noir: The Making of "Blade Runner"* (New York: Harper Prism, 1996). I am indebted to Peter Lev for this reference.

30. Chris McGowan, "An Appreciation of the *Criterion Collection,*" page 1 of 2.

31. Ibid.

32. Ibid.

33. "The Criterion Collection: *Brazil,*" http://www.voyagerco.com/criterion/catalogpage.cgi?brazil, n.d., page 1 of 2 (accessed 8 August 1997).

I realize that these prices are high specifically because the discs are collector's editions. Other discs in the Criterion Collection (discs that aren't collector's editions) cost about half the prices cited here. My point, though, is that dedicated laser disc collection can be costly. Not only are the discs themselves expensive, laser disc culture invites a certain amount of financial investment in home viewing equipment. On the level of cost alone, then, disc culture has a certain class bias built in. The significance of this will become clear later.

34. Of course, fan culture also has obsessive modes of viewing that are quite unlike the modes of viewing generally associated with viewing home movies. Certain films and certain scenes in films are watched repeatedly, studied for previously unnoticed nuances or technical data. And of course, the level of narcissistic involvement is different. When asked what she'd like to watch on television, my friend's three-year-old daughter, Susie, habitually replies, "Susie!" So, into the VCR goes the video that Mom made in Disneyland. For more on home movies, see Patricia Zimmerman, *Reel Families: A Social History of the Amateur Film* (Bloomington: Indiana University Press, 1995).

35. Michael Atkinson, "Obscure Objects: Satisfying Cinephiliac Lusts," *Village Voice,* 22 April 1997, 86.

36. This is a more adversarial market than the "outsider" market that Criterion caters to. I should mention, however, that the markets can overlap. That is, there are collectors who collect both Criterion discs and paracinema tapes. These collectors occupy different collecting sites simultaneously and are addressed differently by each company.

Because the same person can occupy both collecting sites, I'm using "collector" here to refer to the collector as she is constructed by the company—not to essentialize Criterion and paracinema collectors as different kinds of *people*.

37. Paracinema fans share a certain "outlaw" value system with computer hackers who believe that "information should be free." As Michael Weldon writes, "this stuff is out there. You should know about it." So it's not surprising that paracinema magazines and 'zines sometimes include articles about various governments' attempts to control or censor the Net. In addition to articles on Anton LaVey's favorite horror flicks and an article on vintage horror, *Eye* no. 9 includes Lisa Crosby, "Internet Censorship," 15–17, and also an article on chain letters and pyramid schemes, which *Eye* proclaims a "scam." See Thomas Lalli, "Chain Letters and Pyramid Schemes: Don't Get Ripped Off," *Eye*, no. 9, 8–10.

38. "An uncompromising [lit. "rock-hard"] film from master-director, Samuel Fuller." Translation help provided by Manfred Wolf.

39. Once in a very great while, a company will throw in a televised interview with the director. Panaction's version of the *Dario Argento Fashion Show*, for example, contains a TV interview with Argento.

40. Sconce's excellent discussion of excess in paracinema draws on Kristin Thompson's work on excess. Certainly, Thompson's observation—"probably no one ever watches *only* these nondiegetic elements" common to stylistic excess; still the elements "are constantly present, a whole 'film' existing in some sense alongside the narrative film we tend to think of ourselves as watching"—is a wonderful description of the extra critical and fan culture material made available on the discs. See Kristin Thompson, "The Concept of Cinematic Excess," in *Narrative, Apparatus, Ideology: A Film Theory Reader*, ed. Philip Rosen (New York: Columbia University Press, 1986), 132–33. I am indebted to Jeffrey Sconce for this reference.

41. One of the reasons Luminous sells a special documentary about Argento is because he is one of the most beloved and well represented of the paracinema auteurs. Known mainly for making *gialli* (Italian thrillers that are long on affect and short on tightly structured plot) and extremely gory horror films, Argento is a master of mood and suspense. He also creates incredibly beautiful films. His best-known film in the United States is *Suspiria* (1977), a supernatural horror film that's available on commercial video in many video stores. While most of his other films are not available through mainstream venues in the United States, they are readily available through paracinema catalogs. For more information on Argento, see Maitland MacDonagh, *Broken Mirrors/Broken Minds: The Dark Dreams of Dario Argento* (New York: Citadel Press, 1994), or check the Web site for Luminous Film and Video Wurks, http://www.lfvw.com.

42. Compare this to the $49.95 that the Criterion Collection charges for its laser disc of Jack Hill's exploitation classic *Switchblade Sisters* (1974). *Switchblade Sisters* is one of the titles in the special Rolling Thunder series, produced by Quentin Tarantino. Interestingly, the promotional material for the disc features Tarantino as prominently as it does Jack Hill. Tarantino is the Rolling Thunder producer; he provides commentary; he provides "video intro and outro." The disc clearly is

meant to appeal to Tarantino fans as much or even more than it is designed to appeal to exploitation collectors. A special video version of the film, with intro and outro by Tarantino, is available for $79.50, more than the laser.

43. Kadrey, "Director's Cuts," 64.

44. Ibid.

45. The high end of the collection marketplace sometimes fetishizes objects in a way that seems positively screwy to paracinephiles. One of my colleagues showed me a special anniversary edition of *Casablanca* he had purchased. When I asked when he planned to watch it, he looked at me in horror. Apparently, unwrapping the disc and actually watching it was detrimental to its later resale value. He was happy just to have it, still neatly wrapped in cellophane, as part of his collection.

46. As I mentioned earlier, glance theory is riddled with problems. I refer to it here to make clear that even at the "low" end of culture, glance theory has problems.

47. Gazing is a feature of any collector's viewing mode. Many collectors are completists; that is, they collect different versions of the same title and compare them. A tape may be valued simply because it has five minutes of footage not included in the original theatrical release. You have to watch the screen carefully to see all the differences, to know that you've gotten your money's worth.

48. See Marshall McLuhan, *Understanding Media: The Extensions of Man* (New York: McGraw-Hill, 1964), 313–37.

49. Ibid., 22.

50. Ibid., 23.

51. Kadrey, "Director's Cuts," 66.

52. Both paracinema and Criterion Collection materials emphasize auteurism. Here, the director is unproblematically assumed to be the "author," the creative genius behind a work. And the director's stamp—his or her definitive cinematic style and personal obsessions—is assumed to be traceable across the works.

3. Art Houses and Horrorshows

1. Pauline Kael, "Zeitgeist and Poltergeist, or Are Movies Going to Pieces?" in *I Lost It at the Movies,* ed. Pauline Kael, 3rd ed. (Boston and Toronto: Little Brown, 1965), 14; here after cited in text.

2. Writing about Sontag's review of Jack Smith's *Flaming Creatures* (1963), which appeared in *The Nation,* 13 April 1964, Kael observes that "in treating indiscriminateness as a *value,*" Sontag "has become a real swinger." Later in the essay, she observes, "Miss Sontag is on to something and if she stays on and rides it like Slim Pickens, it's the end of criticism, at the very least" (Kael, 19).

3. Kael writes that she was "stunned that so bright a young man could display such shocking taste, preferring a Warner Brothers forties mediocrity to the classics" (Kael, 6). *The Beast with Five Fingers* was also a favorite film of surrealist director Luis Buñuel. Buñuel had worked on the creeping-hand sequences for Warner

Bros., and he paid homage to the film in another film that Kael didn't like, *The Exterminating Angel.*

4. Staiger, *Interpreting Films,* 184–85.

5. Gomery, *Shared Pleasures,* 189.

6. Hoberman and Rosenbaum, *Midnight Movies,* 43.

7. David Skal, *The Monster Show: A Cultural History of Horror* (New York: W. W. Norton, 1993), 15–23.

8. Michael Brodsky, *Detour* (New York: Urizen Books, 1977).

9. Roger Ebert, "Why Movie Audiences Aren't Safe Anymore," *American Film* 6, no. 5 (March 1981): 54–56.

10. See Carol J. Clover, *Men, Women, and Chainsaws;* and Linda Williams, "Film Bodies."

11. Kael begins her essay talking about the frightening, ostentatious display of wealth and power that she sees whenever she goes to Los Angeles. Somehow the Sodom and Gomorrah atmosphere of L.A. is linked to the behavior of movie audiences—to a sort of general lack of taste and "immorality." Roger Ebert takes this a step further in his essay when he reads the frightening behavior of movie audiences at slasher films as part of a disturbing social backlash against women, one that has disturbing moral implications as the audience for *I Spit on Your Grave* seems to approve the most horrific violence being visited on a woman's body. See Ebert, "Why Movie Audiences Aren't Safe Anymore."

12. Hoberman and Rosenbaum, 43.

13. Brodsky, 1.

14. Mikhail Bakhtin, *Rabelais and His World,* trans. Hélène Iswolsky (Bloomington: Indiana University Press, 1984), 153–54.

15. David Gascoyne, *A Short Survey of Surrealism* (San Francisco: City Lights Books, 1982), 40.

16. This marketplace atmosphere had traditionally been a part of movie theater culture. In the early days of cinema, patrons often came in during the middle of a picture. There was entertainment before the program started and during intermissions—raffles, drawings, even bingo games. Theaters sponsored the kinds of promotional gimmicks that we see in grocery stores today. People could get special deals on china, cutlery, and encyclopedia sets by going to the show. During the fifties, however, that began to change.

In an attempt to compete with (and distance themselves from) television, mainstream movie theaters began a program of gentrification and of disciplining the audience. Gimmicks and special entertainment were slowly eliminated; in the 1960s, the introduction of fixed viewing times ("see it from the beginning") gave movies the same profile that theater had always had. For more on this, see Gomery, *Shared Pleasures;* and Richard Maltby and Ian Craven, *Hollywood Cinema: An Introduction* (London: Blackwell, 1995).

17. See Dwight Macdonald, "A Theory of Mass Culture," in *Mass Culture: The*

Popular Arts in America, ed. Bernard Rosenberg and David Manning White (Glencoe, Ill.: Free Press, 1957), 59–73.

18. See Andrew Sarris, "The Birds," in *Confessions of a Cultist,* 84, 86. Essay originally published in *Village Voice,* 4 April 1963.

19. See Andrew Sarris, "Lawrence of Arabia," in *Confessions of a Film Cultist: On the Cinema, 1955–1969* (New York: Simon and Schuster, 1970), 67. Originally published as "Sand Gets in Your Eyes, or The Sheik of Araby," in *Village Voice,* 20 December 1962, 17.

20. Valerie Walkerdine, "Video Replay: Families, Films, and Fantasy," in *Formations of Fantasy,* ed. Victor Burgin, James Donald, and Cora Kaplan (New York: Methuen, 1986), 167.

4. The Scalpel's Edge

1. Philippe Ross, *Les visages de l'horreur* (Paris: Edilig 1985), 63.

2. The quote is taken from Jim Naremore's informal response to an earlier draft of this chapter. Private e-mail memo dated 3 December 1997, Bloomington, Ind.

3. I will be discussing Clarens's, Durgnat's and Rosenbaum's critical positions at greater length later in the chapter.

4. I said that while *Les yeux sans visage* merges with popular horror on some levels, it's still seen primarily as an art film. That is definitely true in the United States, where the film merits inclusion in histories of French cinema and in popular studies of art films, as well as in books about horror cinema. Roy Armes, Alan Lovell, and Alan Williams all mention the film in their studies of French cinema. And as we have already seen, American film critics have embraced the film as an art film and, in many cases, as a masterpiece. It's less clear what kind of "official" position the film holds in France. Many French film histories make no reference to the film at all. Neither René Prédal's *Le Cinéma français depuis* 1945 nor his *Le Cinéma français contemporain* makes any mention of the film, even though between them the two histories note almost all of Franju's other feature titles—as well as several of the documentary shorts. Similarly, René Jeanne and Charles Ford's *Histoire illustrée du cinéma* neglects *Les yeux sans visage* in favor of Franju's feature-length adaptations of classic literary works, *La tête contre les murs* and *Thérèse Desqueyreux* (1962), as well as his short documentaries. Phillippe de Comes and Michel Marmin mention *Les yeux* only as part of a larger discussion of Pierre Brasseur, the actor who played Doctor Génessier in the film. Roger Boussinot's *Encyclopédie du cinéma* includes *Les yeux* as part of Franju's filmography but does not single out the film for special notice. And while Boussinot acknowledges that Franju's best films merit a second look ("[on] gagne à revoir les meilleurs d'entre eux"), he clearly does not share Jonathan Rosenbaum and J. Hoberman's view of *Les yeux* as "possibly Franju's best feature."

Similarly, while the Larousse *Dictionnaire du cinéma* praises Franju's work, it makes no special mention of *Les yeux.* Furthermore, it places the director differently than Anglo-American sources do. The *Dictionnaire* calls Franju the "heir of poetic realism" [héritier du réalisme poétique], linking him to the golden age of Renoir rather than to the surrealism of Bataille, Breton, and Artaud—as Alan Williams, Paul Coates, Raymond Durgnat, and others do. I find this interesting because in a 1959 interview with Truffaut, Franju both admitted the great admiration he had for Renoir's work and expressed his desire to carve out a different aesthetic. "I succeeded [in *Les yeux*]," he told Truffaut, "if the horror reaches the 'poetic uncanny'" [J'y suis arrivé si l'épouvante atteint au fantastique poétique]. Not only is "poetic uncanny" [poétique fantastique] opposed to "poetic realism" [réalisme poétique] in this passage, but it also clearly indicates Franju's own conception of his aesthetic as a fundamentally dreamlike, fundamentally surrealist, fundamentally avant-garde one. In invoking "poetic realism" in its description of Franju's work, then, the *Dictionnaire* both pays him a great compliment (he is the heir to the great tradition established by Renoir) and simultaneously reinscribes him within the classic tradition that he wished to surpass. It denies the revolutionary status that he wished to claim for his concept of cinematic style. And if it makes him seem more respectable, more clearly part of the great French cinematic tradition, it also makes him seem more tame.

There seems to be some lingering uneasiness in French cinema references over Franju's trafficking in a minor or low genre. In many cases, *Les yeux* is notable by its absence in the index listings and discussion; in at least one major work, the style elaborated in the film is reinscribed as part of a classic—rather than surreal—tradition. Even *Cahiers,* which championed the film and tried to build an audience for it, seems uneasy with its status as a horror film and so connects it to the more legitimate aesthetic of film noir. In that sense, *Les yeux sans visage* still seems to exist at the margins of official French film culture. At once too avant-garde and too popular to be included in art cinema discussions, it is, as Paul Coates maintains, a film at the intersection of high and mass cinema. See Roy Armes, *French Cinema* (New York: Oxford University Press, 1985); Alan Lovell, *Anarchist Cinema* (New York: Gordon Press, 1975); Alan Williams, *Republic of Images: A History of French Filmmaking* (Cambridge: Harvard University Press, 1992). Susan Hayward does not mention the film in *French National Cinema.* In fact Franju has only two listings in the index of Hayward's book—one mentioning his connection with Henri Langlois, and one (in conjunction with a longer entry on Alain Resnais) mentioning his short subjects and documentaries. See Susan Hayward, *French National Cinema* (New York: Routledge, 1993).

See also René Prédal, *Le cinéma français depuis 1945* (Editions Nathan, 1991); Prédal, *Le cinéma français contemporain* (Paris: Editions du Cerf 1984); René Jeanne and Charles Ford, *Histoire illustrée du cinéma,* vol. 3 (Verviers, Belgium: Editions Gérard and Marabout Université, 1966); Phillippe de Comes and Michel Marmin, *Le cinéma français, 1930–1960* (Paris: Editions Atlas, 1984); Roger Boussinot, *L'Encyclopédie du cinéma* (Paris: Les Savoirs Bordas, 1995), 805; Jean Loup Passek, ed., *Dictionnaire du cinéma* (Paris: Librairie Larousse, 1986), 266; and Paul Coates,

Film at the Intersection of High and Mass Culture (Cambridge: Harvard University Press, 1994). In what seems to be a clear allusion to Artaud's notion of cinema as a kind of witchcraft, Coates describes Franju's films as a "witchlike fusion of melodrama and expressionism" (Coates, 77). See also Antonin Artaud, "Witchcraft and the Cinema," in *The Shadow and Its Shadow*, ed. Paul Hammond, 113–15. For the context of the original "J'y suis arrivé si l'épouvante atteint au fantastique poétique" quote, see François Truffaut, "Entretien avec Georges Franju," *Cahiers du cinéma* 17, no. 101 (November 1959): 7. The same 1959 issue that contained Truffaut's interview with Franju used a still from *Les yeux* for its cover. The issue came out months before the film officially opened in Paris. See *Cahiers du cinéma* (November 1959).

5. Again, this quote comes from an informal response to an earlier draft of this chapter. Private e-mail memo from James Naremore, 3 December 1997, Bloomington, Ind.

6. Bruno Gay-Lussac, "La Chronique de Bruno Gay-Lussac," *L'Express*, no. 456 (10 March 1960): 36.

7. "A voir, à écouter, à savoir," *L'Express*, no. 456 (10 March 1960): 24.

8. Michèle Manceaux, "La Semaine," *L'Express*, no. 455 (3 March 1960): 38.

9. *Variety*, 26 August 1959.

10. Gay-Lessac, 36.

11. Raymond Durgnat, *Franju* (Berkeley and Los Angeles: University of California Press, 1968), 28; hereafter cited in text.

12. Bataille left Breton's circle in the late twenties and went on to found his own renegade surrealist journal, *Documents*. Running for about two years, *Documents* was instrumental in publishing photographs and literary pieces by artists and writers who were temporarily or permanently out of favor with Breton. It provided an alternative surrealist voice, one that developed alongside mainstream surrealism and, some critics argue, had a profound effect on mainstream surrealism's aesthetic development.

I'm indebted to Adam Lowenstein for his interesting discussion on the way Bataille's aesthetic informs Franju's early work. Adam Lowenstein, "Films without a Face: Surrealism, Horror, and Historical Trauma in the Cinema of Georges Franju," manuscript, 1996. A revised version of this MS was published. See Adam Lowenstein, "Films without a Face: Shock Horror in the Cinema of Georges Franju," *Cinema Journal* 37, no. 4 (summer 1998): 37–58. For more on the relationship between *Documents* and the other ("official") surrealist journals, see Rosalind Krauss, "Corpus Delicti"; and Dawn Ades, "Photography and the Surrealist Text," in *L'Amour Fou: Photography and Surrealism*, ed. Rosalind Krauss (Washington, D.C.: Corcoran Gallery of Art; New York: Abbeville Press, 1985).

13. I'm indebted to Jim Naremore for help with editing and wording this passage.

14. Along with Henri Langlois, Georges Franju cofounded the Cinémathèque Française, an organization dedicated to the preservation and exhibition of great old films. As Hoberman and Rosenbaum note, Langlois was the "dean of 'French' trash

collectors" (*Midnight Movies*, 23), and the programs he orchestrated at the Cinémathèque were often eclectic, paracinematic: Luis Buñuel's Mexican films dubbed into German with Portuguese subtitles, Satyajit Ray's *Apu* trilogy projected out of sequence. But if Langlois seemed determined to institutionalize paracinema aesthetics, he was also determined to give young French cineasts a good understanding of the historical development of film. As Jean-Luc Godard, writing under the pen name of Hans Lucas, or "H.L.," noted, "without Langlois' gigantic effort, today the history of French cinema would be little more than that of Bardèche and Brasillach [authors of the 1935 film history *Histoires du cinéma*]. . . . thanks to Henri Langlois, we now know that ceilings do not date from *Citizen Kane* but from Griffith, of course, and from Gance; that cinéma vérité does not date from Jean Rouch, but from John Ford; the American comedy from a Ukrainian filmmaker; and the photography of *Metropolis* from an anonymous French cameraman who was a contemporary of Bougereau." Jean-Luc Godard, "Grace à Henri Langlois," *Le Nouvel Observateur*, 12 January 1966, 36–37.

As usual with Godard, the reference is as pointedly political as it is aesthetic. Robert Brasillach, one of the authors of the *Histoire*, was considered to be a notorious collaborator with the Nazis. In the trials that followed World War II, he was sentenced to death. According to Germaine Brée, Maurice Bardèche was "just as brilliant, just as disturbed, and just as biased toward fascist social action" as Brasillach. The implication, then, is that without Langlois, film history would have remained the providence of the radical right or—to put it more bluntly—that Langlois liberated film history from the French fascists. See Germaine Brée, *Twentieth Century Literature*, trans. Louise Guiney (Chicago: University of Chicago Press, 1983), 15–17, 70–71. See also Maurice Bardèche and Robert Brasillach, *Histoire du cinéma* (Paris: Denoël et Steele, 1935). For more on Henri Langlois and the Cinémathèque, see Hoberman and Rosenbaum, *Midnight Movies*; Glenn Myrent and Georges P. Langlois, *Henri Langlois: First Citizen of Cinema*, trans. Lisa Nesselson, Twayne's Filmmakers Series (New York: Twayne, 1995); and Richard Roud, *A Passion for Films: Henri Langlois and the Cinémathèque Française* (New York: Viking Press, 1983).

15. Myrent and Langlois, *Henri Langlois*, 26. For more on the surrealist response to these films, see the Surrealist Group, "Some Surrealist Advice," in Hammond, *The Shadow and Its Shadow*, 51–52; and Ado Kyrou, *Le surréalisme au cinéma* (Paris: Le Terrain Vague, 1963), 77, 79, 83, 89.

16. Roud, *A Passion for Films*, 17.

17. Gene Wright, *Horrorshows* (New York: Facts on File Publications, 1986), 70; hereafter cited in text.

18. "House of Pain" comes from Erle C. Kenton's *The Island of Lost Souls* (1933). Here Dr. Moreau, played to terrifying, over-the-top effect by Charles Laughton, changes animals into humans by performing unbearably painful vivisections. The House of Pain is the name that Moreau gives to his operating theater.

19. This will be covered at greater length later in the chapter.

20. Richard von Busack, "Seeing behind the Mask of Horror," MetroActive Web site (20 June 1996), http://www.metroactive.com/papers/metro/06.20.96/eyes-face-9625.html; accessed 17 October 1997, 5.

21. See Michel Foucault, *The Birth of the Clinic: An Archaeology of Medical Perception,* trans. A. M. Sheridan Smith (New York: Vintage Books, 1973), 196; and Loewenstein, 11.

22. Christian de Chalonge's *Docteur Petiot* (1990) also plays on the links between medicine, horror, and the Nazi occupation of France. Based on the case of a real serial killer, the film self-consciously uses historic film footage and copies shots and scenes from classical horror films to make its point. See Guy Austin, *Contemporary French Cinema* (New York: Manchester University Press, 1996), 34–37.

23. During the same period, another Left Bank filmmaker, Alain Resnais, was also making films that dealt with historical memory and the trauma of the war. *La nuit et le brouillard* (Night and Fog, 1955) and *Hiroshima mon amour* (1959) resemble *Les yeux sans visage* both in their anxiety about the way history is constructed and memory is lived and in their depiction of a history played out on and through the body.

24. See Hannah Arendt, *Eichmann in Jerusalem: A Report on the Banality of Evil* (New York: Viking Press, 1963).

25. Alice Yaeger Kaplan, *Reproductions of Banality: Fascism, Literature, and French Intellectual Life* (Minneapolis: University of Minnesota Press, 1986), 19.

26. Guy Austin, *Contemporary French Cinema* (New York: Manchester University Press, 1996), 21. The book is distributed in the United States by St. Martin's Press.

27. Résistancialisme has taken a beating in recent years. The trials of Klaus Barbie and Paul Bousquet and the debate over the wartime activities of the Catholic Church and of François Mitterand have forced the French to reexamine the French role in the deportation of French Jews and to question the myth of universal resistance. See for example, Alain Finkielkraut, *Remembering in Vain: The Klaus Barbie Trial and Crimes against Humanity,* trans. Roxanne Lapidus with Sima Godfrey (New York: Columbia University Press, 1989); and Alice Yaeger Kaplan, *Reproductions of Banality.*

28. James Monaco, *Alain Resnais* (New York: Oxford University Press, 1979), 22.

29. Gay-Lussac, 36.

30. Philippe Ross, *Visages de l'horreur,* 64.

31. Another film that does this is Michael Powell's *Peeping Tom,* in which the main character—a murderous photographer who'd been tormented, experimented on, and psychologically abused throughout his childhood by his renowned father—is played by Carl Boehm, a German actor. In case we fail to get the point, a former colleague of the protagonist's father is also given a German accent.

32. Michel Delahaye, "Gothique flamboyant," *Cahiers du cinéma* 18, no. 106 (April 1960): 48; hereafter cited in text.

33. "Franju se sert du réel pour transcender l'épouvante et de l'épouvante pour transcender du réel" (50).

34. Works on horror generally reprint stills from the operating-room sequence.

35. See James Naremore, *More than Night: Film Noir in Its Contexts* (Berkeley and Los Angeles: University of California Press, 1998).

36. Throughout the late fifties and sixties, Hammer Studios made a series of period color movies that definitively marked the studio's style. Icons such as Dracula, Frankenstein and his monsters, and the Mummy were revived, but in color and with what *The BFI Companion to Horror* calls "a robustness" never seen before. Using highly saturated colors, Hammer put out films that seemed much gorier than the Universal films of the 1930s. At the same time, the studio increased the latent sexual content of the films by featuring buxom women in low-cut dresses. Monsters such as Dracula, portrayed for Hammer by Christopher Lee, were athleticized, eroticized, and perhaps made to seem more cruel. And they did physical battle with their foes. For the French, then, Hammer represented visceral, sensational, and supernatural horror—with supernatural or mythic monsters. For more information on Hammer studies, see the entry in the *The BFI Companion to Horror*, ed. Kim Newman, 145; and Peter Hutchings, *Hammer and Beyond: the British Horror Film* (New York: Manchester University Press, 1993).

37. Manceaux, "La semaine," *L'Express*, no. 455 (3 March 1960): 38.

38. Quoted in Robin Buss, *French Film Noir* (New York: Marion Boyars, 1994), 215. I am indebted to Jim Naremore for this reference.

39. E-mail message from Eric Schaefer, 13 August 1998 ("Childhood Memories").

40. Clarens, *An Illustrated History of the Horror Film*, 138.

41. The Grand Guignol was a French theatrical phenomenon that ran from 1897 to 1962. The theater was noted for its unflinching displays of graphic violence, gore for its own sake. See Mel Gordon, *The Grand Guignol: Theatre of Fear and Terror* (New York: Amok Press, 1988).

42. And he did so in a very Castle-like, gimmicky fashion. See Linda Williams, "Learning to Scream," *Sight and Sound* 4, no. 12 (December 1994): 14–17. For an interesting discussion of *Psycho*'s place in 1950s and early 1960s horror culture, see Mark Jancovich, *Rational Fears: American Horror in the 1950s* (New York: Manchester University Press, 1996), 220–60. Manchester University Press titles are distributed in the United States by St. Martin's Press.

43. See Betty Friedan, *The Feminine Mystique* (New York: Norton, 1963); Philip Wylie, *Generation of Vipers*, 2d. ed. (New York: Rinehart, 1955). Friedan's *Feminine Mystique* became one of the founding texts of the second wave of feminism in the United States. Wylie's *Vipers*, first published in 1942, became the major articulation of Momism.

44. The film that addresses all of these is, of course, *Them* (Gordon Douglas, 1954), a sci-fi thriller in which "atomic testing in the New Mexico desert produces fifteen foot long ants capable of killing humans with massive injections of formic acid" (Clarens, 131–32).

45. I am indebted to Eric Beckstrom for this observation.

46. "'Earth' Hot $17,000, Frisco—'Bird' Big 12 G," *Variety,* 4 April 1962, 10. The following week, *Variety* again estimated box office receipts at $13,000. As for relative comparisons of the term "good," the same issue called *Experiment in Terror* "brisk" and "robust" at $20,000. A double bill of two reissues, *The Guns of Navarone* and *Breakfast at Tiffany's,* brought in $10,000. "'Terror' Robust $20,000 in Frisco," *Variety,* 18 April 1962, 18.

47. "U.S. Premiere of Horror Films," *San Francisco Examiner,* 30 March 1962, 27.

48. Ibid.

49. Loewenstein, 15.

50. Jonathan Rosenbaum, *Eyes without a Face* (capsule review), *Chicago Reader* (1995), reprinted on-line: *Chicago Reader,* On Film: Brief Reviews: http://onfilm. chireader.com/MovieCaps/E/EY/13162_EYES_WITHOUT_A_FACE. html (accessed 17 October 1997). The film is still listed under this title in several of the paracinema catalogs discussed in the introduction. Here it becomes the "uncut" version" of *The Horror Chamber of Dr. Faustus,* a description that drives the medical-cinematic pun on "cut" about as far as it can go.

51. See Judith Halberstam, *Skin Shows: Gothic Horror and the Technology of Monsters* (Durham, N.C.: Duke University Press, 1995).

52. John McCarty, *Splatter Movies: Breaking the Last Taboo of the Screen* (New York: St. Martin's Press, 1984), 1. McCarty identifies *Les yeux sans visage* as an early splatter film, and as Loewenstein points out, "he astutely notes the link between Franju, the Grand Guignol and David Cronenberg" (Loewenstein, 29 n. 56).

53. Steven Shaviro, *The Cinematic Body,* 129.

54. See André Bazin, *What Is Cinema,* vol. 1, trans. Hugh Gray (Berkeley and Los Angeles: University of California Press, 1967–1971). This is a sharp contrast to the New Wave films that were made the same year—*Breathless* and *400 Blows.* As I mentioned earlier, the style of *Les yeux sans visage* is similar to the style that characterizes the other major Left Bank film made the same year, *Hiroshima mon amour,* another film that details—with great precision—the passage of time.

55. In French, too, one speaks of the *opérations* of the camera. And whereas *plan,* the French term for "shot," does not have much medical resonance, *coupures* (cuts) and *masque* (mask) do. Finally, French film theory's use of the word *suture* to connote the complicated psychological process by which a film spectator is "stitched into" the filmic text comes, as Susan Hayward notes, "from the medical term for stitching up a cut or wound." Susan Hayward, *Key Concepts in Cinema Studies* (New York: Routledge, 1996), 371.

56. See Laura Mulvey, "Visual Pleasure and Narrative Cinema," in *Visual and Other Pleasures* (Bloomington: Indiana University Press, 1989); originally published in *Screen* 16, no. 3 (1975): 6–18.

In the years following the publication of this important essay, feminist critics—including Mulvey herself—have tried to broaden the original argument to include female spectatorship, the spectacularization of the male body, and issues of race and

class. Feminist critics working in the areas of pornography and horror have theo-
rized the possibility of a masochistic viewing position and forms of viewer identification other than the ones that Mulvey described. See, for example, Laura Mulvey,
"Afterthoughts on 'Visual Pleasure and Narrative Cinema' Inspired by King Vidor's
Duel in the Sun (1946)," in *Visual and Other Pleasures* (Bloomington: Indiana University Press, 1981); Diane Carson, Linda Dittmar, and Janice R. Welsch, eds., *Multiple Voices in Feminist Film Criticism* (Minneapolis: University of Minnesota Press,
1994); Steven Cohan and Ina Rae Hark, eds., *Screening the Male: Exploring Masculinities in Hollywood Cinema* (New York: Routledge, 1993); Mary Ann Doane,
The Desire to Desire: The Woman's Film of the 1940s (Bloomington: Indiana University Press, 1987); Tania Modleski, *The Women Who Knew Too Much: Hitchcock and
Feminist Theory* (New York: Methuen, 1988); Kaja Silverman, *Male Subjectivity at
the Margins* (New York: Routledge, 1992); Suzanna Danuta Walters, *Material Girls:
Making Sense of Feminist Cultural Theory* (Berkeley and Los Angeles: University of
California Press, 1995).

See also the essays on spectatorship in Manthia Diawara, ed., *Black American
Cinema* (New York: Routledge, 1993); Clover, *Men, Women, and Chainsaws*; E. Ann
Kaplan, *Looking for the Other*; and Linda Williams, *Hard Core*.

57. As Carol Clover points out, Hitchcock seems to equate the on-screen victim specifically with the off-screen audience. In his marginal notes for the shower
scene of *Psycho*, Hitchcock wrote, "the slashing. An impression of a knife slashing,
as if tearing at the very screen, ripping the film." As Clover interprets these remarks,
"not just the body of Marion is to be ruptured, but also the body on the other side
of the film and screen: our witnessing body" (*Men, Women, and Chainsaws*, 52).

58. Michael Powell also does this brilliantly in *Peeping Tom*.

59. Clarens describes *Les yeux sans visage* as "an elusive alliance of poetry and
terror" (*An Illustrated History of the Horror Film*, 155). Even Tohill and Tombs emphasize the film's "poetry" by beginning their chapter on *Les yeux sans visage* with a
quote by Baudelaire: "There is in the act of love a close similarity to torture or to a
surgical operation" (17).

60. Jonathan Rosenbaum, *Eyes without a Face*.

61. Gene Wright, *Horrorshows*, 70.

62. For Breton's elaboration of the *marvellous*, see André Breton, "Manifeste du
surréalisme," in *Oeuvres complètes*, vol. 1, Bibliothèque de la Pléiade (Paris: Gallimard,
1988); translated as "First Surrealist Manifesto," in *Manifestoes of Surrealism*, trans.
Richard Seaver and Helen Lane (Ann Arbor: University of Michigan Press, 1969).

63. In part, this is because we ordinarily think of contemporary horror as
Anglo-American. Continental horror films of the fifties and sixties have the kind of
pacing that we generally associate with European art cinema. For the novice American viewer, the films of Mario Bava and Jess Franco often seem slow.

64. David Bordwell, "The Art Cinema as a Mode of Film Practice," *Film Criticism* 4, no. 1 (fall 1979): 56–64.

65. As I mentioned in Chapter 1, note 73, horror films are often characterized

by a much looser plot structure and a more experimental visual style than main-stream cinema. Tohill and Tombs link the visual style of all European sex-horror to art cinema.

66. Clarens, 154–55.

67. Something Weird Video recently removed *The Horror Chamber of Dr. Faustus* from its list of titles, and Luminous doesn't seem to carry it, so the film's status among horror fans may be changing.

68. Hoberman and Rosenbaum, *Midnight Movies,* 327.

69. I am indebted to Jeffrey Sconce for the wording here, which comes from a private response to an earlier version of this chapter.

5. The Anxiety of Influence

1. As *Anxious Visions,* an art exhibit on the "real-life" inspiration for surrealist painting, made abundantly clear, there is a medical crisis in the wake of every violent war—with too few limbs, faces, wheelchairs, drugs to go around. See Sidra Stich, *Anxious Visions: Surrealist Art* (New York: Abbeville Press; Berkeley, Calif.: University Art Museum, 1990); and Skal, *The Monster Show.*

2. Films that purport to represent real bodies at the limits of pleasure and pain; films that are often "unambiguously delimited as gratuitous sadism for entertainment's sake." Mikita Brottman, *Offensive Films: Toward an Anthropology of Cinéma Vomitif* (Westport, Conn.: Greenwood Press, 1997), 4.

3. Franco was the second unit director of photography for Welles's film.

4. Kim Newman, ed., *The BFI Companion to Horror* (London: Cassell and British Film Institute, 1996), 121; Ginette Vincendeau, *The Encyclopedia of European Cinema* (London: Cassell and BFI), 159.

5. Jim Morton, "Film Personalities," in Jim Morton, guest editor, *Incredibly Strange Films, RE/Search* no. 10, ed. V. Vale and Andrea Juno (San Francisco: RE/Search Publications, 1986), 194.

6. Ibid.

7. Ibid.

8. It should be noted that the ubiquitous references to jazz in relation to Franco's work derive at least in part from the fact that Franco started his artistic life as a musician and still plays music (in fact, he frequently composes and plays part of the jazz scores we hear on his film sound tracks). At least one mail-order house, Video Search of Miami, markets CDs of Franco's music in addition to videos and laser discs of his movies. For more on Franco's thoughts about music, sex, and just about everything else, see Harvey Fenton and William Lustig, "A Different Point of View: The Jess Franco Interview," *Flesh and Blood* 9 (1997): 32–35.

9. One story has it that the Spanish producers for *Chimes at Midnight,* horrified by Welles's choice of second-unit director of photography, dug out *Rififi en la ciudad* (Rififi in the City, 1963) to show Welles just how bad Franco's camera

work could be. Unfortunately for the producers, Welles was charmed by *Rififi*'s obvious homage to *The Lady from Shanghai* (Welles, 1948). See Tohill and Tombs, 87.

10. See Tohill and Tombs, 87.

11. Tim Lucas, "Horrotica! The Sex Scream of Jess Franco," in *The Video Watchdog Book,* ed. Tim Lucas (Cincinnati, Ohio: Video Watchdog, 1992), 74.

12. *Luminous Film and Video Wurks Catalogue 2.0* carried an insert advertising the possible appearance of Jess Franco and his wife, Lina Romay, at the October 1996 Chiller Theater Convention. "Maybe the time has come for the much maligned Jess Franco to garner the attention he deserves. And to seal your fate and make the Chiller attendance unquestionable Jess's newest film, *THE KILLER BARBYS,* might just be making its US premiere sometime during the convention weekend. Judging from the trailer, it looks like a winner for Franco. When have you seen a 35 mm, THX stereo Franco film, projected in a theater? Keep your fingers crossed that it all works out and order your tickets for the October 25, 26, 27th Chiller Theater Convention now!"

13. Tim Lucas, "How to Read a Franco Film," *Video Watchdog,* no. 1 (1990): 23.

14. Lucas, "Horrotica!" 74.

15. Lucas, "How to Read a Franco Film," 19.

16. Andrew Sarris,"Notes on the Auteur Theory in 1962," in Mast, Cohen, and Braudy, *Film Theory and Criticism,* 586. Auteur theory has, of course, undergone radical theoretical formulations in the past thirty years. As I mentioned in Chapter 1, however, paracinema's version of auteurism remains to a large extent rooted in the art cinema discourse and culture of the 1950s and 1960s. For contemporary, updated discussions of the importance and place of auteurism in film theory and criticism, see Dudley Andrew, "The Unauthorized Auteur Today," in *Film Theory Goes to the Movies,* ed. Jim Collins, Hilary Radner, and Ava Preacher Collins (New York: Routledge, 1993), 77–85; and James Naremore, "Authorship and the Cultural Politics of Film Criticism," *Film Quarterly* 44, no. 1 (fall 1990): 14–22. For a good discussion of some of the factors complicating auteurist readings, see Barbara Klinger, *Melodrama and Meaning: History, Culture, and the Films of Douglas Sirk* (Bloomington: Indiana University Press, 1994).

17. Jaglom's film *Always* (1985), for example, is the director's look at marriage and divorce both on-screen and in real life. Written by, directed by, and featuring Jaglom, the film costars his real-life ex-wife Patricia Townsend. *Déja Vu* (1997) is a fictionalized retelling of the director's meeting and falling in love with his wife and collaborator Patricia Foyt. As Stephen Holden, writing for the *New York Times,* puts it, "Henry Jaglom's autobiographical films, with their navel-gazing introspection, require a degree of patience that many moviegoers are loath to extend. But even the most self-indulgent Jaglom films loiter in psychic territory that more mainstream explorations of well-heeled angst often overlook." This seems like a fitting description not only of Franco's films but of most low horror. See Stephen Holden, "How Puppy Love Can Teach New Tricks to Old Dogs," *New York Times* 24 April 1998, B12.

Jaglom's films, like Jess Franco's, are difficult to find. Most of Jaglom's films are available for rental by mail from Facets Multimedia, 1517 W. Fullerton Ave., Chicago, IL 60614; e-mail address: rentals@facets.org.

18. It's also interesting that Jaglom, like Franco, had a curious relationship with Orson Welles. Welles agreed to act in one of Jaglom's early films and then continued to visit Jaglom to watch him work. Welles was apparently fascinated by Jaglom's attempts to move beyond acting and scripting—a process so different from Welles's own.

19. There was also a negative side to coproductions. As Virginia Higginbotham notes in her *Spanish Film under Franco,* "while foreign funds put Spanish film professionals to work, they also raised production costs to levels entirely out of reach of Spanish directors. Actors who had been paid enormous salaries for small parts in Italian and American films were no longer interested in working in low-paying Spanish productions. Most of the lead roles in copros were reserved for famous stars, while Spanish actors and actresses were left with minimal roles." Virginia Higginbotham, *Spanish Film under Franco* (Austin: University of Texas Press, 1988), 15.

20. Tohill and Tombs, 64. It should be noted here that during the 1970s, for many Spaniards, the "weekend" didn't begin until Saturday afternoon.

21. As Marsha Kinder notes, "during the Francoist era, the depiction of violence was repressed, as was the depiction of sex, sacrilege, and politics." Marsha Kinder, *Blood Cinema: The Reconstruction of National Identity in Spain* (Berkeley and Los Angeles: University of California Press, 1993), 138.

22. Ibid.

23. John Hopewell, *Out of the Past: Spanish Cinema after Franco* (London: British Film Institute, 1986), 209.

24. Frédéric Strauss, ed., *Almodóvar on Almodóvar,* trans. Yves Baignères (Boston: Faber and Faber, 1994), 105. It's interesting that Almodóvar refers to Jess Franco by one of the horror director's many Anglicized pseudonyms, Jess Frank.

Jess Franco sees a definite similarity between his work and Almodóvar's. "I find Almodóvar very simpatico," Franco told Lucas Balbo in an interview. "He has the courage to show the public who he really is. . . . I like his earlier films better than *Matador,* because now I think he's beginning to become too serious. . . . I preferred him filming nuns walking tigers in their gardens . . . and his first scatalogical film *Pepa, Luci, Bom y otras chicas del monton* (Pepa, Luci, Bom, and Other Girls from the Masses). It's really excessive, but excessive in the best sense of the word." Lucas Balbo, "Unbearable Films and Terrible Headaches: A Conversation with Jess Franco," *Video Watchdog,* no. 1 (1990): 39–40. For more on Franco's take on the Spanish film industry, see Kevin Collins, "Interview with Jess Franco," *European Trash Cinema,* Special no. 1 (October 1996).

25. Harvey Fenton and William Lustig, "A Different Point of View: Jésus Franco Manera in Conversations with Harvey Fenton and William Lustig," *Flesh and Blood* 9 (1997): 34.

26. Ibid.

27. Tim Lucas, ed., *The Video Watchdog Book,* 87.

28. Ibid., 74.

29. Ibid.

30. A lot has been written on the connections between sex and horror. See David Hogan, *Dark Romance: Sexuality in the Horror Film* (Jefferson, N.C.: McFarland, 1986); Gregory Waller, *The Living and the Undead: From Stoker's "Dracula" to Romero's "Dawn of the Dead"* (Urbana and Chicago: University of Illinois Press, 1986), 170–71; Christopher Craft, "'Kiss Me with Those Red Lips': Gender and Inversion in Bram Stoker's *Dracula,*" *Representations* 8 (fall 1984): 107–33; James Twitchell, *Dreadful Pleasures: An Anatomy of Modern Horror* (New York: Oxford University Press, 1985).

31. McLuhan, *Understanding Media,* 23.

32. Laurie Anderson, "Difficult Listening Hour," on Anderson, *Home of the Brave,* Elliott Abbott, executive producer (Talk Normal, distributed by Warner Brothers, 1986). The piece is not included on the audio recording. I don't mean to suggest here that Anderson specifically referred to Franco's work, but her comments about the demands that "difficult" music makes on the listener are very much in keeping with the kind of demands that Franco's sound tracks make on his viewers.

33. Something Weird Video sells the dubbed American version, which was released by Sigma III in 1964. Video Search of Miami sells the "uncut French version" (which still appears to be missing some footage—there's a jump cut at the end, for example, that seems related more to missing film than to stylistic innovation). The French version includes two nude scenes missing from the SWV edition. But Video Search's edition is much poorer visual quality than the SWV version; the lighting is poor, and the whole tape seems to be washed with a curious green tint. The SWV edition is gorgeous. I should note that according to Michael Weldon, these are the only two editions available from any of the companies that sell the film. See Weldon, *The Psychotronic Video Guide,* 32.

34. *Gialli* are Italian thrillers, whose conventions are similar to those of film noir. While they share many stylistic and thematic conventions with American thrillers, though, *gialli* are usually more explicitly violent and gory than American thrillers, and the plotting isn't as tight.

35. Quoted from the box of Frank Henenlotter's Sexy Shocker release (Something Weird Video).

36. Lucas, "How to Read a Franco Film," 26.

37. See Sergei Eisenstein, "A Dialectic Approach to Film Form," in Mast, Cohen, and Braudy, *Film Theory and Criticism,* 143. For the discussion of "collision," see Eisenstein, "The Cinematographic Principle and the Ideogram," in Mast, Cohen, and Braudy, *Film Theory and Criticism,* 133. Both essays were reprinted from Eisenstein, *Film Form.*

38. Like many European directors, Franco admires the work of Edgar Allan Poe. Sam and Barbara's fate in this film is reminiscent of the fate of Fortunato in

The Cask of Amontillado, an example of the premature burial theme that turns up so frequently in Poe's stories.

Mr. Hallen's decision to book a flight to Paris almost has the status of a trick ending (as the friend watching the film with me said, "You think it's going to end like a Poe story, but then it ends like an O. Henry story instead"). Hallen hears a Christmas telephone message from Sam, saying that he's found Barbara and instructing Mr. Hallen to "call in the marines" if he doesn't hear from them in three days. Hallen does better than call in the marines. He makes plans to go to Paris himself.

39. Robin Wood, "Return of the Repressed," *Film Comment,* July–August 1978, 25–32.

40. Tim Lucas, "Face to Face with *Faceless,*" in *The Video Watchdog Book,* 195–96.

41. Ibid., 195.

42. Peter Bondanella, *Italian Cinema from Neorealism to the Present* (New York: Continuum, 1983), 206.

43. One of the few scenes shown entirely from a victim's point of view is the walling-in sequence, and here the point of view is Sam's. Female victims rarely control the gaze.

44. I am using "mode" here in the way that David Bordwell does in "The Art Cinema as a Mode of Film Practice," to refer to a style of filmmaking that is characterized by certain formalistic (rather than plot) conventions and encourages a specific reading strategy on the part of the viewer. See David Bordwell, "The Art Cinema as a Mode of Film Practice," *Film Criticism* 4, no. 1 (fall 1979): 56–64.

45. Helmut Berger, Anton Diffring, and Stephane Audran are familiar to fans of European art cinema. Howard Vernon and Lina Romay (Franco's wife) are familiar to fans of European horror. And Brigitte LaHaie is familiar to fans of European hard-core entertainment.

46. All the things the French find distasteful about Americans are cited in these sequences—albeit with tongue firmly in cheek: the way we handled Vietnam, our annoying tendency to come in and start running things, our adolescent attitude toward sex, our reliance on violence to solve problems, our gum chewing.

47. Yvonne Tasker, "Dumb Movies for Dumb People: Masculinity, the Body, and the Voice in Contemporary Action Cinema," in *Screening the Male: Exploring Masculinities in Hollywood Cinema,* ed. Steven Cohan and Ina Rae Hark (New York: Routledge, 1993), 230.

48. For more on the *cinéma du look,* see Guy Austin, *Contemporary French Cinema: An Introduction* (New York: Manchester University Press, 1996; distributed in the United States by St. Martin's Press); A. Goodwin, "Music Video in the (Post)Modern World," *Screen* 28, no. 3 (summer 1987): 36–55; and René Prédal, *Le cinéma français depuis 1945* (Paris: Nathan, 1991).

49. "Postmodernism" remains a vexed term. The Anglo-American pop culture postmodern aesthetic I'm discussing here grew in part out of a punk-eighties–New

Wave aesthetic (reflected in films like *Blade Runner, Brazil, Diva, Liquid Sky, Repo Man, Star Struck, Women on the Verge of a Nervous Breakdown,* and *Videodrome*). It's heavily indebted to themes, images, and formal techniques drawn from advertising, comic books, music videos, science fiction, and TV dramas. If it has stylistic antecedents, they're to be found in the historical avant-garde schools of surrealism and dada. This branch of postmodernism is quite different from the coolly formal postmodernism of art directors like Peter Greenaway, Raoul Ruiz, and Lars von Trier, which seems to have its roots in modernist aesthetics.

For more on pop postmodernism, see Jean Baudrillard, *America,* trans. Chris Turner (London and New York: Verso, 1989), and *Cool Memories,* trans. Chris Turner (London and New York: Verso, 1990); Scott Bukatman, *Terminal Identity: the Virtual Subject in Postmodern Science Fiction* (Durham, N.C.: Duke University Press, 1993); Jim Collins, *Architectures of Excess: Cultural Life in the Information Age* (New York: Routledge, 1995); Anne Friedberg, *Window Shopping: Cinema and the Postmodern* (Berkeley and Los Angeles: University of California Press, 1993); Fredric Jameson, *Postmodernism, or The Cultural Logic of Late Capitalism* (Durham, N.C.: Duke University Press, 1991); Angela McRobbie, "Postmodernism and Popular Culture," *ICA Documents* 4 (London: Institute of Contemporary Art, 1986), 54–58; and Christopher Sharrett, *Crisis Cinema: The Apocalyptic Idea in Postmodern Film,* PostModern Positions, vol. 6 (Washington, D.C.: Maisonneuve Press, 1993). For more on the formalist postmodernism that I've linked to modernism, see Ingeborg Hoesterey, ed., *Zeitgesit in Babel: The Postmodernist Controversy* (Bloomington: Indiana University Press, 1991); and Andreas Huyssen, *After the Great Divide: Modernism.* For a discussion of the distinctions between the historic avant-garde and modernism, see Patrick Brantlinger and James Naremore, "Introduction: Six Artistic Cultures," in *Modernity and Mass Culture* (Bloomington: Indiana University Press, 1991), 1–23; and Juan Suárez, *Bike Boys, Drag Queens, and Superstars: Avant-garde, Mass Culture, and Gay Identities in the 1960s Underground Cinema* (Bloomington: Indiana University Press, 1996).

50. In an interview with Kevin Collins, Franco describes the influences that made him want to make films. "I was eight. I was in school and I escaped from school to go to the cinema. But I didn't go to the cinema to see *Popeye* or something like that, no, no. I went to see Raoul Walsh films. My brother was two years younger than me and when I was ten and he was eight we made a list of the directors we loved. And we wanted to go see all of the films by them that we could. And, by chance, all of them were American directors and American films. Because in Europe there's a mistaken belief that a film is a way to talk about politics or social problems or philosophy—and I don't think so. I think a film is a complete thing and when a film ends I think it is important enough, you know to be just a show." Quoted in Kevin Collins, "Interview with Jess Franco," *European Trash Cinema,* special no. 1 (1996): 6.

Of course, when Franco talks about the depiction of sex in the cinema, his take on the superiority of American movies shifts dramatically (they don't show enough, he says).

51. There is a blurring of the boundaries between high art and low culture within the European segment, though. Here, art cinema stars like Stephane Audran play opposite porn stars like Brigitte LaHaie.

52. Bourdieu, *Distinction,* 25.

53. Lucas, "How to Read a Franco Film," 19.

54. Adorno argues that true "mass culture" is one that arises spontaneously from the masses themselves, not one that they have to learn to appreciate. For Adorno, most of what passes as "mass culture" is really just the product of a "culture industry" that has as its goal the inculcation and enforcement of certain hegemonic codes. See Adorno, "The Culture Industry Reconsidered," trans. Anson G. Rabinbach, *New German Critique* (fall 1975): 12–19.

55. Lucas, "How to Read a Franco Film," 19.

56. Lucas, *The Video Watchdog Book,* 74.

57. Lester Bangs, *Psychotic Reactions and Carburetor Dung* (New York: Vintage Books, 1988), 122–23. Quoted in Jeffrey Sconce, "'Trashing' the Academy: Taste, Excess, and an Emerging Politics of Cinematic Style," 371.

6. Exploitation Meets Direct Cinema

1. André Breton, "Second Manifesto of Surrealism," in *Manifestoes of Surrealism,* trans. Richard Seaver and Helen Lane (Ann Arbor: University of Michigan Press, 1972), 125.

2. Polanski made *Break Up the Dance* when he was a film student at Lodz. He described the circumstances surrounding the making of the film to Joseph Gelmis. "After the third year [at the film school] you made a ten minute documentary short. . . . I had no vocation for documentaries, so I tried to make mine a sort of story. Like every school does, we used to organize dances. And I invited a group of bad guys. We used to call them hooligans. . . . I told them to break up the dance. And I filmed it. I was almost thrown out of the school." Joseph Gelmis, *The Film Director as Superstar* (New York: Doubleday, 1970), 144–45.

3. Barbara Haskell and John G. Hanhardt, *Yoko Ono: Arias and Objects* (Salt Lake City: Peregrine Smith Books, 1991), 2; hereafter cited in text.

4. Lennon had been mistakenly informed that Ono's show at the Indica Gallery would be a performance of *Bag Piece* (1962), in which two performers come onstage with a black bag large enough to accommodate both of them. The performers remove their shoes, get into the bag, and remove all their clothing. They then replace their clothes, come out of the bag, and exit the stage, taking the bag and their shoes with them.

5. David Sheff, *The Playboy Interviews with John Lennon and Yoko Ono,* ed. G. Barry Golson (New York: Playboy Press, 1981), 86–87; italics mine.

6. For a description of these, see Yoko Ono, *Grapefruit: A Book of Instructions* (New York: Simon and Schuster, 1970; London: Owen, 1970). Originally published by Wunternaum Press (Tokyo, Bellport, and New York) in 1964.

7. Here too, the similarities between horror and the avant-garde are striking. Lon Chaney suffered physical pain in order to create his most memorable characters, and Boris Karloff suffered permanent damage as a result of the leg braces and heavy shoes he had to wear to portray Frankenstein's monster. See John Brosnan, *The Horror People* (New York: St. Martin's Press, 1976).

8. Barbara Haskell and John Hanhardt argue, for example, that both *Cut Piece* and *Wall Piece for Orchestra* were informed by "proto-feminist questions about the nature of personal violation and violence" (Haskell and Hanhardt, *Yoko Ono: Arias and Objects,* 6).

9. Robert Atkins, *Art Speak: A Guide to Contemporary Ideas, Movements, and Buzzwords* (New York: Abbeville Press, 1990), 80.

10. Ono's songs are characterized, as John Dougan points out, by "noise," "cacophony," and "trademark caterwauling." Charles Shere is more charitable in his description, referring to Ono's singing as a "unique warble." See John Dougan's review of *Onobox* (a compilation of Ono's work since 1969) released on compact disc, *In These Times* 16, no. 25 (20–26 May 1992): 18; and Charles Shere's introduction to the interview with Yoko Ono included in Melody Sumner, Kathleen Burch, and Michael Sumner, eds., *The Guests Go in to Supper* (Oakland and San Francisco: Burning Books, 1986), 170. For an interesting discussion of the relationship between Fluxus musical composition and Fluxus film, see James Peterson, *Dreams of Chaos, Visions of Order: Understanding the American Avant-garde Cinema* (Detroit, Mich.: Wayne State University Press, 1994), 98.

11. In *Add Colour Painting* and *Kitchen Piece,* for example, Ono "conflated viewer and performer by turning over to viewers the responsibility for creating the paintings by adding the proffered materials—colour and food respectively—to the canvases" (Haskell and Hanhardt, 18).

12. For example, in *Laundry Piece,* Ono instructs the reader: "In entertaining your guests, bring out your laundry of the day explain to them about each item. and when it became dirty and why, etc." (quoted in Haskell and Hanhardt, 32).

13. *University Art Museum/Pacific Film Archive Bimonthly Calendar* (University of California at Berkeley, 2625 Durant Ave., Berkeley, CA 94720), vol. 14, no. 4 (July–August, 1991), 6.

14. See Bill Nichols, *Representing Reality: Issues and Concepts in Documentary* (Bloomington: Indiana University Press, 1991), esp. 39–56.

15. The term "cinema verité" has a precise meaning that's often ignored in popular writing on film. Some critics use the terms "cinema verité and "direct cinema" interchangeably, but "cinema verité" refers more properly to the work of ethnographic filmmakers such as Jean Rouch who believed in (and acknowledged in their work) the powerful role of the camera in shaping the reality that unfolds in front of the camera. For them, the camera is a catalyst, and the vérité (truth) that is revealed in front of the lens is one that would not and could not have been revealed without the camera's presence. "Direct cinema" refers to the American group of "vérité" filmmakers—people such as Pennebaker, Wiseman, and Leacock—who

seem to believe that the camera can function simply as an observational tool. Although *off-screen* these filmmakers acknowledge the power of the camera to shape events, their work is characterized by the visual absence of the filmmaker, who rarely steps in front of the lens, and the absence on the sound track of any information about how the film came to be made. In popular American usage and even in some scholarly writing, the two terms are frequently collapsed, so that cinema verité stands for *any* slice-of-life mode of filmmaking, from Wiseman's *High School* to *RealTV.* Because of confusion surrounding the use of the terms, scholars such as Bill Nichols and Michael Renov have preferred to invent different categories for discussing documentary film.

In this chapter, which draws heavily on press reports and reviews, to avoid confusion I have used "cinema verité" to describe both "vérité" and "direct cinema" techniques. See Nichols, *Representing Reality*; and Michael Renov, ed., *Theorizing Documentary* (New York: Routledge, 1993).

16. Nichols, *Representing Reality,* 39.

17. In that sense, the film can be seen as an extension of Yoko Ono's earlier work with Fluxus, an avant-garde movement that, like the surrealists, purposely tried to blur the divisions between "real" life and art.

18. L. Marsland Gander, "Lennon's *Rape* Erratic," *Daily Telegraph and Morning Post,* 26 April 1969, 15.

19. *University Art Museum/Pacific Film Archive Bimonthly Calendar,* 6.

20. See Laura Mulvey, "Visual Pleasure and Narrative Cinema," in *Visual and Other Pleasures* (Bloomington: Indiana University Press, 1989); and E. Ann Kaplan, *Women and Film: Both Sides of the Camera* (New York: Methuen, 1983).

21. See Haskell and Hanhardt, *Yoko Ono: Arias and Objects.*

22. In a way, then, the film is a particularly grim illustration of Duncan Petrie's observation that "in contemporary society, the power of the image is such that the audiovisual media play a fundamental role in the actual construction of realities." Duncan Petrie, "Change and Cinematic Representation in Europe," in *Screening Europe: Image and Identity in Contemporary European Cinema* (London: British Film Institute, 1992), 3.

23. Vivian Sobchack, "*No Lies:* Direct Cinema as Rape," in *New Challenges for Documentary,* ed. Alan Rosenthal (Berkeley and Los Angeles: University of California Press, 1988), 332.

24. Because so few people have seen this film, I am including a detailed description of it here. I am indebted to Shelley Diekman at the Pacific Film Archive for making it possible for me to view the film.

25. All translations are mine. There are no subtitles, a fact that will be discussed in greater detail later in the chapter.

26. It is important to remember here that although we're aware only of the I-camera and its jerky movements, there are other crew members present. Majlata can be surrounded.

27. Because the entire apartment sequence is so poorly lit, I assume that the light crew was left behind.

28. Knowland actually followed Majlata for three days; thus the cemetery sequence, the walk along the Strand, and the apartment sequence could all have been shot on different days. By the time Majlata was locked in the flat with Knowland, Lennon and Ono had had time to tell her sister about the project. "Her sister was in on it," Ono said in an interview, "so when she calls her sister on the phone, her sister is just laughing at her and the girl doesn't understand why." Scott MacDonald, *A Critical Cinema 2: Interviews with Independent Filmmakers* (Berkeley and Los Angeles: University of California Press, 1992), 151.

29. Although both Lennon and Ono have screen credits, Ono considers the film to be primarily hers. In a 1992 interview, Ono said, "By the time that I actually got to make the film, John and I were together, and the reporters were hounding us, but the *Rape* concept was something that I thought of before John and I got together" (Scott MacDonald, 151).

30. Certainly, Majlata's often repeated statement, "Ich möchte allein werden," is reminiscent of Greta Garbo's famous plea that she be let alone.

31. Ono has stated that she had the idea for *Rape* before she met John Lennon and had to learn to contend with the ever-present press.

32. John Berger's influential essay *Ways of Seeing* argues that women—unlike men—are socialized to think of themselves as objects of the gaze, and to accept their position as objects-to-be-looked-at as natural. See John Berger, *Ways of Seeing* (London: BBC and Penguin Books, 1972), especially his discussion of the female nude in Western art, 45–64.

33. The film script does go on to say that several women should be chased and that the chase "may be made with men and boys as well." Since the finished film, however, details the systematic stalking of one woman, these (later) instructions seem to occupy the same peripheral zone (peripheral to the finished project) as the observation that "the cameraman will be taking a risk of offending the girl as the girl is somebody he picks up arbitrarily on the street, *but there is a way around this.*" In the finished film, there is no "way around" offending—and indeed traumatizing— Majlata, just as there are no other women or men or boys chased (Haskell and Hanhardt, 94; italics mine).

34. See Mulvey, "Visual Pleasure and Narrative Cinema." There is, of course, a whole Hollywood tradition of males as objects of the gaze, as well. The male body—Astaire's, for example—is fetishized in musicals, and Westerns generally feature shots in which the body of the male gunfighter becomes an object of scrutiny and fascination for the audience, as well as for his cinematic opponent (typically, the camera will "explore" the gunslinger's body, usually as he is slumped over a bar, traveling up his legs, resting for a time at his hips, and then moving up to his arms, hands and, finally, face and head). The difference between male and female objectification, though, is that pleasure in looking at the male body must always be rationalized in some way. In musicals, the man is generally presented as a performer

(i.e., one who has agreed to be looked at); in Westerns, the gunslinger is presented as a "threat" to the person whose point-of-view shot establishes the gunslinger as the object of the cinematic gaze. No diegetic reason need be provided for gazing at women, however. Women are there, as both Mulvey and Berger argue, simply to be looked at.

Mulvey believed the system of visual pleasure outlined in "Visual Pleasure and Narrative Cinema" was a function largely of Hollywood film. In the article, experimental cinema, which disrupts traditional mechanisms of pleasure, is seen as an *alternative* to the sadistic and fetishizing gaze(s) that, for Mulvey, structure Hollywood cinema. I do not believe that *Rape* can really be read as such an alternative. While the film makes us very aware of the sadistic camera gaze, it does so by literally demonstrating its power.

35. Gander, "Lennon's *Rape* Erratic," 15.

36. Even Roman Polanski, generally an avid publicity seeker, resorted to violence when the paparazzi became intrusive. Polanski, who had alienated his friends by conducting a maudlin media tour through his "house of death" a little more than a week after Sharon Tate's grisly murder, made headlines years later when he assaulted a photographer who snapped an unauthorized photo of him paying a memorial visit to his late wife's grave.

37. The title of the film is telling. When males are stalked by women photographers, the sexual metaphor tends to be very different. For months in 1979, French photographer Sophie Calle followed people at random in the street and photographed them without their knowledge. In January 1980, she met a man at an opening. When she heard that he was planning a trip to Venice, she decided she would follow him and take pictures of him without his knowledge. The photos she took during the adventure were published along with a narrative text—in journal form—of the photographer's activities, thoughts, and emotions during the time she was stalking Henri B. and his wife in Venice. The role of the camera is very different here than it is in *Rape*. Although Sophie Calle's camera, like Nic Knowland's, is a means of violating someone's privacy, she cannot afford to be so directly, so physically, threatening. Hers is a photography of surveillance rather than one of bodily assault. Interestingly, in *Please Follow Me,* a critical essay that accompanies Calle's text, Jean Baudrillard calls Calle's photographic stalking of Henri B. "the cunning demon of *seduction*" [le malin génie de la séduction] and wonders if Sophie secretly wished that Henri B. would kill her. Even when women are behind the camera, it seems, their main role vis-à-vis men is that of seductress or potential victim. See Sophie Calle, *Suite vénitienne*; and Jean Baudrillard, *Please Follow Me* (Paris: Editions de l'Etoile, 1983), 83; italics mine. Published in English as Sophie Calle, *Suite vénitienne;* Jean Baudrillard, *Please Follow Me,* trans. Dany Arash and Danny Hatfield (Seattle: Bay Press, 1983).

38. The question of spectator identification is controversial. Whereas Christian Metz maintains that "the primary identification of the spectator revolves around the camera itself," Carol J. Clover has convincingly argued for circumstances in which

the use of "point of view shots can . . . be pro forma." In a sense, both of them are correct. Regarding the use of POV shots in *Rape*, it seems safe to say that Ono wanted the spectators to feel complicitous in the victimization of Majlata. For the film "to work," however, spectators also have to identify with the victim, to feel her fear. The development of audience identification may be one reason that the film is not subtitled. Although realizing that a certain amount of audience identification with the victim is unavoidable, Ono and Lennon wanted to ensure that non-German-speaking audiences would continue to see Majlata as *other*.

See Christian Metz, *The Imaginary Signifier: Psychoanalysis and the Cinema*, trans. Celia Britton, Anwyl Williams, Ben Brewster, and Alfred Guzzetti (Bloomington: Indiana University Press, 1982), 97; and Clover, *Men, Women, and Chainsaws*, 45.

39. Our attention is drawn not only to the fact that *Rape* is a film but to the lack of continuity between numbers ("four, take one," is followed by "eight, take one," for example), and, by extension, to the fact that the film has been carefully edited for effect. A great deal of footage has obviously been left out.

Because of the obvious constructedness of the piece, some journalists and scholars have questioned whether the film was "real"; that is, was Eva Majlata really brutalized, or was she "in" on a faux-documentary hoax? Yoko Ono has always maintained that the film was real, that the actress did not know what was happening to her. In an interview with Scott MacDonald, Ono said the film "was completely candid—except for the effects we did later in editing. . . . I remember John saying later that no actress could have given a performance that real" (MacDonald, *A Critical Cinema 2*, 151).

40. Vera Dika, *Games of Terror: Halloween, Friday the 13th, and the Films of the Stalker Cycle* (Rutherford, N.J.: Fairleigh Dickinson University Press; London and Toronto: Associated University Presses, 1990), 53; hereafter cited in text. For more information on the stalker film, see Lucy Fischer and Marcia Landy, "*Eyes of Laura Mars*: A Binocular Critique"; Robin Wood, "Returning the Look: *Eyes of a Stranger*"; and Allison Graham, " 'The Fallen Wonder of the World': Brian De Palma's Horror Films," in *American Horrors: Essays on the Modern American Horror Film*, ed. Gregory A. Waller (Urbana and Chicago: University of Illinois Press, 1987).

41. As Dika points out, the stalker film's narrative structure follows a fairly strict formula. See Dika, 59–60.

42. Clover, *Men, Women, and Chainsaws*, 35–41; hereafter cited in text.

43. Majlata did survive and, ironically, prospered as a direct result of her "appearance" in the film.

44. As Linda Williams points out, the film was a hoax. To dispel the rumors surrounding the film, the "murdered" actress gave an interview to the press after the film's release (*New York Times*, March 1976). See Linda Williams, *Hardcore*, 190–95; and David Kerekes and David Slater, *Killing for Culture: An Illustrated History of Death Film from Mondo to Snuff* (San Franciso: Creation Books, 1994), esp. chap. 1.

45. *Something Weird Catalog* no. 1 (1995–1996): 87; hereafter cited in text.

46. The "exquisite corpse" was a name the surrealists invented for an art game that resulted in "collaborative" artistic productions. One member of the group would begin a drawing. He or she would fold the paper so that nobody could see what had been drawn. Without looking at what the previous artist had drawn, the next player would draw the next body part. The drawing would circulate until a full "body" had been completed. Once revealed, it became an "exquisite corpse." Whitney Chadwick has reproduced some of the exquisite corpse drawings in *Women Artists and the Surrealist Movement* (Boston: Little Brown, 1985).

47. For more on Fluxfilms, see Janet Jenkins, ed., *In the Spirit of Fluxus* (Minneapolis: Walker Art Center, 1993). Distributed in the United States by Distributed Art Publishers, New York.

It should be noted that the Findlays split up shortly after *Snuff* was made. Roberta Findlay continues to work in film. Michael Findlay died in a helicopter accident in May 1977.

48. Findlay directed the film under a pseudonym, Marshall Smith.

49. *Satan's Bed* (1965, Prometheus Productions) is available from Something Weird Video, P.O. Box 33664, Seattle, WA 98155.

50. As Gary Indiana notes in his scathing "Home," from the point of view of subculture(s), "home is where pathology meets entertainment. Home is where children of Satan worshippers who love too much and neurosurgeons who've had sex changes turn up on 'Geraldo.' Home is where you shouldn't leave without your American Express card. . . . Home consists of a dysfunctional suburban clan of cartoon characters. . . . Home is where wayward teens are chained to the radiator. Home is where battered women plot their escape. Home has to be investigated." Gary Indiana, "Home," *Aperture* 127 (spring 1992): 56–63. The article is illustrated with glossy color photos of suburban houses, reminiscent of the creepy technicolor shots of middle-America houses in David Lynch's disturbing *Blue Velvet* (1986).

51. Gene Ross, "Sexploitation Films: The 60's Sexplosion!!!" *Adult Video News* 2, no. 1 (March 1987): 82. When I've shown the film in class, male students express some affect at first, but the film wears them down. The proliferation of rapes combined with the absence of any hard-core shots tends to numb them. After-screening discussions are interesting because students quickly move from expressions of boredom with the film to questions of economics, distribution, and production. Who footed the bill for exploitation films? Where were they shown and to whom? And why were they popular? are the questions the students regularly ask. Granted, these are students who've grown up with cable access and R-rated films. As I mention later in the chapter, however, at the time of the film's release, contemporary New Jersey audiences weren't thrilled (or weren't thrilled *enough* to satisfy at least one projectionist), either.

52. Ross, 84.

53. Projectionist's notes for *Satan's Bed*, Fine Arts Theatre, (unidentified town) New Jersey, week of 6 July 1966. I am indebted to Eric Schaefer, the guardian of the note cards, for this information.

54. In fact, in this respect, the hotel room scenes in *Touch of Evil* (1958) are much more menacing and truly shocking than anything shown here.

55. I don't mean to suggest that Ono and Lennon scripted the end of *Rape* or intentionally modeled it on *Satan's Bed.* What interests me is the uncanny similarity between the two films, given the difference in genre.

56. See Trinh T. Minh-ha, "Reassemblage" in *Framer Framed* (New York: Routledge, 1992), 95–105; and Trinh T. Minh-ha, "The Language of Nativism: Anthropology as a Scientific Conversation of Man with Man," in *Woman, Native, Other: Writing, Postcoloniality, Feminism* (Bloomington: University of Indiana Press, 1989), 47–76.

57. This is not always successful, and several critics argue that in effect, she perpetrates some of the very abuses she appears to be questioning. See, for example, Henrietta L. Moore, "Trinh T. Minh-ha: Observed Anthropology and Others," in *Visualizing Theory: Selected Essays from V.A.R.,* ed. Lucien Taylor (New York: Routledge, 1994), 115–25. It should also be noted that Trinh uses the untranslated voices in *Reassemblage* as a means of focusing viewer attention on the rhythm and musicality of language.

58. In the version of *Film Script No. 5* that Haskell and Hanhardt print, the first line of the script is "Rape with camera." See Haskell and Hanhardt, 94.

59. Some prints of the film end with Yoko and the housewife running. Others, including the print used for the videotape, show her getting hit by a car.

60. This is a quote from Sandy Stone's section of *Clicking On,* in which she tries to explain the relationship between the physical body of the computer user and virtual space. Steven Shaviro makes a similar point in *The Cinematic Body* when he writes that "power works in the depths and on the surfaces of the body and not just in the disembodied realm of 'representation' or of 'discourse.'" (viii).

61. Here the tools of French feminist discourse seem to be used against Majlata. As E. Ann Kaplan points out, the work of women filmmakers like Marguerite Duras frequently depict silence as a kind of female resistance in the face of patriarchy. Here, a traditional mode of female resistance is being used—against a woman—to enforce certain patriarchal values. See E. Ann Kaplan, *Women and Film: Both Sides of the Camera* (New York: Methuen, 1983), particularly the chapter on Marguerite Duras, 91–103.

62. Celtic history, for example, is full of stories about the active suppression of Gaelic and other languages in the British Isles and the enforced imposition of English as the official language of the colonies.

63. E. Ann Kaplan, *Looking for the Other: Feminism, Film, and the Imperial Gaze* (New York: Routledge, 1997), xix.

64. Ella Shohat, "Imaging Terra Incognita: The Disciplinary Gaze of Empire," *Public Culture* 3, no. 2 (1991): 41–70.

65. I am indebted to Michael Curtin for pointing this out to me.

66. Scott MacDonald, *A Critical Cinema 2,* 151. In another piece, Ono wrote,

"Nick *[sic]* is a gentleman who prefers eating clouds and floating pies to shooting *Rape*. Nevertheless it was shot." See Haskell and Hanhardt, "On *Rape*," 94.

67. Perhaps the most extreme example of this was the trial of artist Carl Andre for the murder of his wife, artist Ana Mendieta. In collecting evidence for the trial, D.A. Robert M. Morgenthau was amazed at how quickly the art world closed ranks. See Robert Katz, *Naked by the Window: The Fatal Marriage of Carl Andre and Ana Mendieta* (New York: Atlantic Monthly Press, 1990).

In writing this, I don't mean to imply that we should regularly stage witch-hunts against artists. But we give up a lot when we link artistic sympathy and so-phistication so unconditionally to acceptance and support. For one thing, we give the job of cultural watchdog completely to the conservative Right, which has a frightening ideological agenda of its own.

68. Alan Rosenthal, "Introduction to Part 3," in Rosenthal, *New Challenges for Documentary*, 245–46.

69. Sobchack, "*No Lies*: Direct Cinema as Rape," in Rosenthal, *New Challenges for Documentary*, 332.

70. Kerekes and Slater, *Killing for Culture*, 11; hereafter cited in text.

71. In the meantime, Michael Findlay sold the name *Slaughter* to Paramount to avoid confusion with their film *Slaughter* (1972).

72. Williams, *Hard Core*, 192.

73. Richard Eder, "'Snuff' Is Pure Poison," *New York Times*, 7 March 1976, sec. 2, pp. 13, 24.

74. "Morgenthau Finds Film Dismembering Was Indeed a Hoax," *New York Times*, 10 March 1976, p. 41, col. 1.

75. Ibid.

76. Williams, *Hard Core*, 193. It should be noted that despite several attempts by various agencies to confirm the existence of snuff movies, no snuff films have ever been found. See Mikita Brottman, *Offensive Films*, 96.

77. Beverly LaBelle, "*Snuff*—The Ultimate in Woman Hating," in *Take Back the Night: Women on Pornography*, ed. Laura Lederer (New York: William Morrow, 1980), 274.

78. See Susan Brownmiller, *Against Our Will: Men, Women, and Rape* (New York: Simon and Schuster, 1975); Andrea Dworkin, *Pornography: Men Possessing Women* (New York: Putnam, 1981); Catherine MacKinnon, *Pornography and Civil Rights: A New Day for Women's Equality* (Minneapolis: Organizing against Pornography, 1988); Catherine MacKinnon, *Only Words* (Cambridge: Harvard University Press, 1993).

79. It's interesting to note that to some extent, John Lennon resisted the film's reification (ghettoization) as "art." In an interview with Martin Jackson, Lennon said, "This is genuine television." Martin Jackson, "Beatle John's Film Makes the Critics Angry," *Daily Express* (London) 29 April 1969, Entertainment Page.

80. Willi Frischauer, "*Rape!*" *Evening Standard* (London) 1 April 1969, 19.

81. Hitchcock quoted in Donald Spoto, *The Dark Side of Genius : The Life of Alfred Hitchcock* (New York: Ballantine, 1983), 483. Also quoted in Clover, *Men, Women, and Chainsaws,* 42.

82. Steven C. Dubin, *Arresting Images: Impolitic Art and Uncivil Actions* (New York: Routledge, 1992), 1.

7. From Horror to Avant-garde

1. Phil Hardy, Tom Milne, and Paul Willemen, *The Encyclopedia of Horror Movies,* 51. To some extent, *Freaks'* unsavory reputation lingers. In *Eye* no. 9, for example, Satanic Church founder Anton LaVey names *Freaks* as one of his three favorite vintage horror flicks. See Patrick Michael O'Donnell, "Satan on the Silver Screen," *Eye,* no. 9 (1997): 3–7.

2. "Big woman" is the term that Hans uses throughout the film to describe Cleopatra. "She is the most beautiful big woman I ever saw," he tells his fiancée, Frieda, at the beginning of the film.

3. "Not for Children," "The Current Cinema," The *New Yorker,* 16 July 1932, 45.

4. "The Circus Side Show," *New York Times,* 9 July 1932, 7.

5. Ibid.

6. *Variety,* 12 July 1932.

7. "The Circus Side Show," 7.

8. "Not for Children," 46.

9. I have decided to use the word "freaks" despite—or perhaps because of—its derogatory connotations. Whether or not physically challenged people are "freaks" is, after all, one of the crucial questions posed by the film, and it is, I believe, the central issue involved in the film's suppression.

10. "The Circus Side Show," 7.

11. The reviewer's discomfort with the use of real freaks in the film is obvious here. One year after *Freaks* was made, *King Kong*—surely the most fantastic love story of all time—was released to rave reviews. See *Variety,* 12 July 1932.

12. *"Freaks," Time,* 18 April 1932, 17.

13. Ad appeared in the *New York Times,* 9 July 1932, 7.

14. Quoted in William Kittredge and Stephen M. Krauzer, eds., *Stories into Film* (New York: Harper and Row, 1979), 11.

15. Quoted in Leslie Fiedler, *Freaks: Myths and Images of the Secret Self* (New York: Simon and Schuster, 1978), 296; hereafter cited in text. I am indebted to William Nestrick for this reference.

16. As David J. Skal and Elias Savada point out, "MGM delayed the New York opening of *Freaks* until July, presumably to keep it away from the influential national media until it had effectively played the entire country." Skal and Savada, *Dark Carnival: The Secret World of Tod Browning, Hollywood's Master of the Macabre* (New York: Anchor, 1995), 180; hereafter cited in text.

17. *Motion Picture Classic,* March 1928. Quoted in John Brosnan, *Horror People* (New York: St. Martin's Press, 1976), 63–64.

18. Ibid., 64

19. Quoted in Skal, *The Monster Show,* 70.

20. Ibid.

21. Ibid., 71.

22. See ad reprints in Skal, 72.

23. Hoberman and Rosenbaum, *Midnight Movies,* 306.

24. Ibid., 307.

25. Jim Morton calls Esper the "father of modern exploitation." Jim Morton, "Film Personalities," in *Incredibly Strange Films, RE/Search* no. 10 (1986: RE/Search Publications, San Franciso), 193. For more on Esper's involvement with *Freaks,* see Skal and Elias, *Dark Carnival.*

26. It also underscores many of the difficulties the general public had in seeing a clear and sharp distinction between pure "exploitation" cinema and mainstream Hollywood films. See Eric Schaefer, "Resisting Refinement: The Exploitation Film and Self-Censorship."

27. Skal, 290. Skal lists the date as the spring of 1947; Friedman places it two years later, in the spring of 1949.

28. David F. Friedman (with Don DeNevi), *A Youth in Babylon: Confessions of a Trash-Film King* (Buffalo, N.Y.: Prometheus Books, 1990), 63.

29. Ibid., 64.

30. See *L'Age du cinéma* (Paris), nos. 4–5 (August–November 1951): 2.

31. See also John Thomas, *"Freaks," Film Quarterly* 17, no. 3 (spring 1964): 59–61. A good discussion of the reasons for the increased popularity of European cinema in the United States from 1958 to 1963 can be found in Peter Lev, *The Euro-American Cinema,* chap. 1.

32. There is a certain irony here. None of Browning's U.S. obituaries mentioned the film at all, and very few mentioned the work he did with Lon Chaney. Clearly, Browning's association with the malformed was deeply disturbing to the American press, which preferred to remember him as the director of *Dracula.*

33. John Thomas, *"Freaks,"* 59.

34. For more on the historical tradition of putting the blame on Mom for "abnormalities" in fetal development, see Marie-Hélène Huet, *Monstrous Imagination* (Cambridge: Harvard University Press, 1993). For an excellent description of the way the female body has traditionally been viewed as an "inferior" version of the male body, see Thomas Laqueur, *Making Sex: Body and Gender from the Greeks to Freud* (Cambridge: Harvard University Press, 1990). And finally, for an interesting discussion of the way that medical discourses have historically promoted gynophobia (or at least used its tropes) in the interest of maintaining a certain medical control over reproduction, see Barbara Ehrenreich and Deirdre English, *For Her Own Good: 150 Years of the Experts' Advice to Women* (Garden City, N.J.: Anchor/Doubleday, 1978); and Carroll Smith-Rosenberg, "The Abortion Movement and

the AMA, 1850–1880," in *Disorderly Conduct: Visions of Gender in Victorian America* (New York: Alfred A. Knopf, 1985), 217–44.

The habit of linking maternal behavior and guilt to fetal development continues in the contemporary media. While I was doing the final manuscript preparation for this book, A&E (Arts and Entertainment) ran a special "biography" on Jan Schlichtmann, the personal injury attorney who fought a long, protracted legal battle against two companies suspected of polluting the water supply in Woburn, Massachusetts. The polluted water, people believed, was responsible for the leukemia deaths of many of the town's children. At the end of a truly gut-wrenching special (designed to dovetail with the theatrical release of *A Civil Action*), in which the companies in question were shown to be guilty of criminal malfeasance, the A&E announcer came on and said that there was some "irony" to the Woburn case. Although the parents had been correct in suspecting that polluted drinking water caused their children's illness, they were mistaken about *when* the damage to the children had been done. The children had not developed leukemia directly, by drinking bad water themselves. Rather, the genetic blueprint for leukemia had been laid while they were still in their mothers' wombs, when their mothers drank contaminated tap water. "Ironically," the announcer said, the mothers who loved and mourned their children so much were themselves "the cause" of their children's illness.

35. According to David Skal, the documentary filmmaker Emile De Antonio was interested in the film for its "vérité aspects." Skal, *The Monster Show*, 16.

36. Thomas, 59; italics mine.

37. Raymond Durgnat, *"Freaks," Films and Filming* 9, no. 1 (August 1963): 23.

38. Ibid.

39. In his obituary for Anthony Balch in *Sight and Sound*, Derek Hill recalls how impressed Balch was "that one afternoon nobody at all came to see *Yoko Ono No. 4*, the famous bottoms film." See Derek Hill, "Anthony Balch," *Sight and Sound* 49, no. 3 (summer 1980): 143.

40. Complicating the mix still further, Balch also showed the film on a double bill with European sexploitation films such as *Don't Deliver Us from Evil* (Joel Seria) and *The Corpse Grinders*. See Tohill and Tombs, *Immoral Tales*.

41. This speech from *Freaks* foreshadows, to some extent, Balch's later work. He went on to make a series of low-budget horror films and exploitation films, and his career is just one more example of the way in which the avant-garde and horror genres seem to overlap. See Ted Morgan, *Literary Outlaw: The Life and Times of William S. Burroughs* (New York: Henry Holt, 1988). I'll discuss the function of the barker's speech later in the chapter.

42. Program note in the Pacific Film Archive series "Received Images: A Reading of Disability in Cinema," University Art Museum and Pacific Film Archive *Calendar*, July 1990, University of California at Berkeley, © Regents of the University of California.

43. Ibid.

44. For a good discussion of "enfreakment," the cultural process by which

people are categorized as "freaks," see Rosemarie Garland Thomson, "Introduction: From Wonder to Error—a Genealogy of Freak Discourse in Modernity," and Robert Bogdan, "The Social Construction of Freaks," in *Freakery: Cultural Spectacles of the Extraordinary Body,* ed. Rosemarie Garland Thomson (New York: New York University Press, 1996). The anthology also contains interesting essays on the exhibition and marketing of freaks, the careers of people performing in the freak shows, and the marketing and representation of Daisy and Violet Hilton, the Siamese twins who have "courtships" in *Freaks.* It also contains my "'One of Us': Tod Browning's *Freaks,*" an earlier version of this chapter.

The term "enfreakment" derives from David Hevey's groundbreaking work on photographic representations of "disability." See David Hevey, *The Creatures Time Forgot: Photography and Disability Imagery* (New York: Routledge, 1992).

45. Ivan Butler, *Horror in the Cinema,* 2d rev. ed. (1967; reprint, New York: A. S. Barnes, 1970), 65.

46. Hercules consistently refers to Hans as a "little ape" or a "pollywog." And when Mme Tetralini calls her charges "children," Jean is incredulous. "Children!" he cries. "But they are monsters!"

47. Schlitze and Elvira tend to cling to Mme Tetralini, as shy children cling to their mother. And they giggle and duck their heads when Phroso promises to buy them hats in Paris. (As William Nestrick pointed out to me, the scene with Phroso is complicated because of its erotic overtones. Phroso is so flirtatious and seductive in this scene that his motive and relation to the freaks becomes difficult to read.)

48. There is, however, one important difference. In gothic romance, the audience generally occupies the point of view of the female victim. We become suspicious when the female protagonist does; sometimes we become suspicious on her behalf before she does. But we are rarely privy to the plans and point of view of the murderous spouse. In *Freaks,* on the other hand, we are privy to Cleo's plans. The film goes out of its way to ensure that the audience knows that Cleo is a gold digger.

49. The shot of Cleo carrying Hans seems particularly designed to feminize and infantilize him. This is all the more striking because Hans has been trying to establish his manhood with Cleo from the beginning of the relationship. Most big people laugh at him, he tells her, because they don't realize he's "a man."

50. Mary Ann Doane, *The Desire to Desire,* 128–40.

51. In most gothic thrillers, the female protagonist's realization that her husband is trying to kill her only makes her vulnerable to him. Typically, she is alone in the house, knows that he is after her, and is unable to get help (the phone doesn't work, or he surprises her just at the moment when the person she is calling answers). Luckily, there is often another "good" man in the film—one who may or may not be in love with the victim—who bursts in and saves the day. Sometimes the "good" man is a policeman; often he has a group of police officers with him. See Doane, *The Desire to Desire,* chap. 5.

52. Doane, 136.

53. As Doane points out, "Freud refers to the conviction of being watched . . . as the most striking symptom of paranoia" (126).

54. This is similar to the reversal we see at the end of Fritz Lang's brilliant 1931 film *M,* in which a child murderer breaks down and recounts the hell his life has been. As he confesses to his crimes, the murderer, sensitively portrayed by Peter Lorre, is transformed from a criminal into a victim. The audience feels sorry for the haunted man who had previously been portrayed as a monster.

55. For Wood, "horror films . . . are progressive precisely to the degree that they refuse to be satisfied with . . . [the] simple designation of the monster as evil." See Robin Wood, *Hollywood from Vietnam to Reagan* (New York: Columbia University Press, 1986), 192.

56. Yoko Ono's *Rape* is not the only avant-garde film that has this tendency. As Atom Egoyan *(Family Viewing, Speaking Parts, The Adjuster)* points out in a 1992 interview, "a lot of films that deal with ideas of voyeurism [a theme common to both avant-garde and horror cinema] are very critical. But they're not actually doing something within the structure of the film to acknowledge that the filmmakers themselves are involved in the most exhibitionist process of all. You can't be coy about the fact that, as a filmmaker, you're also implicated in that process." The coyness that Egoyan mentions here is, interestingly enough, not a problem that horror shares with avant-garde cinema. Such diverse critics as Walter Kendrick and Carol J. Clover agree that "horror films are among the archest, most self-conscious products of contemporary culture." Traditionally problematizing the gaze, they relentlessly interrogate the terms of their production and consumption. In fact, as Clover points out, one of horror's masterpieces, *Peeping Tom,* ruthlessly calls the production and consumption of *all* cinema—not only of horror—into question. See Michael Fox, "Sex, Slides, and Videotape in Atom Egoyan's Latest," *San Francisco Sunday Examiner Chronicle,* 5 July 1992, 33; Walter Kendrick, *The Thrill of Fear: 250 Years of Scary Entertainment* (New York: Grove Press, 1991), xix; Clover, *Men, Women, and Chainsaws,* chap. 4, pp. 166–230.

57. The lovers, Hans and Frieda, are the notable exception here. They are played by the famous brother and sister pair Harry and Daisy Earles.

58. Leslie Fiedler, *Freaks,* 296.

59. Dilys Powell, "A Fit of the Horrors," *Sunday Times* (London) 16 June 1963, 41.

60. Fiedler, *Freaks,* 294.

61. Quote is taken from the film's prologue.

62. *Freaks* is not alone in this. Many of the works that treat freakishness as a theme tend to play on the audience's primeval and modern fears of difference. The theory here seems to be that if you live with freaks long enough, you will become one. In *X, the Man with the X-Ray Eyes* (1963), for example, a surgeon who has x-ray vision takes refuge in a circus sideshow where—in the guise of a psychic—he hopes to use his strange gift to help people. Soon, however, his gift begins to drive him mad, and he blinds himself. Once blinded, he has no further function in the circus

until he is transformed by the sideshow manager into the circus "geek" (the "big person" who, fueled by massive doses of wood alcohol, bites the heads off of live chickens and rodents). And Katherine Dunn's novel *Geek Love* describes the strange Arturo cult, a group of "normal" people who have fallen under the spell of a megalomaniacal freak and have begun mutilating themselves (in order to turn themselves into freaks). Katherine Dunn, *Geek Love* (New York: Knopf, 1989).

63. In terms of both structure and plot, the shot of the chicken-woman seems like an appropriate place to end. Structurally, it parallels the barker's speech that opens the film and completes the opening sequence's missing shot. Thematically it unveils the monster that the audience has been waiting to see.

64. Some show copies and videotapes do not include it.

65. The identification of Frieda with the maternal and Cleo with the sexual is particularly pointed in the film. Almost immediately after receiving erotic encouragement from Cleo, Hans begins rejecting Frieda's maternal suggestions. When she tells him that he shouldn't smoke such a big cigar at night, he tells her, "Please Frieda, don't tell me what I do. When I want a cigar, I smoke a cigar. I want no orders from a woman." "Ach, Hans," she replies, "this is the first time since we have been engaged you have spoken to me so. Why is it?"

The desexualization of Hans in this scene can also be read in light of conventions from still other film genres. As William Nestrick has pointed out to me, in almost all films in which wayward husbands return to the domestic fold, a similar shift from erotic to maternal love takes place. This observation seems to be one more example of the film's complexity, one more example of the way in which *Freaks* layers genres.

66. Early in the film, Venus leaves the strongman Hercules, with whom she has been living. As she carries her things back to her own wagon, she sees Phroso taking off his makeup. Realizing that he has heard the entirety of her argument with Hercules, Venus lashes out at Phroso. "Women are funny, ain't they?" she says sarcastically. Phroso follows Venus back to her wagon, where he replies, "You dames are all alike . . . how you squeal when you get what's coming to you." He goes on to tell Venus to buck up. "You ain't so hard to look at," he tells her, and advises her not to start drinking. "Say," she responds when his speech is over. "You're a pretty good kid."

67. It is interesting to note that ruining the looks of a woman who sexually betrays her man is also a recurring motif in film noir.

68. Hoberman and Rosenbaum, *Midnight Movies,* 297.

69. See Clover, *Men, Women, and Chainsaws,* 50–53.

70. In fact, Cleo's preference for men who can physically dominate her is one of the few traditional female codes she follows.

71. Butler, 66.

72. For more information see Mary Ann Doane, *Femmes Fatales: Feminism, Film Theory, Psychoanalysis* (New York: Routledge, 1991).

73. See Susan Lurie, "Pornography and the Dread of Woman"; and Barbara

Creed, *The Monstrous Feminine*. Also see my discussion of *Les yeux sans visage*, in chapter 4 of this volume.

74. This seems to have been the case among the freaks playing in the film as well. Schlitze, the childlike pinhead who is consistently portrayed as a girl in the film, was actually played by Schlitze, the man. See Skal, *The Monster Show*, 152.

75. As I have demonstrated elsewhere, the treatment of gender and adultery in *Freaks* presents an interesting variation on the homosocial bonding that Eve Kosofsky Sedgwick describes. See Hawkins, "'One of Us': Tod Browning's *Freaks*," in *Freakery: Cultural Spectacles of the Extraordinary Body*, ed. Rosemarie Garland Thomson (New York: New York University Press, 1996), 265–76; and Eve Kosofsky Sedgwick, *Between Men: English Literature and Male Homosocial Desire* (New York: Columbia University Press, 1985).

76. Fiedler, 298.

77. Hoberman and Rosenbaum, 306.

78. See Susan Rubin Suleiman, *Subversive Intent: Gender, Politics, and the Avant-garde* (Cambridge: Harvard University Press, 1990).

79. See Morgan, *Literary Outlaw*.

80. Clover, *Men, Women, and Chainsaws*, 64.

81. A much-needed book on De Antonio will be published by University of Minnesota Press in 2000. Edited by Douglas Kellner and Dan Streible, the collection will include a lengthy bio of "De," a slew of interviews, reviews, and commentary on each of his documentaries.

82. Bosworth, *Diane Arbus*, 162. Also quoted in Skal, *The Monster Show*, 17.

83. Diane Arbus, *Diane Arbus* (Millerton, N.Y.: Aperture, 1972).

84. Susan Sontag, *On Photography*, 3d ed. (New York: Doubleday Books, 1977), 32; hereafter cited in text.

85. Christoph Grunenberg, *Gothic: Transmutations of Horror in Late Twentieth Century Art* (Boston: Institute of Contemporary Art, 1997), 211.

86. The exhibit was curated by Christoph Grunenberg.

87. Grunenberg, *Gothic*, flyleaf.

8. Monsters in the Art World

1. As Maurice Yacowar, the author of one of the only serious auteurist studies of Morrissey's work, notes, "Warhol allowed his friend's films his famous imprimatur, in order to ease their way into the marketplace, but this generosity helped to delay the recognition of Morrissey's own voice and values." Maurice Yacowar, *The Films of Paul Morrissey* (New York: Cambridge University Press, 1993), 11.

2. Anglo-American sources generally credit Margheriti with "special make-up effects" and list Morrissey as both the writer and director.

3. *The BFI Companion to Horror*, 210–11.

4. Michael Ferguson, *Little Joe Superstar: The Films of Joe Dallesandro* (Laguna Hills, Calif.: Companion Press, 1998), 128.

5. See entry under *Il mostro e in tavola* 1973, p. 279.

6. Although Morrissey seemed to be breaking away from the Factory at this point, it's clear that Warhol still considered him to be part of his entourage. He was present in Rome during the filming of *Frankenstein* and was concerned about the title of the film. See Melton S. Dawes, "Morrissey—from *Flesh* and *Trash* to *Blood for Dracula*," *New York Times,* 15 July 1973, "Arts and Leisure," 9.

7. Valerie Solanas, an author, playwright, and founder and only member of SCUM (Society for Cutting Up Men), shot Warhol in June 1968.

8. Paul Gardner, "Creepy Gothic," *New York Times Film Reviews, 1973–1974* (New York: New York Times and Arno Press, 1975), 237. Originally published in *New York Times,* 14 July 1974, sec. 2, p. 11.

9. Andy Warhol, *The Philosophy of Andy Warhol (From A to B and Back Again)* (New York: Harcourt, Brace, Jovanovich, 1975), 11.

10. Maurice Yacowar, *The Films of Paul Morrissey,* 2; hereafter cited in text. A good example is the filmography in Juan Suárez's *Bike Boys, Drag Queens, and Superstars.* Suárez lists *Flesh, Heat,* and *Trash* in Warhol's filmography, followed by the following note: "The trilogy *Flesh, Heat,* and *Trash* was produced by Andy Warhol and, according to the credits, written and directed by Paul Morrissey. However it is included in all Warhol filmographies." Juan Suárez, *Bike Boys, Drag Queens, and Superstars: Avant-garde, Mass Culture, and Gay Identities in the 1960s Underground Cinema* (Bloomington: Indiana University Press, 1996), 320.

11. Carlo Ponti was the official producer of the film, which had a kind of commercial backing that other Morrissey productions lacked.

12. Dawes, "Morrissey—from *Flesh* and *Trash* to *Blood for Dracula*."

13. Morrissey's post-*Dracula* films include *The Hound of the Baskervilles* (1977), *Madame Wang's* (1981), *Forty-Deuce* (1982), *Mixed Blood* (1984), *Beethoven's Nephew* (1985), and *Spike of Bensonhurst* (1988).

14. For an interesting discussion of Warhol as "auteur" of Morrissey's Factory films, see David E. James, "The Producer as Author," *Wide Angle* 7, no. 3 (1985): 24–33; reprinted in Michael O'Pray, ed., *Andy Warhol Film Factory* (London: British Film Institute, 1989), 136–45.

15. Even in the case of *Frankenstein,* a film for which Warhol had no credited role, Warhol was present during the screening and was concerned with the film's title. See Melton S. Dawes, "Morrissey—From *Flesh* and *Trash* to *Blood for Dracula*."

16. After a passage describing Warhol's title suggestions for the Frankenstein film, for example, Morrissey is quoted as saying, "We don't want our pictures taken seriously." Dawes, "Morrissey—from *Flesh* and *Trash* to *Blood for Dracula*."

17. Yacowar, 3.

18. Ibid., 25.

19. Parker Tyler, *Underground Film: A Critical History* (New York: Grove Press, 1969), 225.

20. Tony Rayms, "Death at Work: Evolution and Entropy in Factory Films," in O'Pray, *Andy Warhol: Film Factory,* 169.

21. Stepehn Koch, *Stargazer: The Life, World, and Films of Andy Warhol,* rev. ed. (New York: Marion Boyars, 1991), 99, 100.

22. Ibid., 79–80.

23. Ironically, Morrissey's anti-art stance brings him remarkably close to Peter Bürger's definition of the "true" avant-garde. For Bürger, the term "avant-garde" refers, or should refer only, to the historic avant-garde, the anti-art dadas and surrealists, because, Bürger says, they're the only ones who successfully challenged the cultural apparatus of art. For Bürger, to be avant-garde is by definition to be anti-art. See Peter Bürger, *Theory of the Avant-garde,* trans. Michael Snow (Minneapolis: University of Minnesota Press, 1987).

24. Interview in Chuck Workman's film, *Superstar: The Life and Time of Andy Warhol* (1990). Paul Morrissey knew Edie Sedgwick.

25. Ibid.

26. In an interview for Chuck Workman's *Superstar,* Dennis Hopper describes his experience working on Warhol's *The Thirteen Most Beautiful Boys* (1965, 40 minutes).Warhol, Hopper said, simply told him the name of the film, turned on the camera, and walked away.

27. P. Adams Sitney, *Visionary Films: American Avant-garde, 1943–1978,* 2d ed. (1974; New York: Oxford University Press, 1979), 372; hereafter cited in text.

28. Jonas Mekas, *Movie Journal* (New York: Macmillan, 1972), 109.

29. Peter Gidal, *Andy Warhol Films and Paintings: The Factory Years* (New York: Da Capo, 1971), 80.

30. Parker Tyler, "Dragtime and Drugtime, or Film à la Warhol," in O'Pray, *Andy Warhol Film Factory,* 94–103. See also Tyler, *Underground Film,* 27–28.

31. Gidal, 90.

32. Ibid., 84.

33. Some exceptional work on Warhol's general relationship with popular culture and with Hollywood has been done by cultural studies critics. See Suárez, *Bike Boys, Drag Queens, and Superstars;* Kathy Acker, "Blue Valentine," Rio Limpo, "Lonesome Cowboys and Gay Cinema," Gary Indiana, "I'll Be Your Mirror," and David James, "the Producer as Author," in O'Pray, *Andy Warhol Film Factory;* and Jennifer Doyle, Jonathan Flatley, and José Esteban Muñoz, *Pop Out: Queer Warhol* (Durham, N.C.: Duke University Press, 1996).

34. See my discussion of glance theory in chapter 2.

35. This is also the kind of viewing encouraged by museums that show Warhol's movies as part of gallery exhibitions. I recently saw some of the screen tests at the Museum of Modern Art in Chicago. Three monitors were set up in a gallery, and viewers could either stroll through, glancing at the monitors, sit on the bench and watch all or part of the display, or move between the film gallery and the adjoining galleries. While I was there, all three kinds of viewing were taking place. Some of the viewing took place in silence. Some was accompanied by discussion. Nico's screen test, which shows Nico literally unable to meet the camera's gaze, made the women spectators terribly uncomfortable. Edie Sedgwick's test brought a

variety of responses from all the spectators who knew Warhol's work. "Art and Film since 1945," Museum of Contemporary Art, Chicago, November 1997. See *Art and Film since 1945: Hall of Mirrors,* organized by Kerry Brougher, ed. Russell Ferguson (Los Angeles: Museum of Contemporary Art; New York: Monacelli Press, 1996).

Because I'm mainly discussing glance and gaze aesthetics here, I'm not attempting to address the other modes of spectatorship that various groups have adopted toward Warhol's movies. Simon Watney writes, for example, that the first time he got busted was together with some two hundred people watching Warhol's *Lonesome Cowboys* (1967) in its first week of screening in London in 1969. "Serious structuralist film critics undoubtedly attended too, but by and large it was a very queer audience indeed, as were the audiences for all Warhol's film screenings in London in the seventies—and to this day." Simon Watney, "Queer Andy," in Doyle, Flatley, and Muñoz, *Pop Out: Queer Warhol,* 20–30. Subsequent references will be to *Pop Out.*

36. Gidal, 95.

37. Corrigan, *A Cinema without Walls,* 32.

38. Gidal, 88–89.

39. Chuck Workman's *Superstar* clearly shows times when Warhol makes one of his famous "uh-I don't know," statements to an interviewer and then laughs as he catches gallery owner Ivan Karp's eye. Warhol was an authority on celebrity and public image, and he managed his own as carefully and perhaps rigidly as the studio managed Garbo's.

40. Gidal, 92–94.

41. Rainer Crone, "Form and Ideology: Warhol's Techniques from Blotted Line to Film," in *The Work of Andy Warhol,* ed. Gary Garrels, Dia Art Foundation Discussion in Contemporary Culture no. 3 (Seattle: Bay Press, 1989), 70–92.

42. Crone, 90.

43. Review included in Kim Evans, *Andy Warhol* (London: London Weekend Television, 1987), prod. Alan Benson.

44. As Suárez has pointed out, there are pop culture elements running through many underground films produced during this period, but few filmmakers embrace the commercialism of the imagery as openly as Warhol does. Warhol "projected his avant-gardism into traditionally non-artistic venues" (Suárez, *Bike Boys, Drag Queens, and Superstars,* 217).

45. Ibid., 223, 225.

46. Paul Gardner, "Morrissey Gives the Director's View," *New York Times,* 14 November 1972.

47. Gerard Malanga, guest editor, *Film Culture,* no. 45 (summer 1967).

48. Suárez, 226.

49. Ibid.

50. Earlier Suárez discusses the ways in which Stan Brakhage's and Jonas Mekas's film aesthetic shares the ideology of the American transcendental movement. See Suárez, 223–25.

51. Suárez, 226.

52. Ibid., 227.

53. See Steven Shaviro, "Warhol's Bodies," in *The Cinematic Body* (Minneapolis: University of Minnesota Press, 1993), 201–41. Not surprisingly, Ultraviolet—one of Warhol's superstars—concurs with this view. See interview in Workman's *Superstar*.

54. As John Cale and Lou Reed note in their song "Starlight," "If Hollywood doesn't call us, we'll be sick" (*Songs for Drella* [U.S: Sire Records, 1990]).

55. Paul Gardner, "Creepy Gothic," *New York Times*, 14 July 1974, sec. 2, p. 11.

56. See the earlier discussions of surrealism, MacMahonism, et cetera in Chapter 1 and 3.

57. Suárez, 91. In his influential 1939 article "Avant-garde and Kitsch," Clement Greenberg defines kitsch as "rear-guard" art, the opposite of avant-garde art. Unlike high art, kitsch "operates by formulas . . . it is vicarious experience and faked sensation. It changes according to style, but remains always the same. Kitsch is the epitome of all that is spurious in the life of our time." He characterized jazz, advertising, Hollywood movies, and commercial illustration in the broad category of kitsch. Where kitsch is simplistic, the avant-garde is demanding. As Suárez points out, like other writers in the Anglo-American tradition, Greenberg defines the avant-garde broadly as any form of modern art that defies traditional modes of representation. The "avant-garde" art he most admires, though, is art that Suárez—and I—would term "modernist"; that is, experimental art that is critical of industrial society and popular culture and—while opposed to a certain view of high art—does not embrace a radically anti-art stance (as the dadas and surrealists did). See Clement Greenberg, "Avant-garde and Kitsch," *Partisan Review* 6, no. 5 (fall 1939): 34–39; reprinted in Clement Greenberg, *Art and Culture* (Boston: Beacon, 1961).

Like Clement Greenberg, in "A Theory of Mass Culture," Dwight Macdonald juxtaposed kitsch or "masscult" to authentic art or modernism. Where Macdonald differs from Greenberg is in identifying a middle ground—an area that Greenberg somewhat problematically defines as "quality kitsch." An example of "quality kitsch" or a "midcult" product would be the *New Yorker*. See Dwight Macdonald, "A Theory of Mass Culture," in *Mass Culture: The Popular Arts in America*, ed. Bernard Rosenberg and David Manning White (Glencoe, Ill.: Free Press, 1958), 59–73.

58. Sitney, 371.

59. Walter Benjamin, "The Work of Art in the Age of Mechanical Reproduction," in *Illuminations*, ed. Hannah Arendt, trans. Harry Zohn (New York: Schocken Books, 1969), 217–53.

60. Andy Warhol and Pat Hackett, *POPism: The Warhol Sixties* (San Diego: Harcourt, Brace Jovanovich, 1980), 34.

61. Ibid., 34–35.

62. Suárez, 253–54.

63. In *Lou Reed: Rock and Roll Heart*, Billy Name claims the nickname was an affectionate one, and that Factory members used it to tease Warhol. Timothy

Greenfield-Sanders, *Lou Reed: Rock and Roll Heart,* American Master Series, produced for PBS by WNET Boston, executive producer of series Susan Lacey (1998).

According to other sources, the vampire nickname was more than just an affectionate, *figurative* label. In *Superstar* people frequently refer to how "strange" or "wonderful" Andy looked—invoking his pallor and his hair. "The question with Warhol," Ultraviolet says at one point, "is was he really alive? When I tried to seduce him, he was so cold, I mean like a dead body" (interview in Workman, *Superstar*).

64. Audio commentary by Udo Kier on Paul Morrissey, *Andy Warhol Presents a Film by Paul Morrissey: Flesh for Frankenstein,* Criterion Collection, CLV (Director's Cut) laser disc (New York: Voyager, 1996), analog audio track 2.

65. I'm using this hyphenated name as a convenient way of referring to the films Paul Morrissey made at—or through the patronage of—the Factory. As others have indicated, Disney films might provide a model for ways to conceive of the "collaboration" between Warhol and Morrissey. David E. James suggests the horror films that Val Lewton made with Jacques Tourneur as another possible model (*Cat People* [1942] and *I Walked with a Zombie* [1943]), but I believe that Lewton had a greater individual (as opposed to studio) hand in shaping the look of those movies than Warhol had in shaping the Morrissey-directed films. See David James, "The Producer as Author."

66. Public tolerance for violence also increased in this era, as *Bonnie and Clyde* (1967), *A Clockwork Orange* (1971), *Straw Dogs* (1971), and *Taxi Driver* (1976) significantly challenged prevailing norms about the amount and kind of violence that could be shown on-screen.

67. See ad, *New York Times,* 21 May 1974, sec. 1, p. 50.

68. Vogel uses this term instead of "transvestite," which would more accurately describe the actress in question.

69. Vogel, *Film as a Subversive Art,* 256–57.

70. Ibid., 235.

71. In large part, of course, this is simply one aspect of the larger upheaval that was taking place in society during this time as various groups came out of the closet and demanded their rights, and as people increasingly ignored traditional moral imperatives and cultural sexual taboos. To this end, the counterculture practiced free love, lived together outside of wedlock, had children outside of wedlock, arranged open marriages, and normalized almost *any* kind of sex between consenting adults. Drug use was accepted and, in many cases, advocated. Traditional notions of patriotism and national loyalty were being questioned. And the government and social institutions (including the family) were increasingly seen as repressive forces rather than as benign or even beneficent agencies of the people's will. This trend was radically reversed in the 1980s, when the American film industry was allowed once again to begin integrating vertically (under vertical intergration, studios can control the means of distribution and exhibition), and when the socio-moral mood of the country shifted.

72. *I Am Curious Yellow* was seized by U.S. customs and banned, following a trial, but the verdict was overturned by the court of appeals. Much of the footage shot was used in the less-interesting companion film, *I Am Curious—Blue.*" See Leslie Halliwell, *Halliwell's 1997 Film and Video Guide,* ed. John Walker (Great Britain: Harper, 1996), 364. It's interesting that Paul Morrissey defended (or tried to) *Blue Movie* from the censors. He had not approved of the film's sexually explicit subject matter and had in fact left the set of the movie after setting up the lighting. See Yacowar, 23.

73. San Francisco's Surf Theater, the neighborhood theater featured at the beginning of Woody Allen's *Play It Again Sam* (1972), played silent films, French New Wave films, Italian neorealist films, Japanese films, and contemporary European art films, as well as Hollywood classics such as *Casablanca* (1942) and *To Have and Have Not* (1945). The concessions stand reflected the mix, selling popcorn, coke, candy, Gauloise cigarettes, pastries, and pastilles. For a long time, black coffee was available—free of charge—in the lobby. And at least twice, the theater tried to attract a before- and after-show crowd by running an adjacent café (which sold espresso drinks, gourmet teas, "regular" coffee, hot chocolate, juice, and pastries). As might be expected, the Surf drew a lot of business from nearby San Francisco State, as well as from the city's Italian, French, and French-Basque populations. But the classic Hollywood films always drew a more mixed crowd, people of different ages who didn't necessarily have an interest in foreign films but loved Hollywood cinema.

74. The mural of whales and dolphins on the outside of the Mitchell Brothers Theater in San Francisco, for example, both established the theater as a "natural" part of the city's landscape and gave it a couples-friendly look.

75. Friends have described seeing both the Warhol-Morrissey films and *Deep Throat* in nonspecialized commercial cinemas in Bloomington, Indiana.

76. *Variety* reported that in 1973, "for the first time in industry annals, 'stag' films found such public acceptance . . . that at least four generated returns in excess of the $1,000,000 rental mark." *Deep Throat* made more than $4 million (according to industry estimates) in 1973. *The Devil in Miss Jones* made more than $2 million, and *Behind the Green Door* made an estimated $1 million by January 1974. The journal predicted that in the wake of a restrictive Supreme Court decision, 1974 would not be such a banner year. Interestingly, however, it also reported that the Supreme Court decision—which ruled that the sale and exhibition of porn may be restricted to conform to local standards—was *not* supported by the majority of Americans polled. According to *Variety*'s figures, 56 percent of those polled completely disagreed with the decision, 20.5 percent had some misgivings about the decision, and only 22.9 percent uncategorically agreed that localities should be allowed to restrict the sale of material sold in other parts of the country. See "Fear of Fines Mums Word on Porno Pix over $1–Mil," *Variety,* 9 Jan 1974, 19; and "'Subsidy' for Films Not Favored by Survey, nor Porno Ruling," *Variety,* 16 Jan 1974, 20.

77. See, for example, D. C. Disney, "Betty and Bruce Had a Sex Hang-Up," *Ladies Home Journal,* October 1969, 20; N. Gittelson, "Erotic Life of the American Wife," *Harper's Bazaar,* July 1969, 76–91; S. Lydon, "Understanding Orgasm," *Ramparts Magazine,* 14 December 1968, 59–63; E. M. Brecher, "We Are All Our Mother's Daughters: What Sex Research Reveals about Unhappy Wives," *Redbook,* November 1969, 71; C. Vincent, "When Married Love Is Disappointing," *Redbook,* April 1970, 82–83; G. Krupp, "Husbands and Wives Talk Frankly about Sex," *Redbook,* July 1970, 69; and, of course, the runaway best-seller, David R. Reuben, *Everything You Always Wanted to Know about Sex but Were Afraid to Ask* (New York: D. McKay, 1969), which—as one reviewer said—helped to dispel the "self-defeating myths about size, endurance, and what Mary McCarthy calls 'the tyranny of the orgasm.'" Marcia Seligson, "The Sex Manual Revolution," *Life,* 5 December 1969, 21.

For an analysis of the ideology of sex literature during this period, see Meryl Altman, "Everything They Always Wanted You to Know: The Ideology of Popular Sex Literature," in *Pleasure and Danger: Exploring Female Sexuality,* ed. Carol S. Vance (London: Pandora Books, 1989), 115–30.

78. As Jeffrey Sconce defines them, "theories of enunciation basically try to explain the discursive relationship between the viewer and the cinematic text; that is, how the film addresses and positions the viewer in relation to the image." Sconce provides a clear and accessible discussion of what he correctly describes as "an often unstable and always volatile combination of Lacanian psychoanalysis, the linguistic theories of Emile Benveniste, and the Marxist aesthetic strategies of Bertolt Brecht." See Jeffrey Sconce, "Spectacles of Death: Identification, Reflexivity, and Contemporary Horror," in *Film Theory Goes to the Movies,* ed. Jim Collins, Hilary Radner and Ava Preacher Collins (New York: Routledge, 1993), 107; subsequent citations will be to Sconce, "Spectacles of Death."

79. Peter Wollen, "Godard and Counter-cinema: *Vent D'Est,*" in *Movies and Methods,* vol. 2, ed. Bill Nichols (Berkeley and Los Angeles: University of California Press, 1985), 500–509.

80. By the 1980s, ironic double-entendre allusions to oral sex had entered commercial Hollywood cinema. In *The Fabulous Baker Boys* (Steve Kloves, 1989), for example, Michelle Pfeiffer tells a curious Jeff Bridges that she only smokes expensive Dunhill cigarettes because she's fussy about what she puts in her mouth. At this particular point in their relationship—which has turned flirty but not yet openly sexual—the line has a definite connotative edge.

81. Peter Travers, "When Shock Has Value," *Rolling Stone* 8 March 1990, 69. Quoted in Sconce, "Spectacles of Death," 104.

82. Sconce, "Spectacles of Death," 115–16. The reason, of course, is that the techniques are used to radically different ends in the two films. In *Freddy's Dead,* as Sconce shows, distancing techniques ironically foster a kind of viewer identification with Freddy—or at least with the visual excitement that Freddy supplies. I suspect the distancing devices used in *Deep Throat* might function in a similar way, enabling male viewers to get off on the film while still allowing female viewers to engage with

the film differently. That is, I suspect the film addresses male and female viewers differently. Which is precisely what made it a successful "crossover" film, something heterosexual couples could share.

83. Morrissey's ironic story lines attracted a youth audience that hadn't always been there for Warhol's "serious" avant-garde productions. *Deep Throat*'s ironic strategies help to break up the traditional porn identification with the phallic male on-screen, a crucial strategy if you want to attract heterosexual couples. It's interesting to note in the same context that both Morrissey's films and *Deep Throat* broke with genre convention by emphasizing narrative.

84. Gilbert and Gubar, *The Madwoman in the Attic*, 228.

85. See Walter Evans, "Monster Movies: A Sexual Theory," in *Movies as Artifacts: Cultural Criticism of Popular Films*, ed. Michael T. Marsden, John G. Nachbar, and Sam L. Grogg Jr. (Chicago: Nelson-Hall, 1982), 129–36.

86. Often Morrissey's statements remind me of what Sconce calls "the caustic rhetoric of paracinema." I keep expecting him to say, as the editors of *Zontar* do, that his films are "*not* for the delicate tastebuds of the pseudo-genteel cultural illiterati who enjoy mind-rotting, soul-endangering pabulum like *Joseph Campbell and the Power of Myth* and the other white boy 'new-age' puke-shit served up from the bowels of PBS during pledge week." Morrissey's rhetoric is usually more genteel—he refers to "half-baked intellectuals"—but the contentiousness and the caustic tone are the same. See Sconce, "'Trashing' the Academy," 372, 371; and Gardner, "Morrissey Gives the Director's View."

87. Taped interview included in Kim Evans, *Andy Warhol*.

88. Dawes, "Morrissey—From *Flesh* and *Trash* to *Blood for Dracula*."

89. This is one of the scenes in the film that is often "received" and perceived very differently by men and women. Many women—including myself—read the scene as a rape. Most of the men I've spoken to see it as a disturbing sex scene, but not rape because Jeanne's consent to try new and even uncomfortable sex games is implied through her continued visits to the apartment. However you read the scene, its juxtaposition with a "revenge" scenario is interesting. After sex, Paul falls asleep, and Jeanne tries to play a record. When Paul wakes up, she tells him the record player won't work. As he grabs the wire in an attempt to fix the phonograph, he gets a nasty electrical shock, and Jeanne laughs.

90. Audio commentary by Morrissey on Paul Morrissey, *Andy Warhol Presents a Film by Paul Morrissey: Flesh for Frankenstein*, analog audio track 2. See also Yacowar, 77; and Ferguson, 119.

91. See for example, Angela Carter, *The Sadeian Woman and the Ideology of Pornography*; Gilles Deleuze, "Coldness and Cruelty," in Deleuze, *Masochism;* Jane Gallop, *Thinking through the Body* and Jane Gallop, *Intersections: A Reading of Sade with Bataille, Blanchot, and Klossowski*. For related discussions on the cultural meaning of sadistic representations, see Georges Bataille, *Visions of Excess: Selected Writings, 1927–1939;* and Linda Williams, "Power, Pleasure, and Perversion: Sado-masochistic Film Pornography," in Williams, *Hardcore*.

92. Georges Bataille, "The Use Value of D. A. F. De Sade," and "The Notion of Expenditure," in *Visions of Excess,* 91–102, 116–29.

93. Yosefa Loshitzky, *The Radical Faces of Godard and Bertolucci* (Detroit, Mich.: Wayne State University Press, 1995), 165.

94. See my discussion of *Snuff,* chapter 6.

95. In "Pornography, Oppression, Freedom: A Closer Look," for example, Helen Longino asserts that "contrary to the findings of the Commission on Obscenity and Pornography a growing body of research is documenting (1) a correlation between exposure to representations of violence and the committing of violent acts generally, and (2) a correlation between exposure to pornographic materials and the committing of sexually abusive or violent acts against women. While more study is needed to establish precisely what the causal relations are, clearly so-called hard-core pornography is not innocent." Helen E. Longino, "Pornography, Oppression, and Freedom: A Closer Look," in Lederer, *Take Back the Night,* 47. Robin Morgan put it more succinctly: "Pornography is the theory and rape the practice." Robin Morgan, "Theory and Practice: Pornography and Rape," in Lederer, 139.

One of the effects of the feminist antiporn discussions of this period was to shut down discussion about women's sexuality, as women saw it—or to confine such discussion to narrowly specified parameters. A key example of this was the feminist antiporn reaction to an academic conference—the Scholar and Feminist IX conference, "Toward a Politics of Sexuality"—held at Barnard College on 24 April 1982. The conference, as Carol S. Vance describes it, "attempted to explore the ambiguous and complex relationship between sexual pleasure and danger in women's lives and in feminist theory." During the week preceding the conference, women identifying themselves as antiporn feminists called the Barnard Administration and "metropolitan area feminists" and denounced the conference organizers for "inviting proponents of 'anti-feminist' sexuality." The protesters were particularly disturbed by the inclusion of a number of S/M practitioners and proponents, to the exclusion—they felt—of "a major portion of the feminist movement." They also felt that the conference wasn't taking women's experience of sexual danger (i.e., rape) seriously enough. The phone calls precipitated a kind of administrative panic. Two days before the conference, college administrators confiscated 1,500 copies of a handbook (which contained "disturbing images") that was to have been distributed to registrants. The conference itself was picketed by Women against Pornography, Women against Violence against Women, and New York Radical Feminists. For more information, see Carol S. Vance, *Pleasure and Danger,* introduction and epilogue.

Finally, for a feminist film that examines female pleasure and the possible liberatory aspects of porn for women, see Bette Gordon, *Variety* (1984).

96. See Clover, *Men, Women, and Chainsaws;* and Williams, *Hardcore.* Laura Kipnis has written about a particularly chilling real-life case that derives in part from our current confusion over fantasy and reality. When Daniel DePew participated in what he thought was an S/M fantasy "scene" with an undercover FBI agent, DePew

was arrested for conspiring to kidnap and molest a child; that is, the fantasy was mistaken for real intent. DePew was sentenced to thirty-three years in prison. See Laura Kipnis, *Bound and Gagged: Pornography and the Politics of Fantasy in America* (New York: Grove Press, 1996), 3–63.

97. See Clover's discussion in *Men, Women, and Chainsaws*, 114–37.

98. Sconce, "Spectacles of Death," 119.

99. Michael Ninn is a porn director whose work, like Godard's and Bertolucci's, problematizes voyeurism and frequently maps larger social concerns onto women's bodies.

Shamway and Augustus Lenzl make a similar point about the uncomfortable similarities between art cinema and porn when they ask "how much of an innovative compulsion has an art-director developed when he progresses, *as a consequence,* to multiple 'set eroticist' of numerous pseudonyms?" The director in question is Stephen Sayadian who, under the name of Rinse Dream, directed *Café Flesh* (1982). Shamway and Augustus Lenzl, "I Know You're Watching Me: Eros, Seminal Rolls, and Coffee," trans. Andy Waller, *Flesh and Blood,* no. 7 (1996): 34; italics mine. For more information on Flesh and Blood Press (FAB) contact Harvey Fenton, P.O. Box 178, Guildford, Surrey, GU3 2YU England or e-mail harvey@fabpress.demon. co.uk.

Finally, Andrew Sarris noticed how much *Last Tango* was lumped together with *Deep Throat* in cocktail party chatter. "'Oh, you're a film critic,' one elegant hostess after another would discover with visible delight. 'What do you think of *Last Tango* and *Deep Throat?*'" Andrew Sarris, "Cock-Tale Parties on the East Side," in *Politics and Cinema* (New York: Columbia University Press, 1978), 135; essay originally published in *Village Voice,* February 1973.

100. Ferguson, 120.

101. Review of "*Flesh for Frankenstein,*" *Variety,* 27 February 1974, 18.

102. Bryanston Films, which distributed the movie, made a slightly less gory R-rated version also available (presumably to capture markets in communities with strict "local standards"). See *Variety,* 14 August 1974, 10. At the time of this rating, the film was playing in only nine cities.

103. Gardner, "Creepy Gothic."

104. Quoted in Ferguson, 157.

105. The Criterion laser disc gives us the unedited European version of the film, which includes at least one full-frontal nude shot of Dallesandro, which, Ferguson points out, was not in the original U.S. X-rated release (Ferguson, 125).

106. Indeed, the film seems to have been cast with the gay audience in mind. Belgian actress Monique Van Vooren, who plays Baroness Frankenstein, was, Michael Ferguson notes, "very popular with gay audiences via a nightclub act" (125). For more discussion of the gay reception of the Warhol-Morrissey films see Simon Watney, "Queer Andy," in Doyles et al., *Pop Out.*

107. This link was strengthened by the fact that the film often played in the same theaters where patrons had seen the other films. In San Francisco, for exam-

ple, the Bridge theater, which exhibited *Frankenstein,* had also shown both *Clockwork Orange* and *Last Tango.*

108. *The Exorcist* was a huge box office success. Not only did it successfully engage with the fear—expressed by many middle-class parents—that American kids were "possessed" and out of control, but it was one of the few films of the period to deal directly with issues of faith and religiosity. As a result, it attracted not only the usual audience for big-budget horror films but also "millions who normally wouldn't be seen dead at a horror movie" (*Encyclopedia of Horror Movies,* 274). For more on demon kid movies and the mood of the times, see Vivian Sobchack, "Bringing It All Back Home: Family Economy and Generic Exchange," *Camera Obscura,* no. 15 (fall 1986): 7–34. The essay also appears in Constance Penley, Elisabeth Lyon, Lynn Spigel, and Janet Bergstrom, eds., *Close Encounters: Film Feminism and Science Fiction* (Minneapolis: University of Minnesota Press, 1991). A shorter version of Sobchack's essay appears in Gregory Waller, ed., *American Horrors: Essays on the Modern American Horror Film* (Urbana and Chicago: University of Illinois Press, 1987), 175–94.

109. Gardner, "Creepy Gothic," 237.

110. Audio commentary by Morrissey on Paul Morrissey, *Andy Warhol Presents a Film by Paul Morrissey: Flesh for Frankenstein,* analog audio track 2.

111. Nora Sayre, "Andy Warhol's Frankenstein," *New York Times,* 16 May 1974, 52.

112. This was emphasized, as Michael Ferguson points out, when it was re-released in May 1982, as part of a 3–D revival (*Jaws 3–D, Friday the 13th Part 3 in 3–D*), when it had a "surprisingly healthy return engagement" (Ferguson, 129).

113. Vincent Canby, "Shock Treatment," *New York Times,* 28 June 1974. Canby mistakes actor Udo Kier's German accent in this scene for a "lisp," a mistake that causes Canby to give the film an even campier reading than he might otherwise have done. In the laser disc analog sound track, Kier talks about his accent working well for the part. "Frankenstein wants a perfect race," he says, "and we know where that comes from." Just in case the listening audience doesn't, he makes the allusion to Hitler clear by mentioning that the zombies are "very Aryan-looking people."

114. Stephen Farber, "Hollywood's New Sensationalism: The Power and the Gory," *New York Times,* 7 July 1974, sec. 2, p. 1.

115. Ibid.

116. Bakhtin, *Rabelais and His World,* 101–2. Also quoted in Paul, *Laughing Screaming,* 45; hereafter cited in text.

117. Mikita Brottman lumps these films together under the heading "cinéma vomitif": films "which purport to represent real bodies at the limits of pleasure and pain; films which are often "unambiguously delimited as gratuitous sadism for entertainment's sake." Mikita Brottman, *Offensive Films: Toward an Anthropology of Cinéma Vomitif* (Westport, Conn.: Greenwood Press, 1997), 4.

118. Bakhtin, 19–20.

119. Audio commentary by Morrissey on Paul Morrissey, *Andy Warhol Presents a Film by Paul Morrissey: Flesh for Frankenstein,* analog audio track 2.

120. For more on dada, see Serge Lemoine, *Dada,* trans. Charles Lynn Clark (New York: Universe Books, 1987).

121. Certainly, *A Clockwork Orange* engages all the ethical questions that typically surround the low splatter genre films. Originally passed by the British Board of Censors in 1971, *A Clockwork Orange* was withdrawn from circulation in Britain by Stanley Kubrick and Warner Brothers Studios because of crimes that the police, judges, and defendants say were inspired by the film. See William E. Schmidt, "Kubrick Keeps a Lid on *Clockwork,*" *San Francisco Chronicle,* 8 February 1993, "Datebook," D1–D2.

122. Zimmerman's review of *Frankenstein* is one of the best-informed reviews to appear in the mainstream press and one of the best discussions I've read of the film. Paul Zimmerman, "Camp Frankenstein," *Newsweek,* 20 May 1974, 105–6.

123. Warhol, *The Philosophy of Andy Warhol,* 92.

Conclusion

1. Jeffrey Sconce, "Spectacles of Death: Identification, Reflexivity, and Contemporary Horror," 113.

2. David E. Williams, "Our Man Flynt," *Film Threat,* no. 2 (February 1997): 27; hereafter cited in text.

3. Laura Kipnis, "Disgust and Desire: *Hustler Magazine,*" 141; hereafter cited in text.

4. This is reminiscent of Huyssen's argument that women are intimately linked to consumer culture in ways that men aren't. See Andreas Huyssen, *After the Great Divide.*

5. Larry Karaszewski and cowriter Scott Alexander also wrote the screenplay for *Ed Wood.*

6. Since I wrote this, Larry Flynt has opened Hustler Hollywood, a large adult emporium that explicitly targets an upscale middle-class market. With its large plate glass windows, store T-shirts, espresso bar, and helpful staff, the store resembles a Barnes and Noble—with dildos. The "cute" and fun sex paraphernalia (flavored jellies, breakaway panties, etc.) are shelved toward the front of the store. The hard-core material is in the back in a special "you must be eighteen or older" section. It will be interesting to see how much or how little the class enunciation of *Hustler* magazine changes as a result of the expansion of Flynt's corporate interests.

7. "Larry has an amazing life story," coscreenwriter Scott Alexander told David Williams, "but it's one that most people don't know because Larry grossed-out so many people on the surface that no one ever took a second look" (Williams, 24).

8. Mark Edmundson, *Nightmare on Main Street: Angels, Sadomasochism, and the Culture of Gothic* (Cambridge: Harvard University Press, 1997).

9. Mark Edmundson, "Art and Imperium," *Nation,* 29 June 1998, 25; hereafter cited in text.

10. An interesting postscript: As *The People vs. Larry Flynt* points out, the first trial against Larry Flynt took place in Cincinnati, and this trial is the most elaborated in the film. Here we see the judge refusing to allow the presentation of evidence that would establish more lenient "community standards" than the ones invoked by the prosecution. And here we see the judge sentencing Flynt to twenty-five years for publishing dirty pictures. Several years later, the same city was the site of another famous smut trial—when the curator of an art gallery was taken to court for displaying "dirty pictures" by renowned photographer-artist Robert Mapplethorpe.

Bibliography

Adorno, Theodor. "The Culture Industry Reconsidered." Trans. Anson G. Rabinbach. *New German Critique* (fall 1975): 12–19.

Anderson, Christopher. *Hollywood TV: The Studio System in the Fifties.* Austin: University of Texas Press, 1994.

Arendt, Hannah. *Eichmann in Jerusalem: A Report on the Banality of Evil.* New York: Viking Press, 1963.

Armes, Roy. *French Cinema since 1946.* Vol. 2, *The Personal Style.* New York: A. S. Barnes, 1966.

Astruc, Alexandre. "The Birth of a New Avant-garde: La Caméra Stylo." In *The New Wave: Critical Landmarks,* ed. Peter Graham, 17–23. New York: Doubleday, 1968.

Atkins, Robert. *Art Speak: A Guide of Contemporary Ideas, Movements, and Buzzwords.* New York: Abbeville Press, 1990.

Atkinson, Michael. "Obscure Objects: Satisfying Cinephiliac Lusts." *Village Voice,* 22 April 1997, 86.

Austin, Guy. *Contemporary French Cinema.* Manchester: Manchester University Press, 1996.

Bakhtin, Mikhail. *Rabelais and His World.* Trans. Hélène Iswolsky. Bloomington: Indiana University Press, 1984.

Balazs, André, ed. *Hollywood Handbook.* New York: Universe Publishing, 1996.

Balbo, Lucas. "Unbearable Films and Terrible Headaches: A Conversation with Jess Franco." *Video Watchdog,* no. 1 (1990).

Bangs, Lester. *Psychotic Reactions and Carburetor Dung.* New York: Vintage Books, 1988.

Bardèche, Maurice, and Robert Brassillach. *Histoire du cinéma.* Paris: Denoël et Steele, 1935.

Barthes, Roland. *S/Z.* Trans. Richard Miller. New York: Hill and Wang, 1974.

Bataille, Georges. *Visions of Excess: Selected Writings, 1927–1939.* Trans. Allan Stoekl with Carl R. Lovitt and Donald M. Leslie Jr. Minneapolis: University of Minnesota Press, 1985.

Baudrillard, Jean. "Please Follow Me." In *Suite Venitienne,* ed. Sophie Calle. Paris: Editions de l'étoile, 1983.

————. *America.* Trans. Chris Turner. London: Verso, 1989.

————. *Cool Memories.* Trans. Chris Turner. London: Verso, 1990.

Bazin, André. *What Is Cinema?* Trans. and ed. Hugh Gray. Berkeley and Los Angeles: University of California Press, 1967.

Benjamin, Walter. "The Work of Art in the Age of Mechanical Reproduction." In *Illuminations,* trans. Harry Zohn, ed. Hannah Arendt, 217–53. New York: Schocken Books, 1969.

Benshoff, Harry M. *Monsters in the Closet: Homosexuality and the Horror Film.* Manchester: Manchester University Press, 1997.

Berger, John. *Ways of Seeing.* London: British Broadcasting Corporation and Penguin Books, 1972.

Bernstein, Michael André. *Bitter Carnival: Ressentiment and the Abject Hero.* Princeton, N.J.: Princeton University Press, 1992.

Bersani, Leo, and Ulysse Dutoit. "Merde Alors: Pasolini's *Salo.*" *October,* no. 13 (summer 1980): 23–35.

Bloom, Harold. *The Anxiety of Influence.* New York: Oxford University Press, 1973.

Bondanella, Peter. *Italian Cinema from Neorealism to the Present.* New York: Continuum, 1983.

Bordwell, David. "The Art Cinema as a Mode of Film Practice." *Film Criticism* 4, no. 1 (fall 1979): 56–64.

Bosworth, Patricia. *Diane Arbus.* New York: Alfred A. Knopf, 1984.

Bourdieu, Pierre. *Distinction: A Social Critique of the Judgment of Taste.* Trans. Richard Nice. Cambridge: Harvard University Press, 1984.

Boussinot, Roger. *L'Encyclopédie du cinéma.* Paris: Les Savoirs Bordas, 1995.

Brée, Germaine. *Twentieth Century Literature.* Trans. Louise Guiney. Chicago: University of Chicago Press, 1983.

Breton, André. *Manifestoes of Surrealism.* Trans. Richard Seaver and Helen Lane. Ann Arbor: University of Michigan Press, 1972.

————. *Oeuvres complètes.* Vol. 1. Bibliothèque de la Pléiade. Paris: Gallimard, 1988.

Brodsky, Michael. *Detour.* New York: Urizen Books, 1977.

Brosnan, John. *The Horror People.* New York: St. Martin's Press, 1976.

Brottman, Mikita. *Offensive Films: Toward an Anthropology of Cinéma Vomitif.* Westport, Conn.: Greenwood Press, 1997.

Brownmiller, Susan. *Against Our Will: Men, Women, and Rape.* New York: Simon and Schuster, 1975.

Bukatman, Scott. *Terminal Identity: The Virtual Subject in Postmodern Science Fiction.* Durham, N.C.: Duke University Press, 1993.

Bürger, Peter. *Theory of the Avant-garde.* Trans. Michael Shaw. Minneapolis: University of Minnesota Press, 1987.

Buss, Robin. *French Film Noir.* London: Marion Boyars, 1994.

Butler, Ivan. *Horror in the Cinema.* International Film Guide Series. New York: A. S. Barnes, 1967.

Caldwell, John Thomas. *Televisuality: Style, Crisis, and Authority in American Television.* New Brunswick, N.J.: Rutgers University Press, 1995.

Cale, John, and Lou Reed. *Songs for Drella.* Audio recording, liner notes, libretto. Sire Records, 1990.

Carroll, David. "Narrative, Heterogeneity, and the Question of the Political," in *The Aims of Representation: Subject, Text, History,* ed. Murray Krieger. New York: Columbia University Press, 1987.

Carter, Angela. *The Sadeian Woman and the Ideology of Pornography.* New York: Pantheon Books, 1978.

Carson, Diane, Linda Dittmar, and Janice R. Welsch, eds. *Multiple Voices in Feminist Film Criticism.* Minneapolis: University of Minnesota Press, 1994.

Chadwick, Whitney. *Women Artists and the Surrealist Movement.* Boston: Little Brown, 1985.

"The Circus Side Show." *New York Times,* 9 July 1932, 7.

Clarens, Carlos. *An Illustrated History of the Horror Film.* New York: Capricorn Books, 1967.

Clover, Carol J. "Her Body, Himself: Gender in the Slasher Film." *Representations* 20 (fall 1987): 187–228.

———. *Men, Women, and Chainsaws: Gender in the Modern Horror Film.* Princeton, N.J.: Princeton University Press, 1992.

Coates, Paul. *Film at the Intersection of High and Mass Culture.* Cambridge: Cambridge University Press, 1994.

Cohan, Steven, and Ina Rae Hark. *Screening the Male: Exploring Masculinities in Hollywood Cinema.* New York: Routledge, 1993.

Collins, Jim. *Architectures of Excess: Cultural Life in the Information Age.* New York: Routledge, 1995.

Collins, Jim, Hilary Radner, and Ava Preacher Collins. *Film Theory Goes to the Movies.* New York: Routledge, 1993.

Collins, Kevin. "Interview with Jess Franco." *European Trash Cinema,* Special no. 1, October 1996.

Comes, Phillippe de, and Michel Marmin. *Le cinéma français, 1930–1960.* Paris: Editions Atlas, 1984.

Cook, David A. *A History of Narrative Film.* 3d ed. New York: W. W. Norton, 1996.

Corrigan, Timothy. *A Cinema without Walls: Movies and Culture after Vietnam.* New Brunswick, N.J.: Rutgers University Press, 1991.

Cotton, Bob, and Richard Oliver. *The Cyberspace Lexicon: An Illustrated Dictionary of Terms from Multimedia to Virtual Reality.* London: Phaidon, 1994.

Craft, Christopher. "'Kiss Me with Those Red Lips': Gender and Inversion in Bram Stoker's *Dracula*." *Representations* 8 (fall 1984): 107–33.

Creed, Barbara. *The Monstrous-Feminine: Film, Feminism, and Psychoanalysis.* New York: Routledge, 1993.

"Criterion Collection: *Blade Runner*." http://www.voyagerco.com/criterion/ catalogpage.cgi? bladerunner, n.d. Accessed 8 August 1997.

"Criterion Collection: *Brazil*." http://www.voyagerco.com/criterion/ catalogpage.cgi?brzil, n.d. Accessed 8 August 1997.

Curtin, Michael. *Redeeming the Wasteland: Television Documentary and Cold War Politics.* New Brunswick, N.J.: Rutgers University Press, 1995.

Delahaye, Michel. "Gothique flamboyant." *Cahiers du cinéma* 18, no. 106 (April 1960): 48–54.

Deleuze, Gilles. "Coldness and Cruelty." In *Masochism,* trans. Jean McNeil. New York: Zone Books, 1989.

Deleuze, Gilles, and Félix Guattari. *Anti-Oedipus: Capitalism and Schizophrenia.* Trans. Robert Hurley, Mark Seem, and Helen R. Lane. Minneapolis: University of Minnesota Press, 1983.

———. *A Thousand Plateaus: Capitalism and Schizophrenia.* Trans. Brian Massumi. Minneapolis: University of Minnesota Press, 1987.

Derry, Charles. *Dark Dreams: A Psychological History of the Modern Horror Film.* New York: A. S. Barnes, 1977.

Diawara, Manthia, ed. *Black American Cinema.* New York: Routledge, 1993.

Dika, Vera. *Games of Terror: Halloween, Friday the 13th, and the Films of the Stalker Cycle.* Rutherford, N.J.: Fairleigh Dickinson University Press; London and Toronto: Associated University Presses, 1990.

Doane, Mary Ann. *The Desire to Desire: The Woman's Film of the 1940s.* Bloomington: Indiana University Press, 1987.

———. *Femmes Fatales: Feminism, Film Theory, Psychoanalysis.* New York: Routledge, 1991.

Doane, Mary Ann, Patricia Mellencamp, and Linda Williams, eds. *Re-vision: Essays in Feminist Film Criticism.* American Film Institute Monograph Series, vol. 3. Frederick, Md.: University Publications of America, 1984.

Doherty, Thomas. *Teenagers and Teenpics: The Juvenilization of American Movies in the 1950s.* Boston: Unwin Hyman, 1988.

Donald, James, ed. *Fantasy and the Cinema.* London: British Film Institute, 1989.

Dougan, John. "Onobox." *In These Times* 16, no. 25 (20–26 May 1992): 18.

Douglas, Mary. *Purity and Danger: An Analysis of the Concepts of Pollution and Taboo.* London: Ark Paperbacks, 1984.

Doyle, Jennifer, Jonathan Flatley, and José Esteban Muñoz. *Pop Out: Queer Warhol.* Durham, N.C.: Duke University Press, 1996.

Dubin, Steven C. *Arresting Images: Impolitic Art and Uncivil Actions.* New York: Routledge, 1992.

Dunn, Katherine. *Geek Love.* New York: Warner Books, 1989.

Durgnat, Raymond. "Freaks." *Films and Filming* 9, no. 1 (August 1963): 22–23.

———. *Franju.* Movie Paperbacks Series. Berkeley and Los Angeles: University of California Press, 1967.

———. *Luis Buñuel.* Berkeley and Los Angeles: University of California Press, 1977.

Dworkin, Andrea. *Pornography: Men Possessing Women.* New York: Putnam, 1981.

Ebert, Roger. "Why Movie Audiences Aren't Safe Anymore." *American Film* 6, no. 5 (March 1981): 54–56.

Edmundson, Mark. *Nightmare on Main Street: Angels, Sadomasochism, and the Culture of Gothic.* Cambridge: Harvard University Press, 1997.

Ehrenreich, Barbara, and Deirdre English. *For Her Own Good: 150 Years of the Experts' Advice to Women.* Garden City, N.J.: Anchor/Doubleday, 1978.

Ellis, John. *Visible Fictions: Cinema, Television, Video.* London: Routledge and Kegan Paul, 1982.

Elsaesser, Thomas. *New German Cinema: A History.* New Brunswick, N.J.: Rutgers University Press, 1989.

Facets Multimedia Catalog no. 14. Facets Multimedia Services, 1517 West Fullerton Avenue, Chicago, Illinois 60614.

Facets Video Catalog no. 12. Facets Multimedia Services, 1517 West Fullerton Avenue, Chicago, Illinois 60614.

Farber, Manny, ed. *Negative Space: Manny Farber on the Movies.* New York: Da Capo Press, 1998.

Fenton, Harvey, and William Lustig. "A Different Point of View: The Jess Franco Interview." *Flesh and Blood* 9 (1997): 32–35.

Ferguson, Michael. *Little Joe Superstar: The Films of Joe Dallesandro.* Laguna Hills, Calif.: Companion Press, 1998.

Ferguson, Russell, ed. *Art and Film since 1945: Hall of Mirrors.* Los Angeles: Museum of Contemporary Art. New York: Monacelli Press, 1996.

Fiedler, Leslie. *Freaks: Myths and Images of the Secret Self.* New York: Simon and Schuster, 1978.

Finkielkraut, Alain. *Remembering in Vain: The Klaus Barbie Trial and Crimes against Humanity.* Trans. Roxanne Lapidus with Sima Godfrey. New York: Columbia University Press, 1989.

Fiske, John. *Television Culture.* London: Methuen, 1987.

Forbes, Elliott. "The 'Lost' World." *Film Comment,* July–August 1991.

Forbes, Jill. *The Cinema in France after the New Wave.* Bloomington: Indiana University Press, 1992.

Ford, René Jeanne, and Charles Ford. *Histoire illustrée du cinéma.* Vol 3. Verviers, Belgium: Editions Gérard and Marabout Université, 1966.

Foucault, Michel. *Birth of the Clinic: An Archaeology of Medical Perception.* Trans. A. M. Sheridan Smith. New York: Vintage Books, 1973.

Fraser, Matthew. "A Question of Culture: The Canadian Solution Resolves a GATT Standoff." *MacLean's* (Canadian ed.), 27 December 1993, 50.

"Freaks." *Time,* 18 April 1932, 17.

Freaks review. *Variety,* 12 July 1932, n.p.

Friedan, Betty. *The Feminine Mystique.* New York: Norton, 1963.

Friedberg, Anne. *Window Shopping: Cinema and the Postmodern.* Berkeley and Los Angeles: University of California Press, 1993.

Friedman, David F. (with Don DeNevi). *A Youth in Babylon: Confessions of a Trash-Film King.* Buffalo, N.Y.: Prometheus Books, 1990.

Gallop, Jane. *Intersections: A Reading of Sade with Bataille, Blanchot, and Klossowski.* Lincoln: University of Nebraska Press, 1981.

———. *Thinking through the Body.* New York: Columbia University Press, 1988.

Gander, L. Marsland. "Lennon's *Rape* Erratic." *Daily Telegraph,* 26 April 1969, 15.

Garrels, Gary. *The Work of Andy Warhol.* Dia Art Foundation Discussion in Contemporary Culture no. 3. Seattle: Bay Press, 1989.

Gascoyne, David. *A Short Survey of Surrealism.* San Francisco: City Lights Books, 1982.

Gay-Lussac, Bruno. "La Chronique de Bruno Gay-Lussac." *L'Express,* no. 456 (10 March 1960): 36.

Gelmis, Joseph. *The Film Director as Superstar.* New York: Doubleday, 1970.

Gidal, Peter. *Andy Warhol Films and Paintings: The Factory Years.* London: British Film Institute, 1989.

Gilbert, Sandra M., and Susan Gubar. *The Madwoman in the Attic: The Woman Writer and the Nineteenth Century Literary Imagination.* New Haven, Conn.: Yale University Press, 1979.

Gomery, Douglas. *Shared Pleasures: A History of Movie Presentation in the United States.* Madison: University of Wisconsin Press, 1992.

Gordon, Mel. *The Grand Guignol: Theatre of Fear and Terror.* New York: Amok Press, 1988.

Greenberg, Clement. *Art and Culture.* Boston: Beacon, 1961.

Grunenberg, Christoph. *Gothic: Transmutations of Horror in Late Twentieth Century Art.* Boston: Institute of Contemporary Art, 1997.

Halberstam, Judith. *Skin Shows: Gothic Horror and the Technology of Monsters.* Durham, N.C.: Duke University Press, 1995.

Hall, Stuart, Dorothy Hobson, Andrew Lowe, and Paul Willis, eds. *Culture, Media, Language.* London: Hutchinson, 1980.

Halliwell, Leslie. *Halliwell's 1997 Film and Video Guide.* Ed. John Walker. Great Britain: Harper, 1996.

Hammond, Paul, ed. *The Shadow and Its Shadow: Surrealist Writings on Cinema.* Edinburgh: Polygon, 1991.

Hamrah, A. S. and Joshua Glenn. "Monsters, Sex, Sci-Fi, and Kung-Fu." *Utne Reader,* July–August 1995, 30.

Hardy, Phil, Tom Milne, and Paul Willemen. *The Encyclopedia of Horror Movies.* New York: Harper and Row, 1986.

Haskell, Barbara, and John G. Hanhardt. *Yoko Ono: Arias and Objects.* Salt Lake City: Peregrine Smith Books, 1991.

Hayward, Susan. *French National Cinema.* New York: Routledge, 1993.

———. *Key Concepts in Cinema Studies.* New York: Routledge, 1996.

Hebdige, Dick. *Subculture: The Meaning of Style.* New York: Routledge, 1987.

Hevey, David. *The Creatures Time Forgot: Photography and Disability Imagery.* London: Routledge, 1992.

Higginbotham, Virginia. *Spanish Film under Franco.* Austin: University of Texas Press, 1988.

Hill, Derek. "Cheap Thrills." *London Tribune,* 29 April 1960, 11.

———. "Anthony Balch." *Sight and Sound* 49, no. 3 (summer 1980): 143.

Hoberman, J., and Jonathan Rosenbaum. *Midnight Movies.* New York: Da Capo Press, 1983.

Hoesterey, Ingeborg. *Zeitgeist in Babel: The Postmodernist Controversy.* Bloomington: Indiana University Press, 1991.

Hogan, David. *Dark Romance: Sexuality in the Horror Film.* Jefferson, N.C.: McFarland, 1986.

Hogue, Peter. "Riders of the Dawn." *Film Comment,* July–August 1991.

Home Film Festival, *Program Guide no. 12* (1996). Home Film Festival, P.O. Box 2032, Scranton PA 18501.

Hopewell, John. *Out of the Past: Spanish Cinema after Franco.* London: British Film Institute, 1986.

Horton, Andrew, and Stuart Y. McDougal. *Play It Again Sam: Retakes on Remakes.* Berkeley and Los Angeles: University of California Press, 1998.

Huet, Marie-Hélène. *Monstrous Imagination.* Cambridge: Harvard University Press, 1993.

Huyssen, Andreas. *After the Great Divide: Modernism, Mass Culture, Postmodernism.* Bloomington: Indiana University Press, 1986.

Indiana, Gary. "Home." *Aperture* 127 (spring 1992): 56–63.

Jameson, Fredric. *Postmodernism, or the Cultural Logic of Late Capitalism.* Durham, N.C.: Duke University Press, 1991.

———. *Signatures of the Visible.* New York: Routledge, 1992.

Jancovich, Mark. *Rational Fears: American Horror in the 1950s.* Manchester: Manchester University Press, 1996.

———. "Cult Fictions: Cult Movies, Subcultural Capital, and the Production of Cultural Distincions." Manuscript, 1998.

Jenkins, Janet, ed. *In the Spirit of Fluxus*. Minneapolis: Walker Art Center, 1993.

Jones, Alan. *Mondo Argento*. London: Midnight Media, 1996.

Kadrey, Richard. *Covert Culture Sourcebook*. New York: St. Martin's Press, 1993.

———. *Covert Culture Sourcebook 2.0*. New York: St. Martin's Press, 1994.

———. "Director's Cuts." *World Art* 3 (1996): 64–68.

Kael, Pauline. "Shoot the Piano Player." *Film Culture* 27, (1962–1963): 14–16.

———. "Zeitgeist and Poltergeist, or Are Movies Going to Pieces." In *I Lost It at the Movies,* 3d ed., ed. Pauline Kael, 3–27.

———. *For Keeps*. New York: Dutton, 1994.

Kaplan, Alice Yaeger. *Reproductions of Banality: Fascism, Literature, and French Intellectual Life*. Minneapolis: University of Minnesota Press, 1986.

Kaplan, E. Ann. *Women and Film: Both Sides of the Camera*. New York: Methuen, 1983.

———. *Looking for the Other: Feminism, Film, and the Imperial Gaze*. New York: Routledge, 1997.

———, ed. *Women in Film Noir*. London: British Film Institute Publishing, 1978.

Katz, Robert. *The Fatal Marriage of Carl Andre and Ana Mendieta*. New York: Atlantic Monthly Press, 1990.

Kendrick, Walter. *The Thrill of Fear: 250 Years of Scary Entertainment*. New York: Grove Press, 1991.

Kerekes, David, and David Slater. *Killing for Culture: An Illustrated History of Death Film from Mondo to Snuff*. San Francisco: Creation Books, 1994.

Kinder, Marsha. *Blood Cinema: The Reconstruction of National Identity in Spain*. Berkeley and Los Angeles: University of California Press, 1993.

Kipnis, Laura. *Ecstasy Unlimited: On Sex, Gender, Capital, and Aesthetics*. Minneapolis: University of Minnesota Press, 1993.

———. *Bound and Gagged: Pornography and the Politics of Fantasy in America*. New York: Grove Press, 1996.

Kittredge, William, and Stephen M. Krauzer, eds. *Stories into Film*. New York: Harper and Row, 1979.

Klinger, Barbara. *Meaning and Melodrama: History, Culture, and the Films of Douglas Sirk*. Bloomington: Indiana University Press, 1994.

———. "The Media Aristocrats: Home Theater and the Domestic Film Experience." *Velvet Light Trap,* no. 42 (fall 1998): 4–19.

Knight, Arthur. Introduction to *Foreign Films on American Screens,* by Michael F. Mayer. New York: Arco, 1965.

Koch, Stephen. *Stargazer: The Life, World, and Films of Andy Warhol*. Rev. ed. New York: Marion Boyars, 1991.

Krauss, Rosalind, ed. *L'Amour Fou: Photography and Surrealism*. Washington, D.C.: Corcoran Gallery of Art; New York: Abbeville Press, 1985.

Kroker, Arthur. *The Possessed Individual: Technology and the French Postmodern*. New York: St. Martin's Press, 1992.

Kuhn, Annette. *The Power of the Image*. London: Routledge and Kegan Paul, 1985.

Kyrou, Ado. *Le surréalisme au cinéma.* Paris: Le Terrain Vague, 1963.

Lalli, Thomas. "Chain Letters and Pyramid Schemes: Don't Get Ripped Off." *Eye,* no. 9 (1997): 8–10.

Laqueur, Thomas. *Making Sex: Body and Gender from Greeks to Freud.* Cambridge: Harvard University Press, 1990.

Lawday, David. "France Guns for Clint Eastwood." *U.S. News and World Report,* 3 December 1993, 72.

Lederer, Laura, ed. *Take Back the Night.* New York: William Morrow, 1980.

Legrand, Gérard. "Female x Film = Fetish." In *The Shadow and Its Shadow: Surrealist Writings on the Cinema,* ed. Paul Hammond. Edinburgh: Polygon, 1991.

Lemoine, Serge. *Dada.* Trans. Charles Lynn Clark. New York: Universe Books, 1987.

Lev, Peter. *The Euro-American Cinema.* Austin: University of Texas Press, 1993.

Levine, Lawrence W. *Highrow/Lowbrow: The Emergence of Cultural Hierarchy in America.* Cambridge: Harvard University Press, 1988.

Lévi-Strauss, Claude. *The Elementary Structures of Kinship.* Boston: Beacon Press, 1969.

Lowenstein, Adam. "Films without a Face: Surrealism, Horror, and Historical Trauma in the Cinema of Georges Franju." Manuscript, 1996.

———. "Films without a Face: Shock Horror in the Cinema of Georges Franju." *Cinema Journal* 37, no. 4 (summer 1998): 37–58.

Loshitzky, Yosefa. *The Radical Faces of Godard and Bertolucci.* Detroit, Mich.: Wayne State University Press, 1995.

Lovell, Alan. *Anarchist Cinema.* New York: Gordon Press, 1975.

Lucas, Tim. "How to Read a Franco Film." *Video Watchdog,* no. 1 (1990).

———, ed. *The Video Watchdog Book.* Cincinnati, Ohio: Video Watchdog, 1992.

Lurie, Susan. "Pornography and the Dread of Woman." In *Take Back the Night,* ed. Laura Lederer. New York: William Morrow, 1980.

Macdonald, Dwight. "A Theory of Mass Culture." In *Mass Culture: The Popular Arts in America,* ed. Bernard Rosenberg and David Manning White. Glencoe, Ill.: Free Press, 1957.

———. "Films: Mostly Bird Watching." *Esquire,* October 1963, 38.

MacDonald, Scott. *A Critical Cinema 2: Interviews with Independent Filmmakers.* Berkeley and Los Angeles: University of California Press, 1992.

———. *Avant-Garde Film: Motion Studies.* New York: Cambridge University Press, 1993.

MacKinnon, Catherine. *Pornography and Civil Rights: A New Day for Women's Equality.* Minneapolis: Organizing against Pornography, 1988.

———. *Only Words.* Cambridge: Harvard University Press, 1993.

Magid, Marion. "Auteur! Auteur! Opposing Camps." *Commentary* 37 (March 1964): 70–74.

Malcolm, Janet. *The Journalist and the Murderer.* New York: Knopf, 1990.

Maltby, Richard, and Ian Craven. *Hollywood Cinema: An Introduction.* Cambridge, Mass.: Blackwell Publishers, 1995.

Manceaux, Michèle. "La Semaine." *L'Express,* no. 455 (3 March 1960): 38.

Marcus, Greil. *Lipstick Traces: A Secret History of the Twentieth Century.* Cambridge: Harvard University Press, 1989.

Marks, Elaine, and Isabelle de Courtivron. *New French Feminisms.* New York: Schocken Books, 1981.

Mast, Gerald, Marshall Cohen, and Leo Braudy, eds. *Film Theory and Criticism.* 4th ed. New York: Oxford University Press, 1992.

Mayer, Michael. *Foreign Films on American Screens.* New York: Arco, 1965.

McCarty, John. *Splatter Movies: Breaking the Last Taboo of the Screen.* New York: St. Martin's Press, 1984.

McDonagh, Maitland. "The House by the Cemetery," *Film Comment,* July–August 1991.

———. *Broken Mirrors/Broken Minds: The Dark Dreams of Dario Argento.* New York: Citadel Press, 1994.

McGowan, Chris. "An Appreciation of the Criterion Collection." http://www.organa.com/Outerspace/Cargo/Lasers/criterion.html, 1994. Accessed 8 May 1997.

McLuhan, Marshall. *Understanding Media: The Extensions of Man.* New York: McGraw-Hill, 1964.

McNeil, Alex. *Total Television: The Comprehensive Guide to Programming from 1948 to the Present.* 4th ed. New York: Penguin Books, 1996.

McRobbie, Angela. "Postmodernism and Popular Culture." In *ICA Documents* 4, 54–58. London: Institute of Contemporary Art, 1986.

Meehan, Thomas. "Not Good Taste, Not Bad Taste, It's Camp." *New York Times Magazine,* 21 March 1965, 30–31.

Mekas, Jonas. *Movie Journal.* New York: Macmillan, 1972.

Metz, Christian. *The Imaginary Signifier: Psychoanalysis and the Cinema.* Trans. Celia Britton, Anwyl Williams, Ben Brewster, and Alfred Guzzetti. Bloomington: Indiana University Press, 1977.

Milne, Tom, ed. and trans. *Godard on Godard.* New York: Da Capo Press, 1972.

Modleski, Tania. "The Terror of Pleasure." In *Studies in Entertainment: Critical Approaches to Mass Culture,* ed. Tania Modleski, 155–67. Bloomington: Indiana University Press, 1987.

———. *The Women Who Knew Too Much: Hitchcock and Feminist Theory.* New York: Methuen, 1988.

Monaco, James. *Alain Resnais.* New York: Oxford University Press, 1979.

Mondo Video. *Mondo Video Catalogue.* Cockeville, Tennessee, n.d.

Moore, Eric. "Guess Who's Coming *as* Dinner?" *TLA Film and Video Quarterly* (spring 1993): 23. TLA Video Management, Inc., 332 South Street, Philadelphia, PA 19147-9923.

Morrissey, Paul. *Paul Morrissey, Andy Warhol Present a Film by Paul Morrissey:*

Flesh for Frankenstein. Criterion Collection (laser disc), CLV (Director's Cut). New York: Voyager, 1996.

Morton, Jim. "A–Z of Film Personalities." *RE/Search* no. 10: *Incredibly Strange Films,* 1986.

Morton, Jim, ed. *Re/Search* no. 10: *Incredibly Strange Films,* 1986.

Mourlet, Michel. "Apologie de la violence." *Cahiers du cinéma* 18, no. 107 (May 1960): 24–27.

Mulvey, Laura. *Visual and Other Pleasures.* Bloomington: Indiana University Press, 1989.

Myrent, Glenn, and Georges P. Langlois. *Henri Langlois: First Citizen of Cinema.* Trans. Lisa Nesselson. Twayne's Filmmakers Series. New York: Twayne, 1995.

Nadeau, Maurice. *Histoire du surréalisme.* Paris: Club des Editeurs, 1956.

Naremore, James. *Filmguide to Psycho.* Bloomington: Indiana University Press, 1973.

———. "Authorship and the Cultural Politics of Film Criticism." *Film Quarterly* 44, no. 1 (fall 1990).

———. *More than Night: Film Noir in Its Contexts.* Berkeley and Los Angeles: University of California Press, 1998.

Naremore, James, and Patrick Brantlinger, eds. *Modernity and Mass Culture.* Bloomington: Indiana University Press, 1991.

Newman, Kim. *Nightmare Movies: A Critical Guide to Contemporary Horror Films.* New York: Harmony Books, 1988.

———, ed. *The BFI Companion to Horror.* London: Cassell and British Film Institute, 1996.

Nichols, Bill. *Representing Reality: Issues and Concepts in Documentary.* Bloomington: Indiana University Press, 1991.

———, ed. *Movies and Methods.* Vol. 2. Berkeley and Los Angeles: University of California Press, 1985.

Nichols, Peter M. "A Hard Sell, Those Little French Films." *New York Times,* 23 June 1996, H29.

"Not for Children." *New Yorker,* 16 July 1932, 45–46.

"Note to the Viewer, A." n.a. http://www.voyagerco.com/criterion/about/note.html. Accessed 8 August 1997.

Obsidian Video. Newspeak. Providence, R.I.

Ono, Yoko. *Grapefruit: A Book of Instructions.* New York: Simon and Schuster, 1970; London: Owen, 1970.

O'Pray, Michael, ed. *Andy Warhol: Film Factory.* London: British Film Institute, 1989.

Orr, John. *Cinema and Modernity.* Cambridge, England: Polity Press, 1993.

Pacific Film Archive. *Pacific Film Archive Bimonthly Calendar.* Vol. 14, no. 4 (July–August 1991). University of California at Berkeley, 2625 Durant Ave., Berkeley, CA 94720.

"Parochial Uproar in Ft. Lee: Panics before Foreign Art Films." *Variety,* 24 April 1960, 24.

Passek, Jean Loup, ed. *Dictionnaire du cinéma.* Paris: Librairie Larousse, 1986.

Paul, William. *Laughing Screaming: Modern Hollywood Horror and Comedy.* New York: Columbia University Press, 1994.

Penley, Constance, Elisabeth Lyon, and Lynn Spigel, eds. *Close Encounters: Film, Feminism, and Science Fiction.* Minneapolis: University of Minnesota Press, 1991.

Peterson, James. *Dreams of Chaos, Visions of Order: Understanding the American Avant-garde Cinema.* Detroit, Mich.: Wayne State University Press, 1994.

Petrie, Duncan, ed. *Screening Europe: Image and Identity in Contemporary European Cinema.* London: British Film Institute, 1992.

Powell, Dilys. "A Fit of the Horrors." *Sunday Times* (London) 16 June 1963, 41.

Prawer, S. S. *Caligari's Children: The Film as Tale of Terror.* New York: Da Capo Press, 1980.

Prédal, René. *Le cinéma français contemporain.* Paris: Les Editions du Cerf, 1984.

———. *Le cinéma français depuis 1945.* France: Editions Nathan, 1991.

Rabinowitz, Lauren. *Points of Resistance: Women, Power, and Politics in the New York Avant-garde Cinema, 1943–1971.* Urbana and Chicago: University of Illinois Press, 1991.

Rebello, Stephen. *Alfred Hitchcock and the Making of "Psycho."* New York: Dembner Books, 1990.

Renov, Michael, ed. *Theorizing Documentary.* New York: Routledge, 1993.

Rosen, Philip, ed. *Narrative, Apparatus, Ideology.* New York: Columbia University Press, 1986.

Rosenbaum, Jonathan. Review of *"Eyes without a Face." Chicago Reader,* 1995. Reprinted on-line: *Chicago Reader* "On Film: Brief Reviews." http:/onfilm.chireader.com/MovieCaps/E/EY/13162_EYES_WITHOUT_A_FACE.html. Accessed 17 October 1997.

Rosenberg, Bernard, and David Manning White, eds. *Mass Culture: The Popular Arts in America.* Glencoe, Ill.: Free Press, 1958.

Rosenthal, Alan. *New Challenges for Documentary.* Berkeley and Los Angeles: University of California Press, 1988.

Ross, Andrew. *No Respect: Intellectuals and Popular Culture.* New York: Routledge, 1989.

Ross, Gene. "Sexploitation Films: The 60's Sexplosion!" *Adult Video News* 2, no. 1 (March 1987).

Ross, Philippe. *Les visages de l'horreur.* Paris: Edilig, 1985.

Roud, Richard. *A Passion for Films: Henri Langlois and the Cinémathèque Française.* New York: Viking Press 1983.

Sammon, Paul M. *Future Noir: The Making of "Blade Runner."* New York: Harper Prism, 1996.

Sanjek, David. "Fan's Notes: The Horror Film Fanzine." *Literature/Film Quarterly* 18, no. 3 (1990): 150–59.

Sarris, Andrew. "The Director's Game." *Film Culture* 22–23 (1961): 68–81.

————. "Notes on the Auteur Theory in 1962." *Film Culture* 27 (1962–1963): 1–8.

————. "Citizen MacDonald." *Village Voice,* 3 October 1963, 13–14.

————. *Confessions of a Film Cultist: On the Cinema, 1955–1969.* New York: Simon and Schuster, 1970.

————. *Politics and Cinema.* New York: Columbia University Press, 1978.

Schaefer, Eric. "Resisting Refinement: The Exploitation Film and Self-Censorship." *Film History* 6, no. 3 (1994): 293–313.

————, ed. *Trash Cinema Reader.* Austin: University of Texas Press, forthcoming.

Schmidt, William E. "Kubrick Keeps a Lid on *Clockwork.*" *San Francisco Chronicle, Datebook,* 8 February 1993, D1–D2.

Sconce, Jeffrey. "Spectacles of Death: Identification, Reflexivity, and Contemporary Horror." In *Film Theory Goes to the Movies,* ed. Jim Collins, Hilary Radner, and Ava Preacher Collins. New York: Routledge, 1993.

————. "'Trashing' the Academy: Taste, Excess, and an Emerging Politics of Cinematic Style." *Screen* 36, no. 4 (winter 1995): 371–93.

Sedgwick, Eve Kosofsky. *Between Men: English Literature and Male Homosocial Desire.* New York: Columbia University Press, 1985.

Self, Robert. "Systems of Ambiguity in the Art Cinema." *Film Criticism* 4, no. 1 (fall 1979).

Sharrett, Christopher. *Crisis Cinema: The Apocalyptic Idea in Postmodern Narrative Film.* PostModern Positions, vol. 6. Washington, D.C.: Maisonneuve Press, 1993.

Shaviro, Steven. *The Cinematic Body.* Minneapolis: University of Minnesota Press, 1993.

Sheff, David. *The Playboy Interviews with John Lennon and Yoko Ono.* Ed. G. Barry Golson. New York: Playboy Press, 1981.

Shohat, Ella. "Imaging Terra Incognita: The Disciplinary Gaze of Empire." *Public Culture* 3, no. 2 (1991): 41–70.

Silverman, Kaja. *Male Subjectivity at the Margins.* New York: Routledge, 1992.

Singer, Daniel. "GATT and the Shape of Our Dreams." *Nation,* 17 January 1994, 54.

Sinister Cinema Catalogue, 1996–1997. P.O. Box 4369, Medford, OR 97501-0168.

Sitney, P. Adams. *Visionary Film: The American Avant-garde, 1943–1978.* 2d ed. New York: Oxford University Press, 1979.

Skal, David J. *The Monster Show: A Cultural History of Horror.* New York: W. W. Norton, 1993.

Skal, David J., and Elias Savada. *Dark Carnival: The Secret World of Tod Browning.* New York: Anchor Books, 1995.

Smith, Gavin. "Foreign Affairs: Which Foreign Films Must Be Seen at All Costs." *Film Comment* 33, no. 4 (July–August 1997).

Smith, Jack. "The Perfect Filmic Appositeness of Maria Montez." *Film Culture* 27 (1962–1963): 28–36.

Smith-Rosenberg, Carroll. *Disorderly Conduct: Visions of Gender in Victorian America.* New York: Alfred A. Knopf, 1985.

Sobchack, Vivian. "Bringing It All Back Home: Family Economy and Generic Exchange." *Camera Obscura,* no. 15 (fall 1986): 7–34.

Sontag, Susan. *Against Interpretation.* New York: Delta, 1966.

———. *On Photography.* 3d ed. New York: Doubleday Books, 1977.

———. "The Decay of Cinema." *New York Times Magazine,* 25 February 1996, 60–61.

Spigel, Lynn. "Television in the Family Circle: The Popular Reception of a New Medium." In *Logics of Television: Essays in Cultural Criticism,* ed. Patricia Mellencamp, 73–97. Bloomington: Indiana University Press, 1990.

Spoto, Donald. *The Dark Side of Genius: The Life of Alfred Hitchcock.* New York: Ballantine, 1983.

Staiger, Janet. *Interpreting Films: Studies in the Historical Reception of American Cinema.* Princeton, N.J.: Princeton University Press, 1992.

Stanley, John. *The Creature Features Movie Guide.* Pacifica, Calif.: Creatures at Large Publishing, 1981.

Stich, Sidra. *Anxious Visions: Surrealist Art.* New York: Abbeville Press; Berkeley, Calif.: University Art Museum, 1990.

Strauss, Frédéric, ed. *Almodóvar on Almodóvar.* Trans. Yves Baignères. London and Boston: Faber and Faber, 1994.

Suárez, Juan A. *Bike Boys, Drag Queens, and Superstars: Avant-garde, Mass Culture, and Gay Identities in the 1960s Underground Cinema.* Bloomington: Indiana University Press, 1996.

Suleiman, Susan Rubin. *Subversive Intent: Gender, Politics, and the Avant-garde.* Cambridge: Harvard University Press, 1990.

Sumner, Melody, Kathleen Burch, and Michael Sumner, eds. *The Guests Go in to Supper.* Oakland and San Francisco: Burning Books, 1986.

Tashiro, Charles. "The Contradictions of Video Collecting." *Film Quarterly* 50, no. 2 (winter 1996–1997): 11–18.

Taylor, Lucien. *Visualizing Theory: Selected Essays from V.A.R.* New York: Routledge, 1994.

Thompson, Kristin. "The Concept of Cinematic Excess." In *Narrative, Apparatus, Ideology: A Film Theory Reader,* ed. Philip Rosen, 130–42. New York: Columbia University Press, 1986.

Thompson, Kristin, and David Bordwell. *Film History: An Introduction.* New York: McGraw-Hill, 1994.

Thomson, Rosemarie Garland, ed. *Freakery: Cultural Spectacles of the Extra-ordinary Body.* New York: New York University Press, 1996.

Tohill, Cathal, and Pete Tombs. *Immoral Tales: European Sex and Horror Movies, 1956–1984.* New York: St. Martin's Griffin, 1994.

Trinh T. Minh-ha. *Woman, Native, Other: Writing, Postcoloniality, Feminism.* Bloomington: Indiana University Press, 1989.

————. *Framer Framed.* New York: Routledge, 1992.

Tudor, Andrew. *Monsters and Mad Scientists: A Cultural History of the Horror Movie.* Cambridge, Mass.: Basil Blackwell, 1989.

Twitchell, James. *Dreadful Pleasures: An Anatomy of Modern Horror.* New York: Oxford University Press, 1985.

Tyler, Parker. *Underground Film: A Critical History.* New York: Grove Press, 1969.

Vale, V., and Andrea Juno. "Introduction." In *RE/Search* no. 10: *Incredibly Strange Films,* ed. Jim Morton. 1986.

Vance, Carol S. *Pleasure and Danger: Exploring Female Sexuality.* London: Pandora Books, 1989.

Variety, 26 August 1959.

Vincendeau, Ginette. *Encyclopedia of European Cinema.* New York: Facts on File, 1995.

Virmaux, Alain, and Odette Virmaux. *Les surréalistes et le cinéma.* Paris: Editions Seghers, 1976.

Vogel, Amos. *Film as a Subversive Art.* New York: Random House, 1974.

"A Voir, à écouter, à savoir." *L'Express,* no. 456 (10 March 1960): 24.

Von Busack, Richard. "Seeing behind the Mask of Horror." MetroActive Web site. 20 June 1996. http://www.metroactive.com/papers/metro/06.20.96/eyes-face-9625.html. Accessed 17 October 1997.

Walkerdine, Valerie. "Video Replay: Families, Films, and Fantasy." In *Formations of Fantasy,* ed. Victor Burgin, James Donald, and Cora Kaplan. New York: Methuen, 1986.

Waller, Gregory. *The Living and the Undead: From Stoker's "Dracula" to Romero's "Dawn of the Dead."* Urbana: University of Illinois Press, 1986.

————, ed. *American Horrors: Essays on the Modern American Horror Film.* Urbana: University of Illinois Press, 1987.

Walters, Suzanna Danuta. *Material Girls: Making Sense of Feminist Cultural Theory.* Berkeley and Los Angeles: University of California Press, 1995.

Warhol, Andy. *The Philosophy of Andy Warhol from A to B and Back Again.* New York: Harcourt, Brace, Jovanovich, 1975.

Warhol, Andy, and Pat Hackett. *POPism: The Warhol Sixties.* San Diego: Harcourt, Brace, Jovanovich, 1980.

Weinraub, Bernard. "A Visit with Roman Polanski." *New York Times Magazine,* 12 December 1971.

————. "Directors Fight for GATT's Final Cuts and Print." *New York Times,* 12 December 1993, 14.

Weldon, Michael. *The Psychotronic Encyclopedia of Film.* New York: Ballantine Books, 1983.

————. *The Psychotronic Video Guide.* New York: St. Martin's Griffin, 1996.

Wexman, Virginia Wright. *Roman Polanski.* Boston: Twayne Publishers, 1985.

Williams, Alan. *Republic of Images: A History of French Filmmaking.* Cambridge: Harvard University Press, 1992.

294 —— Bibliography

Willliams, Linda. "When the Woman Looks." In *Re-vision: Essays in Feminist Film Criticism,* ed. Mary Ann Doane, Patricia Mellencamp, and Linda Williams. American Film Institute Monograph Series, vol. 3. Frederick, Md.: University Publications of America, 1984.

———. *Hard Core: Power, Pleasure, and the Frenzy of the Visible.* Berkeley and Los Angeles: University of California Press, 1989.

———. "Learning to Scream." *Sight and Sound* 4, no. 12 (December 1994): 14–17.

———. "Film Bodies: Gender, Genre, and Excess." In *Film Genre Reader II,* ed. Barry Keith Grant. Austin: University of Texas Press, 1995.

Williams, Tony. "Resource Guide: Video Sales and Rentals." *Jump Cut* 37 (1992): 99–109.

———. "Mail Order and Video Companies II." *Jump Cut* 41 (1997): 110–18.

Wollen, Peter. "The Two Avant-gardes." In *Readings and Writings: Semiotic Counter-Strategies.* London: New Left Books, 1982.

———. "Godard and Counter Cinema: *Vent d'Est.*" In *Narrative, Apparatus, Ideology,* ed. Philip Rosen, 120–29. New York: Columbia University Press: 1986.

Wood, Robin. "Return of the Repressed." *Film Comment,* July–August 1978, 25–32.

———. "Gods and Monsters." *Film Comment,* September–October 1978, 19–25.

———. *Hollywood from Vietnam to Reagan.* New York: Columbia University Press, 1986.

———. "Ideology, Genre, Auteur." In *Film Theory and Criticism,* 4th ed., ed. Gerald Mast, Marshall Cohen, and Leo Braudy. New York: Oxford University Press, 1992.

Wright, Gene. *Horrorshows: The A-to-Z of Horror Film, Television, Radio, and Theater.* New York: Facts on File Publications, 1986.

Wylie, Philip. *Generation of Vipers.* 2d ed. New York: Rinehart, 1955.

Yacowar, Maurice. *The Films of Paul Morrissey.* New York: Cambridge University Press, 1993.

Zimmermann, Patricia. *Reel Families: A Social History of the Amateur Film.* Bloomington: Indiana University Press, 1995.

Select Filmography and Videography

The Act of Seeing with One's Own Eyes. Stan Brakhage, 1972.

Akira. Katsuhiro Otomo, 1987.

Alphaville. Jean-Luc Godard, 1965.

Always, Henry Jaglom, 1985.

Les Amants du Pont-Neuf. Léos Carax, 1991.

Andy Warhol. Kim Evans, 1987 (London Weekend Television).

Andy Warhol's Dracula (Dracula vuole vivere). Paul Morrissey, 1973.

Andy Warhol's Frankenstein (Carne per Frankenstein, Flesh for Frankenstein, Il Mostro e in tavola). Paul Morrissey, 1973.

Les avaleuses (The Swallowers). Jess Franco, 1973.

L'avventura. Michelangelo Antonioni, 1960.

The Awful Dr. Orlof (Gritos en la noche). Jess Franco, 1962.

Baby of Macon. Peter Greenaway, 1993.

Bad Seed. Mervyn Le Roy, 1956.

The Bare-Breasted Countess. Jess Franco, 1973.

Basquiat. Julian Schnabel, 1996.

Beast with Five Fingers. Robert Florey, 1946.

The Beautiful People. Floria Sigismundi, 1997.

Beethoven's Nephew. Paul Morrissey, 1985.

La belle captive. Alain Robbe-Grillet, 1983.

Belle du jour. Luis Buñuel, 1966.

Bill and Tony. Anthony Balch, 1962–1972.

Billy Budd. Peter Ustinov, 1962.

The Birds. Alfred Hitchcock, 1963.

Black Narcissus. Michael Powell, 1947.

Blade Runner. Ridley Scott, 1982.

Blood and Roses. Roger Vadim, 1960.

Blood Sucking Pharaohs of Pittsburgh. Alan Smithey, 1990.

Bloodsucking Freaks (aka *Incredible Torture Show*). Joel Reed, 1978.

Blue Movie. Andy Warhol/Paul Morrissey, 1968.

Blue Velvet. David Lynch, 1986.

Body Double. Brian De Palma, 1984.

The Body Snatcher. Robert Wise, 1945.

Boogie Nights. Paul Thomas Anderson, 1997.

A bout de souffle (Breathless). Jean-Luc Godard, 1959.

The Brain That Wouldn't Die. Joseph Green, 1959.

Brazil. Terry Gilliam, 1985.

Bread and Chocolate. Franco Brusati, 1974.

Break Up the Dance. Roman Polanski, 1957.

The Bride of Frankenstein. James Whale, 1935.

The Bridge on the River Kwai. David Lean, 1957.

Burnin' Love. Lee Bennett Sobel, 1996.

Cabinet of Dr. Caligari. Robert Wiene, 1919.

Café Flesh. Stephen Sayadian (pseud. Rinse Dream), 1982.

Carnival of Souls. Herk Harvey, 1962.

Castle of Fu Manchu. Jess Franco, 1968.

Cat and the Canary. Paul Leni, 1927.

Cat and the Canary. Elliott Nugent, 1939.

Cat People. Jacques Tourneur, Val Lewton, 1942.

Cet object obscur du désir (That Obscure Object of Desire). Luis Buñuel, 1976.

La chagrin et la pitié (The Sorrow and the Pity). Marcel Ophuls, 1972.

The Chelsea Girls. Andy Warhol, 1966.

Un chien andalou. Luis Buñuel and Salvador Dali, 1929.

Chimes at Midnight. Orson Welles, 1965.

Circus of Horrors. Sidney Hayes, 1960.

Citizen Kane. Orson Welles, 1941.

A Civil Action. Steven Zaillian, 1998.

A Clockwork Orange. Stanley Kubrick, 1971.

Close Encounters of the Third Kind. Steven Spielberg, 1977.

La comtesse noire (La comtesse aux seins nus). Jess Franco, 1973.

The Conformist (Il Confomista). Bernardo Bertolucci, 1969.

The Conversation. Francis Ford Coppola, 1974.

The Cook, the Thief, His Wife, and Her Lover. Peter Greenaway, 1989.

The Corpse Grinders. Ted Mikels, 1971.

Count Dracula. Jess Franco, 1971.

The Crazy Ray. René Clair, 1923.

Cría cuervos. Carlos Saura, 1975.

The Crying Game. Neil Jordan, 1992.

The Damned (Caduta degli dei). Lucino Visconti, 1969.

Dario Argento, Master of Horror. Michele Soavi, 1993.

Daughters of Darkness (La rouge aux lèvres). Harry Kuemel, 1971.

David Holzman's Diary. Jim McBride, 1967.

Deadly Sanctuary. Jess Franco, 1970.

Deep Throat. Gerard Damiano (pseud. Jerry Gerard), 1972.

Dekalog. Krzysztof Kieslowski, 1988.

Delicatessen. Jean-Pierre Jeunet and Marc Caro, 1990.

Déjà Vu. Henry Jaglom, 1997.

Dementia. John Parker, 1955.

Il deserto rosso. Michelangelo Antonioni, 1964.

Les diaboliques (Diabolique). Henri-Georges Clouzot, 1954.

Diva. Jean-Jacques Beneix, 1980.

Doctor Petiot. Christian de Chalonge, 1990.

Dr. Blood's Coffin. Sidney J. Furie, 1960.

Dracula. Tod Browning, 1931.

Dracula's Daughter. Lambert Hillyer, 1936.

Dressed to Kill. Brian De Palma, 1980.

Eat. Andy Warhol, 1963.

Empire. Andy Warhol, 1964.

El espíritu de la colmena (Spirit of the Beehive). Victor Erice, 1973.

The Exorcist. William Friedkin, 1973.

Extase (Ecstasy). Gustave Machaty, 1932.

The Exterminating Angel. Luis Buñuel, 1962.

The Eyes of Laura Mars. Irvin Kershner, 1978.

Faceless (Les prédateurs de la nuit). Jess Franco, 1988.

The Fall of the House of Usher (La Chute de la maison d'Usher). Jean Epstein, 1928.

Une femme est une femme (A Woman Is a Woman). Jean-Luc Godard, 1961.

Une femme mariée (A Married Woman). Jean-Luc Godard, 1964.

La femme Nikita. Luc Besson, 1990.

Fireworks. Kenneth Anger, 1974.

The Fisher King. Terry Gilliam, 1991.

Flaming Creatures. Jack Smith, 1963.

Flesh. Paul Morrissey, 1968.

The Fly. Kurt Neumann, Roger Corman, 1958.

Frankenstein. James Whale, 1931.

Freaks. Tod Browning, 1932.

Freddy's Dead: The Final Nightmare (Nightmare on Elm Street 6). Rachel Talalay, 1991.

Germinal. Claude Berri, 1993.

Ghostbusters. Ivan Reitman, 1984.

Glen or Glenda. Edward D. Wood Jr., 1953.

Golem. Julien Duvivier, 1937.

La grande illusion. Jean Renoir, 1937.

Halloween. John Carpenter, 1978.

Harlot. Andy Warhol, 1964.

The Haunting. Robert Wise, 1963.

Heat. Paul Morrissey, 1971.

Henry: Portrait of a Serial Killer. John McNaughton, 1990 (prod. 1986).

High Heels (Tacones lejanos). Pedro Almodóvar, 1991.

High School. Frederick Wiseman, 1968.

Hiroshima mon amour. Alain Resnais, 1959.

Horrors of the Black Museum. Arthur Crabtree, 1959.

Hound of the Baskervilles. Paul Morrissey, 1977.

The House on Haunted Hill. William Castle, 1959.

I Am Curious Yellow (Jag är nyfiken-gul). Vilgot Sjöman, 1967.

I Shot Andy Warhol. Mary Harron, 1997.

I Spit on Your Grave (aka **Day of the Woman**). Meir Zachi, 1977.

I Walked with a Zombie. Jacques Tourneur and Val Lewton, 1943.

I Was a Teenage Frankenstein. Herbert Strock, 1958.

Intervista. Frederico Fellini, 1988.

Island of Lost Souls. Erle C. Kenton, 1933.

Ivan the Terrible. Sergei Eisenstein, 1942.

Jail Bait. Edward D. Wood Jr., 1955.

Jaws. Steven Spielberg, 1975.

La jetée. Chris Marker, 1964.

Juliet of the Spirits. Frederico Fellini, 1965.

Jurassic Park. Steven Spielberg, 1993.

Kika. Pedro Almodóvar, 1993.

King Kong. Merian C. Cooper and Ernest B. Schoedsack, 1933.

King of Hearts. Philipe de Broca, 1967.

Kiss. Andy Warhol, 1963.

Last Tango in Paris. Bernardo Bertolucci, 1972.

Last Year at Marienbad. Alain Resnais, 1961.

Laugh-In. George Schlatter, Ed Friendly, and Paul Keyes, prods., 1968–1973 (NBC).

Legacy of Satan. Gerard Damiano, 1973.

The Life and Death of Colonel Blimp. Michael Powell, 1943.

Lightning Bolt. Antonio Margheriti, 1966.

Lonesome Cowboys. Paul Morrissey, 1967.

Lou Reed: Rock and Roll Heart. Timothy Greenfield-Sanders, 1998.

Love Letters of a Portuguese Nun. Jess (Jésus) Franco, 1976.

Mad Love (aka *Hands of Orlac*). Karl Freund, 1935.

Made in USA. Jean-Luc Godard, 1966.

Maedchen in Uniform. Leontine Sagan, 1931.

Mains d'Orlac. Edward T. Greville, 1960.

The Man Who Could Cheat Death. Terence Fisher, 1959.

The Man without a Body. W. Lee Wilder, 1957.

The Manster. Kenneth Crane and George Breakston, 1959.

The Magnificent Ambersons. Orson Welles, 1942.

Mario Eats a Banana (Mario Banana). Andy Warhol, 1964.

Masculin/féminin (Masculine/Feminine). Jean-Luc Godard, 1966.

Matador. Pedro Almodóvar, 1988.

McCarthy: Death of a Witchhunter. Emilio de Antonio, 1964.

Metropolis. Fritz Lang, 1926.

Millhouse. Emilio de Antonio, 1971.

Midnight Cowboy. John Schlesinger, 1969.

Mod Squad. Aaron Spelling, prod., 1968–1973 (ABC).

Mom and Dad. Kroger Babb, 1944.

Motor Psycho. Russ Meyer, 1965.

Mute Witness. Anthony Waller, 1995.

My Hustler. Andy Warhol, 1965.

My Life to Live. Jean-Luc Godard, 1962.

My World Dies Screaming (aka *Terror in the Haunted House*). Harold Daniels, 1961.

Nadja. Michael Almereyda, 1995.

Near Dark. Kathryn Bigelow, 1987.

Nico Icon. Susanen Ofteringer, 1995.

Night Monster. Ford Beebe, 1942.

Night of Shooting Stars. Paolo and Vittorio Taviani, 1982.

Night of the Hunter. Charles Laughton, 1955.

Night of the Living Dead. George Romero, 1968.

No Lies. Mitchell Block, 1973.

Nosferatu. Friedrich Murnau, 1921.

La notte. Michelangelo Antonioni, 1960.

La novia ensangretada (The Blood-Spattered Bride). Vicente Aranda, 1972.

La nuit et la brouillard (Night and Fog). Alain Resnais, 1955.

Numéro deux, Jean-Luc Godard, 1975.

The Official Story. Luis Puenzo, 1985.

Our Hitler. Hans-Jürgen Syberberg, 1977.

Passion (Passion de Jeanne d'Arc). Jean-Luc Godard, 1982.

Passion of Joan of Arc. Carl Dreyer, 1928.

Peeping Tom. Michael Powell, 1960.

The People vs. Larry Flynt. Milos Forman, 1997.

Pierrot le fou. Jean-Luc Godard, 1965.

The Picture of Dorian Gray. Albert Lewin, 1945.

The Picture of Dorian Gray (Il dio chiamato Dorian, The Evils of Dorian Gray). Massimo Dallamano, 1970.

Pink Flamingoes. John Waters, 1973.

Portrait of Jason. Shirley Clarke, 1967.

Poor Little Rich Girl. Andy Warhol, 1965.

Possession. Andrzej Zulawski, 1981.

Psycho. Alfred Hitchcock, 1960.

Les quatre cent coups (Four Hundred Blows). François Truffaut, 1959.

Rape, Yoko Ono, 1969.

Reassemblage. Trinh T. Minh-ha, 1982.

The Red Shoes. Michael Powell, 1948.

Reefer Madness. Louis Gasnier, 1939.

Repulsion. Roman Polanski, 1965.

Return of the Vampire. Lew Landers, 1943.

The Rocky Horror Picture Show. Jim Sharman, 1975.

The Road to Mandalay. Tod Browning, 1926.

The Road Warrior. George Miller, 1981.

Roma, città aperta (Rome, Open City). Roberto Rossellini, 1945.

Rosemary's Baby. Roman Polanski, 1968.

Rouge aux lèvres (Daughters of Darkness). Harry Kuemel, 1971.

Salò. Pier Paolo Pasolini, 1975.

Salome (Neon Vampires). Gino Marotta.

Samson and Delilah. Cecil B. DeMille, 1949.

Sang des bêtes. Georges Franju, 1948.

Satan's Bed. Michael Findlay and Roberta Findlay, 1965.

Sauve qui peut, la vie (Every Man for Himself). Jean-Luc Godard, 1980.

Scarface. Howard Hawks, 1932.

Screen Test No. 2. Andy Warhol, 1965.

She Demons. Richard E. Cunha, 1958.

Sleep. Andy Warhol, 1963.

Snuff. Michael Findlay, Roberta Findlay, and Allan Shackleton, 1976.

La société de la spectacle (Society of the Spectacle). Guy Debord, 1973.

Spanish Dracula. George Melford, 1931.

The Stepfather. Joseph Ruben, 1987.

Straw Dogs. Sam Peckinpah, 1971.

Succubus. Jess Franco, 1968.

Superstar: The Life and Times of Andy Warhol. Chuck Workman, 1991.

Suspiria. Dario Argento, 1977.

Sweeney Todd: The Demon Barber of Fleet Street. Stephen Sondheim, 1981.

The Tenant. Roman Polanski, 1976.

Tenderness of Wolves. Uli Loemmel, 1973.

La tête contre les murs (Head against the Walls). Georges Franju, 1958.

Texas Chainsaw Massacre. Tobe Hooper, 1974.

Texas Chainsaw Massacre 2. Tobe Hooper, 1986.

Thelma and Louise. Ridley Scott, 1991.

Them! Gordon Douglas, 1954.

The Tingler. William Castle, 1959.

Tirez sur le pianiste (Shoot the Piano Player). François Truffaut, 1960.

Tombs of the Blind Dead. Amando de Ossorio, 1971.

Touch of Evil. Orson Welles, 1958.

Tout va bien. Jean-Luc Godard, 1972.

Tower of Screaming Virgins. François Legrand, 1968.

Towers Open Fire. Anthony Balch, 1963.

Trash. Paul Morrissey, 1970.

Triumph of the Will (Triumph des Willens). Leni Reifenstahl, 1936.

Twelve Monkeys. Terry Gilliam, 1995.

Two Faces of Dr. Jekyll. Terence Fisher, 1960.

Umbrellas of Cherbourg. Jacques Démy, 1964.

The Unearthly. Brook Peters, 1957.

The Unholy Three. Tod Browning, 1925.

The Unknown. Tod Browning, 1927.

Vampyr. Carl Dreyer, 1932.

Variety. Bette Gordon, 1984.

Venus in Furs. Maartje Seyferth and Victor Nieuwenhuijs, 1994.

Vinyl. Andy Warhol, 1965.

Viridiana. Luis Buñuel, 1961.

Vivre sa vie (My Life to Live). Jean-Luc Godard, 1962.

The War Games. Peter Watkins, 1965.

The Washing Machine. Ruggero Deodato, 1993.

The Werewolf and the Yeti. Miguel Iglesias Bonns, 1975.

Weekend. Jean-Luc Godard, 1968.

White Dog. Samuel Fuller, 1981.

White Zombie. Victor Halperin, 1932.

Wild Strawberries. Ingmar Bergman, 1957.

Women on the Verge of a Nervous Breakdown (Mujeres al borde de un ataque de nervios). Pedro Almodóvar, 1988.

X, the Man with the X-Ray Eyes. Roger Corman, 1963.

Les yeux sans visage (Eyes without a Face, The Horror Chamber of Dr. Faustus). Georges Franju, 1959.

Zontar, the Thing from Venus. Larry Buchanan, 1966.

Video Distributors

European Trash Cinema
P.O. Box 12161
Spring, TX 77391-2161

Facets Multimedia (mail-order rentals available to members)
1517 W. Fullerton Ave.
Chicago, IL 60614
(800) 331-6197

The Fang
P.O. Box 1012
Floral Park, NY 11002
(516) 354-3715

Home Film Festival (mail-order rentals available to members)
P.O. Box 2032
Scranton, PA 18501

Luminous Film and Video Wurks
P.O. Box 1047
Medford, NY 11763
http://www.lfvw.com

Scorched Earth Productions (Ronnie Cramer's Cult Films)
P.O. Box 101083
Denver, CO 80250

Sinister Cinema
P.O. Box 4369
Medford, OR 97501-0168
(541) 773-6860
http://www.sinistercinema.com

Something Weird Video
Direct orders to
The Picture Palace
P.O. Box 281
Caldwell, NJ 07006
http://www.picpal.com/swhome.html

TLA Video MGMT
http://www.tlavideo.com
(800) 333-8521

Video Search of Miami
P.O. Box 16-1917
Miami, FL 33116-1917
(888) 279-9773
VSOM@aol.com

Video Vamp
23 Big Spring Circle
Cookeville, TN 38501

Video Watchdog
P.O. Box 5283
Cincinnati, OH 45205-0283

Index

Sendak, Maurice: quote of, 65
Sexploitation, 87, 129, 196
Sexual acts, 188, 196; confronting,
120; cultural value to, 195
Seyrig, Delphine: photo of, 61
Shackleton, Alan: *Snuff* and, 135,
136–37
Shakespeare, William, 8, 9
Sharits, Paul: Fluxfilms and, 130
Shaviro, Steven, 21, 256n60
Shayé, Robert: on mail-order video in-
dustry, 8
Sheff, David, 118–19
Shelley, Mary, 193
Shere, Charles, 250n10
Shock Value (Waters), review of, 205
Shohat, Ella, 134
Shoot the Piano Player, 18, 20
Shot repetition, 106
Sick humor, 208, 209
Sight and Sound, 74
Sigismundi, Floria, 164
Signatures of the Visible, 8
Silence, in visual terms, 177
Sinatra, Frank, 126
Singin' in the Rain, 206
Sinister Cinema, 4, 11, 83; catalog by,
15, 218n6; on *Vampyr*, 14
Sirk, Douglas, 18
Siskel, Gene: splatter movies and, 43
Sitney, P. Adams, 177; avant-garde cine-
ma and, 202; structural films and,
174; on Warhol, 174, 178, 184
Skal, David J., 25, 259n27; on Arbus,
166–67; on Chaney, 145; on De
Antonio, 260n35; on Esper, 146;
freak culture and, 166; on *Freaks*,
147, 148, 258n16; on New Yorker
Theater, 58
Sklar, Robert, 27
Slater, David, 135–36
Slaughter, Findlay/Paramount and,
257n71

Sleep: fixed-frame in, 176; grotesque
realism and, 201; scene from, 176
(photo); viewing, 178
Smith, Gavin, 27
Smith, Jack, 182, 223n54; review of,
54, 233n2
Smith, Marshall. *See* Findlay, Michael
Sneak Previews, splatter movies and, 43
Snuff, 32, 129, 255n47; criticism of,
136, 138, 195; described, 135–39
Sobchack, Vivian: *No Lies* and, 122,
135
Social origin, role of, 29–30
Society of the Spectacle, 220n28
Sodomy: in European intellectual cul-
ture, 195; sadoeroticism and, 195
Solanas, Valerie, 171, 189, 265n7
Solomon, Joe, 136
Something Weird Video (SWV), 11,
243n67, 246n33; *Satan's Bed* and,
129
Sontag, Susan, 35, 40, 41, 44, 57; on
academic bureaucracy, 62; on
Arbus, 167, 168; on art cinema
movement, 13; on *Flaming
Creatures*, 233n2; on modern art,
168; review by, 54
Spanish Dracula, 12
Spanish film industry, 92, 109,
245n19; Hammer takeoffs by, 93
Speaking about/speaking nearby,
132–35
Spectator response, 31, 178–79, 180.
See also Audience participation;
Viewing practices
Spigel, Lynn: discursive rules from,
229n20
Spike of Bensonhurst, 265n13
Splatter films, 14, 65, 80, 241n52
*Splatter Movies: Breaking the Last Taboo
of the Screen* (McCarty), 43
Staiger, Janet: on audiences, 22, 57,
224n66

Joan Hawkins is assistant professor in the Department of Communication and Culture at Indiana University, Bloomington, where she teaches American studies, comparative literature, cultural studies, and film studies.